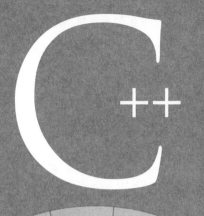

C++

AN ACTIVE LEARNING APPROACH

RANDAL ALBERT
Oregon Institute of Technology

TODD BREEDLOVE
Oregon Institute of Technology

JONES AND BARTLETT PUBLISHERS

Sudbury, Massachusetts

BOSTON   TORONTO   LONDON   SINGAPORE

World Headquarters

Jones and Bartlett Publishers
40 Tall Pine Drive
Sudbury, MA 01776
978-443-5000
info@jbpub.com
www.jbpub.com

Jones and Bartlett Publishers
Canada
6339 Ormindale Way
Mississauga, Ontario L5V 1J2
Canada

Jones and Bartlett Publishers
International
Barb House, Barb Mews
London W6 7PA
United Kingdom

Jones and Bartlett's books and products are available through most bookstores and online booksellers. To contact Jones and Bartlett Publishers directly, call 800-832-0034, fax 978-443-8000, or visit our website www.jbpub.com.

Substantial discounts on bulk quantities of Jones and Bartlett's publications are available to corporations, professional associations, and other qualified organizations. For details and specific discount information, contact the special sales department at Jones and Bartlett via the above contact information or send an email to specialsales@jbpub.com.

Production Credits
Acquisitions Editor: Timothy Anderson
Editorial Assistant: Melissa Potter
Production Director: Amy Rose
Production Intern: Ashlee Hazeltine
Senior Marketing Manager: Andrea DeFronzo
V.P., Manufacturing and Inventory Control: Therese Connell
Composition: Northeast Compositors, Inc.
Photo Researcher: Lee Michelsen
Cover Design: Kristin E. Ohlin
Cover Image: © Jamesmmm/Dreamstime.com
Printing and Binding: Malloy, Inc.
Cover Printing: Malloy, Inc.

Library of Congress Cataloging-in-Publication Data
Albert, Randal.
    C++ : an active learning approach / Randal Albert, Todd Breedlove.
        p. cm.
    ISBN-13: 978-0-7637-5723-6 (pbk.)
    ISBN-10: 0-7637-5723-3 (pbk.)
    1. C++ (Computer program language) I. Breedlove, Todd. II. Title.
    QA76.73.C153A4165 2008
    005.13'3—dc22
                                        2008027307

6048

Printed in the United States of America
12 11   10 9 8 7 6 5 4 3 2

To our better halves, Linda and Jamie, and to all of our kids—
the students in the Computer Systems Engineering Technology
programs at Oregon Institute of Technology

Preface

Welcome to our textbook! After many years of teaching C and C++ and continually searching for the "perfect book," we have finally decided to write our own.

C++: An Active Learning Approach is designed to teach beginning programming at the college level. It has a strong focus on procedural programming using the C++ language. Additionally, at the end of most chapters we show how these concepts apply to the C programming language. The textbook serves as an introduction to programming for use within such curricula as Computer Science, Software Engineering, Information Technology, and Management Information Systems, or it can be used by individuals on their own. The text can be used for either a one-semester course or a two-quarter term sequence.

Prerequisites

The text is targeted at the broad base of students taking their first programming course. Although it assumes no prior programming knowledge, due to the mathematical nature of some of the programming assignments, students should have an understanding of algebraic concepts.

How We Are Different

Over the past few years we have used several texts within our introductory courses for programming students. Every few years we tend to alternate among these texts, only to find that they all fall short of our objectives. Our text is different in the following ways:

1. We include a more hands-on approach to presenting materials.

2. Throughout the text, exercises are presented for the students to complete as they work through a specific topic.

3. We clearly stress a more procedural approach to learning programming.

4. At the end of most chapters, we point out the corresponding C language constructs related to the specific topic being presented.

5. The writing style seeks to actively engage the reader in a "learn-by-doing" fashion and makes extensive use of various aspects associated with using the debugger to help solidify concepts.

6. The writing style presents information concisely and makes use of many code examples to help present the topics.

Getting the Most Out of the Text

The distinguishing feature of this text is the applied, hands-on nature of the material presented. It actively involves students in the learning process and provides a practical how-to guide to help them quickly learn and appreciate various fundamental aspects associated with the C++ programming language. It is strongly encouraged that the reader completes all of the Section Exercises and "Learn by Doing" Exercises before moving on to the next section. These exercises allow readers to solidify their understanding before advancing to the next topic.

The Problem Solving Applied and Debugging sections typically contain some of the more difficult concepts our students encounter. These sections have been very helpful to the students in our test group.

One aspect of programming that many students in academia don't have exposure to is using other people's design, code, and specifications. The Team Programming section tries to introduce the student to typical situations found in the team environment of the computer industry.

Chapter Components

The typical chapter format includes the following sections:

- Objectives

- Introduction

- Major Concepts (1.0, 1.1, 1.2, etc.)
  - Code examples
  - Coding style tips
  - Section Exercises
  - Learn by Doing Exercises
- Problem Solving Applied
- C—The Differences
- Summary
- Debugging Exercise
- Programming Exercises
- Team Programming Exercise
- Answers to Chapter Exercises

Within the main body of each chapter, a number of code examples are provided. Most of the samples are short, focusing directly on the concept being presented. A section is also provided after the chapter topics that walks students through the design process. This section includes pseudocode as well as UML class diagrams where appropriate.

Preceding the summary, a section clearly outlines the syntactical differences between C and C++. This is a purely optional section in the text.

Supplements

Example Code—The programs contained within the text are available for students and instructors from the publisher's website at http://www.jbpub.com/catalog/9780763757236/.

PowerPoint Presentations—PowerPoint slides are available to adopters on request from Jones and Bartlett Publishers.

Solutions—The solutions to the Learn by Doing Exercises, Programming Exercises, and Team Programming Exercises are also available for instructors from Jones and Bartlett Publishers.

Acknowledgments

The beta version of the text was used in CST 116 C++ Programming I and CST 126 C++ Programming II at the Oregon Institute of Technology (OIT). The students provided a lot of positive feedback as well as suggestions for improvement.

During the process of writing this text we have received the continual encouragement and support of our colleagues, our current students, OIT alumni, and the OIT administration. We would like to thank the following reviewers: Dmitriy Kupis, St. Joseph's College; Michael I. Schwartz, University of Denver; Deirdre Folkers, Penn State University; and Stacey Dunevant, Jackson State Community College. In addition, we owe a special thank you to Bryan Wintermute, Heath Higgins, Jeanie King, and Marcus Blankenship for their support, careful review, corrections, and invaluable comments on a number of the chapters. A special thank you goes to Tyler Ferraro and Scott Nash for their editing feedback.

A number of other individuals have provided a wide range of support. Marie Murray, Gary Albert, Gregg Albert, Lois Breedlove, Paul Breedlove, Tim Wheeler, and Lennard Wheeler have been invaluable sources of support and encouragement. We would also like to thank Tim Anderson, Melissa Elmore, Melissa Potter, and Amy Rose at Jones and Bartlett Publishers for putting up with our unending stream of questions.

Feedback

We greatly value your opinion and would appreciate hearing about any errors or problems you might encounter in the textual or technical portions of the book. If you should find an error or have concerns, please email us at:

Todd Breedlove: todd.breedlove@oit.edu

Randy Albert: randal.albert@oit.edu

Your comments will help us improve the text. Thanks for any help and feedback you can provide!

Randy and Todd

Contents

CHAPTER 1

Introduction to Computers and Programming

Chapter Objectives

By the end of the chapter, readers will be able to:

- Define what is meant by a modern day computer.
- Understand some of the key milestones in the evolution of computers.
- Explain the major components of a computer.
- Explain what is meant by software.
- Differentiate between an operating system and an application program.
- Discuss the differences and similarities among hardware, software, and embedded systems.
- Explain what is meant by a programming paradigm.
- Discuss significant historic developments associated with both C and C++.
- Explain the components of data hierarchy.
- Discuss the issues surrounding numbering systems.

Introduction

This chapter is designed to introduce you to the exciting and ever-changing world of computers and computer programming. We begin our journey by developing a working definition of computers. Next we briefly examine some of the early milestones in computing history, and then study the various components that make up computers, beginning with hardware.

Once the basic premise behind computer hardware has been introduced, we focus our attention on computer software. Our discussion not only reviews the major categories of software but also introduces two of the more popular programming languages: C and C++. Other issues revolving around computers—such as numbering systems, data hierarchy, and programming paradigms—are discussed.

Be aware that we are providing only a brief introduction to the various topics presented, although some of the material will be discussed in greater detail in the remainder of the text. As you read the chapter, we encourage you to start your browser and further research any area of interest.

1.1 Overview of Computers and Programming

As you are well aware, computers have had a huge influence on almost all phases of our lives. They are everywhere, and additional uses for computers continue to emerge. You see them in classrooms, homes, cars, cell phones, gaming consoles, televisions, and MP3 players. However, before continuing with the remainder of the text, it is important to establish a common understanding of computer terminology.

For our purposes, we refer to a *computer* as an electronically powered physical device that has the ability to store, manipulate, and access data. In addition, our definition includes the fact that a computer can be designed to carry out or follow a specific set of instructions called a *program*. Programs are often referred to as computer *software*.

A computer system is composed of both hardware and software. The physical components, *hardware*, work with the software installed on the computer to accomplish the tasks the user desires. It is necessary to have both hardware and software working together to enable all of the capabilities to which we have become accustomed. These terms and more will be discussed in greater detail in the remainder of the chapter.

1.2 Historical Developments

Using devices to help in performing computations has had a long history. Many scholars date the abacus, with its beads and wires, as being invented by the Chinese thousands of years ago (Figure 1.2.1).

Another step in the computing evolution was due in large part to English mathematician *Charles Babbage*, (1791–1871) often considered the father of computing. During his lifetime Babbage developed detailed plans for a number of machines. The design for one of his machines, the *analytical engine*, contained many of the fundamental features that still exist in today's computers, including the concept of a stored program. Babbage's friend, *Ada Lovelace*, created a program based on the design of his analytical engine, and is therefore thought of as the first programmer. The influence of both of these remarkable individuals is still being felt today.

Some of the earliest electronic computers were developed in the 1940s. These computers were extremely large and heavy, and it was not uncommon for them to be so big that they would take up an entire room. One of the first electronic computers, the ENIAC, was said to weigh approximately 30 tons (Figure 1.2.2). *ENIAC* is an acronym for electronic numerical integrator and computer and had most of its programming done by a group of six women. From that point, a wide variety of hardware advances quickly began to emerge.

One of those advances centered on the development of the *integrated circuit*, or *IC*. An IC is a chip that can contain a large number of different components, such as resistors, transistors, and capacitors. ICs, sometimes referred to as chips, are in a continual state of evolution and enhancement.

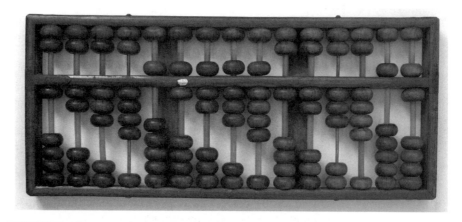

Figure 1.2.1 Abacus. © Lim ChewHow/Shutterstock, Inc.

Figure 1.2.2 ENIAC. Courtesy of U.S. Army

Following the development of the IC was the introduction of the *microprocessor*. A microprocessor is an IC containing components that actually execute a program. The microprocessor, or *processor*, often has a component called a CPU.

The *CPU*, central processing unit, acts as the brains of the computer. It is here where the actual program or set of instructions that tells the computer what to do is interpreted and processed.

> *i*
>
> The **central processing unit** (CPU) is responsible for executing the set of instructions that directs the computer's activities and for managing the various hardware components.

The microprocessor serves as the major component within today's microcomputers, such as a personal computer (PC), and is responsible for directing and managing many of the computer's functions. We will have more to say about the CPU in the next section.

In the late 1970s, the microcomputer became available to a huge segment of the population. By the end of the 1980s, companies like Apple and its competitor IBM were selling a huge number of PCs to a wide range of customers.

Today we see a continuing trend, in which processors are becoming smaller, faster, more powerful, and less expensive. Their use in an ever-widening range of devices continues to expand into such areas as health-related products, consumer goods, and industrial applications.

Section 1.2 Exercises

1. Using the Internet, find and discuss two more significant advances or events in the evolution of computers.

2. Using the Internet, find three people who have had a major influence on computers or programming.

1.3 Computer Hardware

Now that we have briefly traced some of the historical developments related to computers, it's time to explore several of the individual hardware components that make up a computer system, especially as they relate to the PC. The term *computer hardware* encompasses objects that can be felt or seen. Examples include disk drives, keyboards, memory, printers, chips, and monitors. To aid in our discussion of computer hardware, we will group the various hardware pieces into some helpful categories.

1.3.1 Input and Output (I/O) Devices

The first category of hardware devices we'll examine relates to input and output. *Input devices* provide a mechanism with which the user communicates with the computer. In some ways input devices are similar to our individual senses. For example, it is through our sense of hearing that we listen to the instructions or directions people provide us. Likewise, through our eyes we have the ability to gather data or input about a particular situation or event. With computers, input equipment often includes such devices as the keyboard and the mouse. It is through these devices, or interfaces, that we send information to the computer system. Today we continue to see a number of innovative methods for inputting data. Some relatively recent examples of creative input devices include touch screens, light pens, graphic tablets, wired gloves, and the Wii remote control.

Output devices are used to communicate information or processed data from the computer to a user. Examples of popular output devices include printers, speakers, and video displays.

1.3.2 Random-Access Memory (RAM)

Random-access memory (RAM) is memory within a computer that is used for holding the program and any information needed to perform the necessary processing. It is often referred to as short-term memory because the data contained within RAM will be lost when the computer is shut off or loses power. RAM tends to be very fast and is considered to be the computer's *main memory*.

1.3.3 Central Processing Unit (CPU)

As noted, the CPU serves as the brains of the computer. Its main function is to interpret and execute the instructions contained within the software it is currently running. In today's PCs, the CPU is contained entirely on one individual integrated circuit and is commonly referred to as a microprocessor. Three core components of the CPU are the arithmetic logic unit, the control unit, and the registers.

The *arithmetic logic unit* (ALU) performs the arithmetic computations and the logical operations. The arithmetic computations include such activities as addition and subtraction, while the logical operations involve such activities as evaluating two values to check for equality.

The *control unit* (CU) is responsible for the actual execution of instructions and also controls when instructions are executed. In other words, the CU tells the ALU what to do and when to do it.

Registers are unique, high-speed sections of memory within the CPU. Their purpose is to hold or store the data that is being operated on.

While the complexity and speed at which CPUs are able to perform various operations and functions continue to increase, the size requirements continue to decrease. As a result, we see the embedding of these microprocessors into a wide variety of devices, such as cell phones, cars, personal digital assistants (PDAs), MP3 players, and video-game consoles.

1.3.4 Storage Devices

The next category of computer hardware involves the devices available for storing data. This type of equipment includes hard drives, USB flash drives, and CD-ROM drives.

One of the more common methods for storing data is on a disk. The three main categories of disk-based storage are hard drives; the once popular removable floppy disks; and optical disks, such as CD-ROMs and DVDs.

A *hard disk* is an excellent form of media for holding your data, the operating system, and application programs. Data and programs can be easily and quickly written, retrieved, modified, and deleted. Most hard drives are physically fixed within your computer. The capacity of today's hard drives is often referenced in terms of *gigabytes*. When used in relation to a drive, a gigabyte (GB) indicates that the drive can store roughly one billion bytes of information. With the evolution of computer technology, the capacity of disk drives increases while their cost decreases. Today it is common to see PCs and laptops with hard disks containing storage space of anywhere from 80 to 500 GB.

A *floppy disk* is another form of media that can be used to store information. Floppy disks are made up of a flexible piece of material containing a magnetic recording surface that can store data. Like hard disks, floppy disks are a form of nonvolatile storage, meaning they retain information even when the computer is turned off. However, unlike hard disks, floppy disks are easily transportable because of their relatively small size. While "gigabytes" is often used in referring to the size of today's hard drives, the capacity of the 3.5″ floppy is cited in *megabytes* (MB). In relation to storage capacities, a megabyte represents approximately 1,000,000 bytes. The capacity of the 3.5″ floppy disk is approximately 1.44 MB, or 1,474,000 bytes. While very popular up until a few years ago, floppy disks are currently being replaced by higher-capacity flash drives.

USB flash drives are another form of nonvolatile storage. These extremely popular devices, sometimes referred to as *pen* or *thumb drives*, are made up of a relatively small circuit board encased in a protective plastic housing (Figure 1.3.1).

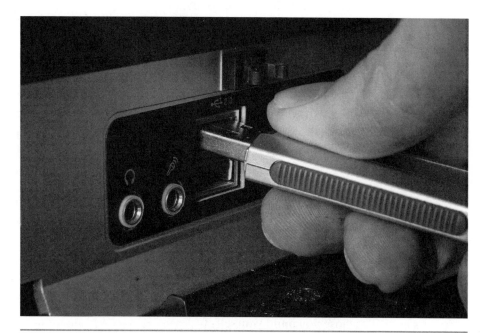

Figure 1.3.1 USB Flash Drive. © Alex Kotlov/ShutterStock, Inc.

These compact and highly portable drives are easily connectable to your PC via a USB port. *USB* (universal serial bus) is a standard interface used by a number of hardware devices to allow them to be easily connected to a PC. In addition to being able to read and write data faster than a floppy disk, flash drives have the ability to hold much more data. Most USB drives today have capacities ranging from 64 MB to as much as 4 GB.

The *CD-ROM* (compact disc read-only memory) is another popular form of nonvolatile, highly portable computer storage. These optical disks are made out of a thin plastic material and use a laser contained within the CD-ROM drive to read the information off the disk's surface. They look exactly like audio CDs and work well for storing large amounts of data. The standard capacity of these disks is usually between 650 and 700 MB of data.

To be able to record information to an optical CD requires either a CD-R or a CD-RW drive. A CD-R (compact disc-recordable) allows the user to write data to the disk only one time but to read the information as often as desired. Likewise, a CD-RW (compact disc-rewritable) provides the ability to read and rewrite information to the disk. The capacity of both CD-R and CD-RW disks is also about 650 to 700 MB.

The final storage medium to note is the *DVD* (digital versatile disc). These optical disks are the same size as regular CDs. However, because they have the capacity to store more than six times the amount of information of a CD, they tend to work well for holding things like movies, music, and large volumes of data. The standard single-sided DVD holds 4.7 GB of data, while the double-sided DVD holds 9.4 GB of data.

As you can see, there are a wide range of options available for storing data. The best choice depends on how much room you need, how fast it needs to be, and how much money you want to spend. No doubt in the future we will continue to see impressive developments in this area.

1.3.5 Motherboard

The *motherboard* contains the circuits necessary to connect all of the various components together. For example, the motherboard has a special CPU slot where the central processing unit simply plugs in. Likewise, there are areas on the board for plugging in additional memory or cards for controlling I/O devices such as monitors or printers. While the CPU is often considered the brains of your PC or laptop, the motherboard is sometimes referred to as its heart because of the key role it plays.

Section 1.3 Exercise

1. What is the best general-purpose computer you can get for $1,000? Look at prefabricated computers as well as those you build yourself.

1.4 Computer Software
· ·

Computer software is responsible for getting the computer hardware to do something. Once we turn on our PCs, the software will be loaded into the computer's memory and will start the execution process.

A program consists of detailed instructions written in a specific *programming language* that actually directs the activities of the computer. This special language must be used so that the computer can understand exactly what the programmer is trying to accomplish.

> *i*
>
> A **programming language** is a language containing a finite list of keywords and constructs that can be used by a programmer to direct the operations of a computer.

Programmers, or software developers, are proficient in one or more programming languages. Their job usually revolves around writing, testing, implementing, and maintaining a variety of software programs. Many people credit Ada Lovelace as being the first programmer for her work with Charles Babbage in the 1840s. The United States Department of Defense named its latest and still widely used programming language after Ada in the 1980s.

In our experience, successful computer programmers are good problem solvers who can meet deadlines and enjoy being part of a team. Unlike the traditional stereotype often portrayed in the film industry, programmers need to work well with others and have strong communication skills. In addition, it is often helpful for individuals who are not planning on becoming software developers to take a programming course or two to help broaden their appreciation and understanding of computer software. Fields such as health informatics, finance, systems analysis, web development, information technology, computer security, and network administration rely heavily on computer software.

For our purposes, we will classify software into two distinct types: application software and system software. While the thrust of this text is on writing application software, both categories of software are briefly examined in the following sections.

1.4.1 Application Software

Application software is an extremely broad area of software development and is targeted toward *users*. Application software can be found in computer games, word processors, spreadsheets, inventory control, grade management,

MP3 players, email, and chat programs. An example of an application program that you will soon become familiar with is Microsoft's Visual Studio, an application designed to develop software.

For these and other application programs to run on your PC, you must have an *operating system*. An operating system is really not an example of application software but falls under the category of system software.

1.4.2 System Software

System software is designed to manage the various hardware components of a computer and to coordinate the loading and execution of application programs. While there are a number of types of system software applications, the most important example is the *operating system* (OS).

Every PC has an operating system that plays a crucial role in running the computer. It is responsible for managing various tasks, such as preparing the computer when the machine is turned on, dealing with various input requests from such devices as the keyboard and the mouse, managing output requests to the display or printers, and managing the overall storage system.

The OS also provides a crucial interface between the computer hardware and the user. It is through the operating system that the user is able to access the various hardware components, such as the disk drive, along with the related file system, which is also managed by the OS. In addition, the operating system is responsible for such activities as scheduling tasks that have been assigned to it and managing the loading and execution of an almost endless range of application programs. Operating systems have continued to expand, and most now include significant components related to such areas as security and networking. Also, most companies that produce operating systems continually strive to provide consumers with a *graphical user interface* (GUI) designed to make the computer system easier to use, manage, and learn.

> Instead of using only text, a **graphical user interface** (GUI) uses pictures and other graphic symbols to help make a program, including operating systems, easier to use. Microsoft Windows and Mac OS X are examples of operating systems that use a graphical user interface.

Some of the more popular operating systems in use today include Windows XP, Windows Vista, UNIX (with its many variations), and Mac OS X. Although most individuals will run only one operating system, they are likely to have a wide variety of applications.

In addition to the operating system itself, there are some utility-type programs that can be used to help manage and control various hardware resources. Examples include file managers and communication-related software.

Section 1.4 Exercises

1. List three operating systems besides the ones mentioned in this chapter.

2. List five applications found on your computer.

1.5 Embedded Systems

Is your watch an example of a PC? Isn't it made up of both computer hardware and software? How about the thermostat in your house or apartment? Well, in reality, these products are more likely to fall into the ever-growing area of *embedded systems*. Unlike your PC, which is designed to be a general-purpose device, embedded systems are designed to perform only one or a limited number of tasks. Most embedded systems include both hardware and software together and can be placed collectively on a single microprocessor. The computer software designed and written specifically for use in an embedded system is often referred to as *firmware*. Since the software is actually located on a chip, it is no longer volatile and thus performs only predefined tasks, unlike a general-purpose desktop computer.

Embedded systems can be found in such products as MP3 players, medical equipment, kitchen appliances, games, vending machines, automobiles, cell phones, and cameras. Clearly the market for embedded systems will continue to grow in the years ahead.

Section 1.5 Exercise

1. Explain the differences between hardware, software, and embedded systems. Give examples of each.

1.6 Programming Paradigms

When examining programming-related problems and the choices that might be available for designing and structuring a specific solution, software developers often have a number of methods available. These different approaches for visualizing a problem's solution or an overall project structure are referred to as *programming paradigms*.

Within this text we begin developing programs based on the *procedural programming paradigm*. The procedural programming paradigm focuses on breaking down a particular programming problem into various pieces, subprograms, or routines. Each of these individual components performs a specific function and is executed as needed. C and Pascal are both examples of languages that adhere to the procedural programming paradigm. Some languages, like C++, actually fall into more than one particular programming paradigm.

Another paradigm discussed within the text is *object-oriented programming* (OOP). In the OOP paradigm, the central component is considered an *object*. Examples of objects surround us in our daily lives. Things like this textbook, a dog, a person, a radio, and your computer are all examples of objects. In this paradigm the focus is on the objects and their relationships and interactions. The first OOP language was called Smalltalk. Today languages such as C++, Java, C# (pronounced "C-sharp"), and Visual Basic all support the OOP paradigm. This doesn't necessarily mean that all programs written with these languages are object-oriented, it just means that they are more capable of creating object-oriented programs.

The final programming paradigm we look at is *functional programming*. This paradigm has its roots in mathematics and centers on the program being made up of a collection of mathematical like functions. A good example of a functional programming language is Lisp. This is probably the least used paradigm.

Section 1.6 Exercise

1. List three examples of programming languages for each of the three paradigms discussed. (Don't list any of the languages already mentioned in the section.)

1.7 Programming Languages

Computer software is made up of very detailed instructions written in a specific programming language designed to tell the computer how to perform an exact task. As noted, a programming language is simply a language designed by people to direct or control the computer. Unlike the language we use in our daily lives, programming languages must be very exact in their meaning because the computer will only do what it has been told. It will not make any assumptions or guesses about what the programmer might have meant by a particular statement that it does not recognize.

While hundreds of programming languages have been created, there are a relatively small number that have become popular and widely used over time. In the past, some of those popular languages included COBOL, FOR-

TRAN, C, BASIC, and Pascal. Today, the most widely used languages include Java, C, C++, Visual Basic, Python, Ada, and C#. Each of these languages has its own strengths and weaknesses. The best language to use for a particular application is usually based on the individual software problem being addressed.

Once introduced, most popular programming languages evolve over time. For example, C++ continues to be reviewed by a standardization committee and is updated to reflect new needs or requirements every few years. Likewise C#, introduced only a few years ago by Microsoft, has already been updated to include new features and additional functionality.

Within this text our emphasis will be on C++, along with an optional section in most chapters showing some comparable C syntax. Given that C++ has its roots in C, we briefly review the history of both languages in the following sections.

1.7.1 The C Programming Language

The programming language *C* was developed between 1969 and 1973 by Dennis Ritchie (Figure 1.7.1). Ritchie, who was working at Bell Telephone Labs, developed the language to be used in parallel with the development of the UNIX operating system. It was called C because a number of the language's characteristics came from an earlier language called B.

Although originally targeted toward the UNIX operating system, the use of C, commonly used in writing application software, has spread to many other operating systems as well, making C a highly portable language.

C became a widely used language and is still used today, especially in the area of systems programming. In addition, because it has the power to access

Figure 1.7.1 Dennis Ritchie. Courtesy of Dennis Ritchie

hardware relatively easily, it continues to be widely used in developing embedded systems. While some people still write traditional user-based applications in C, most programmers have found that languages like C++ are better designed for this particular purpose.

Unlike Pascal, which was developed by a college professor named Niklaus Wirth to teach programming to students, both C and C++ were developed for professional programmers, making them extremely powerful and capable of providing the programmer with the tools to do exactly what he or she wants—even if it is wrong or causes a problem. As a result, you will sometimes see places within both languages that allow you to get into trouble rather easily and perhaps without warning. Within the text we try to make you aware of these potentially dangerous areas.

1.7.2 The C++ Programming Language

In the late 1970s another individual from Bell Labs, Bjarne Stroustrup, augmented C to create a new programming language (Figure 1.7.2). Stroustrup called the first version of the language C with Classes, but after internal use of the language at AT&T in 1983, the name was changed to C++.

Often it is helpful to think of C++ as having two main characteristics or advantages over C:

1. C++ offers an easier-to-use and enhanced version of C. For example, the syntax for reading data in C++ is considerably easier to use than that for C. Many of the additional language features that help make C++ "a better C" are discussed throughout the remainder of the text.

Figure 1.7.2 Bjarne Stroustrup. Courtesy of Bjarne Stroustrup

2. C++ facilitates object-oriented programming by including *classes*. In addition, it provides excellent support for powerful object-oriented activities such as inheritance and polymorphism.

Similar to other popular programming languages, C++ has been standardized by an international organization. The current version was last revised in 2003, and a new standard is expected to be published in 2009.

Today C++ continues to be the language of choice for a variety of applications because of the power and functionality it offers. While there are other programming languages that are easier to learn, being taught C++ as your first programming language will provide you with a strong programming background.

Section 1.7 Exercise

1. Find and bookmark Bjarne Stroustrup's website.

1.8 Data Hierarchy

Data hierarchy is a way of grouping data or information. We commonly think of data hierarchy as consisting of bits, bytes, fields, records, and files.

The smallest piece of data to examine is a *bit*. In the data hierarchy a bit, or binary digit, can hold either 0 or 1. A bit is the elementary unit of storage found in digital computers. Similar to a light switch found in your dorm room or home, a bit is either on, represented by a 1, or off, denoted by a 0. Typically, a grouping of eight bits is called a *byte*.

Today, by far the most common size for an individual byte is eight bits. The term "byte" is often used to refer to the amount of computer memory needed to represent or hold one character.

A collection of related bytes is referred to as a *field*. A field holds all of the characters or data for a specific piece of information. For example, to hold the first and last name of a student, along with their student ID number, we could create three separate fields.

A group of related fields is called a *record*. To hold the information for 30 students, we would have a set of 30 records. Each record contains a first name field, a last name field, and an ID number field.

The individual records for each of the 30 students in a specific section of a programming course represents a *file*. A data file is simply a group of related records physically stored on a disk or some other storage media.

One final piece that can be added to the data hierarchy view is a *database*. In our example, we might have a separate file for each particular section of each of the classes on campus, a file containing a record for each of the faculty members on campus, a separate file listing all the courses offered in a particular term, and so on. Because managing all of these separate files becomes unwieldy, a database can be used to manage the data. A *database management system* (DBMS) provides tools that assist in handling the maintenance of all of the data.

Throughout the remainder of the text, many of the terms just introduced will be reviewed and expanded on. Having an understanding of the hierarchy will serve you well in helping to visualize how data can be arranged and referenced.

Section 1.8 Exercises

1. What are two common database management systems?

2. Using the Internet, what is one-half of a byte called?

1.9 Numbering Systems

Ever since we were old enough to count we have been using a *numbering system*. Humans typically count using the decimal numbering system. The decimal system uses 10 different digits, 0–9, and is therefore considered a "base 10" numbering system. Computers, however, only know two things: on and off. Therefore, computers need numbering systems that work well with those two states.

The three common numbering systems for computers are binary (base 2), octal (base 8), and hexadecimal (base 16). Notice that 8 and 16 are both powers of two and are therefore very compatible with binary systems. Even though it may be intimidating to learn new numbering systems, the process isn't any different from the one we already know except for the digits used. The following sections explain how to count in different numbering systems, how to convert to base 10 from some other base, and how to convert from base 10 to a different base.

1.9.1 Counting

Counting in base 10 is so commonplace for us that we often no longer think about the mechanics of the process. However, if the process is broken down into its simplest form, we can extend the same procedure to other bases.

In base 10, we start at zero and increment that single digit until we reach nine. At that point the digit to the left of that digit is then incremented. The least significant digit is then reset to zero. This process is easily understood by examining an automobile's odometer. Figure 1.9.1 demonstrates this process.

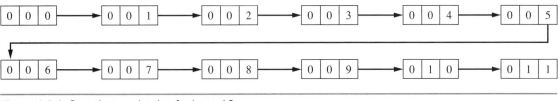

Figure 1.9.1 Counting mechanics for base 10

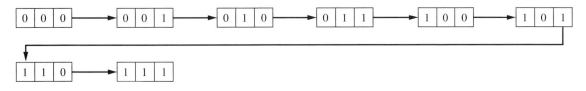

Figure 1.9.2 Counting mechanics for a binary numbering system

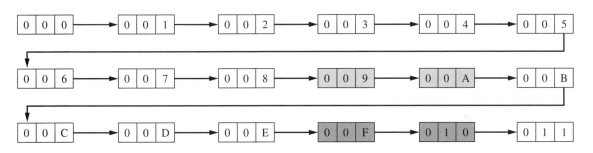

Figure 1.9.3 Counting in hexadecimal

Notice from Figure 1.9.1 that the value of the largest digit is one less than the base. Therefore, in a base 10 numbering system the largest digit is a nine, whereas in a binary numbering system the largest digit is a one. The nice thing about this process is that it can be applied to any base. Figure 1.9.2 shows an example of counting in binary.

The only anomaly to this method is any base greater than 10. The reason for this difference is that there are only 10 numbers we can use for digits. Hexadecimal, base 16, requires six more digits. The additional digits come from the English alphabet. The letter *A* is used to denote a value of 10; *B* is used for 11; *C* for 12, and so on. Figure 1.9.3 shows how to count in hexadecimal.

The boxes with 009 and 00A in Figure 1.9.3 show the transition from a numeric digit to a character. The boxes with 00F and 010 demonstrate the process of adding a second digit to the number. Notice that the least significant digit becomes zero while the second digit is incremented to a one. This is the same process that we use for a base 10 numbering system.

Extending the concept shown in Figure 1.9.3, it becomes apparent that there are a variety of other bases that could be created by using the remaining letters in the alphabet. Although binary, octal, decimal, and hexadecimal are the four most common bases, other bases have been used. In 1993 Telegrafix created RIPscript, a graphics protocol used to send drawing commands to a remote computer via what they called a meganum—a base 36 number, which used digits 0–9 and letters A–Z.

1.9.2 Converting from a Base to Base 10

The conversion from any base to base 10 is a fairly simple process. The first step is to label the digits with their position, starting from the least significant digit. The number shown and labeled in Figure 1.9.4 is assumed to be a hexadecimal number (C3A).

The next step is to multiply the value of each digit with the current base, raised to the position of that digit. Any non-number digit must be converted to its base 10 value. This process is shown in Figure 1.9.5.

The last step is to add those values together to get the result in base 10. This step is shown in Figure 1.9.6.

Notice that in Figure 1.9.6 the subscript number after the result designates the base of that number. Although this example used a hexadecimal value, the same process will work with any base.

1.9.3 Converting from Base 10 to a Different Base

Since we used multiplication to determine the value of a digit, it makes sense that we will need to use division to convert a base 10 number to some other base. The process involves dividing the base 10 number by the target base. The

$$C^2 3^1 A^0$$

Figure 1.9.4 Step 1: Labeling the digits

$$
\begin{aligned}
A \times 16^0 &= 10 \times 1 &&= 10 \\
3 \times 16^1 &= 3 \times 16 &&= 48 \\
C \times 16^2 &= 12 \times 256 &&= 3{,}072
\end{aligned}
$$

Figure 1.9.5 Step 2: Determining digit value

$$10 + 48 + 3{,}072 = 3{,}130_{10}$$

Figure 1.9.6 Step 3: Determining the result

$$\begin{array}{r} 195 \\ 16\overline{)3,130} \end{array} \text{ Remainder: 10 (A)}$$

$$\begin{array}{r} 12 \\ 16\overline{)195} \end{array} \text{ Remainder: 3}$$

$$\begin{array}{r} 0 \\ 16\overline{)12} \end{array} \text{ Remainder: 12 (C)}$$

Figure 1.9.7 Converting from base 10 to hexadecimal

remainder of the division operation becomes the least significant digit in the result. If the remainder is greater than or equal to 10, this value is translated to its corresponding letter. This process continues using the quotient from the previous step until the quotient becomes zero. This process is shown in Figure 1.9.7, using the base 10 number determined in Figure 1.9.6. The target base will be 16 to prove that the process produces the correct hexadecimal value.

Converting the values to their corresponding hexadecimal digits results in $C3A_{16}$, the original value we started with. Similar to the process of converting to base 10, this process also works with any base.

Section 1.9 Exercises

1. Using the octal numbering system, list the first 20 numbers.

2. Convert each of the following numbers to base 10.

   a. 123_8

   b. 10101010_2

   c. $FAB4_{16}$

   d. $ZZTOP_{36}$

3. Convert 1199_{10} to each of the following bases.

   a. binary

   b. octal

   c. hexadecimal

   d. base 5

   e. base 36

1.10 SUMMARY

This chapter began by introducing a number of fundamental terms and by examining a few of the early historical developments in computers. While exploring some of the major developments, we also presented a number of important events and individuals, including the father of computing, Charles Babbage.

Next we looked at some of the key hardware components that make up a PC. These include I/O devices, such as keyboards and monitors, as well as storage devices, such as flash drives and hard disks. In addition, we discussed the brains of the system—the central processing unit and RAM. Once we covered the key hardware components, the idea of a motherboard was introduced as a way to connect the various pieces together.

After investigating the functionality of computer hardware, our focus changed to software. Even though this text is targeted toward writing application software, we discussed the role that system software plays within a computer system. We also briefly explored embedded systems and noted how most embedded systems today are made by combining both hardware and software in one device.

We introduced the concept of programming paradigms, which help programmers develop solutions to various software problems. After presenting a few of the paradigms, we directed our attention to exploring the history and developments associated with two individual programming languages: C and C++.

Next we presented the data hierarchy, to show one way programmers and software developers can group related data. The last topic covered the concept of numbering systems and explained how numbers can be converted from one base to another.

Now that some of the key historical developments and fundamental aspects associated with computer systems have been presented, you are ready to move forward into the rest of the text. While the major focus will be centered on developing software, you will no doubt find many of the terms and concepts presented here helpful.

1.11 Answers to Selected Chapter Exercises

Section 1.5

1. Hardware is the physical equipment used within a computer system. Examples include the monitor, keyboard, hard disk, and CPU.

   Software is the set of detailed instructions that tells the computer what to do. Examples include the OS, solitaire, an email application, and Visual Studio.

   An embedded system is designed to perform one or just a few tasks and contains both the hardware and the software. Examples include the chip in an MP3 player or a cell phone.

Section 1.8

1. SQL Server, Sybase, DB2, and Oracle

2. Nyble

Section 1.9

1. 0, 1, 2, 3, 4, 5, 6, 7, 10, 11, 12, 13, 14, 15, 16, 17, 20, 21, 22, 23

2.

    a. 83

    b. 170

    c. 64,180

    d. 60, 457, 993

3.

    a. 10010101111

    b. 2257

    c. 4AF

    d. 14244

    e. XB

CHAPTER 2

Program Design and Development

Chapter Objectives

By the end of the chapter, readers will be able to:

- Explain the characteristics of the procedural programming paradigm.
- Understand the components of problem solving, program design, and algorithm development.
- Understand the characteristics associated with flowcharts and pseudocode.
- Understand the role of stepwise refinement in developing algorithms.
- Distinguish between the types of errors encountered in building, compiling, and running programs.
- Understand the steps required in both compiling and building an executable file.
- Understand how to key in, build, and execute a program within Microsoft Visual Studio.
- Explain the role of desk checking and debugging in the development of programs or solutions.

Introduction

This chapter introduces some of the fundamental skills and tools necessary to design, develop, and implement computer programs. These skills are not language specific but are essential for any programmer; whether you are going to write a program in C++, C, Visual Basic, or C#, the fundamental skill set required is the same. The chapter also introduces how to create, debug, and execute a program using a software development tool from Microsoft called Visual Studio. Following this, we present and explore an assortment of errors a programmer could encounter. Finally, we conclude the chapter by beginning the process of familiarizing you with Visual Studio.

> **Remember:** A **program** is a specific set of structured (or ordered) operations to be performed by a computer.

2.1 Procedural Programming

Over the past number of years, a wide variety of programming paradigms have evolved. Programming paradigms are simply methods or approaches used to conceptualize how we might solve a specific problem or design and structure a program. Countless books and articles continue to discuss the advantages and disadvantages of individual paradigms. However, our personal experience, as well as that of other educators and industrial partners, has clearly shown that if you are new to programming, you are likely to have the most success by learning programming from a procedural point of view.

Procedural programming performs, or presents, the steps needed to solve a problem in a very sequential and logical manner. For example, in a recipe to bake a cake, the steps need to be followed in the order presented. Deviating from those steps could lead to disastrous results.

In addition, procedural programming provides us an easy way to point out potential problem areas and to make useful suggestions for helping develop good programming habits from the very start. Finally, procedural programming lends itself well to various aspects of learning about problem solving, program design, and algorithm development.

Section 2.1 Exercises

1. Define the term "procedural programming."

2. Define the term "program."

2.2 Problem-Solving Overview

Perhaps one of the most difficult activities for beginning (and even some advanced) programmers to appreciate is the need to make sure they clearly understand the problem they are trying to solve. At first glance this appears to be a very easy task, but upon further digging and review it becomes apparent that identifying the problem may not be nearly as obvious (or easy) as one might hope. It is imperative as we progress in our exploration of C++ that you continue to refine your skills in identifying and defining the problem at hand. Your teacher (or boss) will not appreciate having spent time and effort on the development of a solution for a problem they never asked you to solve. This is a waste of your time—and your employer's money. If you do not have a clear goal of where you are headed, how will you know when the problem has been solved?

Too often beginning programming students want to immediately "code" or type commands into their editor instead of making sure they understand the problem. Obviously you wouldn't leave for a spring-break road trip with your buddies to go from Madison, Wisconsin to Keno, Oregon, without looking at a map. With the high price of gas, it would be a huge misuse of your money. Plus, you just don't have the time to waste by accidentally ending up in Virginia.

Before writing a program in C++ or any other language, it is crucial for you to have an overall strategy for solving the problem. We all know that developing a plan (or looking at the map) takes time; however, it will most definitely save time in the long run.

The next section offers a suggested guideline to follow in developing your programs. This method requires completing each step sequentially. Notice that you do *not* write any code until the fourth step. The goal of the steps is to help develop effective problem-solving skills. In addition, by following these steps, you will find that you are able to create programs in a timelier fashion, which will prove to be more accurate, efficient, and maintainable.

2.2.1 Development Process

There are many methodologies geared to aid in program design and general problem solving. One thing to realize is that we unconsciously solve problems every day of our lives. The techniques used to plan a road trip are really no different from those used to develop a program to keep track of employee payroll information.

The following steps illustrate one of several possible problem-solving approaches. These steps attempt to clarify the approach by walking through the process involved in dealing with a relatively common event.

Step 1: <u>Define the Problem.</u> In this step, determine what you are trying to accomplish. Although this sounds simple, it is one of the most crucial and challenging steps in solving the problem. An error here would prove to be an extremely costly mistake in relation to both time and money.

As an example, suppose your friend has asked you to be responsible for planning a small party for her 21st birthday. She really doesn't want anything big or fancy, but just a few friends to get together for some beverages and dessert. To restate the problem definition in more concise terms, "Plan a friend's birthday party."

Step 2: <u>Requirement Specification.</u> In this step, remove all ambiguities (unclear or not well-defined statements) from the problem definition. Also determine what output or results are required. Lastly, determine what input is needed as well as the source of that input (for example, from the keyboard or from a file) to achieve the desired results or output.

It is essential that the following steps be performed on a small subset of the program. Do *not* attempt to perform the following steps on the entire program. In general, you can't produce output until you perform some type of processing, and you can't process something until you get the appropriate input. Therefore, the input phase is a good place to start. For this very reason, a lot of procedural programs often contain three stages.

$$\text{Input (I)} \rightarrow \text{Process (P)} \rightarrow \text{Output (O)}$$

Continuing with the example started previously, the second step of our birthday-party illustration involves further refining and identifying requirements for the party. This is what is known so far:

- 21st birthday
- Female friend

- Small group of attendees

- Dessert and beverages will be provided

Further clarification of the requirements is necessary to help in the planning. For example, the number of attendees needs to be solidified so that the appropriate amount of food can be obtained. After some deliberation, the decision is made to begin by concentrating on making a dessert—angel food cake—for the party.

Another element related to the overall party relates to finalizing the date and time for the big event. Once you have identified this information, the process can continue on to the next step, having established a clear goal and anticipated timeline.

At the conclusion of this step in our example, we have a much clearer problem statement, which now includes the following requirements:

- 21st birthday

- Female friend

- 14 attendees

- Angel food cake (use Grandma's Devilishly Good Angel Food Cake recipe)

- Fruit punch

- Party will be Friday, August 2 at 7:00 p.m.

- Calvin's place is the location of the party

The ingredients for Grandma's recipe are the inputs needed to produce the desired output, Grandma's Devilishly Good Angel Food Cake. The source of these ingredients will be our cupboards as well as the local market. We are now finished with Step 2 because we have identified the inputs and output for our solution. Also, all ambiguities have been removed from the problem statement.

Step 3: <u>Design.</u> In this phase, develop an algorithm for a small piece of your program or problem. This text focuses on using pseudocode to represent the algorithm. Pseudocode is a written list of the individual steps needed to solve the problem, independent of any programming language. This list should include all the necessary details to clearly outline the solution.

i　An **algorithm** is a finite set of instructions that leads to a solution.

Once the algorithm has been completed, use some sample data and attempt to validate the results by hand. (This simply refers to test data being used to determine if the outlined steps achieve the desired results.)

The process of verifying the logic of your solution is often referred to as **desk checking**.

The desired results of this third step are to provide enough detail to prove you have

1. accounted for all required input,

2. completed all the necessary processing steps,

3. addressed all of the issues required to generate the output or solution identified in the Requirement Specification (Step 2).

Applying Step 3 to our example requires us to determine the amount and type of ingredients necessary to make Grandma's cake. The amount of ingredients is based on the number of attendees. Since our cupboards are bare, we will need to go to the store with the list of ingredients. Once back from the store, all of the ingredients are measured and arranged. Writing the pseudocode for this process results in the following list of steps:

1. Calculate the amount and type of ingredients

2. Go to store

3. Purchase ingredients

4. Come home

5. Measure and arrange all ingredients

Keep in mind that the design of the algorithm created in Step 3 may not be implemented by you. Therefore, the design must be clear and concise enough for someone who hasn't been involved in the design process to be able to implement the solution.

In our example, we are fortunate that Grandma has already created the algorithm for baking the cake—it's included with the recipe. If we assume you were suddenly called away right after assembling all the needed items, our process should be able to be continued by someone else without much of a problem. Indeed, because we have a detailed recipe (i.e., pseudocode) clearly outlining the remaining steps, you can quickly ask one of your friends to complete the dessert. From your friend's perspective, all she or he would really need to do is follow the recipe by mixing the various ingredients together as outlined, and bake our dessert as explained in the recipe. Because of the preliminary work and documentation provided, your sudden departure two hours before the party would not be cause for failure.

Step 4: <u>Implementation.</u> Write the source code based on the algorithm developed in Step 3. Once the pseudocode has been translated to the desired programming language, integrate the newly generated code into any existing source code. Again, please resist the temptation to immediately jump to this step before completing Steps 1–3.

> **Remember:** Write the pseudocode **before** writing the source code. Use pseudocode to help generate your program. This will save you time, especially as the problems become more challenging.

We now enter the final phases of the development of our birthday cake. Your friend follows the steps as outlined in the recipe and bakes the cake as directed. Once the cake is placed in the oven, we have completed almost all of the steps required—except, of course, the one that many of us would say is the best of all.

At this point we now have our cake in the oven and are ready to focus our attention on following a similar process as just described, only this time with an objective to developing the frosting for our dessert. As you can see, it's the accumulation of these individual components, or subpieces, that will help make our dessert an ultimate success.

Step 5: <u>Testing and Verification.</u> In this step, make sure the program works and produces the correct output. This step involves good news and bad news. The bad news: This is not nearly as easy as it sounds, but it is crucial that you verify your results, including checking their accuracy by hand. The good news: Because you have been doing this each step of the way, any error is generally localized to the last section designed and implemented. If the testing and verification reveals the algorithm was incorrect, return to Step 3. Resist the urge to bypass the design step. Going directly to Step 4 without redesigning your algorithm leads to "hacking," which is an undesirable form of programming that some beginning students unfortunately slip into. Hacking is a trial-and-error method of programming, which typically leads to a less robust program that is extremely difficult to debug and maintain, and usually results in a huge amount of time being wasted. After all, would you go on a long road trip or design a new car by using a trial-and-error method?

In relating this step to our example, you need to double-check the cake after it has finished baking. Once the cake is done, remove it from the oven, take it out of the pan, and let it cool. This would be the perfect time to check your final results by sampling the crumbs that remain inside the pan and verifying that the cake is indeed perfect.

Step 6: <u>Repeat Steps 3–5.</u> Once you have tested your code sufficiently, determine the next piece of the solution to be implemented and repeat Steps 3–5. The size of the piece is usually determined by the complexity of the solution and the experience of the programmer.

For the next item in our menu for the party, you would now repeat the previous steps (3–5), only this time focusing your energies on making the punch. Assuming our cake has cooled and we have completed Steps 3–5 for our punch, we can now serve our food.

Step 7: <u>Maintenance.</u> Once you have completed your program, including the required testing and verification, your job isn't over really. Usually the program will need to be revised and enhanced over time. Keeping the design documents as well as providing readable source code makes this phase of the process more productive and less time consuming. This is indeed a crucial step of the development process. To stress the importance of this step, you will be given an exercise at the end of each upcoming chapter for which you will be requested to modify, enhance, or test someone else's code. We call this section the Team Programming Exercise.

We have found that students who get into the habit of following the steps as outlined save considerable time and frustration in learning programming. Particularly when they begin developing more complex and robust applications, the development process becomes a crucial tool.

Comparing the preparation of the dessert (and punch) with the overall maintenance phase might involve altering or experimenting with some of the ingredients we used in making the dessert. For example, maybe we can try to reduce the number of calories each piece of cake contains by substituting artificial sweeteners for sugar the next time. While not perhaps a real crowd-pleasing idea, you no doubt get the point.

Remember:

Step 1: Define the problem

Step 2: Requirement specification

Step 3: Design

Step 4: Implementation

Step 5: Testing and verification

Step 6: Repeat steps 3–5

Step 7: Maintenance

Section 2.2 Exercises

1. In which steps would you find each of the following activities?

   a. Writing pseudocode.

   b. Clarifying the problem statement with your client.

   c. Writing C++ code.

   d. Determining what information will be needed from the user.

   e. Determining what problem needs to be solved.

   f. Identifying what outputs or actions are generated by the program.

   g. Running the program and determining if it works correctly.

2. As referred to in this chapter, what does IPO stand for?

2.3 Algorithm Representation

As previously noted, pseudocode is an important tool to help illustrate the specific steps required to accomplish a particular task. Perhaps the best-known example of an algorithm is a recipe, as demonstrated in the previous section. The ingredients and steps are all clearly defined and outlined in an effort to provide the chef with a road map to follow in making the specific food item. There are a number of ways to represent an algorithm, including flowcharts and pseudocode.

To help illustrate the concepts that follow, assume we want to ask (prompt) a person to enter a score on a test. Our goal is to print out a message that says

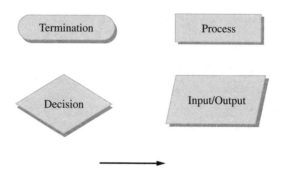

Figure 2.3.1 Flowchart symbols

"Excellent job" if the test taker had a score above 90. If, however, the test taker scores at or below 90, we want to print out a message suggesting they "Try a little harder".

Notice in the preceding problem statement that we can clearly identify the problem or objective—to display a message directly tied to the results of the individual grade entered. Remember, defining the problem is the first step in the development process outlined in the last section. The second step involves identifying what the desired outputs are and what input we need to achieve those results. The output in our short sample will only be one of two messages—either "Excellent job" or "Try a little harder". To display the messages correctly, we only need one input—the score—which will then be evaluated based on the criteria outlined. The third step requires us to develop an algorithm. Next we introduce two options for representing the algorithm.

2.3.1 Flowchart

A flowchart is a graphical or pictorial representation of an algorithm. It is a series of standardized shapes, each with their own meaning, arranged to represent the overall flow of the program. Although there are many other symbols, Figure 2.3.1 shows some of the basic flowcharting shapes and their purpose.

Termination—marks the start or the end of the flowchart

Process—denotes any activity associated with manipulating the data

Decision—illustrates the flow of the solution based on either a true or a false condition

Input/Output (I/O)—shows reading data or displaying results

The arrow illustrates the flow of control.

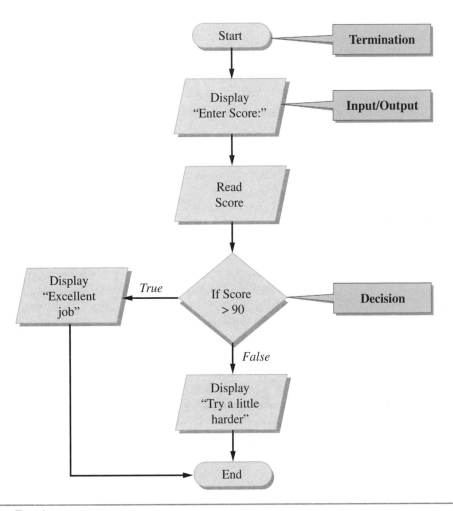

Figure 2.3.2 Flowchart

Figure 2.3.2 shows a flowchart that demonstrates the design of the grade program.

Looking at the flowchart in Figure 2.3.2, you quickly see the flow is from the top down. Notice also how a diamond is used to denote a choice or conditional path, which leads to only one of two possible choices based on a specific condition. Flowcharts can be used to demonstrate the flow of any system, from a program's algorithm to a college's admissions process. However, we will focus our attention on representing algorithms using pseudocode to help us identify and outline the steps needed in solving a specific problem.

```
Display Prompt "Enter Score: "
Read Score from keyboard
If Score > 90
    Display "Excellent job"
Else
    Display "Try a little harder"
```

Figure 2.3.3 Pseudocode

2.3.2 Pseudocode

Pseudocode is an English representation of an algorithm. Pseudocode, like flowcharting, is just another tool we can use to help in our quest to clearly outline the specific steps we must take to solve a problem. Unlike flowcharting, however, it does not require the use of any special predefined symbols.

Pseudocode provides you with the capability to develop an algorithm in English (not in C++ or any other programming language), so you can focus on the problem at hand without regard to the syntax of a specific language. This is the method of representing an algorithm we will use within this text. Figure 2.3.3 demonstrates the use of pseudocode to solve the test-score problem previously discussed.

A **prompt** is text displayed to the user asking (prompting) him or her to do something.

We will return often to the topic of pseudocode as additional programming concepts are introduced in the remaining chapters. Because we view this topic as such a crucial component in programming, we include a section in each chapter called Problem Solving Applied, which will contain examples of the development process, including pseudocode. Based on our experience, we have found that in the development process, design and pseudocode are vital to student success in learning to program, regardless of the language.

Remember: One of the biggest mistakes we have seen beginning students make is not providing enough detail in their pseudocode. Ideally there should be almost a one-to-one translation between lines of pseudocode and source code. Pseudocode should explain *how* to accomplish a task, not just *what* task needs to be performed.

Figure 2.3.4 demonstrates Step 4 and the idea of using pseudocode or a flowchart to represent your solution. Remember, Step 4 of the development process requires you to translate your algorithm to C++, as illustrated in the figure.

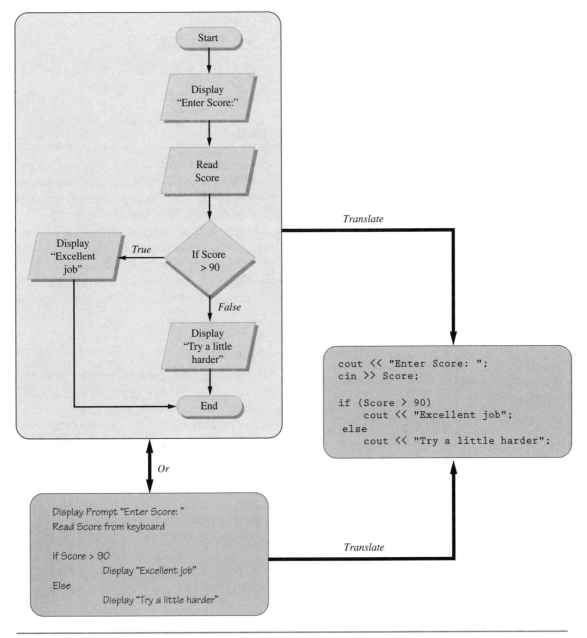

Figure 2.3.4 Translation process

Section 2.3 Exercises

1. What is an algorithm?

2. What form of algorithm representation uses symbols?

3. What form of algorithm representation is English-like?

4. When in the development process do we develop the algorithm?

5. You read a flowchart from _____ to _____.

6. What symbol is used to mark the beginning and end of a flowchart?

2.4 Algorithm Development

Even though the test-score example in Figure 2.3.4 is very straightforward, hopefully it can help you understand the steps required in actually developing an algorithm. Did you notice how we needed to get the input before we could check the score to see what message to display? Did you also notice that we included a clear message telling the person using our solution what specific data needed to be entered (i.e., our prompt)? Once we had collected all the input and done all the required processing, we were only left with our final task—displaying the output as requested in the original problem definition. As you can see, we have now accomplished all three of the I → P → O phases discussed earlier.

2.4.1 Value of Algorithm Development

Although developing your algorithm will take time, please remember it should be done before you ever attempt to write any code. The time you spend working on and testing your algorithm will greatly reduce the total time it takes to complete your problem-solving task or program. As the problems become more complex, you will see the value of your pseudocode increase dramatically.

2.4.2 Stepwise Refinement

This is a methodology that greatly aids in decreasing the time required to create a program. While this technique takes some effort and practice, when done correctly, it is an incredible time saver.

The key to stepwise refinement is to break the program down into smaller, more manageable, and detailed pieces. Then take the first piece and design, implement, and test it. If it is correct, move on to the next piece, if it is not correct, fix it before continuing.

That's about all there is to it, but it is one of the best techniques to use in developing programs. This technique not only saves time but has the added benefit of confining any errors introduced into your program to a smaller area, making them easier to find. Stepwise refinement meets the objective of Step 6 in the development process.

2.5 Compilation Process

Once your solution has been coded using a programming language (like C++), it needs to be turned into a form the computer can understand. Computer languages will perform this process in one of three ways: compilation, interpretation, or a combination of both.

Compilation translates the entire program to machine language and creates a file that can be executed by the operating system. Since translation is done at compilation time, a compiled program runs faster than an interpreted program. Also, the translation process only needs to be completed once (or until changes are made to the source code). However, since each operating system (Windows, UNIX, Macintosh) has a unique command set, the executable compiled on one operating system will not work on a different one. Therefore, the program must be recompiled to run on different operating systems. C and C++ are commonly compiled languages.

Interpretation takes the source code line by line, translates it, and then executes that line immediately. This all takes place when the program is running, so interpreted programs tend to execute slower than other forms of language translation. An advantage of an interpreted program is that as long as you have an interpreter for your platform, you can run your program on any operating system. HTML, LISP, and Forth are languages that are usually interpreted. The disadvantage of this translation method is that every time you execute or run the program it must be reinterpreted.

The last form of translation is a hybrid of interpretation and compilation. The program is compiled into an intermediate form. This intermediate form is then interpreted when executed. Since much of the translation process is done during the compilation phase, the speed during execution is greatly improved over that of a true interpreted language, but retains much of the platform independence of the interpreted languages. Java is an example of a hybrid language.

Since C and C++ are typically compiled, this book focuses on the compilation process. There are many C/C++ compiler products available today.

Microsoft, Borland, and MetroWerks all offer commercial products, while groups such as the GNU Foundation offer a free compiler used by many professional programmers. While the code samples in this text will work on these platforms, they have been tested using Microsoft's Visual Studio.

2.5.1 Editor

Once you have developed your algorithm as discussed previously, you need to translate the pseudocode solution into C++ and then type the source code into an editor. We advise beginning programmers to write out their source code using paper and pencil to help reduce the tendency to program using a trial-and-error approach, often called *hacking*. Once that's done, the code can be entered into an integrated development environment (IDE) focused on C++ development. An IDE combines many development tools in one application. Most of today's IDEs provide a great deal of support to help programmers along the way, including color-coded keywords and automatic text formatting. Using the editor, you are creating a text file with a .cpp file extension containing your source code.

> **Remember:** A text editor is different than a word processor. A text editor, such as Notepad and UNIX's vi editor, will create a file that consists of text only. Word processors, such as Word and WordPerfect, allow you to include many advanced formatting features, such as bolding, special fonts, tables, and image-handling capabilities. Word processors, by default, save their files in a binary format, whereas text editors save their files as text.

2.5.2 Preprocessor

After your C++ code has been written, the first step in the translation process is to run your code through the preprocessor. The preprocessor identifies special commands within your code—called preprocessor directives—and performs the tasks specified by the directives. Preprocessor directives are easy to recognize because they all begin with a pound sign (#). Some of the more common preprocessor directives are #include and #define. These statements will be discussed in more detail later in the text.

2.5.3 Language Translator

Once the preprocessor phase has been completed, the language translator (compiler) takes over. The compiler takes the source code that has been processed by the preprocessor and translates it into something called object code. Object code is mostly machine code that is understandable by the CPU. The object code is stored in an object file. An object file is a binary file with the filename extension .obj. If desired, you can use Windows Explorer to see that this file now exists.

2.5.4 Linker

Once the object files have been created (yes, there can be multiple), the linker combines them into one executable file. In Windows, the file will have the extension .exe. The reason there can be multiple object files is that larger programs are often broken into many separate source-code files. Each source-code file needs to be translated; and an object file, created. This step in the process is often called *building* your program. Assuming the process doesn't encounter any errors, you now have an executable file and can run your program.

Figure 2.5.1 shows how all of these components fit into the compilation process.

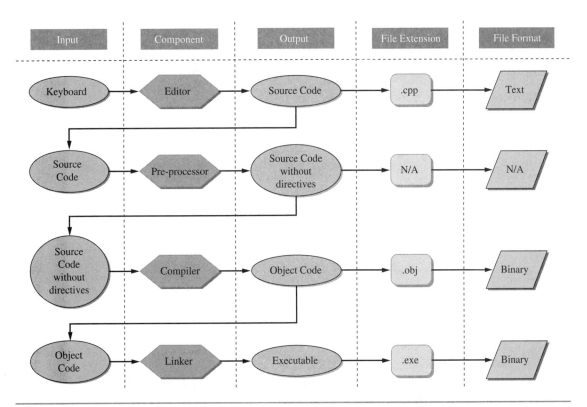

Figure 2.5.1 Compilation process

Section 2.5 Exercises

1. What is the filename extension for each of these files?

   a. C++ source code

   b. executable file

   c. object file

2. What step in the compilation process generates object code?

3. What step in the compilation process creates an executable file?

4. What file format are the following files?

   a. source code

   b. executable

   c. object file

   d. Word document

5. `#define` and `#include` are examples of _____ directives.

6. What step in the compilation process is commonly referred to as building?

7. What step in the compilation process is commonly referred to as compiling?

8. List in order the components used in the compilation process.

2.6 Program Development in Microsoft Visual Studio

Visual Studio is a suite of tools developed by Microsoft to aid in various programming activities. Programs can be written in Visual Studio using many different languages, including C++, Visual Basic, C#, and J#. Recent versions of Visual Studio can be used to build applications targeted for Windows, mobile devices, and the World Wide Web.

2.6.1 Using an Integrated Development Environment (IDE)

Visual Studio is often referred to as an integrated development environment, and like most modern IDEs, it includes an editor for entering your source code, a language translator, a debugger, and many additional tools used in program development. We will focus mainly on using the editor, compiler, and debugger in this text.

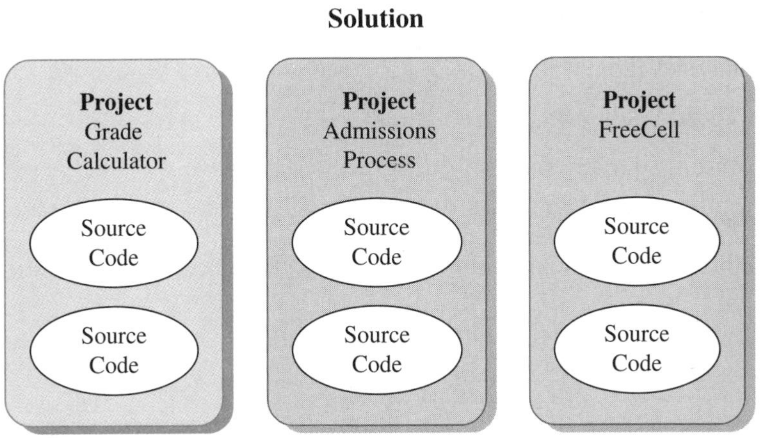

Solution

Figure 2.6.1 Microsoft Visual Studio hierarchy

To use Visual Studio, it is necessary to understand the hierarchy involved in creating a program. The current hierarchy was introduced by Microsoft in the .NET version of their IDE in 2003.

A *solution* encapsulates one or more *projects*. Each project can encapsulate one or more *source-code files*, as shown in Figure 2.6.1. Although only one project can be active at any given time, each individual project represents one complete program.

When you build the program, the *active project*, represented by the rectangle at the far left in Figure 2.6.1, is actually the one that gets created. In addition, the name of the executable will mirror the name of the active project you are building. For example, for the project named Grade Calculator, the name of the executable will be `GradeCalculator.exe`.

As previously mentioned, Visual Studio allows you to quickly build a wide range of applications. In this text, we use it to help us develop our understanding of C++ by actually using it to create, debug, and test our console-based applications.

> *i*   A **console application** is a text-based application. Usually a console application doesn't include any of the familiar graphical user interface (GUI) features, such as buttons, menus, or even mouse control.

Section 2.6 Exercises

1. What does IDE stand for?

2. In Visual Studio, what is a solution?

3. In Visual Studio, what is a project?

4. Where does the name of the executable come from?

5. In this text we will be writing _____-based console applications.

2.7 Running the Program

Once you have built your program, there are several ways to execute it. You can run the executable either from the operating system or through the IDE. To run your application from the operating system, double-click on the executable from Windows Explorer or run it from the Command Prompt (under All Programs—Accessories). However, while you are still in the development mode of Visual Studio, you will find it much quicker and easier to run your program from within the IDE.

2.8 Errors

While we would all like to think we can write error-free code, chances are extremely good that you will encounter some type of error. Some errors will be easy to find and fix, while others may take a long time to locate and resolve. The following sections address the types of errors a programmer will encounter.

2.8.1 Syntax Error

A *syntax error* is caused by something incorrect in the mechanics of the statement(s). For example, in the English language, a sentence without appropriate punctuation at the end would be considered syntactically incorrect. An executable cannot be created until all syntax errors are corrected.

A syntax error is found during the compilation process. These errors are identified and displayed by the compiler. Most modern development environments allow the programmer to jump to the line of source code that the compiler "thinks" the error is on. The IDE will also display an error message—although it is sometimes fairly cryptic—and provide help on the typical causes of the error. Remember, the compiler is working on the programmer's behalf to locate any syntax errors. Unfortunately, with most other types of errors, the burden of locating them rests squarely on the shoulders of the programmer.

The compiler also determines the severity of the syntax problem. If the infraction is minor, the compiler will flag it as a warning. A program with warnings still compiles but may or may not run correctly. Even if the program may run correctly, it is best to remove all warnings as well as errors before running it. In fact, in our classes we stress that all warnings will be treated as errors and should be corrected before running, or turning in, a program.

It is important to understand how the compiler actually works in relation to errors. When a line of source code is translated, it is checked for syntax errors. If there is an error, the compilation process doesn't stop. Instead, the compiler makes assumptions as to what you were trying to accomplish, and the compilation process continues using those assumptions. Most of the time, however, the assumptions are incorrect. This makes it seem like there are more errors than there actually are. The correction of one error may actually remove many error messages. It is extremely important that you correct the first error the compiler identified and then recompile. This will save you a lot of time in chasing phantom errors.

Remember: Always correct the first error or warning in the compiler-generated list and recompile before moving on to the next item in the list.

2.8.2 Linker Error

Another type of error is called a *linker error*, identified by the linker during the build process. These error messages are often very cryptic and hard to understand for beginning programmers, but with practice you can usually find and correct them. Unfortunately, since the linker's job is to build the executable from the object code, there are no tools that allow you to jump to the line that caused the error. Linker errors seldom appear until you start writing your own functions, as shown in Chapter 9. Like syntax errors, all linker errors must be corrected before an executable can be created.

2.8.3 Run-Time Error

Once your program has been built into an executable file, you can now finally run it. Unfortunately, this doesn't mean your program will work correctly. One type of error that may still exist is a *run-time error*. If your program abruptly terminates, or crashes, during execution, you have a run-time error. The cause of the error could be anything from dividing a number by zero to accessing memory that doesn't belong to your program. For finding the cause of this error, the debugger will become an extremely valuable tool and your new best friend. The *debugger* is a set of tools that helps the programmer locate errors, or bugs. (A *bug* is the common term used for an error in a program.)

2.8.4 Logic Error

The most difficult type of error to find is the dreaded *logic error*. A logic error occurs if your program compiles, links, and runs without crashing but doesn't produce the correct results. The debugger is a crucial tool for helping locate logic errors. Stepwise refinement also helps by confining the logic error to a more localized area, making the place where the error was first introduced into your program much easier to find.

> **Remember:** Stepwise refinement breaks large tasks into smaller ones. Each small task is then designed, developed, and tested before moving on to the next small task.

You need to recognize when you do have a logic error. Appropriate desk checking—validating the results by hand—is absolutely vital to your success.

Section 2.8 Exercises

1. What types of errors must be resolved before an executable can be created?

2. What types of errors does the debugger help find?

3. Why is it important that the first syntax error be corrected and then the program recompiled?

4. What type of error would you get if you forget to include a required semicolon at the end of a statement?

2.9 Desk Checking

One of the most fundamental activities you can undertake in relation to locating errors is to mentally simulate and draw out by hand the overall flow of your program *before* you actually run it. This process, often referred to as *desk checking*, can act as a valuable tool in identifying and catching various bugs and problems in your code on paper—well before they enter into the compilation of your program.

Remember: A **bug** is a phrase coined by Grace Hopper, which refers to an error or a flaw found in a computer or computer program.

To desk-check your program, examine your completed source code and write the values of your data on a piece of paper. This is done with the intent to confirm your program's accuracy or to find and correct bugs. Freely draw various boxes to represent your data, and create the necessary test values to see if your calculations are indeed correct.

While this can be a time-consuming process, it is often very helpful for beginning programmers to incorporate desk checking into their development process. This has proved to be an excellent learning tool over the years, and we would suggest you take the time to complete this step. A picture is indeed worth a thousand lines of code and many wasted hours of valuable development time.

Once your program is compiling and apparently executing correctly, it is imperative that you verify your results by hand. To verify that the results of your program are correct, determine ahead of time exactly what your results and calculations should look like, then compare that information against the data generated by your program. Make sure to always double-check some of your calculations as well as your totals on reports to confirm their accuracy. There is obviously nothing worse in programming than generating a report and then finding that you have made an error in the calculations.

Remember: Make it a point to verify your results on all programs you write.

2.10 Using Visual Studio (VS)

As previously mentioned, Visual Studio (VS) is also referred to as an integrated development environment (IDE). The material presented here is simply designed to help get you started using this very powerful and professional tool. Before we get too far, please remember to relax and have fun with this package. Remember, any time you spend learning how to use this application will be time well spent. Figures 2.10.1–2.10.10 were done using Microsoft Visual Studio 2008 Professional Edition.

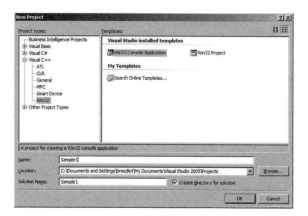

Figure 2.10.1 New project window

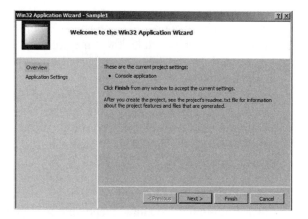

Figure 2.10.2 Win32 application wizard

2.10.1 Getting Started

1. Launch Visual Studio (Start → All Programs → Microsoft Visual Studio). Then select Microsoft Visual Studio 2008.

2. Select File → New → Project → and click on the "+" sign to the left of Visual C++ (under Project types). The results are shown in Figure 2.10.1.

3. Now click on Win32 under Project types. On the right-hand side under Templates, select Win32 Console Application. Enter the name of your new project in the Name field. For illustrative purposes we have called our project "Sample1". Click the OK button. Figure 2.10.2 shows the window that is now displayed.

4. You will now see the Win32 Application Wizard. On the left side you will

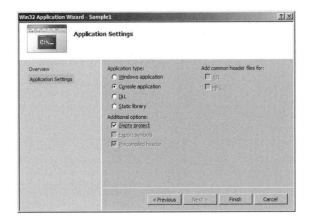

Figure 2.10.3 Application settings

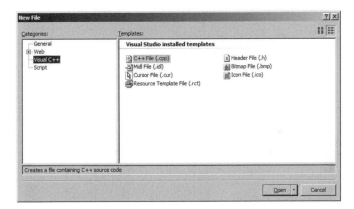

Figure 2.10.4 New file window

find the link called Application Settings. Under Application Settings/
Additional options, check the box that says Empty project. Make it a point
to verify that the Console application radio button has been selected for
you. This is illustrated in Figure 2.10.3.

Click the Finish button. We have now created a solution. As you may recall,
a solution is composed of one or more projects (i.e., applications).

5. Under File, select New → File causing a new file dialog box to appear, as
shown in Figure 2.10.4.

6. Under Categories, be sure to click on Visual C++, and under Templates, be
sure to select C++ File (.cpp). Now press the Open button.

7. By default, the name of your new file is called `Source1.cpp`. Immediately
save this file to the same directory as your solution but give it a new name,

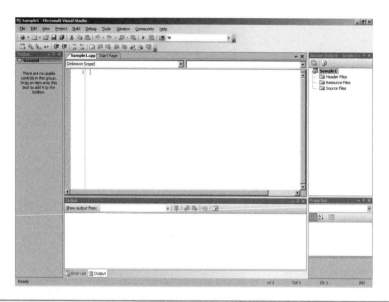

Figure 2.10.5 Visual Studio with Sample1.cpp

as we did: `Sample1.cpp`. Visual Studio should now appear as shown in Figure 2.10.5.

8. Now go to the File menu option and select the Move `Sample1.cpp` into → 1 Sample1 project. This is directly above the Exit menu option at the bottom of that menu. The menu system is shown in Figure 2.10.6.

9. You are now in the editor, and the file `Sample1.cpp` has been added to this project.

   Type in the program as shown in Figure 2.10.7.

10. Notice the use of the colored text in relation to the syntax highlighting in your IDE. Your code should look something similar to that in Figure 2.10.7.

    Notice an asterisk appears to the right of the filename, indicating that the file has not yet been saved.

11. Under the Debug menu option, select Start without Debugging.

12. You may see a dialog box appear, noting that Visual Studio is working on your behalf to monitor the changed state of your application. If you have indeed made changes, you will be asked if you would like to build your application; click the Yes button. This is shown in Figure 2.10.8.

13. Notice that once you start the build process, the Output window at the bottom of Visual Studio provides status information. The Output window is shown in Figure 2.10.9.

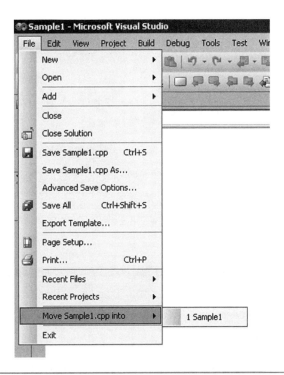

Figure 2.10.6 Including source file

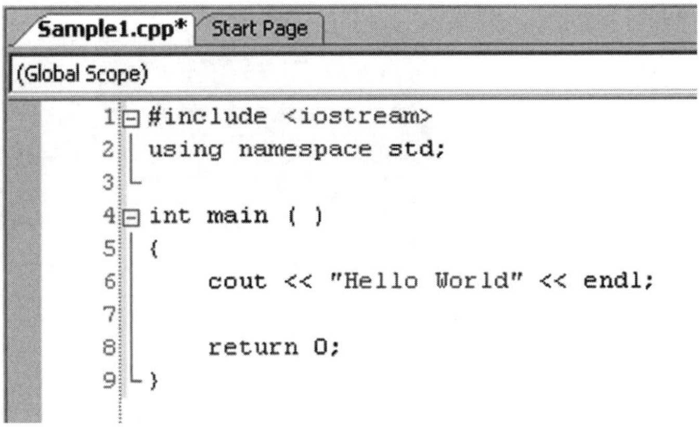

Figure 2.10.7 Unsaved source code

Figure 2.10.8 Project out-of-date confirmation window

Figure 2.10.9 Output window

Figure 2.10.10 Console window

14. As you can see, your application has launched a new console application and displays the text "Hello World". Remember, to terminate the console application, you need only press any key. The console window is shown in Figure 2.10.10.

Congratulations! You have now just entered, compiled, built, and executed your first C++ program!

We will have much more to say about using Microsoft's Visual Studio in the future, but for now you can indeed be proud of your progress. If you ran into any errors in the compilation process, correct them and repeat the process, beginning with Step 11.

2.11 Debugging

Debugging is the process of removing run-time and logic errors from a program. There are many tools available to aid in the debugging process. These tools, which are integrated into the IDE, will not find the errors for you but will allow you to analyze the situation to determine whether the results of the code being examined meet the expectations.

> ⚠ **Remember:** Debugging tools only help you find logic and run-time errors in running applications. All syntax and linker errors must be corrected before using debugging tools.

Most modern developer environments have some form of these debugging tools. It is crucial for you to learn the tools available in your specific IDE. We will begin to explore the various debugging tools integrated into Visual Studio in Chapter 5.

2.12 Problem Solving Applied

Problem statement: One of your friends, Jamie, who is majoring in physics, operates a small computer business on the side to help her pay for her college expenses. She has asked you to create an algorithm that outlines the steps needed to calculate her total mileage expenses for her federal tax return. This year the IRS allows 58.5 cents a mile for business-related travel. However, since that amount is subject to change ever year, your solution should simply ask her for that information. Unfortunately the IRS will not allow the deduction of her mileage accrued while traveling for the softball team. She would like to be able to enter in the amount of miles she traveled for business and calculate the total mileage expenses.

Please develop the necessary pseudocode solution outlining the steps needed to solve the problem of calculating and displaying her mileage expenses for last year.

Requirement Specification:

Input(s):

Input Type	Data	Source
Decimal	MilesTraveled	Keyboard
Decimal	MileageRate	Keyboard

Output(s):

Output Type	Data	Destination
Decimal	MilesTraveled	Screen
Decimal	MileageRate	Screen
Decimal	MileageExpenseAllowance	Screen

Design:

Required formulas:

MileageExpenseAllowance = MilesTraveled * MileageRate

Pseudocode:

— **I**nput Phase —

Display prompt "Please enter in the miles you traveled for business: "
Read MilesTraveled

Display prompt "Please enter in the IRS mileage rate: "
Read MileageRate

— **P**rocess Phase —

MileageExpenseAllowance = MilesTraveled * MileageRate

— **O**utput Phase —

Display "Miles Traveled: "
Display MilesTraveled

Display "Mileage Rate: "
Display MileageRate

Display "Total IRS Mileage Allowance: "
Display MileageExpenseAllowance

Testing and Verification:

Desk Checking:

Are all inputs accounted for? **Yes**
Are prompts self-describing? **Yes**
Has all required processing been completed? **Yes**

Is all of the processing correct? Use test values of 496 miles @ 58.5 cents a mile.

— Validation —

MileageExpenseAllowance = 496 * .585 = 290.16

— Validation Correct —

Is all output from the Output Phase self-describing? **Yes**

— Pseudocode Correction —

None needed

2.13 SUMMARY

Many of the concepts presented in this chapter will be the basis for much of the material in the remainder of the text. While some of these concepts might appear abstract or theoretical at this time, it is imperative that you become familiar with them.

This chapter illustrates various aspects associated with procedural programming. In addition, we have outlined a series of steps you should follow in the development of your programs.

After completing the design overview, we presented information related to actually entering, compiling, and running your application within Microsoft's Visual Studio. It is during this process that various errors will be encountered, including those related to syntax and program logic. Although there are many available debugging tools, covered later in the text, your best resource in finding errors currently lies in the desk-checking process.

2.14 Debugging Exercise

1. Given the following problem statement and pseudocode, verify (desk-check) that the solution is correct. If it is not correct, make the necessary changes and rewrite the pseudocode.

Problem: Read a test score and determine what letter grade the student should receive based on the following grading scale:

$90+ \rightarrow A$
$80+ \rightarrow B$
$70+ \rightarrow C$
$60+ \rightarrow D$
Score of less than $60 \rightarrow F$

Solution:

   Input(s): A decimal number for the test score.

   Output(s): A letter signifying the grade.

Pseudocode:

```
Print prompt "Enter Test Score: "
Read score
If score > 90
    Print "A"
If score > 80 and score < 90
    Print "B"
If score > 70 and score < 80
    Print "C"
If score > 60 and score < 70
    Print "D"
If score < 60
    Print "F"
```

2. Based on the following recipe for making French onion soup, answer the following questions:

   a. Does the recipe appear complete and easy to follow?

   b. What specific items are lacking?

   c. Would you eat it?

Recipe for Marie's World-Famous French Onion Soup:

Ingredients (Inputs)

4 medium fresh onions
3 tablespoons butter
4 cups beef broth
1 teaspoon Worcestershire sauce
2 slices toasted French bread
¼ cup grated Parmesan cheese

Activities (Process)

- In a covered large saucepan, cook the onions in the butter over low heat, stirring occasionally
- Uncover and add the beef broth to the saucepan
- Add Worcestershire sauce to the saucepan
- Heat to boiling
- Reduce heat, cover, and simmer
- Place ½ slice of toasted bread in each of 4 soup bowls; pour hot soup over bread and sprinkle generously with Parmesan cheese

Serve and enjoy (Output)

2.15 Programming Exercises

1. Write the pseudocode to find the average of three fixed numbers (10, 100, and 1,000) and print the results.

2. Assume you take three exams during the term. Write the pseudocode solution that prompts you to enter the score for each of your three exams, calculates the sum and average of your exam scores, and prints the final total and average to the screen.

2.16 Team Programming Exercise

A long time pen pal of yours from another country has recently come to stay with you and attend your school for one academic term. She asks you to review a pseudocode solution she has been working on to help her determine if it appears to be logically correct. Even though we have just touched the surface in relation to using and writing algorithms, you agree—perhaps somewhat reluctantly—to help her out. Basically your friend is trying to write a pseudocode solution to find the sum of the first five natural numbers. The problem statement and her solution follow, preceded by some questions to aid you in your evaluation:

1. Is the solution proposed logically correct? If not, what is wrong and how would you correct it?

2. How might you be able to actually prove that her solution works?

3. What suggestions do you have to improve the overall readability of her pseudocode?

Problem: Construct an algorithm to find and print out the sum of the first five positive, non-zero integer numbers.

SET x to 0
Set n to 0
WHILE $n < 5$
ADD n to x
Print out x

Write your response to each of the preceding questions (1–3). In addition, rewrite the entire solution, addressing all of your concerns and correcting any errors.

2.17 Answers to Chapter Exercises

Section 2.1

1. Procedural programming performs, or presents, the steps needed to solve a problem in a very sequential and logical manner.

2. A program is a specific set of structured (or ordered) operations to be performed by a computer.

Section 2.2

1.

    a. Step 3: Design

    b. Step 2: Requirement specification

    c. Step 4: Implementation

    d. Step 2: Requirement specification

    e. Step 1: Define the problem

    f. Step 2: Requirement specification

    g. Step 5: Testing and verification

2. Input → Process → Output

Section 2.3

1. An algorithm is a finite set of instructions that leads to a solution.

2. flowchart

3. pseudocode

4. Step 3: Design

5. top; bottom

6. oval

Section 2.5

1.

    a. `.cpp`

    b. `.exe`

    c. `.obj`

2. language translation

3. linking

4.

  a. text

  b. binary

  c. binary

  d. binary

5. preprocessor

6. linking

7. language translation

8. editor, preprocessor, language translator (compiler), linker

Section 2.6

1. integrated development environment

2. A solution in Visual Studio encapsulates one or more individual projects.

3. A project in Visual Studio is part of a solution and contains all the necessary files for a particular application. You could have a solution called `MyInLabs` that contained a number of weeks' InLab projects (`InLabWeek1`, `InLabWeek2`, etc.)

4. The name of the executable file will be the same name as that of the active project within your solution.

5. text

Section 2.8

1. There are two different categories of errors that must be fixed before an executable file can be created: syntax (compiler) errors and linker errors.

2. run-time and logic errors

3. Because the correction of one error may indeed remove a number of other error related messages.

4. syntax error

Getting Started with C++

Chapter Objectives

By the end of the chapter, readers will be able to:

- Understand the case sensitivity and semicolon rules of C++.
- Understand how whitespace is used to increase readability.
- Comment source code.
- Understand the role of `main`.
- Use `#include` statements.

Introduction

Up to this point, everything we have covered has been language independent. Now it is time to write some actual C++ code. This chapter discusses some of the fundamental aspects of C++ programs.

3.1 C++ Basics

One of the first things to understand about C++ is that it is a case-sensitive language. This means the word "cat" is different from the word "Cat"—or any other variations related to capitalization. Not all languages are case sensitive. Visual Basic and Ada are two examples of languages that are case *in*sensitive.

Second, you should be aware that all programming languages are composed of a series of *reserved words* that have a special or predefined meaning within the language and therefore cannot be used as user-defined identifiers.

Remember: All C++ reserved words are lowercase.

Another C++ language requirement is the use of semicolons to end or terminate most statements. If the statement is an instruction, the semicolon *must* be included. The omission of the semicolon is one of the most common errors we have seen in teaching C++ (and C as well).

Some categories of statements that don't require semicolons are:

- Preprocessor directives

- Function headers

- Control statements

Except for "preprocessor directives," none of these terms will make much sense yet. Rest assured, however, that throughout the following chapters, the meaning of these terms will become much clearer.

Remember: A **preprocessor directive** is a command executed by the preprocessor. You can recognize preprocessor directives because the first character on the line is a number sign (#).

3.2 Whitespace

Whitespace usually refers to empty spaces inserted around related items. In the area of computer science and programming, the term refers to an empty or non-visible character (i.e., a space or tab), including blank lines. We will use white-space to improve the readability and maintainability of our programs. Example 3.2.1 shows two identically functional and correct programs, the first using an appropriate amount of whitespace and the second using no whitespace other than what is required to make the program compile.

Example 3.2.1 Whitespace example

```
Example 1:

int main ( )
{
    return 0;
}

Example 2:

int main(){return 0;}
```

Clearly the first example is much more readable, even with just these few lines of code. Imagine how much more difficult it would be to read a program with 100,000 lines of code written using only the minimum required white-space.

Some beginning programmers are apprehensive about putting whitespace in their code because of the misguided notion that it will increase the size of the executable program. While we appreciate their good-hearted intentions to save disk space and memory, this is not true. Whitespace is ignored by the compiler and therefore removed from the executable, resulting in no difference in file size.

3.3 Comments

Comments are lines of C++ code that are ignored by the compiler. Like white-space, using comments has no impact on the overall behavior, flow, or size of your program. These lines are used to document the source code for you or for other programmers. Comments aid in the readability and maintainability of your code.

There are two types of comments available for programmers in C++: *inline* and *block*. An inline comment starts with a double forward-slash (//) and continues until the end of the line. Example 3.3.1 shows an inline comment. Note that an inline comment can only span one line.

Example 3.3.1 Inline comment

```
// This is an inline comment.
```

The block comment starts with a forward-slash and asterisk combination (/*) and ends with an asterisk and forward-slash (*/). This style of comment is sometimes referred to as a C-style comment. Unlike the inline comment, the block comment can span multiple lines of source code, as demonstrated in Example 3.3.2.

Example 3.3.2 Block comment

```
/* This is a
    multiple
      line
    comment. */
```

Section 3.3 Exercises

For each of the following code fragments, indicate if there are any errors. If there is an error, specify how you would fix it.

1. `\\ This is an inline comment`

2. `/* This is a comment`

3. `/* This is another comment /*`

4. `/* Isn't this /* a fun */ comment */`

5. `// This is a`
   `multiline`
   `comment`

3.4 The main Function

When you run a program, how does the computer know where in the program to start? Many beginning programmers incorrectly assume that the first physical line of code in the file executes first. However, a C++ program always starts its execution at the function named *main*. It doesn't matter if main is physically located at the beginning or end of your source code—its contents will always be the first executed. For this reason, we often see main listed as the first function in a program.

> *i* The term **function** refers to a task or job. For example, the function of a waiter is to serve food. In programming, a function is a group of related statements that together perform a specific task or job.

If you were to type the code in Example 3.4.1 into your IDE, some words would be blue. They are reserved words, meaning they already have a predefined purpose in C++.

Example 3.4.1 The main function

```
int main() // Function header, no semicolon
{// Start of function body

    return 0; // C++ statement, requires semicolon
}// End of function body
```

> *i* A **function header** is the first line in a **function definition**. The function definition is the combination of the function header and the **function body**, the statements enclosed in curly braces.

Even though Example 3.4.1 compiles and runs, it doesn't do anything constructive; it is just used to illustrate the overall format of `main`.

 Remember: You will always have only one function per program called `main`.

Observe that `main` is always written in lowercase and that no semicolon is used after the function header. Notice also that parentheses and curly braces always come in pairs. If there is an opening parenthesis or brace, there must be a matching closing parenthesis or brace. The job of the braces is to group statements together and to define the beginning and end of the function body.

There are some issues with `main` that we have not yet addressed, such as the meaning of the **int** before `main` and the **return** statement. Although at this point the underlying meanings are not important, they will be addressed in more detail in later chapters. For now, just remember that they are necessary for creating a C++ program.

Section 3.4 Exercises

For each of the following code fragments, indicate if there are any errors. If there is an error, specify how you would fix it.

1. ```
int Main ( )
```

2. ```
int main ( );
```

3. ```
int main()
(
        return 0;
)
```

4. ```
int main()
{
        Return 0;
}
```

5. ```
int main ( )
}
        return 0;
{
```
```

3.5 The #include **Preprocessor Directive**

The preprocessor directive *#include* allows the programmer to access external or separate files called *header files*. These header files contain the information necessary to access many of the predefined C++ routines. While header files are not required to create a valid C++ program, virtually all C++ programs use them because of the powerful constructs to which the header files provide access.

> *i* A **predefined routine** is not part of the core language but is an extension to the language. These routines are part of the C++ standard and are accessed through header files.

At language translation (compile) time, all of the information for using predefined routines must be provided. Although the implementation of the routines is found in the Standard C++ Library, the header file is required to access these routines.

There are two forms of the #include:

1. #include <header_file>

2. #include "header_file"

While both of these forms accomplish the same thing, they look for the header file in physically different locations. The first looks for the header file in the include directory, established when the compiler was installed. If the default path was chosen when Visual Studio was installed, you will find the include directory at: C:\Program Files\Microsoft Visual Studio 9.0\VC\include. Header files are just text files, so feel free to open them to see what they contain. However, we strongly suggest you don't change anything in the header file.

The second form looks for the header file in the current directory (the directory where the .cpp file exists) or within the directory specified as a path in the #include statement. This form is generally used to access programmer-created header files. Creating your own header files will be discussed later in this text.

The header file used in most of the programs you will write for this text is <iostream>. Although the full explanation of this file and its associated routines will be left for Chapter 5, we will use it to demonstrate the use of the #include.

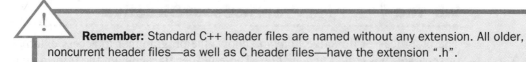

Remember: Standard C++ header files are named without any extension. All older, noncurrent header files—as well as C header files—have the extension ".h".

In Example 3.5.1 we use the #include to allow us to use the predefined routine cout, which prints or displays text to the screen.

Example 3.5.1 The #include **directive**

```cpp
#include <iostream> // Allows access to Input/Output routines

int main()
{
     // Outputs "Hello World!" to the screen
     std::cout << "Hello World!";

     return 0;
}
```

3.5.1 Namespaces

In Example 3.5.1, notice the "std::" prefix to the cout statement. This prefix allows access to a named area (namespace) within the Standard C++ Library. As you might expect, having to preface all of the predefined routines with "std::" might become cumbersome after a while. Fortunately, there are a couple of ways of accessing the necessary routines without using the prefix. Example 3.5.2 shows the easiest way to access the needed information.

Example 3.5.2 The using namespace **statement**

```cpp
#include <iostream>
using namespace std; // Replaces std:: prefix

int main()
{
     cout << "Hello World!";

     return 0;
}
```

However, the easiest way is not necessarily the best. Another method is shown in Example 3.5.3.

Example 3.5.3 The `using` **statement**

```
#include <iostream>
using std::cout; // Replaces std:: prefix for cout only

int main()
{
    cout << "Hello World!";

    return 0;
}
```

Example 3.5.3 doesn't look so difficult, but there is a catch: you have to have a `using` statement for each routine needed. In some cases, this could quickly create a fairly long list of `using` statements. In Example 3.5.3 we are bringing into the scope of the program only those specific statements we will be using from the `<iostream>` header file. By including `using namespace std;` in Example 3.5.2, we are bringing in many additional routines that may not even be used.

---

i   A **namespace** is a method provided in C++ that allows us to group or structure related entities inside one category.

Another thing to keep in mind is that some header files and their associated routines don't require the use of namespaces. An example of such a header file is `<cmath>`, which allows access to some predefined math routines. These routines are actually a holdover from the C language.

STYLE NOTE   Of the three methods available to access routines contained within a namespace, which is the preferred? The answer depends on your organization, which is responsible for dictating the method you should use.

Section 3.5 Exercises

For each of the following code fragments, indicate if there are any errors. If there is an error, specify how you would fix it.

1. `#Include <iostream>`

2. `#include "iostream"`

3. `#include (iostream)`

4. `#include <iostream>;`

5. `#include <IOstream>`

6. `#include <iostream>`
   `Using namespace std`

7. `using namespace std;`
   `#include <iostream>`

8. `#include <iostream>`
   `using std:cout;`

9. `#include <iostream>`
   `using std::cout`

3.6 Problem Solving Applied

Problem statement: Develop a pseudocode solution to calculate the gross pay for I. M. Sample. Mr. Sample is paid on an hourly basis, does not receive overtime, and is in the 20 percent tax bracket. He has been working for the company for the past six months. Please display his gross pay, the amount of taxes withheld, and his net pay.

Requirement Specification:

Input(s):

Input Type	Data	Source
Decimal	Wage	Keyboard
Decimal	Hours	Keyboard

Output(s):

Output Type	Data	Destination
Decimal	GrossPay	Screen
Decimal	TaxesWithheld	Screen
Decimal	NetPay	Screen

Design:

Required formulas:

GrossPay = Hours * Wage

TaxesWithheld = GrossPay * 20%

NetPay = GrossPay – TaxesWithheld

Pseudocode:

— Input Phase —

Print prompt "Enter wage: "

Read Wage

Print prompt "Enter hours worked: "

Read Hours

— Process Phase —

GrossPay = Hours * Wage

TaxesWithheld = GrossPay * 20%

NetPay = GrossPay – TaxesWithheld

— Output Phase —

Display GrossPay

Display TaxesWithheld

Display NetPay

Testing and Verification:

Desk Checking:

Are all inputs accounted for? **Yes**

Are prompts self-describing? **Yes**

Has all required processing been completed? **Yes**

Is all of the processing correct? Use test values of 40 hours @ $10.00/hr.

— **Validation** —

GrossPay = 40.0 * 10.00 = **400**

TaxesWithheld = 400 * .20 = **80**

NetPay = 400 – 80 = **320**

— **Validation Correct** —

Is all output from the Output Phase self-describing? **No**

— **Pseudocode Correction** —

Display "Gross Pay: "

Display GrossPay

Display "Taxes Withheld: "

Display TaxesWithheld

Display "Net Pay: "

Display NetPay

3.7 C—The Differences

Beginning with this chapter, we will provide a unique section for those readers interested in learning some of the fundamental elements associated with the C programming language. The objective of this section is to present and illustrate the C language statements that correspond to the C++ language material presented thus far in the chapter. The focus will clearly be on showing the syntax of the C language. This section is truly optional but provides some additional information for those who need to learn C as well as C++. Although no exercises will be provided in this section, you can use the C++ exercises to practice the C language constructs.

For illustrative purposes, Example 3.7.1 is the C version of the classic "Hello World" program in Example 3.5.1.

Example 3.7.1 The C version of the "Hello World" program

```c
#include <stdio.h> // Allows access to Input/Output routines

int main( void )
{
    // Outputs "Hello World!" to the screen
    printf( "Hello World!" );

    return 0;
}
```

You are likely to see the word "void" in the parentheses. The word "void" means that main is passed or receives no value or data. It is equivalent to ( ) in C++. Finally, preprocessor directives are very important in C. Like in C++, they basically tell us where we can locate the definitions or meanings of the predefined routines used in our code. The header files would include, however, ".h" extensions, as shown in Example 3.7.1. Notice that namespaces aren't used with C header files.

3.8 SUMMARY

Chapter 3 introduced you to a number of the fundamental components associated with a C++ program. Our discussion started with some C++ basics, including comments, the important role of `main`, and the use of header files.

As discussed, a couple of different options are available for including comments in your code, such as the `/* ... */` and the `//`. Appropriately commented code, as well as the proper use of whitespace, greatly increases the readability and maintainability of your program.

The function `main` is required in any C++ program. It is the one function all of our programs will include and the first function to be executed by your program, regardless of its physical location within your code. Obviously, we will have a lot more to say about functions in the following chapters.

Our next topic focused on using header files and provided a brief discussion of namespaces. We will periodically revisit the topic of namespaces and additional header files in the remainder of the text, as their use becomes warranted.

So now you have seen the full implementation of a complete, albeit very small, C++ program. This overall structure will continue to be expanded and discussed in more detail in the remaining chapters of this text. If you are feeling comfortable with the material presented, you are ready to continue on your C++ journey. If not, please make it a point to review the material presented, firing up your compiler and actually walking through some of the examples. With these fundamental concepts out of the way, it's about to get really exciting!

3.9 Debugging Exercise

Problem: Rewrite your friend's directions in pseudocode form, removing any extraneous information to make them easier to read. Verify that Storm hasn't left anything out and that the directions make sense.

Your friend Storm has invited you to go riding in the dunes with him. He has written you an email with the details on how to get to Spinreel Park on the Oregon dunes.

Hey!

Here are the directions from Klamath Falls to Spinreel Park. First take Hwy 140 west to Medford. You might want to fill up here, gas was much cheaper in Medford than any place else on the trip. Take I-5 North for a little over 100 miles until you get to the second exit at Sutherlin. Take this exit and at the end of the off-ramp take a left (west) on Hwy 138, which ends at Elkton. Take a left here, this is Hwy 38. When you are going through Elkton stop off at the Pastry Mill. Their Cranberry, Walnut, Carmel, Orange Sticky Buns are incredible! ;-) Take Hwy 38 to Reedsport where it T-bones into Hwy 101. Take Hwy 101 until you get to the exit that announces Spinreel Park. This is about 12 miles from Reedsport.

I'm really looking forward to this weekend. It should be a blast!

Storm

3.10 Programming Exercises

1. Write the pseudocode for asking a user to input the radius of a circle. Once you have the radius, do the necessary calculation and display the area of the circle. For the value of pi, please use 3.1416.

2. To gain some additional experience with your particular development environment, enter in, build, debug (if necessary), and execute the following program. (Notice the use of the '\n' in the following code.)

```
#include <iostream>

int main()
{
    std::cout << "Modified version of original C program "
            << " (by Kernighan & Ritchie)\n";

    std::cout << "Hello World!";

    return 0;
}
```

3. Write a C++ program to display your name and your age (hint: you will need to use `cout`). Make it a point to include the `<iostream>` header file.

3.11 Team Programming Exercise

Remember your old pen-pal friend from another country (you know, from the last chapter)? Well, now she is wondering why it is that while most of the world uses the metric system, the United States does not. While you don't necessarily want to debate the various political issues associated with this topic, you are willing to help her with the conversion of miles to kilometers problem. As you can see, the complexity of the problem is a bit more challenging than the last. She asks you to review the following pseudocode solution for outlining the steps required to convert a given distance entered by someone in kilometers to miles and help her determine if it is logically correct. Even though we just got started with pseudocode, you again agree to help her out.

In an effort to help you judge the accuracy of the algorithm below, your friend tells you the following information:

- She prefers the metric system
- A kilometer is 1000 meters
- One kilometer is less than one mile
- Kilometers per mile is approximately 1.6093 kilometers

Use the following questions to aid in your evaluation:

1. We know that 15 miles is approximately 24.14 kilometers. Using this information, how might you be able to actually prove that her solution is logically correct? If there is a problem, fix it!

2. What suggestions do you have to improve the overall readability of her pseudocode?

Problem: Write the pseudocode to ask a person to enter a distance in miles and then display the converted distance in kilometers. You will likely need to refer to some of the preceding background information.

DISPLAY PROMPT "PLEASE ENTER IN THE MILES YOU WANT TO CONVERT: "

READ MILES

KILOMETERS = MILES * 1.3069   DISPLAY MILE

DISPLAY "MILES = "

DISPLAY KILOMETER   DISPLAY " KILOMETERS"

Write your response to each of the preceding questions (1 and 2). In addition, rewrite the entire solution, addressing all of your concerns and correcting any errors. Make it a point to keep readability in mind as you rewrite your solution.

3.12 Answers to Chapter Exercises

Section 3.3

1. Wrong slashes, change to //.

2. For an inline comment, change to //; for a block comment, add the */ at the end of the comment. The /* */ is a matched set; you can't have one without the other.

3. Replace the ending /* with */.

4. You can't nest block comments. One comment must end before the next one starts.

5. The // is for single-line comments only. To fix, either replace the // with the /* and */ combination or place the // at the beginning of each line.

Section 3.4

1. Remember, C++ is case sensitive; therefore, the "M" in "Main" must be lowercased.

2. No semicolons after function headers.

3. Curly braces are used to encapsulate statements, not parentheses. The return statement should be placed between { and }.

4. The "R" in "Return" needs to be lowercased.

5. The braces are reversed.

Section 3.5

1. The "I" in "Include" needs to be lowercased.

2. Although legal with the default settings in VS, it may not work for all compilers. It is always recommended to reserve the " " for user-defined header files. Replace the " " with < >.

3. Wrong symbols; replace the ( ) with < >.

4. Remember, no semicolons after preprocessor directives.

5. In Windows, everything is fine. In a case-sensitive operating system like UNIX, the compiler would not be able to find the header file. Therefore, it is safer to make all header files lowercase.

6. "Using" must be all lowercase, and there must be a semicolon after the `using` statement.

7. The `using` statement must be after the `#include`.

8. There is a colon missing. The :: is required between "`std`" and "`cout`".

9. There needs to be a semicolon at the end of the `using` statement.

Literals, Variables, and Constants

Chapter Objectives

By the end of the chapter, readers will be able to:

- Understand the types and use of literals.
- Explore the role of data types in programming.
- Describe some of the key primitive data types found in C++.
- Understand the requirements and conventions used in naming identifiers.
- Differentiate between initialization and assignment.
- Use and interpret an ASCII chart.
- Understand the use of constants.
- Understand the use of variables.

Introduction

In this chapter we will explore how to store information in memory so that our program has access to the information when needed. Several other chapters focus on the same issue, but they all require the basic concepts introduced in this chapter.

To explain the difference between literals, variables, and constants, let's look at the mathematical formula to calculate the circumference of a circle: $2\pi r$. The character *r* is a variable that represents the radius of the circle. The symbol π represents the constant for pi, and the character 2 is a numeric literal. We will refer to this example throughout the chapter.

4.1 Literals

A *literal* is a value that is interpreted exactly as it is written. In our introductory example of the circle circumference formula, the 2 is a numeric literal. It is not a variable or a constant, as explained later in this chapter, because it has no name associated with it.

There are three types of literals: numeric, character, and string. In C++, a *numeric literal* is represented exactly as suspected. Examples of numeric literals would include 14, −457, and 3.14. A *character literal* is a single character enclosed by single quotation marks, such as 'a', 'Z', and '9'. A *string literal* is composed of multiple characters surrounded by double quotation marks ("). You have already been exposed to string literals in the previous chapters. For example, in the following statement, the string literal would be "Hello World".

```
std::cout << "Hello World";
```

Table 4.1.1 shows examples of the different types of literals.

In Table 4.1.1, the fourth numeric literal, 0xFF, specifies that the value following the x is a hexadecimal value. Notice that the fifth numeric literal starts with a zero, which designates that the literal is an octal value.

Also notice that in the third example of string literals, "A" is a single character surrounded by double quotation marks. Although perfectly legal, it should be avoided because of the additional overhead required. We will have more to say about this later in the text.

Literal Type	Examples
Numeric	0
	3.12
	-5
	0xFF
	0777
Character	'A'
	' '
String	"Hello World"
	"Ralph"
	"A"

Table 4.1.1 Literals

Section 4.1 Exercises

In the following exercises, find the illegal literals. If the literal is legal, state what type of literal it is.

1. -12.34

2. 'Hello'

3. "F"

4. "1234"

5. '1'

6. A

7. "Marcus'

4.2 Character Escape Sequences

An exception to the rule that literals are interpreted exactly as they are written is an *escape sequence*. Character escape sequences also violate the rule that a character literal be a single character surrounded by single quotation marks. All escape sequences start with a backslash (\) followed by one or more characters.

Escape Sequence	Character Representation
\n	Carriage return and line feed (new line)
\t	Tab (eight characters wide)
\"	Double quote
\'	Single quote
\\	Backslash
\0	Null character

Table 4.2.1 Character escape sequences

The reason for character escape sequences is that it is difficult to use some characters as literals. Escape sequences allow us to use a special notation to represent a specific character or a control character. Some escape sequences, such as \n and \t, are referred to as *control characters* because they don't display anything but control the position of the text displayed. Table 4.2.1 shows some of the more commonly used escape sequences.

i   A **null character** is a special character, used—among other things—to give a character variable an initial value.

!   **Remember:** C++ is case sensitive. Therefore, the escape sequences shown in Table 4.2.1 must be used as written.

Example 4.2.1 demonstrates how to use escape sequences.

Example 4.2.1 Character escape sequences

```
cout << "This is on one line\n This is on another\n";
cout << "\tHe said, \"Stop!\"";
// Output
This is on one line
 This is on another
        He said, "Stop!"
```

Section 4.2 Exercise

1. Given the following text, make a legal string literal using escape sequences.

   This is a "backslash" \, this is a forward slash /.

   The way to remember is to stand up and turn to your right.

   If you lean "back", you become a backslash; if you lean

   "forward", you become a forward slash.

   This is Randy's surefire method!

4.3 Variable Declarations

We will use mathematics to help introduce the concept of *variables*. A variable is nothing more than a placeholder whose contents can change. The placeholder is given a name (many times x in mathematics), which we use to reference the value stored in the variable. If we again refer to the circumference formula, the r is a variable representing the radius. Programming has taken this concept and added some other features.

In order to use a variable in any of our programs, we must first *declare* it. Declaring a variable has several purposes:

- Informs the operating system how much internal memory (RAM) the variable will need

- Identifies the memory address to use for that variable

- Identifies the type of data to be stored in that physical memory location

- Indicates what operations (+, -, /) can be performed on the data contained within that variable (or memory location)

This is a very crucial concept, and it is imperative that by the end of this section you fully understand variables and their usage. The basic syntax for a variable declaration is:

```
<data type> identifier;
```

The previous `<data type>` needs to be replaced with any data type, many of which are discussed in the next section. This declaration creates a variable with the name `identifier`. This form of declaration is shown in Example 4.3.1.

Example 4.3.1 Basic variable declaration

```
int salary; // Notice the semicolon
```

A variable declaration can be written in a variety of ways. For example, we can declare many distinct variables in a single statement as long as they are all the same data type.

```
<data type> identifier1, identifier2, identifier3;
```

This form of variable declaration is illustrated in Example 4.3.2.

Example 4.3.2 Multiple variable declarations

```
int age, iq, shoe_size;
```

In C++, variables can be declared anywhere within your code as long as they are declared before they are used. However, at this point we strongly suggest that all of your variable declarations be placed directly after the opening curly brace of main.

4.3.1 Variable's Initial Value

So what is the initial value stored in the variables declared in Example 4.3.2? The value in each variable is unknown, often referred to as undefined and commonly thought of as garbage. The reason for the unknown value is that memory will never be guaranteed to be clean or empty when given to your variable. Therefore, when we request memory for a variable, the variable may contain whatever was there previously. We can initialize variables to either a constant or a literal, which allows us to provide a known value to a variable during its declaration. This is also referred to as *initializing* the variable. The syntax is shown here.

1. `<data type> identifier = <literal>;`

2. `<data type> identifier = <constant>;`

Both of these forms are demonstrated in Example 4.3.3.

Example 4.3.3 Variable declaration with initialization

```
int sum = 0;
int Ralphs_age = RETIREMENT_AGE;
```

Interestingly enough, we can even initialize our new variable to another variable's value as long as the variable we are using to obtain the initial value is declared before being used. Assuming that `identifier` has already been declared and, preferably, initialized, the syntactical example that follows initializes `identifier2` with the value stored in the variable `identifier`.

```
<data type> identifier2 = identifier;
```

Although this form is not used as often as that in the examples shown previously, Example 4.3.4 illustrates this style.

Example 4.3.4 Variable declaration using another variable

```
int base_salary = 30000;
int num_dependents, staff_salary = base_salary;
```

Be careful, however; in Example 4.3.4, only `base_salary` and `staff_salary` are initialized. The other variable, `num_dependents`, remains uninitialized, and its value is unknown or indeterminate.

i

Initialization is the process of giving a variable a value during its declaration. As a result, the variable will always be in a known state.

It is legal in C++ to use an additional form of variable initialization. Notice the parentheses in the following syntax diagrams.

```
1. <data type> identifier (<literal>);
```

2. `<data type> identifier (<constant>);`

3. `<data type> identifier1, identifier2 (identifier);`

Example 4.3.5 Alternate initialization form

```
int base_salary( 30000 );
int num_dependents, staff_salary( base_salary );
```

The style shown in Example 4.3.5 is the preferred style of some programmers, while others choose the style discussed previously. Just remember—the parenthetical form can only be used with initialization.

4.3.2 Initialization

One of the principles good programmers adhere to is to always know the state, or value, of all variables. If you declare a variable without initializing it, the value stored in the variable is unknown (or undefined). Even if the variable is assigned a value later, there is still a period of time during which the value is unknown. Therefore, it is always a good practice to give all variables an initial value at the time they are declared.

The most common value used to initialize numeric variables is zero. Character variables are usually initialized to the null character (\0).

Remember: The null character actually has the ASCII value of 0. Therefore, initializing a character to null is in essence initializing it to 0.

4.3.3 Data Types

A data type is a key piece to any variable declaration. It specifies the type of data to be stored in the variable, the amount of memory the variable uses, and the operations (+, −, *, /) that can be used on the variable. There are many different data types to choose from, some of which are shown in Table 4.3.1. All of the data types shown are *primitive* data types.

A **primitive data type** is a data type whose definition is built into the language.

C++ Data Type	Description of Data	Memory Allocated	Range
char	Character	1 byte	−128 to 127
int	Integer	OS dependent	OS dependent
float	Floating point (decimal)	4 bytes	3.4E +/− 38 with 7 digits of accuracy
double	Double precision floating point	8 bytes	1.7E +/− 308 with 15 digits of accuracy
bool	Boolean data	1 byte	true or false
short (or short int)	Smaller integer	2 bytes	−32,768 to 32,767
long	Larger integer	4 bytes	−2,147,483,648 to 2,147,483,647
long double	Larger double	8 bytes	1.7E +/− 308 with 15 digits of accuracy

Table 4.3.1 Data types

A **Boolean** value is either true or false.

Table 4.3.1 is sure to raise some questions. First, the size of an int is dependent on which operating system the program is running. For example, an int in Windows 3.1, which is a 16-bit operating system, is allocated two bytes (16 bits). On the current version of Windows XP, which is a 32-bit operating system, an int is allocated four bytes (32 bits) of memory. Starting to see the pattern? What would happen if we were running our program on one of the newer 64-bit operating systems?

The amount of memory allocated is the key to determining the range of values an int can hold on the platform you are targeting with your program. On a 32-bit operating system, an int is 32 bits in size. Since each bit only has two possibilities, a 0 or a 1, we could calculate the number of different possibilities as 2^{32}. However, the most significant bit (MSB) is used as a sign bit, eliminating that bit from our calculations. Therefore, we are left with $\pm 2^{31}$, which equates to the range of −2,147,483,648 to 2,147,483,647. We can use the same idea with a 16-bit operating system: $\pm 2^{15}$, which equates to the range of −32,768 to 32,767.

Some of you might be concerned about the one bit that can't be used as data. There is a remedy! The **unsigned** prefix allows you to use the MSB as data rather than as a sign bit for all *integral data types*. This means you can have: `unsigned char`, `unsigned short`, `unsigned int`, and `unsigned long`.

> An **integral data type** is any data type that can hold only whole numbers. The `char` data type is an integral data type because under the hood, a `char` holds an ASCII number representing a character.

The next thing many beginning students often find confusing is the `long` and `long double` data types. These data types are guaranteed to be equal to or bigger than an `int` and a `double`. Both of the larger data types are exactly the same size as the smaller data types (assuming a 32-bit operating system).

STYLE NOTE   One of the lost arts of programming to resurface in recent years relates to memory management. When computers had a very limited amount of memory, programmers were forced to be very conservative. Now that computers have much more memory, some programmers forget that they should still not waste resources. One thing to remember as you declare variables is to use the smallest (most efficient) data type that will work for your projected needs. For example, there is no reason to declare a variable as an `int` if all you are going to do is hold a person's age. A `short int` (or just `short`) would work fine and conserve two bytes of memory.

One of the exciting areas continuing to emerge today is embedded systems. An embedded system is a very small, specialized computer that is a part of a larger system. A good example is a cell phone. There is at least one, and sometimes more, embedded systems in each phone.

One common aspect of all embedded systems is that they typically have very few resources, including memory. This is driving a resurgence of the increased awareness on the part of programmers in resource conservation.

4.3.4 The `sizeof` Operator

There is an easy way to determine how many bytes of memory are reserved for either a variable or a data type. The `sizeof` operator returns the number of bytes set aside for whatever parameter you pass it, as shown in Example 4.3.6.

Example 4.3.6 The `sizeof` **operator**

```
// Part 1
cout << sizeof( char ) << '\n';

// Part 2
unsigned short age = 21; // Variable declaration/initialization
cout << sizeof( age ) << '\n';

// Output
1
2
```

In Example 4.3.6, Part 1 will print a 1 on the screen, while Part 2 will print a 2.

4.3.5 Numeric Literal Suffixes

Numeric literals have a feature that allows you to explicitly specify the type of certain values. This feature, called a *suffix*, uses special characters to specify the type of literal. A numeric literal with the suffix *F* specifies that the number is to be treated as a `float`. Likewise, the *L* suffix specifies that the number is to be treated as a `long`.

This feature is mostly used in the initialization of variables. Since all floating-point numeric literals are treated as `doubles`, the compiler will generate a warning if a `float` variable is initialized or even assigned a floating-point literal. This is because a `double` is eight bytes and a `float` is four bytes; therefore, it would be like trying to stuff eight pounds of sand into a four-pound sack. Without the suffix, the compiler will flag that line with the warning: "initializing : truncation from double to float". The *F* suffix changes the literal from the default type of `double` to a `float`. Example 4.3.7 demonstrates the use of suffixes.

Example 4.3.7 Numeric literal suffixes

```
float money = 123.45F;
float avg = 95.5f;
long flag = 0L;
long salary = 500001; // The last character is not a one but a
                      // lowercase L.
```

Notice in Example 4.3.7 that the suffix can be upper- or lowercase. However, as shown with the declaration of *salary*, it is much more readable to use the uppercase letter for the suffix since it is difficult to distinguish between the lowercase *L* and the numeral 1. Although there are a few other suffixes, *F* and *L* are by far the most commonly used.

4.3.6 Naming Rules

There are certain rules in any programming language that we must adhere to when naming variables. The following are the rules for C++.

- Variables can only be made up of letters, digits, and underscores.

- Variables can't start with a digit (i.e., they must begin with a letter or an underscore).

- Variables can't be a reserved word (e.g., `if`, `else`, `while`, `for`).

Although legal, it is best not to start a variable name with two underscores. The double underscore is usually reserved for special predefined identifiers.

STYLE NOTE ▷ Although not a requirement of the C++ language, all variable names should be descriptive of their purpose. This greatly increases both the readability and the maintainability of your program—by others as well as yourself. Sometimes beginning programmers fall into the trap of having single-character variable names, such as `a`, `b`, or `c`. If working with a well-known mathematical formula that uses these variables—such as the quadratic formula, in which they represent the coefficients of the *x* terms—then they might be appropriate. Generally, though, these short names are not representative of most of the data we tend to use, such as a person's age or test score. Use descriptive variable names like `age` or `test_score` to make your code more readable.

Section 4.3 Exercises

1. Calculate the range for the following data types.

   a. `unsigned char`

   b. `unsigned short`

   c. `unsigned int` (on a 16-bit operating system)

   d. `unsigned int` (on a 32-bit operating system)

e. `unsigned int` (on a 64-bit operating system)

f. `int` (on a 64-bit operating system)

g. `unsigned long`

h. `short int`

2. Which of the following are invalid variable names? For each invalid name, state why it is illegal.

a. `a`

b. `tot-pay`

c. `tot_pay`

d. `avg`

e. `One&Two`

f. `One_and_Two`

g. `1day`

h. `temp1`

i. `One and Two`

j. `ss#`

k. `short`

3. What is wrong with each of the following statements?

a. `int a, int b;`

b. `int a = b;`

   `int b = 0;`

c. `int a = 0, b = 3.5;`

d. `char grade = "A";`

e. `char c = 1;`

f. `int a, b, c, d, e, f;`

g. `char x = "This is a test.";`

Section 4.3 Learn by Doing Exercises

The following exercises are intended to be short, hands-on programs emphasizing topics covered in this section. Write, compile, and run the following program.

1. Write a program to create variables for each of the following items. Be sure to use the smallest data type appropriate for each situation.

   a. A person's age (initialize to 19)

   b. A person's shoe size (initialize to 8.5)

   c. The altitude specified in feet (initialize to 0)

   d. A person's gender (initialize to 'F')

   e. A person's weight in pounds (initialize to 175)

4.4 ASCII Characters

As mentioned previously, all data is stored in memory as ones and zeros. For the most part, we can easily see how to convert numbers to their binary equivalent. However, how are characters stored as binary? The answer lies in what is called an *ASCII chart*. The American Standard Code for Information Interchange (ASCII) chart associates each character with a number. Take a few minutes now to review the ASCII chart in Appendix A.

As you can see from the chart, related characters tend to be grouped together. For example, capital letters start at 65 while lowercase letters start at 97. A common mistake is to think that the uppercase letters are represented by a higher number than the lowercase letters. Personally we agree, but we weren't consulted in 1967 when the chart was developed.

The basic ASCII chart has values ranging from 0 to 127. However, there is an extended ASCII chart that includes 256 unique characters. These additional characters are typically line-drawing characters or special characters for foreign languages. Examples of these characters are ê, ë, è, ï, and î.

So, how are characters stored in memory? Each character is associated with a numeric value that is stored in memory as binary. This process is shown here.

$$\text{'A'} \rightarrow 65 \rightarrow 1000001$$
$$\text{'a'} \rightarrow 97 \rightarrow 1100001$$

Although not used as often as character escape sequences, engineers sometimes need to use numbers specified in a different base other than base 10. Therefore, two numeric escape sequences that allow the programmer to specify ASCII values in either hexadecimal or octal bases are shown in Table 4.4.1.

Escape Sequence	Numeric Representation
\x####	Hexadecimal number
\o####	Octal number

Table 4.4.1 Numeric escape sequences

Be careful when using the escape sequences shown in Table 4.4.1. The value specified must not exceed 255_{10}. Therefore, the largest hexadecimal value would be FF_{16}, and the largest valid octal value would be 377_8. Example 4.4.1 demonstrates how to use numeric escape sequences.

Example 4.4.1 Numeric escape sequences

```
cout << "Hexadecimal ASCII character: " << "\x4E" << endl;
cout << "Octal ASCII character: " << "\77" << endl;

cout << "Hexadecimal number: " << 0x4E << endl;
cout << "Octal number: " << 077 << endl;

//Output
Hexadecimal ASCII character: N
Octal ASCII character: ?
Hexadecimal number: 78
Octal number: 63
```

Remember: A hexadecimal number is a base 16 number and uses the characters 0–9 and A–F. An octal number is a base 8 number and uses the characters 0–7 only. The hexadecimal value FF equates to 255_{10}, and the octal value 777 equates to 511_{10}.

Section 4.4 Exercises

1. Convert the following statement to ASCII numbers. Display the numbers in base 10.

   Hello World!

2. Convert the following number sequence to text.

   67 43 43 32 82 111 99 107 115 33

4.5 Constants

Literals are a common occurrence in any program. We saw in the formula $2\pi r$ that the 2 is a literal but the π (pi) is a *constant*. The difference between a constant and a literal is that a constant has a name (e.g., PI) whereas a literal doesn't.

Creating constants for specific values, such as pi, not only makes your code more readable, it also makes it more easily modifiable as well. For example, seeing the literal 65 in a formula may not mean much, but what if you were to use the constant SPEED_LIMIT instead? It is much more readable. Now let's assume 65 can refer to the maximum speed limit as well as to a person's retirement age. If the retirement age were to change to 67, we would have to search through all of the instances of 65 within our code and change only those that refer to the retirement age to 67. This could be an extremely time-consuming task in a program that may have several hundred thousand lines of code. If we used constants, however, all we would need to do is change the value associated with that specific constant and recompile.

> **Remember:** A constant is different from a variable in that it contains a value that cannot change during the execution of the program. Like a variable, however, the compiler does indeed allocate the necessary memory.

Example 4.5.1 shows how to declare constants in C++.

Example 4.5.1 C++ constants

```
const int SPEED_LIMIT = 65;
const int RETIREMENT_AGE = 67;
const double PI = 3.1416;
```

It is a common mistake for beginning programmers to forget to include the data type when declaring a constant. Although syntactically legal, the compiler assumes you wanted to create a constant integer. Therefore, if you initialized the constant to a decimal number, you will get a compiler warning about a type mismatch.

> ⚠️ **Remember:** Since the value of a constant cannot be changed, all constants are required to be initialized.

STYLE NOTE ▸ Notice in Example 4.5.1 that the names of the constants are uppercase. It is common practice to use uppercase letters to name constants and lowercase letters to name variables to easily and quickly differentiate between constants and variables.

Section 4.5 Exercises

What is wrong with each of the following statements?

1. `const PI = 3.14;`

2. `const int DAYS_IN_YEAR;`

3. `const char AUTHOR = "Randy Albert";`

4.6 `const` **Versus** #define

We have already seen how to create a constant using the reserved word `const`. Another method is using the #define preprocessor directive, which has its roots firmly planted in the C programming language.

Here is the syntax for creating a constant using #define.

    #define *identifier* <value>

The `<value>` in the syntax diagram can be replaced with any literal: numeric, character, or string. Notice a couple of things about the preceding statement:

1. There isn't a semicolon at the end

2. There isn't an equals sign used to associate the value with the identifier

3. No data type is provided

During the compilation process, when the preprocessor encounters a #define statement, the preprocessor searches through the entire program looking for the existence of the identifier. When it is found, the preprocessor textually replaces the identifier with the value we associated with it. Example 4.6.1 illustrates how to create constants using the #define directive.

Example 4.6.1 #define **constants**

```
#define SPEED_LIMIT 65     // Notice no = or semicolons
#define RETIREMENT_AGE 67
#define PI 3.14
```

Be careful not to use semicolons or equals signs in a #define directive. If you do, you introduce undesirable characters via your #define directive, as shown in Example 4.6.2.

Example 4.6.2 Invalid #define

```
#define PI = 3.14;

int main()
{
    int circumference = 0, radius = 5;
    circumference = 2 * PI * radius;
    return 0;
}
```

Except for the #define, everything looks syntactically correct. However, the compiler tells us we have an error, but on a line of code we might not expect. The error is on the line:

```
circumference = 2 * PI * radius;
```

Although this line of code appears syntactically correct, look what happens when we expand PI as the preprocessor would.

```
circumference = 2 * = 3.14; * radius;
```

Even with your limited experience with mathematical expressions in C/C++, you can probably tell that the line of code is malformed. The problem is that we weren't able to locate the error until we manually expanded the #define directive. This type of syntax error is extremely difficult to find—even for experienced programmers.

> **Remember:** If a line of code is flagged by the compiler as having an error, but the line of code looks syntactically correct, look at the syntax of any #define directives in the statement.

We have now seen how to create constants using #define. Next, let's explore the added benefits of using const versus #define. First, using const allows us to associate a data type with a constant, and allocates the same amount of memory a variable of the same type would receive. Second, constants created with const provide the added benefit of type checking. Last, although it doesn't mean much now, constants declared using const have scope, meaning we can hide the constant from other parts of our program. Constants declared with #define are always going to be seen by all parts of our program.

Given these added benefits, we suggest all C++ constants be made using the const reserved word. The potential dangers of #define even caused a change in the C language specifications. The newer versions of C allow the use of const to create constants.

4.7 Bringing It All Together

Now that we have covered many of the fundamental concepts associated with declaring and initializing variables, it's time to make sure you can visualize exactly what is happening behind the scenes. Assume you have declared the variables shown in Table 4.7.1.

In Example 1, we requested the compiler to declare a variable in memory that we are calling age. The memory will be the size of a short integer, or two bytes. Because we did not initialize the contents of the variable age, its value is currently unknown or undefined.

Imagine Figure 4.7.1 illustrates a contiguous section of the computer's RAM. Assuming each box represents one byte, we know the variable age would require two adjacent memory locations to hold its contents, or value.

The type of this variable has been declared a short int; thus, the size is two bytes. At any given time, the variable age can hold one value. The range of

Example Number	Variable and Constant Declarations
1	`short int age;`
2	`char grade = 'A';`
3	`float gpa(0.0);`
4	`const float PI = 3.14F;`

Table 4.7.1 Declaration examples

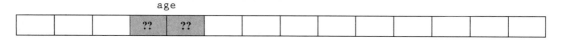

Figure 4.7.1 Memory diagram

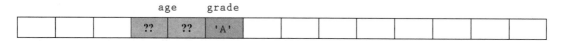

Figure 4.7.2 Memory diagram

that value is −32,768 to 32,767. Should we put a value that is too large into this variable, we will have a definite problem. The contents of the variable would depend on how much out of range the value is. Regardless, the resulting value is going to be incorrect. We will indeed be in for a very long day as we try to figure out what just happened.

The process just described is somewhat similar to making a reservation in a fancy restaurant for dinner this Friday night. You call ahead and tell the restaurant you will need a table for 4 people at 7:00 p.m. However, when you arrive at the restaurant with your group of 16 people (not the 4 you reserved), you may find that the establishment is filled to capacity and a problem clearly exists!

In the second example in Table 4.7.1, you requested the compiler to find you a single byte of memory and associate the variable name `grade` with that particular section of memory. In this case, we did the right thing and initialized the value to a known state. Remember, because of the `char` data type we asked for, we can only store one character at a time in the variable we call `grade`. Attempting to put more than one value in this location would be an error. Your memory might now look somewhat like that in Figure 4.7.2.

Figure 4.7.3 Memory diagram

The third example in Table 4.7.1 requests room in memory to hold a value associated with a variable called `gpa` that is four bytes long. Similar to what we had done in Example 2, we again initialized the variable; however, this time we used the C++ parentheses as the initialization syntax.

For the last example in Table 4.7.1 we created a constant called `PI`. As required when declaring constants, we initialized it to a known state. Figure 4.7.3 is the final illustration showing one possible interpretation of how our memory might look with some imagination on your part.

4.8 Variable Declarations in Pseudocode

One thing that may seem a little confusing is that variable declarations are not represented in pseudocode. Pseudocode is reserved for executable statements, and variable declarations are not executable. While the declarations serve an important purpose, they don't actually do anything. This is also why we don't see any #includes or constant declarations in our pseudocode. Also, data types and #includes are C++ specific. Remember, pseudocode should be programming-language independent.

4.9 Problem Solving Applied

Problem statement: Develop the pseudocode solution to calculate the weekly developmental billing report for local radio station WJJQ's biggest client, a car dealership. WJJQ has been in operation for over 30 years, and recently Alexis Blough has taken over as general manager. The station has a format of contemporary rock and country music.

WJJQ uses the following rate structure for the car dealership account:

Production	$100.00 per hr
Pre-production	$60.00 per hr
Producer's fee	$40.00 per hr

The car dealership will be billed for the following time during the past week:

Production	1.5 hours
Pre-production	2 hours
Producer's fee	3 hours

Alexis needs you to display the amount due for each respective activity and to display the overall total owed by the car dealership.

Requirement Specification:

Input(s):

Input Type	Data	Source
Decimal	ProductionHours	Keyboard
Decimal	PreProductionHours	Keyboard
Decimal	ProducersHours	Keyboard

Output(s):

Output Type	Data	Destination
Decimal	ProductionCost	Screen
Decimal	PreProductionCost	Screen
Decimal	ProducersCost	Screen
Decimal	TotalCost	Screen

Constants:

Type	Data	Value
Decimal	PRODUCTION_RATE	100.00
Decimal	PRE_PRODUCTION_RATE	60.00
Decimal	PRODUCERS_RATE	40.00

Design:

Required Formulas:
ProductionCost = ProductionHours * PRODUCTION_RATE
PreProductionCost = PreProductionHours * PRE_PRODUCTION_RATE
ProducersCost = ProducersHours * PRODUCERS_RATE
TotalCost = ProductionCost + PreProductionCost + ProducersCost

Pseudocode:
— Input Phase —
Display prompt "Enter Production Hours: "
Read ProductionHours

Display prompt "Enter Pre-Production Hours: "
Read PreProductionHours
Display prompt "Enter Producer's Hours: "
Read ProducersHours
— **P**rocess Phase —
ProductionCost = ProductionHours * PRODUCTION_RATE
PreProductionCost = PreProductionHours * PRE_PRODUCTION_RATE
ProducersCost = ProducersHours * PRODUCERS_RATE
TotalCost = ProductionCost + PreProductionCost
— **O**utput Phase —
Display "Production Cost: "
Display ProductionCost
Display "Pre-Production Cost: "
Display PreProductionCost
Display "Producer's Cost: "
Display ProducersCost
Display "Weekly Total Cost: "
Display TotalCost

Testing and Verification:

Desk Checking:

Are all inputs accounted for? **Yes**
Are prompts self-describing? **Yes**
Has all required processing been completed? **Yes**
Is all of the processing correct? **No**
Use test values below:

1.5	hours for Production
2.0	hours for Pre-production
3.0	hours for Producer's Fee

— **Validation** —
ProductionCost = 1.5 * 100
PreProductionCost = 2.0 * 60
ProducersCost = 3.0 * 40
TotalCost = ProductionCost + PreProductionCost

— **Pseudocode Correction** —
Line with Error: TotalCost = ProductionCost + PreProductionCost
Corrected Version: TotalCost = ProductionCost + PreProductionCost
                                                          + ProducersCost

Is all output from the Output Phase self-describing? **Yes**

4.10 C—The Differences

There are only a few differences between C and C++ in the topics discussed in this chapter. First, there isn't a Boolean (`bool`) data type and therefore no predefined `true` and `false` values in C. Many advanced C programmers make their own data type that simulates a Boolean data type, but the `bool` data type does not exist. Don't be disheartened; by the end of this text you will be able to create your own Boolean-like data type in C if needed.

Another difference is that you can't use the parentheses form of initialization (i.e., `int x(1);`) in C. That, too, was one of the enhancements made by the developers of C++, and we will see its use again later in the text.

In older versions of C, unlike in C++, you must declare variables as the first statements in a block of code. Therefore, the variable declarations must come directly after an opening curly brace.

The current C standard allows a programmer to use `const` to create constants. However, legacy C programs written prior to the current standard must use `#define` to create constants.

4.11 SUMMARY

We began our discussion in this chapter with a quick look at literals and found that, with the exception of escape sequences, they are interpreted as they are presented. We also discussed the three types of literals: numeric, character, and string. We then examined escape sequences and how they offer us the ability to use a special notation to represent a specific character or perform some predetermined action.

The next discussion centered on the use of variables and how they are used to store data in memory. The concept of a data type was also introduced along with a number of the fundamental data types available to us. We also stressed that a data type is the central piece to any variable declaration because it indicates the type of data stored in the variable, the amount of memory the variable uses, and the specific operations that can be performed on the variable. Remember, when creating your variable names, you must follow the rules outlined. Time was also spent stressing the importance of initializing your variables.

The ASCII chart was introduced to help facilitate your understanding of how character data is represented in memory. An ASCII chart is included in Appendix A.

Next, we began our discussion of constants, and the important role they play within programming. As we learned, constants are unchangeable values used to enhance the readability and maintainability of your program. Finally, we concluded the chapter with an overview of the `#define` statement, which is a preprocessor directive sometimes used to create constants. However, because of the added benefits of the `const` reserved word, it is best to not use a `#define` to declare constants unless programming in C.

As done in previous chapters, we made you aware of the problems our students encounter when creating and using variables, constants, and literals. Many of the concepts presented in this chapter are crucial to your understanding of the language and will become the building blocks for much of the material that follows. As usual, make sure you feel pretty confident about the material presented. If you feel good about the information we just provided, you are ready to continue your journey.

4.12 Debugging Exercise

Find and correct the logic errors in the following pseudocode examples. You will need to desk-check these problems carefully to locate the errors.

1. **Problem:** Your brother has decided to give all of the employees in his small company a 6% raise. A novice programmer, he wants to create a program that calculates the new wages. He has created the following pseudocode and has asked you to look it over for errors.

```
Display "Enter old wage: "
Read Old_wage

New_wage = Old_wage * .06

Display Old_wage
Display " + 6% = "
Display New_wage
```

2. **Problem:** Last term your grade in math was lower than you, or your parents, expected. You want to create a program to check your professor's calculations. The course syllabus states that all of the assignments were worth 30% of the total grade, the three tests were worth 15% each, and the final exam was worth 25%. Look over the following pseudocode for correctness.

```
Display "Enter Assignment average: "
Read Assignment_avg

Display "Enter Test 1: "
Read Test1

Display "Enter Test 2: "
Read Test1

Display "Enter Test 3: "
Read Test3

Display "Enter Final: "
Read Final
```

Test_avg = Test1 * .15 + Test2 * .15 + Test3 * .15 / 3
Class_score = Assign_avg * .20 + Test_avg * .40 + Final * .25

Display "Final score: "
Display Class_score

4.13 Programming Exercises

1. In Section 4.9, Problem Solving Applied, we provided a solution for WJJQ's billing program. Based on that pseudocode solution, please declare the variables and constants needed.

2. Just to keep you in practice using your development environment, type in the following program, then compile and run it. The output will make you smile.

```cpp
#include <iostream>
using std::cout;

int main()
{
    char ascii = 1;

    cout << ascii << '\n';

    ascii = 2;
    cout << ascii << '\n';

    ascii = 3;
    cout << ascii << '\n';

    return 0;
}
```

3. Write a C++ program to calculate how old you are in days. Declare an integer variable and initialize it to your age. Also, declare a constant that represents the number of days in a year. Make sure you write your pseudocode solution before attempting to write your code. HINT: Here is an example of an assignment statement that might be similar to what you will need to perform the actual calculation: `gross = hours * RATE;`. Of course you will also need to use `cout`.

4.14 Team Programming Exercise

Well, your old pen pal continues to need your assistance. In the last chapter you helped her with the pseudocode solution to convert a given distance in kilometers to miles. With some additional time and your help, she was able to construct the expanded, although rough, pseudocode solution. Now, however, she needs your assistance to help her in identifying the different C++ variables and constants needed in this program.

Based on the following solution, your job is to declare all the variables and constants needed. Remember to initialize your variables as previously discussed. Here is some additional background information related to the program that you may find helpful.

    a. A decimeter (dm) is 0.1 meter.

    b. A kilometer is 1000 meters, or meters per kilometer (MPK) is 1000.

    c. One kilometer is less than one mile.

    d. KPM stands for kilometers per mile.

    e. There are approximately 1.6093 kilometers per mile (KPM).

    f. Your friend is thinking of changing her major from physics to software engineering.

```
Display prompt "Please enter in the miles you want to convert to kilometers: "
Read miles

Display prompt "Please enter in the meters you want to convert to kilometers: "
Read meters

KilometersFromMiles = miles * KPM
KilometersFromMeters = meters / MPK

Display mile
Display " miles  = "
Display Kilometers
Display " Kilometers"

Display meters
Display " meters  = "
Display Kilometers
Display " Kilometers"
```

4.15 Answers to Chapter Exercises

Section 4.1

1. legal; numeric

2. illegal; you can't enclose more than one character in single quotation marks.

3. legal; string

4. legal; string

5. legal; character

6. illegal; you must enclose the character in either single or double quotation marks.

7. illegal; you must enclose the group of characters in double quotation marks.

Section 4.2

1. "This is a \"backslash\" \\, this is a forward slash /.\n\tThe way to remember is to stand up and turn to your right.\n\tIf you lean \"back\", you become a backslash; if you lean\n\t\"forward\" you become a forward slash. \n\tThis is Randy\'s surefire method!"

Section 4.3

1.

   a. 0 to 255

   b. 0 to 65,535

   c. 0 to 65,535

   d. 0 to 4,294,967,295

   e. 0 to 18,446,744,073,709,551,615

   f. $-9,223,372,036,854,775,808$ to $9,223,372,036,854,775,807$

   g. 0 to 4,294,967,295

   h. $-32,768$ to $32,767$

2.

   a. legal

   b. illegal; dash (-) is an illegal character

   c. legal

   d. legal in C++; however, use with caution, as it may be a reserved word in some languages

   e. illegal; ampersand (&) is an illegal character

   f. legal

   g. illegal; can't start with a digit

   h. legal

   i. illegal; spaces are illegal characters

   j. illegal; pound sign (#) is an illegal character

   k. illegal; reserved word

3.

    a. Either replace the comma with a semicolon or remove the second `int`.

    b. You can't use *b* to initialize *a* because *b* hasn't been declared yet.

    c. The literal 3.5 is an invalid value for an integer.

    d. Replace the double quotation marks with single quotation marks.

    e. This is legal, although you are probably not going to get the results you had anticipated. Since the 1 is a numeric literal, it will be used as the ASCII value 1 instead of the character '1'. ☺

    f. Legal, but not ideal as variable names.

    g. You cannot store more than one character in a `char` variable.

Section 4.4

1. Hello World! = 72 101 108 108 111 32 87 111 114 108 100 33

2. C++ Rocks!

Section 4.5

1. There is no data type; therefore, it defaults to an `int`, and the literal 3.14 is not valid for an `int`.

2. All constants must be initialized to a value.

3. You cannot store more than one character in a `char` constant.

Input and Output Streams

Chapter Objectives

By the end of the chapter, readers will be able to:

- Understand and use input and output streams.
- Understand the difference between `endl` and `'\n'`.
- Format output streams using manipulators.
- Format output streams using member functions.
- Understand the value of using various debugging tools.
- Set and remove breakpoints.
- Use watches to examine the contents of variables.

Introduction

In the previous chapters we have written text to the screen using `cout` without a detailed explanation of how `cout` works. Although there are other forms of input and output (I/O), this chapter focuses on how to write output to the console window (the screen) and read input from the keyboard using *streams*. Remember, input and output were two of the key aspects of the IPO phases discussed in Chapter 2.

5.1 Input and Output Streams

The basic form of I/O in C++ incorporates the use of streams, similar to a stream found in a forest. A C++ stream, however, is a flow of information instead of water. The flow can run either from the input device (keyboard) into your program or from your program to an output device (console window or screen). All of the streams in this chapter require including the header file `<iostream>`.

> ⚠️ **Remember:** To include a header file in your program, you must use the `#include` preprocessor directive, in this case `#include <iostream>`.

5.1.1 Namespaces and I/O Streams

Don't forget that the namespace rules must be followed in order to access the individual components of the header file, as shown in Example 5.1.1. While all the methods shown would work, the third method is the preferred approach, as discussed in Section 3.5.1.

Example 5.1.1 Using `namespace` **options**

```
// Method 1
#include <iostream>
using namespace std;

...
cout << "Hello World";
```

```
// Method 2
#include <iostream>

...
std::cout << "Hello World";
// Method 3
#include <iostream>
using std::cout;

...
cout << "Hello World";
```

5.1.2 The cout Statement

The cout statement allows us to display information to the screen. The information we can write using cout includes literals, constants, and variables. Example 5.1.2 shows how to use the cout statement to write a string literal, "Hello World", to the screen.

Example 5.1.2 Displaying a string literal

```
cout << "Hello World";
```

 Remember: The term **cout** stands for <u>c</u>onsole <u>out</u>put.

Because we are inserting the string literal "Hello World" into the cout stream, the operator << associated with the cout statement is called the *insertion operator*. As previously noted, the cout statement is not limited to displaying string literals. Example 5.1.3 demonstrates using the cout statement to display the contents of variables.

Example 5.1.3 Displaying a variable

```
int int_exp = 99;

cout << int_exp;
```

Displaying variables of other data types with `cout` is just as easy. The only data type that might produce some unexpected results is the `bool`. Instead of printing `true` or `false`, `cout` actually prints a 1 for true values and a 0 for a false value. Another feature of the `cout` statement is that we can write multiple pieces of data using a single statement, as shown in Example 5.1.4.

Example 5.1.4 Displaying multiple pieces of data

```
char grade = 'B';
float class_avg = 88.5;

// Notice there isn't a semicolon at the end of the first line
cout << "Your average is: " << class_avg
     << "\nYour grade is: " << grade;

// Output
Your average is: 88.5
Your grade is: B
```

 Remember: The '`\n`' is an escape sequence that moves the cursor to the next line.

STYLE NOTE▶ Because a single `cout` statement can be lengthy, they can become a little difficult to read. There are various techniques that increase the readability of the `cout` statement. Notice in Example 5.1.4 that there is an optional space on either side of the insertion operator. Also notice that the second line of the `cout` statement is on a new line, tabbed over so that the insertion operators line up. Both of these techniques greatly increase the readability and maintainability of the `cout` statement.

Remember: Always put a space between any operator and its operands to improve readability.

5.1.3 The `cin` Statement

The `cin` statement reads data from the input stream, which is the keyboard by default, and stores that value, if possible, in the variable used in the `cin` statement. Example 5.1.5 shows how to use `cin` to read from the keyboard.

Example 5.1.5 Reading a value from the keyboard

```
int score = 0;

cin >> score;
```

 Remember: The term **cin** stands for **c**onsole **in**put.

Notice that we use a different operator (>>) with `cin` than we did with `cout`. Because we are removing, or extracting, information from the data stream, this operator is called the *extraction operator*. The right operand of the extraction operator must be a variable or variables. Like `cout`, `cin` can handle multiple values from the keyboard using a single statement, as demonstrated in Example 5.1.6.

Example 5.1.6 Reading multiple values from the keyboard

```
int score1 = 0, score2 = 0;

cout << "Enter two scores: ";

cin >> score1
    >> score2;
```

The two scores entered in Example 5.1.6 must be whitespace delimited. This simply means that when the two values are entered, they must be separated by some form of whitespace. Whitespace can be one or more spaces, a tab, or carriage return. When all of the input has been typed in, press the enter key to signify that the input process is finished.

STYLE NOTE ▶ Even though it is possible to read multiple values using the same `cin` statement, it is better for the user of your program to provide a prompt for each individual input. Example 5.1.6 has been modified to the preferred style, as shown in Example 5.1.7.

Example 5.1.7 Reading multiple values from the keyboard—a better way

```
int score1 = 0, score2 = 0;

cout << "Enter first score: ";
cin >> score1;

cout << "Enter second score: ";
cin >> score2;
```

Section 5.1 Exercises

1. Show the output generated by the following lines of code:

   a. `cout << "C++ is ";`

     `cout << "very cool";`

   b. `cout << "Hello\n";`

     `cout << "World";`

   c. `cout << "Computers are useless. \n";`

     `cout << "They can only give you answers.\n"`

        `<< "Pablo Picasso\n";`

2. What header file do you need to include in your program when using `cin` or `cout`?

   a. `<iostream.h>`   b. `<ihni>`   c. `<iostream>`   d. `<cmath>`

3. Earlier in the text we discussed I → P → O. Which of the following C++ statements relate to the output phase?

   a. `cin`   b. `cout`   c. `namespace`   d. `scanf`

4. Assume you wanted to read data from the keyboard. Which of the following C++ statements would you use?

   a. `cin`   b. `cout`   c. `namespace`   d. `scanf`

5. Which of the following statements are invalid? For each invalid statement, state what is wrong with it.

a. `cout >> "Hello World";`

b. `cout << "Almost over\n"`

c. `cin >> "Enter name: " >> name;`

d. `cin >> age >> soc_security_#;`

e. `cout << Enter size\n;`

f. `cout << "\n\n\tHello";`

g. `cin >> "\n" >> age >> shoe_size;`

h. `cin >> done >> "\n";`

i. `cin >> first >> last;`

Section 5.1 Learn by Doing Exercises

The following exercises are intended to be short, hands-on programs that emphasize the topics covered in this section. Write, compile, and run the following programs.

1. Write a program to display a prompt and read a person's age.

2. Take the following code fragment and convert it to a more appropriate style. Don't forget to make the variable names more descriptive. Be sure to write the entire program.

```
int bros, siss;

cout<<"Enter brothers and sisters:";
cin>>bros>>siss;
```

5.2 The end1 Manipulator

We have already seen the use of the `'\n'` escape sequence to move the cursor to the next line. The `end1` *manipulator* also moves the cursor to the next line and has an additional characteristic, as you will soon see. Example 5.2.1 demonstrates the use of `end1`.

A **manipulator** is a command that is directly placed into the stream.

Example 5.2.1 The `endl` **manipulator**

```
float money = 123.45F;

cout << "You have $" << money << endl;
cout << "Your turn to buy!" << endl;

// Output
You have $123.45
Your turn to buy!
```

 Remember: The term **endl** stands for **end l**ine.

5.2.1 The `endl` Manipulator Versus `'\n'`

As stated before, `endl` and `'\n'` seem to do the same thing. However, `endl` does something `'\n'` does not. In order to understand the difference, we need to know what really happens under the hood when we print to the screen.

There is actually an intermediate step between the execution of the `cout` statement and the text appearing on the screen. All of the information inserted into the stream is sent to an area in memory called the *output buffer*. The buffer holds the information until a signal is received to write the entire buffer to the screen. This process is called *flushing the buffer*. The `endl` manipulator is one way to flush, or dump, the contents of the output buffer to the screen. While `'\n'` does indeed move the cursor to the next line, it doesn't flush the buffer. The buffer is also flushed when your program ends. There is also another way to flush the buffer, which we will discuss in Section 5.4.4.

So which method is preferred? It really depends on your situation. There is more overhead to `endl`; therefore, it is more expensive, in relation to speed. Use the `'\n'` when possible unless you need to flush the output buffer. One thing you should never do is have more than one `endl` per `cout` statement. The additional performance cost doesn't justify having the extra `endl`s. Use an `endl` only at the end of a `cout` statement.

Section 5.2 Exercises

1. Which of the following moves the screen cursor to the next line and flushes the output buffer?

   a. `flush_now`   b. `\t`   c. `\n`   d. `endl`

2. What output would be displayed in each of the following lines?

   a. `cout << "\nn New Year's is coming \n";`

   b. `cout << "\n Hello\nWorld" << endl;`

   c. `cout << "goodbye my friend\n" << endl;`

5.3 Input and Output Buffers

In programming, the term *buffer* is often used to refer to a specific area of memory that holds data. The input buffer contains data that is going to be read via a `cin` statement, while the output buffer holds data generated by a `cout` statement.

The reason for the output buffer is to speed up the process of writing to the screen. It is always quicker and less resource-intensive to perform one write to the screen with a lot of information than multiple writes with just one piece of information.

This process is similar to when Troy moved a pile of gravel for his dad. He started by carrying a shovel full of gravel to the new location and then went back to the original pile and repeated the process. Troy's dad informed him it would be much quicker if he were to fill a wheelbarrow with the gravel and use it to dump the gravel at the new location. Troy did as he was told, even though he preferred the other method because he was being paid by the hour.

The input buffer is used to temporarily store data typed from the keyboard so it can be manipulated and assigned to variables. It is much quicker and easier to work with the data in the buffer than to process each individual keystroke. We will have more to say about the input buffer in Chapter 10.

5.4 Formatting the Output Stream

Up to this point, we had to accept the default way our output appeared. Now we will see several ways to format the output to fit our specific needs. There are two syntactically different techniques for formatting the output stream (`cout`).

The first method involves using *member functions*, in which the function can only be accessed through `cout`. There is a lot more going on here, which we will discuss later in the text. The following shows the syntax for using a `cout` member function:

```
cout.<function_name> ( <parameters> );
```

Member Function	Manipulator	Description
`<iostream>`	`<iomanip>`	**Required header files**
`.width`	`setw`	Set the total width for the displayed data
`.precision`	`setprecision`	Places to the right of the decimal point
`.setf( ios::right )`	`right`	Right justify
`.setf( ios::left )`	`left`	Left justify
`.setf( ios::fixed )`	`fixed`	Decimal notation
`.setf( ios::scientific )`	`scientific`	Scientific notation
`.setf( ios::showpos )`	`showpos`	Show the sign of all numbers even if positive
`.setf( ios::showpoint )`	`showpoint`	Show trailing zeros
`.flush`	`flush`	Flush the output buffer

Table 5.4.1 Formatting member functions and manipulators

The preceding syntax example uses the term *parameters*. A parameter is the data we supply to the function so that it has all the information it needs to perform its task.

The second method of formatting the output uses manipulators. We have already seen an example of manipulators when we discussed `endl`. Remember, a manipulator is a command placed directly into the output stream.

Both member functions and manipulators allow you to format the output stream; they are just two different ways to accomplish the same thing. Table 5.4.1 shows some of the more common member functions and the corresponding manipulators.

5.4.1 The `.width` Member Function and `setw` Manipulator

When data is printed to the screen, all of the data is printed without any additional *padding*.

> *i* **Padding** is placing spaces on either side of the data.

The `.width` member function and `setw` manipulator allow you to specify how much space a piece of data will occupy on the screen. If the data isn't big enough to fill the allotted space, the data will be padded with spaces. The side of the data the spaces will appear on depends on the justification of the data. If the data is right justified, spaces will appear on the left side of the data. If the data is left justified, spaces will appear on the right side of the data. By default, all data is right justified or aligned.

> **Remember:** If the data is larger than the specified width, the data will not be truncated; it will simply not appear with any padding.

Strings are typically left justified, so the beginning of each string appearing on separate lines will line up. Numbers, however, should always be right justified so that the decimals line up. Figure 5.4.1 shows an example report that uses appropriate justification.

```
Willy          Makit            1.92
Marcus         Sunkenship       3.75
Calvin         Cowboy            .56
```

Figure 5.4.1 Sample justification

Example 5.4.1 demonstrates the .width member function and how the output will be displayed on the screen.

Example 5.4.1 The .width **member function**

```
float money = 123.45F;
cout << "You have $";

cout.width( 20 );
cout << money << endl;

// Output
You have $              123.45
```

Example 5.4.2 shows the corresponding form using the `setw` manipulator. In order to use formatting manipulators, include the header file `<iomanip>` and use the appropriate namespace rules.

Example 5.4.2 The `setw` manipulator

```
#include <iostream> // Needed for cout
#include <iomanip>  // Needed for setw
using std::cout;
using std::endl;
using std::setw;
int main()
{
    float money = 123.45F;

    cout << "You have $";
    cout << setw( 20 ) << money << endl;

    return 0;
}
// Output
You have $                 123.45
```

Notice the extra spaces, or padding, between the literal and the value stored in `money`. We set the width for 20 total spaces and the data takes up 6; therefore, there are 14 spaces used as padding.

Remember: It is a common mistake to not include the decimal point as a character when counting the total space required for your output.

The width setting is volatile, meaning the setting is applied only to the next output statement. After that statement, the width setting is automatically reset.

5.4.2 The `.precision` Member Function and `setprecision` Manipulator

The `.precision` member function and `setprecision` manipulator set the number of digits displayed to the right of the decimal place. Unlike `.width` and `setw`, `.precision` and `setprecision` are not volatile. Therefore, the precision remains set until a different value is given.

5.4.3 The .setf Member Function

The .setf member function can be used to perform many formatting tasks by incorporating the concept of *flags*. A flag is a value that represents a specific setting or state.

 Remember: The term **setf** stands for **set flag**.

To format the output stream, a flag representing the specific formatting function is passed to .setf. Example 5.4.3 shows an example of how to use .setf. An entire program is provided so that you can see the required header files and related namespace rules.

Example 5.4.3 The .setf **member function**

```
#include <iostream>
#include <iomanip> // Needed for manipulators

using std::cout;
using std::endl;
using std::setprecision;
using std::ios;     // Needed for formatting flags

int main()
{
    float money = 123.45F;

    cout << "You have $";

    cout.setf( ios::fixed ); // Decimal notation
    cout << setprecision( 2 ) << money << endl;

    return 0;
}
// Output
You have $123.45
```

For every flag passed to .setf, there is a corresponding manipulator with the same name as the flag, as shown in Example 5.4.4.

Example 5.4.4 The `fixed` **manipulator**

```
using std::fixed;
...

cout << fixed << setprecision( 2 ) << money << endl;
```

⚠ **Remember:** Any flag that is set, or turned on, can be unset using the member function **unsetf**.

5.4.4 The `.flush` Member Function and `flush` Manipulator

When discussing the `endl` manipulator, we presented the concept of the output buffer. We also mentioned that `endl` flushes the output buffer and moves the cursor to the next line. But what if we want to flush the output buffer without moving the cursor to the next line? That is where the `.flush` member function or `flush` manipulator comes in. The `.flush` member function and the `flush` manipulator both flush the output buffer without creating a new line, as shown in Example 5.4.5.

Example 5.4.5 The `.flush` **member function and** `flush` **manipulator**

```
// Member function
cout.flush();

// Manipulator
cout << flush;
```

Section 5.4 Exercises

1. You can use a couple of different options for formatting the output stream. However, all of these methods are only used with:

   a. `cin`   b. `cout`   c. `endl`   d. `'\n'`

2. What are the two main categories or techniques available for formatting the output stream?

3. The predefined identifier `endl` is an example of which of the following?

   a. stream   b. member function   c. manipulator   d. precision

4. The code fragment `.setf( ios::right )` is an example of which of the following?

   a. stream   b. member function   c. manipulator   d. precision

5. Both `.setf( ios::right )` and the manipulator `right` do what?

   a. right-justify a field   b. truncate right digits

   c. round-off digits   d. align text on the left side

6. The `.width` member function and `setw` manipulator allow you to specify how much space a piece of data will occupy on the screen. If the data or value isn't large enough to fill the requested space, the data will be padded with what?

   a. 0s   b. 1s   c. *s   d. spaces

7. By default, all data is _____ justified.

   a. left   b. right   c. not   d. decimal-point

8. Based on the following section of code, please display the data generated. Use 'b' in your output to represent spaces.

```
float gpa = 3.45F;
cout << "Your GPA is: ";
cout << setw(8) << gpa << endl;
```

9. When displaying the total spaces you requested for your output, you must remember to include the decimal point in your count.

   True   False

10. If the data you attempt to display is bigger than the size of the width you specified, the data will be truncated.

   True   False

11. What header file do you need to include to use formatting manipulators?

   a. `<stdio.h>`   b. `<iomanip>`   c. `<iostream>`   d. `<cmath>`

Section 5.4 Learn by Doing Exercises

The following exercises are intended to be short, hands-on programs that emphasize the topics covered in this section. Write, compile, and run the following programs.

1. Write a program that accepts as input from the keyboard a decimal number representing a person's temperature. Display the person's temperature on the screen, formatted so that it reserves six total spaces on the screen and will always show one decimal place, even if it is zero.

2. Write a program that generates the following report and displays it to the screen. Use literals for all data. Make sure to display appropriate column headings. In the following sample, the

fields are first name, GPA, class, major, and number of credits. Be sure to refer to Table 5.4.1 for help.

```
Bob        3.23    Freshman     Software Engineering        23

Jamie      0.98    Freshman     Underwater Basket Weaving   15

Marcus     4.00    Freshman     Management                   3

Phong      3.75    Junior       Encryption                 101

Webster    2.00    Sophomore    Wildlife Management         56
```

5.5 Debugging

Now that you are starting to write larger programs, you will encounter more runtime and logic errors. As mentioned earlier, the debugger will quickly become your new best friend in locating and correcting these errors. The debugger is actually a set of tools that allows you to analyze your program line by line while it is running. This way you can narrow down where the errors were introduced into your program. This section introduces some of the tools commonly encountered in most programming environments. Section 5.9, Debugging Exercise, will extend your knowledge by guiding you step-by-step through a practical application of the debugger.

> **Remember:** The debugger can only help find logic and runtime errors. All syntax errors must be resolved before an executable is built.

5.5.1 Step Into, Step Over, and Step Out

These tools allow you to execute your program line by line. The Step Into tool executes the current line in the execution process. This line is designated in Visual Studio by a yellow arrow in the left margin, as shown in Figure 5.5.1.

If the current line is a function call or routine, using Step Into will attempt to step into the code within that function or routine. Although usually undesirable, this can be interesting if the function or routine is predefined. For example, using Step Into as shown in Figure 5.5.1 will take you to the code for the insertion operator. This might be interesting, although it is guaranteed to be

```
 1   #include <iostream> // Needed for cout
 2   #include <iomanip>  // Needed for setw
 3   using std::cout;
 4   using std::endl;
 5   using std::setw;
 6
 7   int main ( )
 8   {
 9       float money = 123.45F;
10
11       cout << "You have $";
12       cout << setw( 20 ) << money << endl;
13
14       return 0;
15   }
16
```

Figure 5.5.1 Current line of execution

Tool	Icon	Hot Key
Step Into		F11
Step Over		F10
Step Out		Shift+F11

Table 5.5.1 Visual Studio tools

highly confusing. It is usually better to use Step Over when the current line of execution includes a predefined routine.

Step Over executes the current line without stepping into the code within that function or routine. Using Step Over in Figure 5.5.1 will execute Line 11 and advance the arrow to Line 12. If you accidentally find yourself in some code you really don't want to be in, such as `cout`, using Step Out will take you back to where you entered the undesirable code. Visual Studio has toolbar icons as well as hot keys to access these tools, as shown in Table 5.5.1.

5.5.2 Run to Cursor

Although the step tools are very useful, in large programs it could be quite time consuming to step over each line until an error is encountered. If there are lines of code that have been proven to be correct, you can bypass these lines by plac-

```
 1 #include <iostream> // Needed for cout
 2 #include <iomanip>  // Needed for setw
 3 using std::cout;
 4 using std::endl;
 5 using std::setw;
 6
 7 int main ( )
 8 {
 9     float money = 123.45F;
10
11     cout << "You have $";
12     cout << setw( 20 ) << money << endl;
13
14     return 0;
15 }
16
```

Figure 5.5.2 Breakpoints

ing the cursor—not to be confused with the mouse cursor—on any executable line and selecting Run to Cursor. The program will then run normally until that line of code has been reached. Execution will then stop, and you will be able to continue from that line of code using the step tools to resume the line-by-line execution.

Visual Studio hides this tool; however, it can be executed by right-clicking in the code window and choosing the correct option from the popup menu. You can also use the Ctrl+F10 hot key to initiate the Run to Cursor process.

5.5.3 Breakpoints

Breakpoints accomplish the same basic functionality as Run to Cursor. The added benefit of breakpoints is that you can have multiple breakpoints located strategically throughout your code. Using the Start Debugging option in Visual Studio runs to the first breakpoint. Once the program has been started using any of the debugging tools, the Resume option will jump to the next breakpoint.

To place a breakpoint on a line of code is very simple in Visual Studio. By clicking in the left margin on the desired line, a reddish circle will appear. This designates that the line now has a breakpoint associated with it. Figure 5.5.2 shows an example program with two breakpoints, the first one having been encountered, which stopped the program execution on that specific line.

There are several other options that are important in managing breakpoints from within Visual Studio.

- Toggle Breakpoints (F9): Sets or removes a breakpoint on the current line, as designated by the cursor.

- Delete All Breakpoints (Shift+Ctrl+F9): Removes, permanently, all breakpoints from your program.

- Disable/Enable All Breakpoints: Temporarily turns all breakpoints on or off.

Breakpoints have other, more powerful features that will be discussed in later chapters, when their usage will make more sense.

5.5.4 Watches

Watches allow you to examine the contents, or the state, of variables, constants, and expressions. These watches often give important clues as to what is causing your errors. If the data in a variable, for example, doesn't match what is expected—as determined through desk checking—watches can greatly narrow down where you went wrong in your program. In most cases, all of the other tools discussed get us to the spot where we can use watches to examine the variables in the general location of the error.

Most IDEs, including Visual Studio, have some method of providing watches. There are several windows provided by Visual Studio: Autos, Locals, and Watch 1 through Watch 4. The Autos window shows any variables within a few lines of the current line of execution. The Locals window shows any variables within the current *scope*. The variables shown are automatically determined by Visual Studio. Although scope is a topic that will be expanded on later in the text, it can be thought of as the area in which a variable can be seen.

The last four windows (Watch 1 through Watch 4) are available for programmers to examine variables of their own choosing. Figure 5.5.3 shows the Autos watch window for our example program.

Visual Studio also allows you to view the contents of a variable by hovering over it with the mouse while debugging. Doing so displays a popup window, which contains the variable's name and value.

5.5.5 Importance of Debugging

Although the preceding sections discussed many Visual Studio specific commands, most IDEs have equivalent tools. The names and how they are accessed may differ, but the concepts remain the same.

With the size and complexity of the programs you have written so far, the topic of debugging may seem unnecessary. However, as your programs increase in complexity, so too will the time you spend finding and correcting errors. At that point, if you haven't learned the debugging tools available in

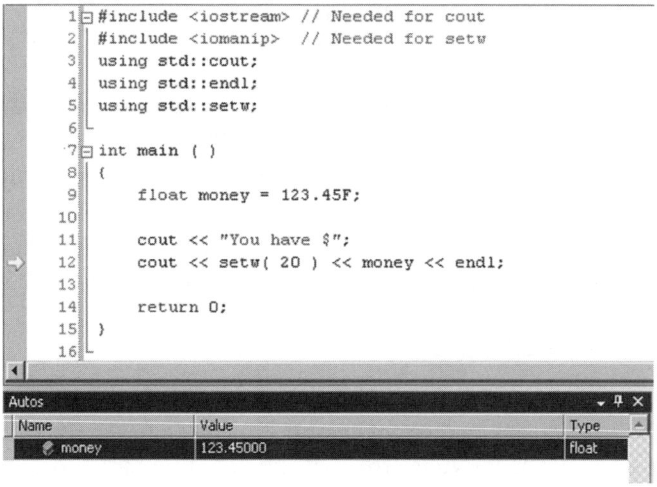

```
1 #include <iostream> // Needed for cout
2 #include <iomanip>  // Needed for setw
3 using std::cout;
4 using std::endl;
5 using std::setw;
6
7 int main ( )
8 {
9      float money = 123.45F;
10
11     cout << "You have $";
12     cout << setw( 20 ) << money << endl;
13
14     return 0;
15 }
16
```

Name	Value	Type
money	123.45000	float

Figure 5.5.3 Autos watch window

your environment as well as the techniques associated with debugging, you will find yourself getting overly frustrated and bogged down.

Because this is such an important topic, almost every chapter contains an exercise in it to help develop your debugging skills. Up to this point the debugging exercises consisted of locating errors within pseudocode. While this is an important skill, starting with this chapter we are providing a program that can be loaded off of the book's website to help reinforce these critical concepts. Instructions and tips are provided within the source code file in the form of comments.

5.6 Problem Solving Applied

Up to this point we have provided you with a complete example illustrating the steps required in designing a solution to a problem, making it a point to show you all the necessary steps along the way. Now we have added the additional phase of converting your algorithm, or pseudocode, to C++ source code. Below is the full solution, including the C++ translation that was easily written based on the pseudocode.

Updated problem statement: Translate the pseudocode solution from Section 4.9 to C++ source code. Please make it a point to include a report title in the output. You will notice that the conversion process will take advantage of all the hard work done in the pseudocode phase.

Original problem statement: Develop the pseudocode solution to calculate the weekly developmental billing report for local radio station WJJQ's biggest client, a car dealership. WJJQ has been in operation for over 30 years, and recently Alexis Blough has taken over as general manager. The station has a format of contemporary rock and country music.

WJJQ uses the following rate structure for the car dealership account:

Production	$100.00 per hr
Pre-production	$60.00 per hr
Producer's fee	$40.00 per hr

The car dealership will be billed for the following time during the past week:

Production	1.5 hours
Pre-production	2 hours
Producer's fee	3 hours

Alexis needs you to display the amount due for each respective activity and to display the overall total owed by the car dealership.

Requirement Specification:

Input(s):

Input Type	Data	Source
Decimal	ProductionHours	Keyboard
Decimal	PreProductionHours	Keyboard
Decimal	ProducersHours	Keyboard

Output(s):

Output Type	Data	Destination
Decimal	ProductionCost	Screen
Decimal	PreProductionCost	Screen
Decimal	ProducersCost	Screen
Decimal	TotalCost	Screen

Constants:

Type	Data	Value
Decimal	PRODUCTION_RATE	100.00
Decimal	PRE_PRODUCTION_RATE	60.00
Decimal	PRODUCERS_RATE	40.00

Design:

Original Pseudocode

C++ Source Code

```cpp
#include <iostream>
using std::cout;
using std::endl;
using std::cin;
```

SEE REQUIREMENT SPECIFICATIONS
FOR VARIABLES AND CONSTANTS

```cpp
const float PRODUCTION_RATE = 100.00F;
const float PRE_PRODUCTION_RATE = 60.00F;
const float PRODUCERS_RATE = 40.00F;

int main()
{
    double  ProductionHours,
            PreProductionHours,
            ProducersHours,
            ProductionCost,
            PreProductionCost,
            ProducersCost,
            TotalCost;
```

Display prompt "Enter Production Hours: "
Read ProductionHours

```cpp
    cout << "Enter Production Hours: ";
    cin >> ProductionHours;
```

Display prompt "Enter Pre-Production Hours: "
Read PreProductionHours

```cpp
    cout << "\nEnter Pre-Production Hours: ";
    cin >> PreProductionHours;
```

Display prompt "Enter Producer's Hours: "
Read ProducersHours

```cpp
    cout << "\nEnter Producer's Hours: ";
    cin >> ProducersHours;
```

ProductionCost = ProductionHours *
          PRODUCTION_RATE
PreProductionCost = PreProductionHours *
          PRE_PRODUCTION_RATE
ProducersCost = ProducersHours *
          PRODUCERS_RATE

```cpp
    ProductionCost = ProductionHours *
                        PRODUCTION_RATE;
    PreProductionCost = PreProductionHours *
                        PRE_PRODUCTION_RATE;
    ProducersCost = ProducersHours *
                        PRODUCERS_RATE;
```

TotalCost = ProductionCost +
       PreProductionCost +
       ProducersCost

```cpp
    TotalCost = ProductionCost +
                PreProductionCost +
                ProducersCost;
```

Display "Production Cost: "
Display ProductionCost

```cpp
    cout << "\n\t\tCar Dealership Bill\n";
    cout << "\n\nProduction Cost: ";
    cout << ProductionCost;
```

Display "Pre-Production Cost: "
Display PreProductionCost

```cpp
    cout << "\n\nPre-Production Cost: ";
    cout << PreProductionCost;
```

Display "Producer's Cost: "
Display ProducersCost

```cpp
    cout << "\n\nProducer's Cost: ";
    cout << ProducersCost;
```

Display "Weekly Total Cost: "
Display TotalCost

```cpp
    cout << "\n\nWeekly Total Cost: ";
    cout << TotalCost << endl;

    return 0;
}
```

5.7 C—The Differences

A whole chapter could be devoted to the differences in I/O routines between C and C++. C doesn't perform input or output the same way as C++. For example, C does not include `cin`, `cout`, or namespaces. All I/O in C is accomplished using a series of functions. Although there are many functions available in C to perform I/O tasks, the more common ones are discussed in this section.

> **Remember:** The term **function** refers to a task or job. For example, the function of a waiter is to serve food. Similarly, in programming, a function is a group of related statements that together perform a specific task or job.

All of the examples in the following sections are direct translations of the examples previously shown in the C++ I/O sections.

5.7.1 The `printf` Function

The `printf` function allows a programmer to print formatted output to the screen. Example 5.7.1 shows a very simple `printf` function call.

> **Example 5.7.1 The `printf` Function**
>
> ```
> printf( "Hello World" );
> ```

The `printf` function supports the use of format specifiers to determine the type of the data to be printed. Table 5.7.1 shows data types and some of their respective format specifiers.

The syntax of `printf` using format specifiers is as follows. Be sure to include the header file `<stdio.h>`.

```
printf ( <format_string>, <argument_list> );
```

The `printf` function requires a formatting string, usually a string literal designated by the programmer. If the formatting string contains any of the format specifiers listed in Table 5.7.1, an argument list must be supplied. There has to be a matching argument for every format specifier in the format string. Think of the format specifier as a placeholder for its corresponding argument. Example 5.7.2 demonstrates how to print the contents of a variable.

Data Type	Format Specifier	Example
int	%d or %i	123
float	%f	3.140000
double	%f or %lf	12.4567878
char	%c	A
String	%s	Hello

Table 5.7.1 Format specifiers

Example 5.7.2 Printing a variable using `printf`

```
int int_exp = 99;

printf( "%d", int_exp );

// Output
99
```

Example 5.7.3 demonstrates how to print the contents of multiple variables.

Example 5.7.3 Printing multiple pieces of data

```
char grade = 'B';
float class_avg = 88.5;

printf( "Your average is: %f\nYour grade is: %c", class_avg, grade );

// Output
Your average is: 88.500000
Your grade is: B
```

Notice there are two format specifiers, %f and %c, in the formatting string; therefore, there are two arguments in the argument list. The first specifier corresponds to the first argument, class_avg, the second specifier corresponds to the second argument, grade.

! **Remember:** Never mix C and C++ I/O routines. If you are writing a C++ program, use C++ routines. Likewise, use only C routines when writing C programs.

5.7.2 Formatting the `printf` Statement

Formatting output with `printf` is accomplished in a much different manner than using the C++ equivalent techniques associated with `cout`. No member functions or manipulators are needed to format the output. If used, width specifiers and alignment adjustments are placed directly into the formatting string of `printf`. A number placed between the percent (%) and the character representation of the data type acts as a width specifier. Examine Example 5.7.4 to see how `printf` formats different types of data.

Example 5.7.4 Formatted output with `printf`

```c
#include <stdio.h> // Needed for printf

int main( void )
{
    int int_exp = 123;
    float float_exp = 98.7653F;

    // Print an integer with 5 total spaces, right aligned
    printf( "%5d\n", int_exp );

    // Print a decimal with 6 total places including the decimal
    // with two places to the right
    printf( "%6.2f\n", float_exp );

    // Print the string literal left justified with a total
    // width of 25
    printf( "%-25s\n", "Calvin" );

    // Print the decimal with 4 total spaces with two to the right of the
    // decimal point
    printf( "%4.2f\n", .346 );
    return 0;
}
// Output
  123
 98.77
Calvin
0.35
```

Notice in Example 5.7.4 that the third example printed the data left justified. This is due to the negative sign (−) being used in the format specifier. The default is to right-justify the text. Also notice that the last `printf` statement rounded the results.

5.7.3 Flushing the Output Buffer

Similar to C++, C also needs a way to flush the output buffer. The `flushall` function clears all buffers, including the output buffer. The header file `<stdio.h>` needs to be included to use this function. Example 5.7.5 demonstrates the `flushall` function.

Example 5.7.5 Flushing the output buffer

```
printf( "Hello World" );
flushall();
```

5.7.4 The `scanf` Function

The `scanf` function allows us to read information from the keyboard. The `scanf` function uses the same idea of format specifiers discussed in Section 5.7.1. The only difference is that the formatting string should *only* contain format specifiers and spaces. Also, each argument in the argument list—except for strings, as discussed in Chapter 10—must be prefaced with an ampersand (&).

The ampersand used in this context is called the "**address of**" operator.

The `scanf` function requires an address to be passed to the function in the argument list. That is why each argument is prefaced with the *address of* operator. Example 5.7.6 demonstrates how to read a value from the keyboard and place it at the address associated with the variable `score`.

Example 5.7.6 Reading a value from the keyboard

```
int score = 0;

scanf( "%d", &score ); // Don't forget the &
```

Example 5.7.7 shows how to read multiple values from the keyboard. Similar to the C++ `cin` statement, the two scores entered must be delimited by whitespace. When all the input has been typed in, press the enter key to signify the input process is finished.

Example 5.7.7 Reading multiple values from the keyboard

```
int score1 = 0, score2 = 0;

printf( "Enter two scores: " );
scanf( "%d %d", &score1, &score2 ); // Place a space between each
                                    // specifier
```

As you can see, using C's `printf` and `scanf` functions to output and input data is a bit more complicated than using C++'s `cout` and `cin`. However, you should be aware that many C++ programmers who originally learned C still miss the various output formatting options. Another popular option for reading data from the keyboard, although not part of the ANSI C standard, is provided with the `getch` function.

i The **A**merican **N**ational **S**tandards **I**nstitute (ANSI) formed a committee to standardize the C programming language. Therefore, any non-ANSI C functions may not be available in strict ANSI C environments.

5.7.5 The `getch` Function

For all of the input routines discussed so far, the enter key must be pressed to signify you are done entering data. The `getch` function, however, doesn't require the enter key to be pressed because it only reads a single character from the keyboard. Example 5.7.8 shows the `getch` function.

Example 5.7.8 Reading a single character with `getch`

```c
#include <stdio.h> // Needed for printf
#include <conio.h> // Needed for getch

int main( void )
{
    char char_exp;

    printf( "Enter character: " );
    char_exp = getch();

    printf( "\nYou entered: %c\n", char_exp );

    return 0;
}

// Output
// Notice that the character entered doesn't appear on the screen
Enter character:
You entered: d
```

A related function to `getch` is `getche`. This function is identical to `getch` except that it displays the character typed. Notice that you must include the header file `<conio.h>` to be able to use either `getch` or `getche`.

> ⚠ **Remember:** The term **getch** stands for **get ch**aracter; the term **getche** stands for **get ch**aracter with **e**cho, which means that the character entered is displayed (echoed) to the screen.

5.8 SUMMARY

Within this chapter we have introduced the concept of streams and their use in helping us perform input- and output-related tasks. To help illustrate streams, we showed you two fundamental options. Reading information from the keyboard was accomplished using `cin`, while directing output to the screen was achieved by using `cout`. We will see a lot of other examples using streams as we continue our exploration of C++, but you have now been introduced to two of the most popular methods available.

Another topic examined related to `cout` compared the use of the `'\n'` escape sequence and the `endl` statement. As you recall, both `'\n'` and `endl` provide us with a method to move the cursor down to the next line, but `endl` also flushes the output buffer.

If you are like most of our beginning programming students, once you learned how to output information to the screen, you wanted to see how to format your results to make them more readable and physically attractive to users. To help with that task, we introduced a variety of formatting options, including some of the fundamental manipulators, like `setw` and `setprecision`, and some member functions, like `.precision` and `.width`, to help dress up your output. Most people new to C++ are often a bit overwhelmed with all the various options. However, you will quickly get used to using the numerous member functions and manipulators presented; it will just take some practice.

The next topic we covered was the crucial topic of debugging. We stressed the importance of debugging as well as some of the tools used in the process. Although the text provides many Visual Studio specific commands and tool names, there are equivalents in most other environments. Remember, the best way to learn debugging is to practice.

Before moving on to the next chapter, please make it a point to fire up your compiler and practice with the material just presented. You need not get bogged down in trying to memorize all the different manipulators and functions. However, do make sure you feel good about the fundamental aspects of reading data in from the keyboard and displaying your results in a formatted fashion to the screen. Once you actually try implementing this material, you will find that it will make much more sense and that your users will become more impressed with the overall look and feel of your applications.

5.9 Debugging Exercise

Download the following file from this book's website and run the program following the instructions noted in the code.

```
/***********************************************************************
 * File: Chap_5_Debugging.cpp
 *
 * General Instructions: Complete each step before proceeding to the
 * next.
 *
 * Debugging Exercise 1
 *
```

```
* 1) On the lines indicated in the code below, insert a breakpoint.
* 2) With the program not in debugging mode, start debugging by
*    using the Step Into tool.
* 3) Click on the Watch 1 tab.
* 4) With the cursor in the Name column, type money and press enter.
*    This adds a programmer-defined watch on the variable money.
* 5) Step into until you reach the first cout statement. With
*    the current line being that cout statement, step into again.
* 6) What happened? Where are we now? What is all of this nasty-
*    looking code?
* 7) Remember, stepping into a predefined routine takes you to the
*    code for that routine. If the debugger can't find the code, it
*    will show the assembly code for that routine.
* 8) How do we get out of this mess? Use the Step Out tool.
* 9) In Visual Studio, you will be taken back to the same cout
*    statement. Use the Step Over tool to take you to the next
*    line.
* 10) Step over the next cout statement. Now look at the console
*     window. What was printed?
* 11) Select Stop Debugging from either the Debug menu or from your
*     toolbar.
*
* Debugging Exercise 2
*
* 1) With the program stopped, run to Breakpoint 1 by selecting
*    the Start Debugging menu option or the toolbar icon, or press F5.
* 2) Step over the cout.
* 3) Step over the cin. Notice that you can now enter a value.
* 4) Enter the value .1 and press enter.
* 5) Notice that the current line of execution is now at the
*    calculation.
* 6) Look at your watch. What is the value of money?
* 7) Hover your mouse pointer over raise. What is its value?
* 8) Step over the calculation. Notice the watch on money is now
*    red. This designates that the variable just changed its value.
* 9) What happened to our money? I thought a raise was supposed
*    to increase our money? Stop debugging and fix the calculation.
*
* Debugging Exercise 3
*
* 1) Choose Disable All Breakpoints from the Debug menu.
* 2) With the cursor on the calculation, employ Run to Cursor. Remember
*    that the Run to Cursor tool can be accessed by right-clicking
*    in the code window and choosing the correct menu option.
* 3) Step over the calculation and verify that this time
*    you end up with more money than before the raise.
* 4) Stop debugging. Now run the entire program by choosing the menu
*    option Start Without Debugging.
*
*********************************************************************/
```

```
#include <iostream>
#include <iomanip>
using std::cout;
using std::cin;
using std::endl;

int main()
{
    float money = 123.45F;
    float raise;

    cout << "You have $";
    cout << money << endl;

    // Breakpoint 1
    // Put a breakpoint on the following line
    cout << "Enter percent raise: ";
    cin >> raise;

    money = money * raise;

    cout << "After your raise you have $";
    cout << money << endl;

    return 0;
}
```

5.10 Programming Exercises

1. Download the following file from this book's website. Fix, compile, build, and execute the code.

```
/****************************************************************
* File: PE 5_10 Q_1.cpp
* Have fun with these errors!
****************************************************************
#include <iosteam>
using std::cout;
using std::cin;

int Main( )
{
    double  ProductionHours
            PreProductionHours,
            ProducersHours,
            ProductionCost,
            PreProductionCost,
            ProducersCost,
            TotalCost;
```

```
    cout >> "Enter Production Hours: ";
    cin << ProductionHours;

    cout << "\nEnter Pre-Production Hours: ;
    cin >> PreProductionHours;

    cout << "\nEnter Producer's Hours: ";
    cin >> "\n" >> ProducersHours;

    ProductionCost = ProductionHours * PRODUCTION_RATE;
    PreProductionCost = PreProductionHours * PRE_PRODUCTION_RATE;
    ProducersCost = ProducerHours * PRODUCERS_RATE;

    TotalCost = ProductionCost + PreProductionCost + ProducersCost

    cout << "\n\t\tCar Dealership Bill\n\";
    cout << "\n\nProduction Cost: ";
    cout << ProductionCost ;

    cout << "\n\nPre-Production Cost: ";
    cout << PreProductionCost;

    cout << "\n\nProducer's Cost: ";
    cout << ProducersCost;

    cout << "\n\nWeekly Total Cost: ";
    cout << TotalCost << endl;

    return 0;
}
```

2. Using the entire development process discussed in Chapter 2, write a working program that accepts as input the radius and height of a cylinder. From this input, calculate the volume of the cylinder. Be sure that you complete all phases of the development process and that your output is self-documenting and correct.

3. Using the following code, add the necessary formatting to make the various values align properly and the overall report look good. Use manipulators for the output in Part 1 and member functions for the output in Part II. See the code itself for some additional information.

```
/*******************************************************************
 * File: PE 5_10 Q_3.cpp
 * Make it a point to have all the output look good by
 * making sure it is properly aligned. Please display the GPA to
 * two places beyond the decimal point.
 *******************************************************************/
#include <iostream>
using std::cout;
using std::endl;
```

```
int main()
{
    // Part I
    cout << "\n Income versus GPA \n";
    cout << "Name              \t Income    \t GPA  \n\n";
    cout << "Jamie             \t 12300.00  \t 3.4   \n\n";
    cout << "Linda             \t 14500     \t 3.92 \n\n";
    cout << "Bob               \t 9400      \t 3.12 \n\n";
    cout << "Marie             \t 15129.00  \t 4     \n\n\n";
    cout << "** End of Report 1 ** \n\n";

    //Part 2
    cout << "\n Income versus Age \n";
    cout << "Name       \t Income     \t Age \n\n";
    cout << "Jamie      \t 12300.00   \t 19  \n\n";
    cout << "Linda      \t 14500      \t 22  \n\n";
    cout << "Bob \t 9400         \t 21   \n\n";
    cout << "Frank      \t 19129.00   \t 51  \n\n\n";
    cout << "** End of Report 2 ** \n\n";

    return 0;
}
```

5.11 Team Programming Exercises

1. Your newest team member Troy has begun developing the solution for a short grade process-ing program. A copy of his pseudocode and his idea of what the output might look like follow. Based on his notes and the algorithm provided, please write the C++ program. Make sure you verify the accuracy of your code by actually building, running, and testing it using your own compiler. Hopefully, Troy has provided the correct pseudocode solution. However, you should double-check that too!

Display "Quiz Calculator"

Prompt "Enter in your score on quiz 1: "
Read Quiz1

Prompt "Enter in your score on quiz 2"
Read Quiz2

Prompt "Enter in your score on quiz 3"
Read Quiz3

TotalQuizPoints = Quiz1 + Quiz2 + Quiz3

AverageQuizScore = TotalQuizPoints / 3

Display "Your three scores were: "
Display Quiz1 " " Quiz3 " "Quiz3
Display "Your total points were:
Display TotalQuizPoints
Display "Your average score was: "
Display AverageQuizPoints

Sample Run/Output:
Quiz Calculator

Enter in your score on quiz 1: *88*

Enter in your score on quiz 2: *94*

Enter in your score on quiz 3: *85*

Your three scores were: *88 94 85*

Your total points were: 267

Your average score was: 89.0

Additional info from Troy
—*Could probably use a constant if desired—not sure*
—*Was rushed so never got a chance to double-check
  algorithm*
—*Supposed to format the output where appropriate to 1
  decimal place*
—*Next Friday is dad's birthday. Send card!*
—*Need the working (and documented) C++ solution
  soon.*

2. Well, here we go again! This time your pen pal has a new request. She was given some pretty
rough legacy code written in C and has asked you to convert it for her to C++. Once you have
it converted, please type your solution into your compiler to prove it actually works.

```
/* Filename:  earnings.c    */
#include <stdio.h>
int main( void )
```

```
{
    int hours = 0;
    float rate = 8.75;
    float gross_pay = 0;

    printf( "Please enter hours worked: " );
    scanf( "%d", &hours );

    gross_pay = hours * rate;

    /* Print a decimal with 7 total places including the decimal
     * with two places to the right for the rate and 8 total spaces
     * including the decimal for the gross pay                    */

    printf( "\n\nYou worked %d hours at $%7.2f per hour\n", hours, rate );
    printf( "and earned a total of $%8.2f.\n\n", gross_pay );

    printf( "\n\n\t\t ** END OF REPORT **\n\n" );

    return 0;
}
```

5.12 Answers to Chapter Exercises

Section 5.1

1.

   a. C++ is very cool

   b. Hello
      World

   c. Computers are useless.
      They can only give you answers.
      Pablo Picasso

2. c. `<iostream>`

3. b. `cout`

4. a. `cin`

5. a. invalid; should use `<<` instead of `>>`

      `cout << "Hello World";`

   b. invalid; needs semicolon

      `cout << "Almost over\n";`

c. invalid; should not put a string literal in a `cin` statement

```
cout << "Enter name: ";
cin >> name;
```

d. invalid character in variable name '#'

```
cin >> age >> soc_security_no;
```

e. invalid; requires double quotation marks around the string literal "Enter size".

```
cout << "Enter size\n";
```

f. valid

g. invalid; should not put a string literal in a `cin` statement

```
cin >>  age >> shoe_size;
```

h. invalid; cannot include a string literal in the input stream

```
cin >> done;
```

i. valid

Section 5.2

1. d. `endl`

2. a.

   n New Year's is coming

   b.

      Hello

   World

   c. goodbye my friend

Section 5.4

1. b. `cout`

2. member functions and manipulators

3. c. manipulator

4. b. member function

5. a. right-justify a field

6. d. spaces

7. b. right

8. YourbGPAbis:bbbbb3.45

9. True

10. False

11. b. `<iomanip>`

Mathematical Operations

Chapter Objectives

By the end of the chapter, readers will be able to:

- Distinguish between well-formed and malformed mathematical expressions.
- Relate the use of *l*-value and *r*-value to mathematical expressions.
- Understand and use standard arithmetic operators.
- Understand the order of precedence.
- Understand the differences between pre- and post-increment and decrement operators.
- Distinguish between a counter and an accumulator.
- Use some predefined mathematical functions.
- Use type-casting techniques.

Introduction

In Chapter 2 we discussed the overall components that most procedural programs follow: **I**nput → **P**rocess → **O**utput. In Chapter 5 we explored the input and output pieces of the puzzle. This chapter examines mathematical expressions that are crucial to the process portion of many programs.

6.1 Mathematical Expressions

Mathematical expressions are not unfamiliar. Since our first algebra class, we have seen mathematical expressions involving variables. C++ mathematical expressions have a few more rules, but conceptually they are the same as what you already know. For example, in mathematics, the following equation is valid.

$$0 = -4y + 5$$

However, this expression violates a couple important C++ rules. First, every operation must be represented by an operator. The "$4y$" implies multiplication in math, but all it would do in C++, and most other programming languages, is produce a syntax error. Second, the left side of the equals sign must be a variable. Placing either a literal, in this case 0, or a constant on the left side of the *assignment operator* (=) produces a syntax error.

Not to pick on mathematicians, but how many ways can you represent multiplication in a mathematical expression? Here are just a few of the different methods mathematical expressions can denote multiplication.

1. $-4y$

2. $-4 \cdot y$

3. $-4 \times y$

4. $-4 * y$

In C++, there is only one valid way to represent each mathematical operation. Example 4 would be the only valid, syntactically correct expression because the asterisk is the only operator that represents multiplication in C++.

We also noted that in C++, the left side of the assignment operator must be a variable. To be more technical, the left side of the assignment operator must represent an appropriate *l-value*. An *l*-value is nothing more than a variable location, or a place to store data. The assignment operator changes the value stored in the variable on the left with the results of the expression on the right, called the *r-value*. The *r*-value is simply the results of any expression or data contained within a variable, constant, or literal.

There are two types of mathematical operators in C++: *unary* and *binary*. Although this might be intimidating at first glance, the difference is simple: a unary operator has one operand, while a binary operator has two operands. In our previous example, "$-4 * y$", the negation operator ($-$) is a unary operator with "4" as its operand. The multiplication operator (*) has two operands, "4" and "y".

As previously discussed, every variable contains a value whose size is based on the number of bytes reserved for the data type specified. Most values can be stored as more than one data type. For example, the value 10 can be stored as an `int`, `float`, `double`, or even a `char` because any value can automatically be stored in a variable with a large enough data type. This is called a *widening conversion*.

The opposite type of conversion is called a *narrowing conversion*. This occurs when a value is stored in a variable having a smaller data type. You may lose information in a narrowing conversion, but not in a widening conversion. For example, the value 10.5121212116 is treated as a `double` because it is a numeric literal. If we tried to store that value into a `float`, we could possibly lose significant data because a `float` is a smaller data type than a `double`. For safety purposes, the data type of the *l*-value should match the largest data type associated with the *r*-value.

Another thing to be careful of is to not store floating-point numbers in an integer variable. These are two different types of data with different memory representations. Therefore, trying to store a `float` or a `double` into an `int` will result in a compiler warning. The rule of thumb is, if the *r*-value contains a decimal number, the *l*-value should be a variable declared with a floating-point data type.

Section 6.1 Exercises

For each of the following statements, identify which ones are valid in C++. If the statement is invalid, state why it is invalid. Assume all variables are declared and initialized.

1. `y = 5x + 1;`

2. `x² + 2x + 1 = 0;`

3. `x = 5 * a + 4;`

4. `0 = -15 * b;`

6.2 Assignment Operator (=)

In its most elementary form, the assignment operator simply assigns a single value to a variable. In the example below, the value 123 is assigned to the variable var_a.

```
var_a = 123;
```

The *r*-value, 123, is being assigned to var_a. If var_a already had a value, it would be replaced by 123. The assignment operator is always executed from right to left. As an example, the following statement assigns the value 1 to all five variables.

```
var_a = var_b = var_c = var_d = var_e = 1;
```

The following example uses an assignment operator with two variables: var_a and var_b.

```
var_a = var_b;
```

After the execution of the statement, the previous value in var_a is replaced with the value in var_b. The variable var_b is assumed to have a valid value; otherwise, both variables will now contain unknown values.

6.3 Standard Arithmetic Operators (+, -, *, /, %)

C++ provides a wide range of mathematical operators for you to use. Table 6.3.1 lists these operators and demonstrates their use.

> ⚠ **Remember:** The modulus operator (%) requires that both operands be integers. Only integer division results in a remainder.

As noted, these symbols are used for addition, subtraction, multiplication, and division and follow the basic understanding you already have of their functionality. The final symbol (%), the modulus operator, provides the remainder of a division of two integer values. In the following example, the variable var_a will be assigned a value of 2 since 2 would be the remainder after dividing 5 by 3.

```
var_a = 5 % 3;
```

Operator	Type	Description	Example
+	Binary	Addition	`a = b + 5;`
−	Binary	Subtraction	`a = b - 5;`
−	Unary	Negation (changes sign of value)	`a = -b;`
*	Binary	Multiplication	`a = b * 5;`
/	Binary	Division	`a = b / 5;`
%	Binary	Modulus (remainder of dividing right operand into left operand)	`a = b % 5;`

Table 6.3.1 Standard arithmetic operators

Be aware that integer division in C++ differs from that in mathematics. In C++, the result of integer division will be an integer. Therefore, the following example will result in zero being assigned to `var_a`. In math, `var_a` would be the floating-point equivalent: $.5\overline{55}$.

```
var_a = 5 / 9;
```

One thing you should never try to do is divide by zero. Doing so results in a runtime error. Later chapters will discuss ways to ensure that this error doesn't happen.

STYLE NOTE   Notice the spacing in the Example column of Table 6.3.1. A space should be placed between a binary operator and its operands. However, we suggest you not place spaces between a unary operator and its operand. Following this form of spacing greatly increases the readability of your code.

Section 6.3 Exercises

What is stored in the variable `a` in each question?

1. `a = 5 + 10 * 2;`

2. `a = (5 + 10) * 2;`

3. `a = 5;`
   `a = a + (5 + 10) * 2;`

4. `a = 10 % 5;`

5. `a = 10 % 3;`

6. `a = 5.2 % 2.3;`

7. `2 - 5 + 7 = a;`

Section 6.3 Learn by Doing Exercises

1. Write a program that converts the following expressions to legal C++ syntax.

   a. $x^2 + 3x + 2 = c$

   b. $\dfrac{10 + 6.0}{9.0} * 3.5 = a$

   c. $\dfrac{-6 + \dfrac{7}{4}}{3.0} = b$

2. Write a program that accepts as input a value representing U.S. currency. Use the Internet to search for the currency exchange rates to convert this value to the following currencies:

   a. Euro

   b. Canada

   c. Mexico (pesos)

   d. Japan (yen)

   e. India (rupees)

   f. Russia (rubles)

6.4 Increment and Decrement Operators (++, - -)

The *increment* (++) and *decrement* (- -) operators are unary operators that increase or decrease their operand's value by one. The two statements shown in Example 6.4.1 are equivalent.

Example 6.4.1 Increment operator

```
++int_exp;                 // pre-increment operator
int_exp = int_exp + 1;
```

The increment operator shown in Example 6.4.1 is called a *pre-increment operator* because the operator appears to the left of its operand. A *post-increment* or *post-decrement operator* appears to the right of its operand.

There are some subtle differences between the pre- and post-increment and decrement operators. Used by themselves, there is no difference in the results between the two forms, as shown in Example 6.4.2.

Example 6.4.2 Stand-alone increment operator

```
int int_exp = 0;

++int_exp;
cout << int_exp << endl; // Displays a 1

int_exp++;
cout << int_exp << endl; // Displays a 2
```

However, when these operators are used as part of a compound statement, the impact on the compound statement is much different. The pre-increment or pre-decrement operator changes the value stored in memory first and then uses the new value in the remainder of the compound statement. The post-increment or post-decrement operator uses the original value in the compound statement but still changes the value in memory when done. Example 6.4.3 demonstrates the differences between the pre- and post- versions of the increment operator.

Example 6.4.3 Difference between pre- and post-increment operator

```
int int_exp = 0;

cout << ++int_exp << endl; // Displays a 1
cout << int_exp++ << endl; // Displays a 1
cout << int_exp << endl;   // Displays a 2
```

Notice that the second `cout` statement in Example 6.4.3 displays a 1 because it uses the current value in the variable to print. Remember, though, that the value in memory is still changed by the post-increment operator. The last `cout` statement in the example displays a 2 because the previous statement modified the memory and changed the value of the variable from 1 to 2.

> **!**
>
> **Remember:** Although all of the examples in this section use the increment operator (++), the pre- and post-decrement operator (− −) has the same syntax but **decreases** the value by one.

Make sure you are very comfortable with the pre- and post-increment and decrement operators, as they are commonly used.

Section 6.4 Exercise

1. Identify the output of the following code fragment.

```
a = 0;
cout << a++ << endl;
cout << ++a << endl;
cout << a + 1 << endl;
cout << a << endl;
cout << --a << endl;
```

6.5 Compound Assignment Operators (+=, -=, *=, /=, %=)

We saw in Section 6.2 the standard mathematical assignment operator (=). There are several other assignment operators that incorporate additional functionality. These compound operators combine the functionality of the binary arithmetic operators with the functionality of the standard assignment operator. These operators provide us with another, shorter method to modify the contents of a variable and include +=, -=, *=, /=, and %=. These compound operators are shortcuts that can be used to replace longer statements, as shown in Table 6.5.1.

Notice that the *l*-value appears as part of the *r*-value expression when expanded, as shown in the Expansion column of Table 6.5.1. Make special care to understand the order of operations. In the /= and *= expansions, parentheses must be used to achieve the same results as the shortcut, because the entire

Operator	Statement	Expansion
+=	a += 5;	a = a + 5;
-=	a -= b;	a = a - b;
*=	a *= b + .1;	a = a * (b + .1);
/=	a /= b + c;	a = a / (b + c);
%=	a %= 2;	a = a % 2;

Table 6.5.1 Compound assignment operators

r-value is evaluated before being applied to the value stored in the variable represented by a.

Section 6.5 Exercises

Convert each of the following statements so that they use either the compound assignment operators or the increment and decrement operators.

int a(10), b(20), c(30);

1. a = 25 + a;

2. b = b * a * 2;

3. b = 1 + b;

4. c = c % 5;

5. b = b / a;

Section 6.5 Learn by Doing Exercise

1. Write a program to prove that the expansions in Table 6.5.1 are correct. Write each compound statement and the expansion to compare the values. As further proof, remove all parentheses from the expansions and rerun. Assume each statement starts with the following values: a = 5; b = 3; c = 10;

6.6 Accumulators Versus Counters

In the previous sections we discussed the increment operator and the compound addition assignment operator. These powerful operators are often used in a couple of rather unique situations. The increment operator works well when used as a *counter*, while the compound addition assignment operator is often used as an *accumulator*. A counter adds one to itself whereas an accumulator adds some value other than one.

The distinction between a counter and an accumulator is significant because when solving problems, the terminology used will determine the type of action we need to take. If the solution calls for counting the number of people in a classroom, we would recognize that an increment operation is required. Likewise, if the solution called for summing up a student's loans, we would recognize the need for an accumulator. Example 6.6.1 shows a counter and an accumulator.

Example 6.6.1 Counter and accumulator

```
int number_students = 0, student_loan = 0;

// Counter
number_students = number_students + 1;
// or
number_students++;

// Accumulator
student_loan = student_loan + 5000;
// or
student_loan += 5000;
```

⚠ **Remember:** You must always initialize your counters and accumulators to a known value. Zero is the most common starting point for these variables.

6.7 Order of Precedence

As you learned in math, there is an established order that must be adhered to when evaluating expressions with multiple operations. This order of operations, or order of *precedence*, applies to all C++ expressions as well. Table 6.7.1 shows the operators we have covered, listed from highest to lowest order of precedence. The operators with the highest level of precedence are evaluated first within an expression.

If there are multiple operators in an expression with the same level of precedence, they are evaluated from left to right. Parentheses can be used either to clarify an expression or to temporarily change the order of evaluation. If paren-

```
postfix ++, postfix − −

prefix ++, prefix − −, unary −

*, /, %

+, −

=, *=, /=, %=, +=, −=
```

Table 6.7.1 Operator order of precedence

theses are nested, the innermost parentheses are evaluated first. One difference between algebraic expressions and C++ expressions is that algebra allows the use of brackets ([ ]) and parentheses interchangeably while C++ only allows parentheses.

STYLE NOTE   Parentheses should be used to help clarify expressions; however, an expression gets cluttered and can become hard to read if there are too many levels of nested parentheses. If an expression starts to get cluttered, break it up into multiple, smaller expressions to improve the readability of your code. Example 6.7.1 shows a cluttered statement and then a more readable form.

Example 6.7.1 Parentheses in expressions

```
// Cluttered
root = ((-b + sqrt( (b * b) - (4 * a * c)) ) ) / (2 * a));

//Not cluttered
discriminant = b * b - 4 * a * c;
denominator = 2 * a;

root = (-b + sqrt( discriminant ) )  / denominator;
```

Section 6.7 Exercises

What is stored in each of the three variables used in the following mathematical expressions? For each of the exercises, assume the variables have been declared and initialized. Use the initial values for each of these exercises.

```
int a = 1, b = 2, c = 3;
```

1. `a = b * c + 3 / 2;`

2. `a += ((b - c) * -4 / (a * 2)) + 10 % 2;`

3. `a %= ++b - c-- * -.5 / 2;`

4. `a -= b-- - --c * -5 / -2;`

6.8 Mathematical Functions

There are some common mathematical operations, such as exponentiation, that do not have associated operators. These operations are provided as functions in an external header file called `<cmath>`. When a function is included in an expression, it is evaluated with the highest level of precedence (i.e., first). The following sections show a few of the more common mathematical functions.

Remember: The term **function** refers to a task or job. For example, the function of a waiter is to serve food. Similarly, in programming, a function is a group of related statements that together perform a specific task or job.

Functions often require the programmer to provide values on which the function will operate. These values are called *parameters*.

A **parameter** is a value passed to a function. This is also sometimes called an **argument**.

6.8.1 The `pow` Function

A lot of mathematical equations and formulas use exponentiation. This is easily accomplished in C++ by using the `pow` function, the syntax of which is shown here.

    `<1-value> = pow( <base>, <power> );`

In mathematics, the preceding syntax would be shown as: *lvalue = base^{power}*. The base parameter can be any numeric data type *except* an `int`, but the power parameter can be any numeric data type. Some compilers support having an `int` for the base, but they are less compliant with the current standard. Remember to make sure there is enough room in the *l*-value to accommodate the results from the function. Example 6.8.1 illustrates how to use the `pow` function.

Example 6.8.1 The `pow` function

```cpp
#include <iostream>
using std::cout;
using std::endl;
#include <cmath> // Needed for pow

int main()
{
    const float PI = 3.141592F;
    float radius = 5;
    double area = 0;

    area = PI * pow( radius, 2 );

    cout << area << " sq. in." << endl;

    return 0;
}

// Output
78.5398 sq. in.
```

Notice that Example 6.8.1 does not directly store the result of the `pow` function in a variable. Instead, the value returned by the `pow` function is directly used in the expression. The results of the calculation are then assigned into the variable `area`.

Also notice that the `<cmath>` header file automatically takes care of the namespace requirements for you. Therefore, once you include the `<cmath>` header file, all of the functions referenced in the file are available for use.

STYLE NOTE In Example 6.8.1 we raised the base to the power of two by using the `pow` function. However, we could have just as easily multiplied the base by itself. In fact, it would have been more efficient to do so. Every time a function is called or executed, there is a certain amount of cost involved. Multiplying the value by itself would have avoided that additional performance degradation. If you are squaring a single variable, it is better and faster to multiply that value by itself.

6.8.2 The `sqrt` Function

Another function commonly needed relates to finding the square root of a value. The function that accomplishes this task is the `sqrt` function. The syntax of how to use the function is shown here.

```
<floating_point_1-value> = sqrt( <floating_point_value> );
```

Although you might expect that the parameter passed to the `sqrt` function could be any data type, it actually needs to be a floating-point value (`float`, `double`, or `long float`). Therefore, if you need to take the square root of an integer, use type casting to convert the integer to a floating-point value (discussed further in Section 6.9). Also, remember your math! It is invalid to take the square root of a negative value. In Visual Studio the value will become "−1.#IND", basically representing an invalid value. Example 6.8.2 demonstrates the `sqrt` function.

Example 6.8.2 The `sqrt` **function**

```
double value = 5;
double square_root = 0;

square_root = sqrt( value );

cout << "Square root: " << square_root << endl;

// Output
Square root: 2.23607
```

6.8.3 The `abs` Function

In C++, the `abs` function returns the absolute value of the parameter passed to the function. The syntax of the `abs` function is shown here.

```
<numeric_1-value> = abs( <numeric_r-value> );
```

Example 6.8.3 demonstrates the `abs` function.

Example 6.8.3 The `abs` function

```
double value = -5;
double square_root = 0;

square_root = sqrt( abs( value ) ); // Notice the nested function

cout << "Square root: " << square_root << endl;

// Output
Square root: 2.23607
```

In Example 6.8.3, the absolute value is determined first, and then the square root of that value will be calculated. Finally, the square root is assigned to the variable `square_root`.

Now that you have seen how some of the math functions in `<cmath>` work, there are many others you can use as needed. Table 6.8.1 shows some additional functions.

There are many math functions available besides those shown in Table 6.8.1. Use your online help or the Internet to find additional functions.

Section 6.8 Exercises

What value is stored in the variable `a` after each mathematical expression?

1. a = sqrt(9.0);
2. a = sqrt(-9.0);

Function	Description
sin	Returns a floating point value that is the sine of the floating-point parameter.
cos	Returns a floating point value that is the cosine of the floating-point parameter.
tan	Returns a floating point value that is the tangent of the floating-point parameter.
asin	Returns a floating point value that is the arcsine of the floating-point parameter.
log	Returns a floating point value that is the natural log of the floating-point parameter.
ceil	Returns the smallest integer greater than or equal to the floating-point parameter.
floor	Returns the largest integer less than or equal to the floating-point parameter.

Table 6.8.1 Mathematical functions

3. ```a = pow(2.0, 5);```

4. ```a = pow(2.0, -2);```

5. ```a = ceil(5.1);```

6. ```a = ceil(5.9);```

7. ```a = floor(5.1);```

8. ```a = floor(5.9);```

9. ```a = sqrt(pow(abs(-2), 4));```

Section 6.8 Learn by Doing Exercise

1. Write a program that accepts as input two sides of a right triangle. Solve for the length of the hypotenuse using the Pythagorean theorem, which states that the square of the hypotenuse is equal to the sum of the squares of the two sides, or $c^2 = a^2 + b^2$, where c is the hypotenuse. Display the length of all three sides.

6.9 Type Casting

There are some situations that require us to convert from one data type to another. This technique, called *type casting*, can be used to force a value to be converted from one type to another. Example 6.9.1 demonstrates how to use one form of type casting to convert the value returned from the `pow` function from a `double` to an `int`.

Example 6.9.1 Type casting

```
double base = 5;
int squared = 0;

squared = static_cast<int>( pow( base, 2 ) );

cout << "Squared: " << squared << endl;

// Output
Squared: 25
```

The conversion forces the type change. However, the change may not always be considered safe. Although type casting helps avoid conversion warnings, it sometimes just hides an underlying problem. There are often very valid reasons why the compiler issued a warning; therefore, care should be taken when using type casting. Example 6.9.2 demonstrates other uses of the `static_cast`.

Example 6.9.2 Additional type casting

```
float score = 0;
double rvalue = 71.5;
char grade = '\0';
int val = 67;

score = static_cast<float>( rvalue );
grade = static_cast<char>( val );
```

```
cout << "Score: " << score << '\n'
     << "Grade: " << grade << endl;

// Output
Score: 71.5
Grade: C
```

In Example 6.9.2, the first cast converted a `double` to a `float`. The second cast converted an `int` to a `char`, in essence converting an ASCII value to its associated character value. It is important to understand that type casting does not change the contents or data of the variable being cast.

There are other, older, forms of type casting. Example 6.9.3 shows these older styles.

Example 6.9.3 Older forms of type casting

```
score = (float)rvalue;
score = float(rvalue);
```

Although still available in many environments, be sure to only use the first form from Example 6.9.3 in C programs. The second example is seen in a lot of legacy code but should be avoided when writing programs. When writing C++ code, use `static_cast` when converting between primitive data types.

6.10 Problem Solving Applied

In the previous chapters an attempt was made to show and discuss the steps necessary for designing and developing a complete solution. In the last chapter, an additional section was added showing how easy it is to convert an algorithm—assuming it was correct—to actual source code. From this point on, a few modifications to the material presented in this section will be made. First, we will continue to focus on the design and implementation details, but will make it a point to stress the latest concepts and material covered within the chapter. Second, in our translation of the algorithm to source code, we will include only the newer concepts and statements just covered.

Problem statement: A friend has asked you to provide a short report that displays the results for a number of different mathematical calculations and functions. Your friend would like a program that can achieve the following functionality:

- Find the average of a series of numbers
- Find the remainder when dividing one number by another
- Raise a number to a power
- Find the square root of a number
- Find the sine of a number

Be sure your report, or output, correctly presents the results of these calculations.

Requirement Specification:

Input(s):

Input Type	Data	Source
Decimal	Test1	Keyboard
Decimal	Test2	Keyboard
Decimal	Test3	Keyboard
Integer	TotalSeconds	Keyboard
Decimal	Base	Keyboard
Decimal	Power	Keyboard
Decimal	Discriminant	Keyboard
Decimal	Angle	Keyboard

Output(s):

Output Type	Data	Destination
Decimal	Average	Screen
Integer	Minutes	Screen
Integer	RemSeconds	Screen
Decimal	RaisedValue	Screen
Decimal	SquareRoot	Screen
Decimal	Sine	Screen

Constants:
No constants are used within this problem.

Design:

Original Pseudocode

WE WILL NOW ONLY SHOW THE UNIQUE ASPECTS IN
RELATION TO THE C++ SOURCE CODE SECTION ON THE
RIGHT OF YOUR SCREEN.

Average = (Test1 + Test2 + Test3) / 3

Minutes = TotalSeconds divided by 60
RemSeconds = The remainder after the division of
TotalSeconds by 60

RaisedValue = call power function (Base and Power)

SquareRoot = call square root function (Discriminant)

Sine = call sine function (Angle)

C++ Source Code

```
// #includes
...

int main()
{
    double Average, RaisedValue, SquareRoot,
        Sine, Test1, Test2, Test3,
        Discriminant, Angle, Base, Power;
    int TotalSeconds, Minutes, RemSeconds;

    // Input
    ...

    Average = (Test1 + Test2 + Test3) / 3;

    Minutes = TotalSeconds / 60;
    RemSeconds = TotalSeconds % 60;


    RaisedValue = pow( Base, Power );


    SquareRoot = sqrt( Discriminant );


    Sine = sin( Angle );

    // Output
    ...

    return 0;
}
```

6.11 C—The Differences

The only differences between C and the C++ techniques discussed in this chapter involve the mathematical functions just presented. First, the header file you would need to include is `<math.h>`. Next, the `pow` function is always passed two `double` values and returns a `double`. Likewise, the `sqrt` function is always passed a `double` and returns a `double`.

The biggest difference, however, is the process required to find the absolute value of a number. There are separate functions for each numeric data type. Table 6.11.1 shows the functions and their associated data types.

Another difference is how C type-casts. In C++, the `static_cast` keyword is used to convert from one data type to another. C, however, places parentheses around the target data type, placed in front of the value to be converted. Example 6.11.1 clearly shows the differences between a C++ and a C cast.

Function	Data Type
abs	int
fabs	double
labs	long

Table 6.11.1 C absolute value functions

Example 6.11.1 C++ versus C type casting

```
double y = 5.0;
float x = static_cast<float>(y); // C++ type casting

float x = (float)y;              // C type casting
```

6.12 SUMMARY

This chapter presented a variety of topics, most related to developing expressions and using existing mathematical functions. Along the way, we presented the standard C++ arithmetic operators—the fundamentals of which you were already familiar with, such as operator precedence. Next, we demonstrated some crucial aspects associated with using the assignment operator, and took a quick peak at the core characteristics associated with variables, including examining *l*-values and *r*-values.

We presented pre- and post-increment and decrement operators, as well as the differences between them. We also provided a descriptive comparison between counters and accumulators and which operators are used in these types of expressions. Next, we presented several mathematical functions that you can use in developing your own programming solutions. The chapter concluded with a discussion of type casting and how this technique forces data type conversion.

You will have plenty of time to practice with these various operators and functions, not only in the following exercises but as the text progresses. Much of the material just presented will be used extensively when discussing more advanced concepts later in the text.

6.13 Debugging Exercise

Download the following file from this book's website and run the program following the instructions noted in the code.

```
/*********************************************************************
 * File: Chap_6_Debugging.cpp
 *
 * General Instructions: Complete each step before
 * proceeding to the next.
 *
 * Debugging Exercise 1
 *
 * 1) On the lines indicated in the code below, insert a
 *    breakpoint.
 * 2) Run to the breakpoint.
 * 3) Put watches on both fahrenheit and celsius.
 * 4) When asked for a temperature, enter 212.
 * 5) Verify that the value you entered is stored
 *    correctly.
 * 6) Step over the conversion calculation. What is the value
 *    in celsius? Is that the correct value? No.
 * 7) Remember your order of precedence. Put parentheses
 *    around fahrenheit - 32. This needs to be done before
 *    the multiplication.
 * 8) Stop debugging and recompile.
 *
 * Debugging Exercise 2
 *
 * 1) Run to Breakpoint 1.
 * 2) When asked for a temperature, enter 212.
 * 3) Verify that the value you entered is stored
 *    correctly.
 * 4) Step over the conversion calculation. What is the value
 *    in celsius? Is that the correct value? No.
 * 5) Look at the division. This is integer division.
 *    Therefore,
 *    5 / 9 = 0. This is not the result we are looking for.
 * 6) Modify the calculation so that it does floating-point
 *    division.
 *    There are three different ways we have discussed:
 *            a) Use the F suffix on the literals
 *            b) Type-cast the literals
 *            c) Replace the 5 with 5.0 and the 9 with 9.0
 * 7) Stop debugging, recompile, and run to verify that it
 *    now works correctly.
 *
 *********************************************************************/
```

```
#include <iostream>
#include <iomanip>
using std::cout;
using std::cin;
using std::endl;

int main()
{
    float fahrenheit = 0;
    float celcius = 0;

    cout << "Enter temperature in Fahrenheit: ";
    cin >> fahrenheit;

    // Breakpoint 1
    // Put a breakpoint on the following line
    celcius = 5 / 9 * fahrenheit - 32;

    cout << fahrenheit << " degrees F = "
         << celcius << " degrees C" << endl;

    return 0;
}
```

6.14 Programming Exercises

The following programming exercises are to be developed using all phases of the development method. Be sure to make use of good programming practices and style, such as constants, whitespace, indentation, naming conventions, and commenting. Make sure all input prompts are clear and descriptive and your output is well formatted and looks professional.

1. Calvin is shopping for a circular, above ground swimming pool. He is currently looking at a pool that is 25′ in diameter and 5′ deep. Assume the Klamath Falls Water Department charges $1.80 per unit of water, and a unit is considered 748 gallons. Write a program that determines how much it will cost Calvin to fill his swimming pool. He will want to be able to enter different dimensions each time he runs the program so that he can determine which pool to buy. Here are some formulas and conversions that may help.

   1 gallon (U.S.) = 231 cubic inches

   1 cubic inch = 1/1,728 cubic foot

   volume of a cylinder: $\pi r^2 h$

2. Paul is building a workshop and has already figured out how much lumber he needs. The following table shows the cost at one of the local lumberyards for each item as well as the number

of items Paul needs. Write a program that creates a report that lists each item, the quantity of each item, the cost per item, and the total cost for that item. The report should also include the total cost of all materials. Because Paul wants to determine which lumberyard will give him the best deal, he will need to be able to specify the cost of each item. Be sure to test your program with the sample data.

Description	Cost per Unit	Quantity Needed
Joists	75.99	25
2 × 6	8.90	100
2 × 4	4.95	25
4 × 4	12.95	20
4 × 8 sheet plywood	22.00	100

Table 6.14.1 Sample data

3. Jeanie recently decided to go shopping for a newer 4-wheel drive Jeep to use for commuting to school. She is hoping to put $1,000 or so down on her new purchase. Your job is to develop the necessary program to calculate and display what her payment would be based on the cost of the car, the amount of money she puts down, the time period of the loan, and the interest rate. The formula might look similar to:

$$payment = \frac{(P - DP)(r/12)}{(1 - (1 + r/12)^{-m})}$$

where P is the principal, DP represents the down payment, r is the interest rate, and m is the number of monthly payments.

4. Your friend is working with various circle-related calculations and has asked for your help. Your job is to write a short program that will prompt the user to enter the radius from the keyboard. Once you have the radius, calculate and display the circumference and area of the circle. Use 3.14159 for pi.

The formula for the circumference is: $C = 2\pi r$

The formula for the area is: $A = \pi r^2$

6.15 Team Programming Exercise

Remember Troy, the guy from the last chapter who recently joined your team? Well, now he has begun developing the solution for a short program dealing with various math-related operations. He has provided you with a copy of his partially completed pseudocode. Unfortunately, Troy did not get a chance to double-check his work, so you will need to check the accuracy of his algorithm before writing the C++ code. And as you can see, he also did not get the chance to complete all of the details required in the pseudocode related to the processing needed. Your job is to double-check his algorithm; complete the necessary parts related to the processing phase; and write, test, and debug the C++ program.

Display "Some Math Examples"

Prompt "Enter the first (integer) number: "

Read FirstNumber

Prompt "Enter the second (integer) number:"

Read SecondNumber

Prompt "Enter the third (integer) number:"

Read ThirdNumber

Prompt "Enter number (x): "

Read NumberX

Prompt "Raise 'x' to what power:"

Read PowerNumber

— Processing Section – need to finish this up —

SumOfNumbers = FirstNumber + SecondNumber + 3rdNum

…

Display "Your three numbers entered were: "

Display FirstNumber " " SecondNumber " " ThirdNumber

Display "Sum of the numbers is: "

Display SumOfNumbers

Display "Average of the three numbers is: "

Display AverageOfNumbers

Display "Product of the 3 numbers is: "

Display ProdOfNumber

Display "Square Root of the Sum of the numbers is: "

Display SquareRoot

Display "The remainder of the sum of the numbers / 3 is: "

Display Reminder

Display "** ALL DONE **

6.16 Answers to Chapter Exercises

Section 6.1

1. Invalid. Each operation has a specific operator. This expression can be rewritten as:

   ```
   y = 5 * x + 1;
   ```

2. Invalid. This statement has so many problems it needs to be completely rewritten. First, the left side of the assignment operator is not a variable. Second, the multiplication is not being represented correctly; it needs the multiplication operator. Finally, there is no C++ operator to represent exponentiation.

3. Valid.

4. Invalid. The left side of the assignment operator must be a variable, not a literal.

Section 6.3

1. 25

2. 30

3. 35

4. 0

5. 1

6. Invalid expression. The modulus operator cannot be used with floating-point values.

7. Invalid expression. The left side of the assignment operator must be a variable.

Section 6.4

1.

   0

   2

   3

   2

   1

Section 6.5

1. `a += 25;`

2. `b *= a * 2;`

3. `b++; or b += 1;`

4. `c %= 5;`

5. `b /= a;`

Section 6.7

1. a: 7; b: 2; c: 3

2. a: 3; b: 2; c: 3

3. Will not compile because the *r*-value is a double, which cannot be used with a modulus operator.

4. a: 4; b: 1; c: 2

Section 6.8

1. 3.0

2. You cannot take the square root of a negative number.

3. 32

4. .25

5. 6

6. 6

7. 5

8. 5

9. 4

Conditional Statements

Chapter Objectives

By the end of the chapter, readers will be able to:

- Create and recognize well-formed conditions using both relational and logical operators.
- Understand the truth tables associated with logical operators.
- Develop solutions using standard C++ conditional statements.
- Discuss the issues dealing with scope.
- Understand and write C++ selection statements.
- Use the ternary conditional operator.

Introduction

In this chapter we will introduce constructs that conditionally execute one or more statements. Up to this point our programs have almost exclusively executed sequentially, starting at `main` and executing line by line until the end of the program. However, in the development of many algorithms, it is necessary to perform a specific task if a particular condition occurs. To handle this situation, conditionals need to be used. In this chapter we will also introduce and discuss the operators required to build valid conditions, which determine the statement(s) that will be executed.

7.1 Conditional Expressions

Conditions compare the values of variables, constants, and literals using one or more of the *relational operators* found in Table 7.1.1. These are binary operators, which means that a variable, a constant, or a literal must appear on each side of the operator. The comparison determines whether the expression is true or false.

> **Remember:** A **constant** is similar to a variable except that the value can't change. A **literal** is a number, character, or string without a name associated with it.

Relational Operator	Description
==	Equality (be sure to use two equals signs)
!=	Inequality
<	Less than
>	Greater than
<=	Less than or equal to
>=	Greater than or equal to

Table 7.1.1 Relational operators

7.1.1 Relational Operators

Table 7.1.1 shows the operators used in creating conditions. All of these operators return a Boolean value, either **true** or **false**.

> ⚠️ **Remember:** A single equal sign (=) is an assignment and a double equal sign (==) represents a test for equality.

Example 7.1.1 illustrates the use of various relational operators.

Example 7.1.1 Relational operators

```
const int CONST_INT_EXP = 9;
int int_exp1 = 0, int_exp2 = 5;
float float_exp = 9.0;
char char_exp = 'a';

bool result;

result = int_exp1 == 0;            // true
result = int_exp2 >= int_exp1;     // true
result = int_exp1 > CONST_INT_EXP; // false
result = float_exp == CONST_INT_EXP; // true
result = char_exp <= int_exp1;     // false, remember ASCII
                                   //        values?

result = int_exp1 != int_exp2;     // true
result = char_exp == 'a';          // true

// --- ILLEGAL OR MALFORMED CONDITIONS ---

result = int_exp1 < int_exp2 < float_exp;
// Malformed condition. May or may not compile depending on
// compiler used. Even if the compiler will compile
// this condition, it should NEVER be written in this manner.

result = char_exp == "a";
// Illegal. Attempting to compare a character to a string
// literal.
```

> **Remember:** The **ASCII** table shows the association between a character and a number. The number is how the character is stored in memory and therefore is used in the comparison. See Appendix A for an ASCII chart.

7.1.2 Logical Operators

Logical operators, as shown in Table 7.1.2, are used to combine multiple relational operators into a larger composite condition.

The || (OR) and && (AND) are binary operators, whereas the ! (NOT) is a unary operator. The && results in a true value *only* if the conditions on both sides of the operator are *true*. The || results in a false value *only* if the conditions on both sides of the operator are *false*. The ! operator reverses the logic of the single condition.

Tables 7.1.3 and 7.1.4 show the truth tables that are the result of combining various logical operators.

Logical Operator	Description
&&	AND
||	OR
!	NOT

Table 7.1.2 Logical operators

Condition 1	Condition 2	&& Result	|| Result
true	true	true	true
true	false	false	true
false	true	false	true
false	false	false	false

Table 7.1.3 Logical AND and OR truth table

Condition	! Result
true	false
false	true

Table 7.1.4 Logical NOT truth table

> *i*
>
> A **truth table** displays the Boolean results produced when the operator is applied to the specified operands.

The order of precedence gives the && operator a higher level of importance than the || operator; therefore, it is evaluated before the || operator when both appear in the same expression. Interestingly enough, the ! operator has the highest level of precedence of all the logical operators and even places higher than the relational operators.

If more than one logical operator of the same level of precedence appears in a condition, they are evaluated from left to right. Parentheses not only change the precedence, as we've seen in mathematical expressions, but also help clarify and simplify any complicated conditions for the programmer reading the code.

As soon as the outcome of the condition can be determined, the evaluation terminates. Therefore, some conditions may not be evaluated. This is called *short-circuit evaluation*. For example, if the first part of an && expression is false, there is no need to proceed because the result *must be* false. In the case of an || expression, if the first condition is true, the final result *must also* be true. The code provided in Example 7.1.2 illustrates the use of various logical operators.

Example 7.1.2 Logical operators

```
int int_exp1 = 0, int_exp2 = 5;
float float_exp = 9.0;
char char_exp = 'a';
const int CONST_INT_EXP = 9;

bool result;
```

```
result = int_exp1 < int_exp2 && float_exp == 9.0;        // true
result = int_exp1 > CONST_INT_EXP || float_exp == 9.0;   // true
result = !(float_exp == 9.0 || int_exp1 > CONST_INT_EXP); // false

// Short-Circuit Evaluation
result = float_exp == 9.0 || int_exp1 > CONST_INT_EXP;   // true
```

The concept of short-circuit evaluation is important because if used correctly, it can help improve the efficiency of your program. To help facilitate this, you should place the most common condition first. In essence you are saying, in the case of &&, "If this condition is false, *do not* go any further."

STYLE NOTE ▶ Do not forget the old saying, "Just because you *can* do something, doesn't mean you *should*." Just because you can make very complicated conditions by chaining multiple logical operators doesn't mean you should. Make the conditions more readable by using parentheses to help clarify the condition and to avoid any unnecessary confusion and uncertainty. Be careful not to make overly complicated conditions by combining a series of logical operators.

Section 7.1 Exercises

Assume the following declarations for the exercises that follow:

```
int int_exp1 = 0, int_exp2 = 1;
char char_exp = 'B';
```

Evaluate the following conditions. For the ones that are incorrect, describe what is wrong with them and show their corrected forms.

1. `int_exp1 => int_exp2`

2. `int_exp1 = int_exp2`

3. `int_exp1 =! int_exp2`

4. `char_exp == "A"`

5. `int_exp1 > char_exp`

6. `int_exp1 < 2 && > -10`

7.2 The if **Statement**

The if statement uses conditions to determine whether a specific action will be executed. It is similar to saying, "If this condition is true, execute this statement."

The general form for the if statement is shown here:

```
if ( <condition> )
    <action>
```

The <condition> represents any valid expression, built either from the relational and logical operators or from the evaluation of a single variable. So how can a float variable be evaluated as true or false? To the computer, zero is considered false while any nonzero value is considered true.

The <action> in the preceding syntax example represents any valid C++ statement. Let us emphasize: any *single* statement. If more than one statement needs to be executed, you *must* enclose multiple statements in curly braces { }. The braces create a block of statements, thus allowing the if statement to control the execution of the action block. Example 7.2.1 illustrates both a single-line and a multiple-line action block.

Example 7.2.1 The if statement

```cpp
// Example 1
if ( test >= 80 && test < 90 )
    cout << "You have earned a B" << endl; // Action block

// Example 2
if ( test >= 90 )
{       // Start of the action block
    cout << "You have earned an A" << endl;
    cout << "Excellent work!" << endl;
}       // End of the action block

// Example 3
if ( test >= 70 && test < 80 )
{       // Start of the action block
    cout << "You have earned a C" << endl;
}       // End of the action block
```

Notice in Example 7.2.1 that there are no semicolons after the condition components of the if statements. Although it is syntactically correct to include them, the results will leave you scratching your head. Since a semicolon is used to terminate a statement, if it is used after the condition, the `if` statement will be terminated at that point. In other words, the action block will be separated from the `if` statement. Therefore, any statements in the action block will always be executed, regardless of the condition's results.

STYLE NOTE ▷ The physical position of the opening curly brace has long been debated. Some programmers like to put it on the same line as the `if` statement. Others put it on the next line under the `if` statement, as shown in Example 7.2.1. It is not the intention of this book to waste the reader's time debating this issue. However, our personal preference is to follow the style illustrated in Example 7.2.1.

Another difference in style relates to the usage of curly braces when only a single statement is associated with a control statement, such as an `if` statement. Some programmers prefer to use curly braces even if there is only a single statement, while others don't. It is our preference to use curly braces only when the action contains multiple statements.

One point most, but not all, programmers agree on is indentation. The statements associated with the `if` statement are indented, three or four spaces, to show that the action statements are associated with a specific `if` statement. Fortunately, the default tab size of most development tools and editors is three or four spaces, although they can be customized.

In relation to style issues, it basically comes down to two things:

1. Follow the style guide of the organization for which you are programming. As a student, you are programming for your instructors, and therefore you need to follow their style.
2. Be consistent. If your organization doesn't have a preference, choose the style you feel looks the best, and stick with that style.

7.2.1 The `else` Statement

The `else` statement is an optional part of the `if` statement. It cannot stand alone; it always has to be associated with an `if` statement.

```
if ( <condition> )
      <action 1>
else
      <action 2>
```

The `else` statement has no condition or expression associated with it, relying instead on the results of the condition associated with the `if` statement. The `else` statement executes its action only if the condition is false. In other words, "If the condition is true, execute action 1; otherwise, execute action 2." As previously noted, an action block can contain one or more statements, but if there is more than one statement, the action must be enclosed in curly braces. In Example 7.2.2, the variable `pass` will be set to true only if the value in the variable `grade` is greater than or equal to 60.

Example 7.2.2 The `else` statement

```
if ( grade >= 60 )
    pass = true;
else
{
    pass = false;
    cout << "Hope you do better next time." << endl;
}
```

7.2.2 The `else if` Statement

Often the need will arise to check another condition when the `if` statement fails. To do this, we embed another `if` statement in the action block of the `else` statement. Notice in Example 7.2.3 how a second condition is embedded within the `else` statement.

Example 7.2.3 Nested `if` statement

```
if ( avg >= 90 )
    cout << "A" << endl;
else
    if ( avg >= 80 )
        cout << "B" << endl;
```

In C++, there isn't a reserved word representing an `else if` statement. That is not true with all languages, however. Both Ada and Visual Basic, just to name two, have specific reserved words to represent an `else if` statement.

As you can see in Example 7.2.3, the indentation could cause the code to become difficult to read once several `else if` statements are added. Therefore, it is a common practice to move the `if` statement to the same line as the `else` statement, as shown here.

```
if ( <condition 1> )
      <action 1>
else if ( <condition 2> )
      <action 2>
else if ( <condition 3> )
      <action 3>
...


else // Optional
      <last action>
```

The checking of the individual conditions stops when the first true condition is evaluated or the action associated with the final `else` statement is executed. So, "If condition 1 is true, execute action 1; otherwise, check condition 2. If condition 2 is true, execute action 2; otherwise, evaluate condition 3. If all of the conditions are false, execute the last action." Note that only one action block will be executed for a given `if` control structure. However, it is possible to not have *any* action block executed if there isn't the optional, final `else` statement.

> ⚠ **Remember:** The `else` statement is always optional and must be placed at the end of the `if` statement.

Using `else if` statements is much more efficient than using a number of separate `if` statements. Study Example 7.2.4 and count how many unique comparisons need to be evaluated if the contents of the variable `avg` are equal to 80.

Example 7.2.4 Inefficient `if` statement

```
if ( avg >= 90 )
    cout << "A" << endl;

if ( avg >= 80 && avg < 90 )
    cout << "B" << endl;
```

```
if ( avg >= 70 && avg < 80 )
    cout << "C" << endl;

if ( avg >= 60 && avg < 70 )
    cout << "D" << endl;

if ( avg < 60 )
    cout << "F" << endl;
```

Since all `if` statements need to be assessed, a total of eight conditions are evaluated. In fact, no matter what the value of `avg` is, eight individual conditions are evaluated. Now, how many conditions are evaluated in Example 7.2.5 if the contents of `avg` equal 80?

Example 7.2.5 The `else if` statement

```
if ( avg >= 90 )
    cout << "A" << endl;
else if ( avg >= 80 )
    cout << "B" << endl;
else if ( avg >= 70 )
    cout << "C" << endl;
else if ( avg >= 60 )
    cout << "D" << endl;
else
    cout << "F" << endl;
```

Since the evaluation stops after the first true condition in Example 7.2.5, a total of two conditions are evaluated. Even better, if the contents of `avg` happen to be 90, only a single comparison is made. Since comparisons are processor intensive, this is potentially a significant time saver.

Added efficiency can also be gained if the most commonly true condition is placed higher in the `else if` list. Doing so would increase the probability that the first or second condition would be evaluated as true, thus terminating the evaluation.

The flow associated with an `if-else if-else` statement is illustrated in Figure 7.2.1. The flowchart graphically illustrates Example 7.2.5.

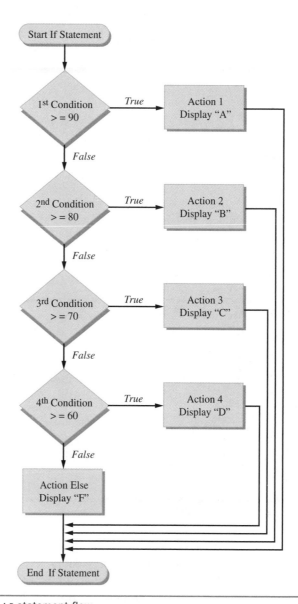

Figure 7.2.1 if statement flow

Another form of the `if` statement uses a series of *nested* `if` statements to do multiple comparisons. In Example 7.2.6, the action(s) taken will be determined by a combination of true and false conditional expressions.

 A **nested** control statement has another control statement in its action block.

Example 7.2.6 Properly nested `if` statement

```
if ( gpa >= 3.75 )
    if ( credits > 25 )
        if ( money < 30000 )
        {
            scholarship = 5000;
            cout << "Way to go!" << endl;
        }
        else
            scholarship = 2000;
    else
        scholarship = 1000;
else
{
    scholarship = 0;
    cout << "You're on your own." << endl;
}
```

When using the format illustrated in Example 7.2.6, remember that you must map your most nested `if` statement with the nearest unmatched `else` statement. Assuming your GPA is 3.76 and your credits are 19, the value of the variable `scholarship` would become 1000. Clearly you can see the importance of consistent indentation and use of curly braces to clarify a complicated set of statements as shown in the example. While the compiler doesn't care about indentation, the more readable code would definitely make your teacher, boss, and teammates much happier. Be careful that you don't get carried away with the number of levels of nesting. Try to keep things as clean and concise as possible.

Section 7.2 Exercises

Examine the following code fragments for errors. If there is an error, identify the type of error (syntactical, logical, runtime) and how you would fix it. If you are unsure or wish to confirm your evaluation, type it into your compiler and run it!

1.
```
if ( a > 0 );
     cout << "a is greater than 0" << endl;
```

2.
```
if ( a = 1 )
     cout << "a is equal to 1" << endl;
```

3.
```
if ( a != 0 || a != 1 )
     cout << "a is not equal to 0 or 1" << endl;
```

4.
```
if ( b < c )
     cout << "b is less than c" << endl;
     cout << "b came before c" << endl;
```

5.
```
if ( a == 0 )
     cout << "a equals 0" << endl;
   elseif( a == 1 )
     cout << "a equals 1" << endl;
```

6.
```
if ( a == b )
     cout << "a equals b" << endl;
   else if ( b == c )
     cout << "b equals c" << endl;
   else ( a != b && b != c )
     cout << "a is not equal to b and "
           << "b is not equal to c" << endl;
```

7.
```
if ( a == 0 ) cout << "a equals 0" << endl;
```

Section 7.2 Learn by Doing Exercise

1. Write the program to determine the level of membership for a local credit union. There are four levels: Platinum, Gold, Silver, and Copper. If members have $25,000 or more, they are Platinum members. If they have more than $10,000 but less than $25,000 and have two different types of accounts, checking and savings, they are Gold members. If they have more than $10,000 but only have one type of account, they are Silver members. Those members with $10,000 or less are Copper members. Prompt for the amount of money as well as a character representing whether they have checking or savings accounts. For output, display the membership level.

7.3 Variable Scope

There are two central concepts associated with variables:

- What code has the right to access or change the variable?

- How long will the variable exist, or live?

In programming, this concept is often referred to as the *scope* of the variable. In its most elementary form, the scope of a variable is what determines where, within your code, the variable can be referenced and used.

In Example 7.3.1, `var_a` and `var_b` are both defined within the scope of our block indicated by the curly braces. As you can see, `var_a` and `var_b` are both accessible within the block where they are defined. However, in the final line of code we would receive an error message from the compiler because `var_b` is not defined; its scope is only within the block in which it was declared.

Example 7.3.1 Variable scope

```
{
    int var_a = 5, var_b = 10;
    var_a++;
    cout << "var_a: " << var_a << endl;
}
cout << "var_b: " << var_b; // Error: undeclared identifier
                            // var_b
```

As a result of the physical location of the variable declarations, their scope is only within that section of code—the code enclosed by the curly braces. Any code outside of this block will not have access to the variables because they don't exist outside the block.

In Example 7.3.1, the lifetime of `var_a` and `var_b` began when the variables were declared within that section of code. When the execution of the program leaves that block of code, `var_a` and `var_b` will no longer exist, they will have indeed reached the end of their lifetimes.

Example 7.3.2 illustrates additional aspects associated with the concept of scope. Notice the physical placement of our constant `PI` along with the variable called `global_area` at the top of our source code. Because of their placement, outside of any function, they are said to be placed at the *global* level. All code within the entire source file, including from within the function main, can access them. Global variables are to be avoided because of their ability to be changed from anywhere within your code. This leads to instability and vulnerability to incorrect values within the variables. Variables declared within braces are considered to have *local* scope.

Example 7.3.2 Global versus local scope

```cpp
#include <iostream>
using std::cout;
using std::endl;
#include <cmath> // Needed for pow


const float PI = 3.141592F;    // global scope
float global_area = 0;         // global scope

int main()
{
    float radius = 5;          // local scope
    global_area = static_cast<float> (PI * pow( radius, 2 ));

    cout << global_area << " sq. in." << endl;

    return 0;
}

// Output
78.5398 sq. in.
```

In the future, we will place only our constants at the global level. All of our variables will always be defined within the specific scope where they are used or needed. We will have a lot more to say about the scope of variables later in the text.

One difference between local and global variables is that global variables are automatically initialized. The initial value of all global variables is set to zero.

7.4 The switch Statement

Another form of a conditional statement is the switch statement, sometimes called a selection statement. Unlike if statements, which allow for very complicated conditions, the switch statement only checks for equality and only for one variable. This statement works well when you want to check the contents of a variable for a rather limited set of values. Also, the switch statement only works with *ordinal* data types. Ordinal data types are those that can be translated into an integer to provide a finite, known number set. Some examples of ordinal data types are int, bool, char, and long. The general form of the switch statement follows:

```
switch ( <variable> )
{ // Required
        case <literal or constant 1>:
                <action 1>
                break;
        case <literal or constant 2>:
                <action 2>
                break;
        ...

        default: // Optional
                <default action>
}// Required
```

When the first line in the switch statement is encountered, the value of the variable is determined. The execution of the program then jumps to the case that corresponds to the value of the variable being examined. The execution of the switch statement then continues line by line until either a break statement is encountered or the end of the switch statement is reached. Example 7.4.1 illustrates a valid switch statement with all necessary break statements included.

Example 7.4.1 The switch **statement**

```
switch ( test_item )
{       // Required when using a switch statement
    case 1:
        cout << "You have chosen a 1." << endl;
        break;
    case 2:
        cout << "You have chosen a 2." << endl;
        break;
}    // Required when using a switch statement
```

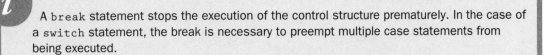

A break statement stops the execution of the control structure prematurely. In the case of a switch statement, the break is necessary to preempt multiple case statements from being executed.

Be careful, however; if a `break` is erroneously left out of the entry `case`, the action for that `case` will execute and continue until a `break` is encountered. Although the `break` statement is not specifically part of the `switch` statement, many programmers believe it is poor programming to use a `break` anywhere outside the context of a `switch` statement.

The optional `default` statement is only executed if the value of the variable doesn't match any of the previous cases. Think of `default` as a type of catchall or "case else." Also, notice that since `default` in Example 7.4.2 is the last case, a `break` statement isn't required because the end of the `switch` statement will be encountered after all of the statements associated with `default` are executed.

> ⚠ **Remember:** Although you can technically use the default case in any position in the list of cases, it should always appear as the last one in the `switch` statement. Likewise, the cases should be logically ordered to aid readability.

In Example 7.4.2, the `switch` statement evaluates the contents of the variable named `menu_item`. If the value of `menu_item` is 1, the `cout` associated with `case 1` will execute. If the value of `menu_item` is 2, the `cout` associated with `case 2` will execute, and so on. If the value doesn't match any of the cases, the `cout` associated with the `default` case will execute.

Example 7.4.2 The `switch` statement

```
int menu_item = 0;

...

switch ( menu_item )
{
    case 1:
        cout << "You have chosen option 1." << endl;
        break;
    case 2:
        cout << "You have chosen option 2." << endl;
        break;
    case 3:
        cout << "You have chosen option 3." << endl;
        break;
```

```
        default:
            cout << "Invalid menu option." << endl;
}
```

Even though leaving a break out of a case is a common mistake, it is sometimes done intentionally. This would allow a programmer to simulate a logical OR using a switch statement. Notice in Example 7.4.3 that the text "Stop!" and "Proceed when light is green." will be displayed if the value in the variable light_color is either 1 or 2.

Example 7.4.3 The switch statement using constants

```
const short GREEN = 0;
const short YELLOW = 1;
const short RED = 2;

short light_color = GREEN;

switch ( light_color )
{
    case GREEN:
        cout << "Go!" << endl;
        break;
    case YELLOW: // Let fall through
    case RED:
        cout << "Stop!";
        cout << "Proceed when light is green." << endl;
        break;
    default:
        cout << "Stop!";
        cout << "Power is out!" << endl;
}
```

Also note that a single character can be used for case values. When using a single character, the case values are surrounded with single quotation marks to designate a character literal. This is demonstrated in Example 7.4.4.

Example 7.4.4 The `switch` **statement using characters**

```
char letter_grade;

cout << "Enter letter grade: ";
cin  >> letter_grade;

switch ( letter_grade )
{
    case 'A':
        cout << "Excellent!" << endl;
        break;
    case 'B':
        cout << "Above average." << endl;
        break;
    case 'C':
        cout << "Average." << endl;
        break;
    case 'D':
        cout << "Below average." << endl;
        break;
    case 'F':
        cout << "Failed!" << endl;
        break;
    default:
        cout << "Invalid letter grade." << endl;
}
```

Remember: It is only possible to use a `switch` statement with integers or single characters.

Although there are many uses for the `switch` statement, one of the most common is in the creation of menu-driven programs. A sample menu for a student grade application is shown in Example 7.4.5.

Example 7.4.5 Sample main menu

Student Grade Program

  - Main Menu -

  1. Enter name

  2. Enter test scores

  3. Display test scores

  9. Exit

Please enter your choice from the list above:

STYLE NOTE Because of the inclusion of the `break` statement in the `switch`, it is unnecessary to surround multiple statements inside a specific `case` with curly braces.

Remember: You must include the entire body of the `switch` statement within braces.

Section 7.4 Exercises

Use the following code fragment for the exercises that follow:

```
short guess;

cout << "Enter a number between 0 and 5";
cin >> guess;

switch ( guess )
{
    case 0:
        cout << "Zero" << endl;
        break;
```

```
case 1:
    cout << "One" << endl;
case 2:
    cout << "Two" << endl;
case 3:
    cout << "Three" << endl;
case 4:
    cout << "Four" << endl;
    break;
default:
    cout << "Invalid guess entered." << endl;
}
```

What is the output generated by the program when the following inputs are provided? Try it first and then prove your results by actually running the code fragment.

1. 0

2. −1

3. 4

4. 2

5. 1

Section 7.4 Learn by Doing Exercises

1. Write the program that generates the menu shown in Example 7.4.5. In addition, repeat back to the user which option was selected from the menu using a `switch` statement.

2. Claude owns a gas station and wants you to write a program to determine the type of fuel, depending on the octane level. Assume the following values: 87—Regular Unleaded; 89—Unleaded Plus; and 92—Premium. If the octane entered is any other value, the fuel type to be displayed is Diesel.

7.5 Conditional Operator

When we discussed mathematical operators in Chapter 6, we noted the differences between unary and binary operators. The *conditional operator* is considered a *ternary* operator, meaning that it has three operands. A few other languages such as Java and C#, whose roots are in C++, also have a ternary operator. The conditional operator is sometimes called an "inline if", and the basic syntax is shown here.

<condition> ? <true expression> : <false expression>

In the preceding syntax, one of the expressions is returned based on the evaluation of the condition. In Example 7.5.1, we are finding the larger of two numbers and storing the largest value in a variable called `larger`.

Example 7.5.1 Conditional operator

```
int a = 5, b = 0;

int larger = a > b ? a : b;

cout << larger << endl;

// Output
5
```

To help clarify what is happening with the conditional operator in Example 7.5.1, Example 7.5.2 accomplishes the same thing using an `if` statement.

Example 7.5.2 Equivalent `if` statement

```
int a = 5, b = 0;
int larger;

if ( a > b )
    larger = a;
else
    larger = b;
```

Another use of the conditional operator is shown in Example 7.5.3. We use this ternary operator to ensure that each portion of the printed-out time consists of two digits. Inspect the example closely. We hope you will enjoy the added challenge.

Example 7.5.3 More challenging conditional operator

```
short hour = 9, minute = 10, second = 5;

cout << (hour < 10 ? "0" : "")   << hour   << ":"
     << (minute < 10 ? "0" : "") << minute << ":"
     << (second < 10 ? "0" : "") << second << endl;

// Output
09:10:05
```

Did you notice the empty quotation marks in Example 7.5.3? These tell cout to print nothing. In other words, if the condition is false (i.e., the hour is 10 or greater), print nothing.

Section 7.5 Exercises

1. What is wrong with the following code fragment?

```
int a = 0;

(a == 0) : cout << "Zero" ? cout << "Non-Zero";
```

2. Use the following code fragment for the exercises that follow:

```
int age = 75;


cout << ((age < 13) ? "Pre-Teen" :
         (age < 20  ? "Teen" :
         (age > 72  ? "Senior" : "Adult"))) << endl;
```

What is the output when age equals the following values?

a. 11

b. 18

c. 75

d. 30

7.6 Problem Solving Applied

Problem statement: You recently got a part-time job working for one of your teachers on campus. She has asked for your help in writing a program that can be used to determine the grade assigned to an individual student based on the results of three exam scores. You will need to ask the user for the student's ID—a five-digit number created by the school—and the scores for each of the three exams. Once you have all the necessary input, please calculate the individual student's overall average and letter grade. The cutoffs for the letter grades are as follows:

```
A >= 92.0    B >= 84.0    C >= 75.0    D >= 65.0    F < 65.0
```

Requirement Specification:

Input(s):

Input Type	Data	Source
Integer	student_id	Keyboard
Decimal	exam_1	Keyboard
Decimal	exam_2	Keyboard
Decimal	exam_3	Keyboard

Output(s):

Output Type	Data	Destination
Integer	student_id	Screen
Decimal	exam_1	Screen
Decimal	exam_2	Screen
Decimal	exam_3	Screen
Decimal	overall_average	Screen
Character	letter_grade	Screen

Constants:

Type	Data	Value
Decimal	A_GRADE	92.0
Decimal	B_GRADE	84.0
Decimal	C_GRADE	75.0
Decimal	D_GRADE	65.0

Design:

| **Original Pseudocode** | **C++ Source Code** |

```
// #include
...
const float A_GRADE = 92.0F;
const float B_GRADE = 84.0F;
const float C_GRADE = 75.0F;
const float D_GRADE = 65.0F;

int main()
{
    double exam_1, exam_2, exam_3,
           overall_average;
    char letter_grade;

    // Input
     ...
    // Processing
    overall_average = (exam_1 + exam_2
                       + exam_3) / 3;

    if ( overall_average >= A_GRADE )
        letter_grade = 'A';
    else if ( overall_average >= B_GRADE )
        letter_grade = 'B';
    else if ( overall_average >= C_GRADE )
        letter_grade = 'C';
    else if ( overall_average >= D_GRADE )
        letter_grade = 'D';
    else
        letter_grade = 'F';

    // Output
     ...
    return 0;
}
```

NEW CONCEPTS FROM THIS CHAPTER

Calculate overall_average = (exam_1 +
     exam_2 + exam_3) / 3

If overall_average >= 92
  letter_grade = 'A'
else if overall_average >= 84
  letter_grade = 'B'
else if overall_average >= 75
  letter_grade = 'C'
else if overall_average >= 65
  letter_grade = 'D'
else
  letter_grade = 'F'

7.7 C—The Differences

The only difference between C and C++ in this chapter is that C doesn't have a Boolean data type. This also means that there isn't a predefined **true** or **false** as part of the C language. Because of the lack of the Boolean data type, all relational operators return either a zero for false or a nonzero value—usually one—for true. C programmers often create their own Boolean data type, as shown in Example 7.7.1.

Example 7.7.1 Making your own Boolean data type

```c
#define BOOL int
#define TRUE 1
#define FALSE 0

int main( void )
{
    BOOL done = FALSE;

    return 0;
}
```

Although the C99 version of the ANSI standard includes a Boolean data type, at this time it is not supported by Visual Studio.

7.8 SUMMARY

This chapter introduced the concept of control statements. A control structure is a statement that controls, or alters, the flow of the program. You will see many other ways of controlling the flow of a program in the following chapters. However, most of these statements rely on the basic constructs just discussed.

We have explored three different control structures: the `if` statement, the `switch` statement, and the ternary conditional operator. Each statement offers some specific benefits over the others. At times, choosing the right statement will be obvious. At other times, you will need to give it some careful thought. Use the correct tool for the job—that is, choose the best option for your situation. For example, the `switch` statement tends to lend itself well to use within menu-related code sections, while the `if` is a much more flexible option.

The bottom line is to always remember to keep your code easy to read and modify. To aid in the readability of your program, avoid complex compound expressions in your program and use a consistent indentation style.

7.9 Debugging Exercise

Download the following file from this book's website and run the program following the instructions noted in the code.

```
/*****************************************************************************
 * File: Chap_7_Debugging.cpp
 *
 * General Instructions: Complete each step before proceeding to the
 * next.
 *
 * Debugging Exercise 1
 *
 * 1) Insert a breakpoint on the lines indicated in the code.
 * 2) Run to Breakpoint 1.
 * 3) When prompted, enter your age.
 * 4) When the execution stops, add a watch on age and verify that
 *    the value in age is what you typed in.
 * 5) Step over the if statement.
 * 6) Why did the value in age change?
 * 7) Fix the problem and repeat Steps 2 - 5 to verify that the
 *    problem was corrected.
 * 8) Stop debugging.
 *
 * Debugging Exercise 2
 *
 * 1) Run to Breakpoint 1.
 * 2) When prompted, enter the value 25 for your age.
 * 3) Step over the if statement. Execution of the program should
 *    continue on the else if statement.
 * 4) Verify that 25 is still stored in age.
 * 5) Step over the else if.
 * 6) Why is the program going to print "Teenager" for an age of 25?
 * 7) Fix the problem and repeat Steps 1 - 5 to verify that the
 *    problem was corrected.
 * 8) Stop debugging.
 * 9) Remove Breakpoint 1.
 *
 * Debugging Exercise 3
 *
 * 1) Run the program without debugging.
 * 2) When prompted, enter the value of 10 for your age.
 * 3) Why does the program print both "Child" and "Adult"?
```

```
* 4) Re-run the program this time with debugging and run to
*     Breakpoint 2.
* 5) Why is the action with the else executing?
* 6) Fix the problem and re-run to verify that the problem was corrected.
********************************************************************/

#include <iostream>
using std::cout;
using std::endl;
using std::cin;

int main()
{
        int age = 0;

        cout << "Enter your age: ";
        cin  >> age;

        // Breakpoint 1
        // Put a breakpoint on the following line
        if ( age = 1 )
            cout << "First Birthday" << endl;
        else if ( age >= 12 || age <= 19 )
            cout << "Teenager" << endl;
        else if ( age < 12 )
            cout << "Child" << endl;
        else if ( age > 62 )
            cout << "Senior" << endl;
        // Breakpoint 2
        // Put a breakpoint on the following line
        else;
            cout << "Adult" << endl;

        return 0;
}
```

7.10 Programming Exercises

The following programming exercises are to be developed using all phases of the development method. Be sure to make use of good programming practices and style, such as constants, white-space, indentation, naming conventions, and commenting. Make sure all input prompts are clear and descriptive and that your output is well formatted and looks professional.

1. Write a program that accepts two integers that represent the numerator and denominator of a fraction. Display the fraction in an acceptable form in regard to negative signs. Also, if the numerator is larger than the denominator, display the number as a mixed fraction.

2. Write a program that accepts both the interest rate and the amount of a loan. Check to make sure the interest rate of the loan is between 1% and 18% and that the amount of the loan is between $100 and $1000. If the data fails either of these conditions, display an appropriate error message and end the program. Determine the cost of the loan fees. If the amount of the loan is between $100 and $500, there is a fee of $20. If the loan is more than $500, the fee is $25. Calculate the amount of interest paid on the loan, and display the requested amount of the loan, the interest rate, and the sum of the interest and fees.

3. Given a quadratic equation in the form of $ax^2 + bx + c = 0$, solve for the roots of the equation using the following formula:

$$\frac{-b \pm \sqrt{b^2 - 4ac}}{2a}$$

Be sure to verify that it is a valid quadratic equation by checking a to make sure it is not zero. If it is zero, display an appropriate error message. Also, if the discriminant—the expression in the square root—is less than zero, display an error message stating that the roots will be complex, imaginary numbers. If the discriminant is zero, the roots will be the same, so display the root and the fact that the roots are identical. **Hint:** You will need to use the square root math function to solve this problem.

Extra Challenge: Instead of just displaying an error message if the roots are complex, display the complex roots in the correct format for complex numbers.

4. Write a program that converts 24-hour military time to standard time. Accept the hours, minutes, and seconds from the user, and verify that the inputs are correct. If any of the inputs are invalid, display an error message and end the program. Otherwise, display the output so that each portion of the time is displayed with two digits and the appropriate AM or PM. Use the conditional operator to both display the time as well as determine whether to use AM or PM.

5. Display a menu to the user that has the following options:

— Main Menu —

1. Calculate Area

2. Calculate Volume

Write a `switch` statement that handles the user's choice. For each of the main menu options, display a submenu that has the following options.

— Area Menu —   — Volume Menu —

a. Rectangle   a. Cylinder

b. Circle   b. Sphere

c. Right Triangle

Write nested `switch` statements to handle each of the submenus. For all of the `switch` statements, use the default case to handle any incorrect menu options. If you are unsure of the correct formulas, research them on the Internet or in your math books. Display the results of each of the calculations based on the appropriate user input.

7.11 Team Programming Exercise

An old buddy of yours, Marcus, has three children now. He wants to create a program that helps his kids learn some basic number manipulations. Although he used to be a pretty awesome programmer back in the day, he has been in management so long that his skills are more than a little rusty. He started the program but got frustrated and asked you to help him out. Here is what he has so far:

```cpp
#include <iostream>
using std::cin;
using std::cout;

int main( )
{
    int menu_choice;
    int number;

    cout << "Enter number: ";
    cin >> number;

    cout << "1) Is the number odd or even?/n"
         << "2) Is the number positive or negative?/n";
         << "3) What is the square root of the number?/n/n;

    cout << "Enter a menu choice: ";
    cin >> menu_choice;

    if ( menu_choice = 1 )
        // Process
        // Display Odd, even, or zero
    if ( menu_choice == 2 )
        // Process
        // Display positive, negative, or zero
    if ( menu_choice == 3 );
        // Process
        // Display square root

    return 0;
}
```

As you can see, he didn't get very far before he gave up. To help him out, convert Marcus's `if` statements to a more efficient `switch` statement. Also, complete the necessary number manipulations. Remember, even though you are jumping into the middle of a program that is already written (well, almost), don't forget the development process. Treat each menu item as a separate solution, and perform all phases of the development process before moving on to the next menu item. By the way, after looking at his code, Marcus's supervisor informed him that he will be getting a promotion—to keep him away from programming even more.

7.12 Answers to Chapter Exercises

Section 7.1

1. The symbols in the operator are reversed.

   Corrected: `int_exp1 >= int_exp2`

2. Should have a double = sign.

   Corrected: `int_exp1 == int_exp2`

3. The symbols in the operator are reversed.

   Corrected: `int_exp1 != int_exp2`

4. You can't compare a string literal using relational operators. To designate a character literal, you must use single quotation marks.

   Corrected: `char_exp == 'A'`

5. Everything is correct. The integer will be compared to the ASCII value of the character.

6. Relational operators are binary operators and therefore require an operand on each side of the operator.

   Corrected: `int_exp1 < 2 && int_exp1 > -10`

Section 7.2

1. **Error type:** logical

   Fix: Remove the semicolon after the condition of the `if` statement.

2. **Error type:** logical

   Fix: There is a single = in the condition where there should be two. (A single = is used for assignments, while the == is required when checking for equality.)

3. **Error type:** logical

   Fix: Should be an `&&` instead of an `||`.

4. **Error type:** logical

   Fix: If you want both statements to execute if the condition is true, enclose the statements in curly braces.

5. **Error type:** syntactical

   Fix: Put a space between the `else` and the `if`.

6. **Error type:** syntactical

   Fix: There is never a condition associated with the `else` statement.

7. **Error type:** none

   Fix: None needed, indentation is for the programmer, not the compiler.

Section 7.4

1. Zero

2. Invalid guess entered.

3. Four

4. Two

   Three

   Four

5. One

   Two

   Three

   Four

Section 7.5

1. The `:` and the `?` are reversed. Also, it would be better to embed the conditional operator in the `cout` rather than the `cout` in the conditional operator. The correct syntax follows.

   ```
   cout << (a == 0 ? "Zero" : "Non-Zero");
   ```

2. a. Pre-Teen

   b. Teen

   c. Senior

   d. Adult

Repetition Statements

Chapter Objectives

By the end of the chapter, readers will be able to:

- Recognize the value of using repetition control statements.
- Understand the syntax for the three different types of loops.
- Implement the `while` loop, `do-while` loop, and `for` loop structures.
- Understand the flow of a nested loop.
- Understand how to set conditional breakpoints within loops.
- Determine the correct situational usage for each type of loop.

Introduction

The previous chapter discussed conditional statements and how they allow a programmer to conditionally execute one or more statements. In this chapter we extend these concepts to show how to conditionally repeat one or more statements or actions. This concept of repetition, or looping, is an extremely important and powerful programming component in that it allows the reuse or repetition of existing sections of code. We will examine three basic looping constructs: `while`, `do-while`, and `for`. The use of these constructs allows for the development of more complex and interesting algorithms.

The process of looping or repetition is also referred to as **iteration**.

Like many of the concepts covered so far, information provided in this chapter will also directly apply to numerous other programming languages, including C, C#, Java, and Visual Basic. The only real difference is the specific syntax for each language.

Please pay careful attention to the material presented in this chapter because loops are the most error-prone programming constructs. Many errors are caused by malformed loops, including infinite loops, empty bodies, and off-by-one errors.

8.1 General Repetition Concepts

Repetition control structures, or loops, allow the programmer to conditionally repeat the execution of specific statements. There are two general types of loops: pre-test and post-test. A *pre-test loop* checks the condition prior to executing the statements associated with the loop's body or action. A *post-test loop* checks the condition after executing the body of the loop the first time. Therefore, the body of a post-test loop will execute a minimum of one time, whereas the body of a pre-test loop may never be executed. As you will soon find, the distinction between pre- and post-test loops is very important.

The statements associated with a loop are called the **body** of the loop.

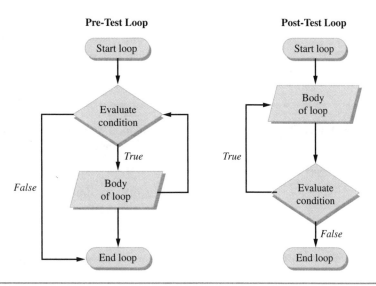

Figure 8.1.1 Pre-test loop versus post-test loop

Figure 8.1.1 uses flowcharts to illustrate the differences between pre- and post-test loops.

These looping structures must have each of the following components or aspects:

1. A variable with an initial value that controls whether the body of the loop is executed; this variable is often referred to as the *control variable*

2. A conditional expression involving the control variable

3. A statement within the body where the control variable is modified or altered each time the body of the loop is executed

One undesirable situation a lot of beginning programmers encounter is an *infinite loop*. While this is often a mistake on the programmer's part, the infinite loop may indeed be a valuable, although debatable, tool.

i

An **infinite loop** is a loop that continuously executes. When this happens, the program or loop has to be terminated by the user or programmer.

The most common cause of an infinite loop is the programmer's failure to manipulate the control variable in the body of the loop. A control variable usually determines when the loop stops and therefore must appear in the condition of the loop. The key thing to remember here is that the control of the loop is determined by the contents of a variable that must change during the execution of the program.

> **Remember:** If you discover an infinite loop while running your program, pressing Ctrl+C will terminate the execution of the program from within Microsoft Visual Studio.

So what kind of statements can appear in the body of a loop? Almost any— yes, even another loop. This concept of a *nested loop* is extremely powerful, and we will cover it in this chapter.

> *i*   A loop embedded in another loop is called a **nested loop**.

Once any loop has finished executing, the flow or control of the program is transferred to the statement following the loop.

8.2 The `while` Loop

The first repetition statement examined is the `while`, which is a pre-test loop that has the following syntax:

```
while ( <condition> )
      <action>
```

The action or body of the loop will execute as long as the condition continues to be true. Fortunately, the condition and the action block in this syntax are exactly the same as those you saw in the last chapter for the discussion on conditional statements. Likewise, if you need to execute more than one statement, enclose them within curly braces. Example 8.2.1 demonstrates how to use a `while` loop.

> **Remember:** Sometimes students will encounter a while loop written as `while ( 1 )` { ... }. Because the numeric literal 1 is treated as a true condition and will never change, this is an infinite loop and would require an additional statement within the body of the loop to terminate it. Although there are reasons to use this type of loop, it should only be used by experienced programmers and then only with due consideration.

Example 8.2.1 The while loop

```cpp
char again = '\0';
int operand1 = 0, operand2 = 0;

cout << "\nDo you wish to multiply two numbers (y/n)? ";
cin  >> again; // Priming read

while ( again == 'y' || again == 'Y' ) // Notice no semicolon
{ // Start of the loop body (action)
    cout << "Enter first number: ";
    cin  >> operand1;

    cout << "Enter second number: ";
    cin  >> operand2;

    cout << "Result: " << operand1
         << " * " << operand2
         << " = " << operand1 * operand2 << endl;

    cout << "\nDo you wish to multiply two more numbers (y/n)? ";
    cin  >> again; // Don't forget to change the control variable
} // End of the loop body (action)
cout << "The End" << endl;
```

In Example 8.2.1, we prompt the user to determine if he or she wants to multiply two numbers. If a 'y' or a 'Y' is entered, the user will be prompted for two numbers, which will be multiplied and the results displayed. The user will then be asked if he or she wants to multiply two more numbers. If another 'y' or 'Y' is entered, the user will be prompted again for two different numbers. If an 'n' or 'N' is entered, or anything else for that matter, the loop terminates, and control flows to the statement located after the action—in this case, the last cout statement. If an 'n' or 'N' had been entered at the initial prompt, the user would not have been asked for the two numbers because the body of the loop would have never executed, since a while loop is a pre-test loop.

An additional aspect of Example 8.2.1 is the prompt prior to encountering the loop. This is typically called a *priming read*, and it ensures that the control variable has a user-provided value before evaluating the condition. With priming reads, there must be a corresponding prompt as the last statement in the body of the loop.

If we neglected to include a priming read, the loop would not have executed because the control variable was initialized to the null character and would not evaluate to true when the condition was checked. If the read at the end of the body was left out, we would have an infinite loop because the control variable would not be changed within the body of the loop.

Section 8.2 Exercises

For each of the following code fragments, indicate if there are any errors. If there is an error, identify what type of error it is (syntactical, logical, runtime) and how you would fix it. If the code fragment would compile and run, what would be the output? If you are unsure or would like to see the proof, type it into your compiler and run it.

1.
```
int count = 0;
while ( count < 5 );
{
    cout << count++ << endl;
}
```

2.
```
int count = 0;
while ( count < 5 )
{
    cout << count + 1 << " ";
}
```

3.
```
int count = 0;
while ( count < 5 )
{
    cout << count-- << " ";
}
```

4.
```
int count = 0;
While ( count < 5 )
{
    cout << count++ << endl;
}
```

5.
```
int count = 0;
while ( count > 5 )
{
    cout << count-- << endl;
}
cout << "Hello World" << endl;
```

Section 8.2 Learn by Doing Exercise

1. Write a program that prompts the user to enter an integer between 1 and 50. The program should then display all of the even integers starting with the number and working back to 0.

8.3 The do-while Loop

The next looping structure is the do-while. This type of loop is an example of a post-test loop, meaning that the body of the loop always executes at least once. The general syntax of the do-while loop is as follows:

```
do
        <action>
while ( <condition> );
```

As always, if the action requires more than one statement, you must enclose the statements in curly braces. Example 8.3.1 demonstrates a common use of a do-while loop: a menu-driven program.

Example 8.3.1 The do-while loop

```
char menu_choice;
float number;

cout << "Please enter a number: ";
cin  >> number;

do
{
    cout << "\n1) Square the Number\n"
         << "2) Cube the Number\n"
         << "3) Exit\n\n"
         << "Please enter menu choice: " << endl;
    cin  >> menu_choice;

    switch ( menu_choice )
    {
        case '1':
            cout << number << " Squared = "
                 << number * number << endl;
            break;
```

```
        case '2':
            cout << number << " Cubed = "
                << number * number * number << endl;
            break;
        case '3':
            cout << "Goodbye" << endl;
            break;
        default:
            cout << "Invalid menu option" << endl;
    }
} while ( menu_choice != '3' ); // Notice the semicolon
```

In Example 8.3.1, the menu is displayed at least once. As demonstrated in the example, a `do-while` is the preferred loop for menu-driven programs because these types of programs should always exit from one of the menu options. Therefore, the menu should always be displayed, allowing the user to decide when to quit. Notice that the priming read is not necessary because it is a post-test loop.

Section 8.3 Exercises

For each of the following code fragments, indicate if there are any errors. If there is an error, identify what type of error it is (syntactical, logical, runtime) and how you would fix it. If the code fragment would compile and run, what would be the output? If you are unsure or would like to see the proof, type it into your compiler and run it.

1. ```
   int count = 0;
   do ( count < 5 )
   {
        cout << count++ << endl;
   } while;
   ```

2. ```
   int count = 0;
   do
   {
        cout << count++ << endl;
   } while( count < 5 )
   ```

3. ```
   int count = 0;
   do
   {
        cout << count++ << endl;
   } while( count > 5 );
   ```
   ```

4. ```
int count = 0;
do
     cout << count << endl;
while (count <= 5)
```

5. ```
int count = 0;
do
{
     cout << ' ' << count++;
} while ( 1 );
```

Section 8.3 Learn by Doing Exercise

1. Modify the program from Section 8.2 Learn by Doing Exercise so that it uses a `do-while` to test for a valid range. If the user enters an invalid value, an error message should be displayed and the user re-prompted for the value.

8.4 The `for` Loop

The `for` loop is the final looping structure we will discuss. A `for` loop is generally used when the specific number of iterations are known. This is not a rule but something of a style issue. Since both `while` loops and `for` loops are pre-test loops, they can be used interchangeably. However, most programmers only use the `for` loop when the loop will execute a known number of times. The syntax of the `for` loop is as follows:

```
for ( <init-expr> ; <condition> ; <post-loop-expr> )
     <action>
```

Although there are four different sections to the `for` loop, the only components required are the two semicolons and the body or action.

> **Remember:** One of the more common errors we have seen students make is to put a semicolon after the closing parenthesis. Although legal, the semicolon terminates the loop, just like it would in any other statement. In effect, it takes the place of the body of the loop. This is often a difficult error to find.

When the execution of the program encounters the `for` loop, the `<init-expr>` section is executed. This is the expression that is generally used to initialize, and sometimes even declare, the control variable for the loop. The

`<init-expr>` section is executed only once for the duration of the loop. Multiple expressions can be contained in this section by separating the expressions with a comma.

The C++ standard states that the scope of any variable declared in this section is visible only within the body of the loop. Although your compiler may or may not follow this standard, you should always assume the variable will go out of scope when the loop terminates.

> ⚠️ **Remember:** The scope of a variable is what determines where within your code it can be referenced and used.

After the initialization section is executed, the condition is evaluated. Since the condition is evaluated before the body of the loop is performed, the `for` loop is an example of a pre-test loop. If the condition is true, the body of the loop is executed. If the condition is false, the body of the loop is never executed.

Once the body of the loop is finished executing, the `<post-loop-expr>` section is evaluated. This section is generally used to change the control variable. One of the most common operators found in this section is the increment operator. Again, if multiple expressions are desired, separate the expressions with a comma. Once this section has finished executing, the condition is checked again to determine if the loop is to continue.

Figure 8.4.1 uses a flowchart to illustrate the flow of the `for` loop shown in Example 8.4.1. Please make it a point to pay careful attention to the detail associated with the overall flow of each of the components.

Example 8.4.1 The `for` loop for Figure 8.4.1

```
for ( int i = 0; i < 5; i++ )
    cout << i << ' ';

// Output
0 1 2 3 4
```

In Example 8.4.1, we used the post-increment operator. The results would have been the same if we had used the pre-increment operator because the entire section is evaluated before moving on to the condition. It is up to the

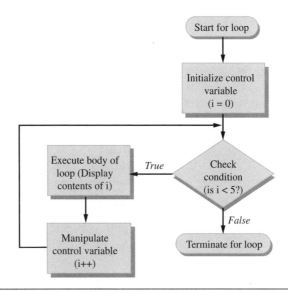

Figure 8.4.1 A for loop flowchart

programmer whether to use pre- or post-increment operators with primitive data types. Example 8.4.2 shows several for loops.

Example 8.4.2 The for loop

```
// Example 1
for ( int i = 0; i < 5; i++ ) // Notice no semicolon
    cout << i << endl;

// Example 2
// Notice the multiple expressions
for ( int i = 0, j = 5; i < 5; i++, j-- )
    cout << i << ' ' << j << endl;

// Example 3
int sum = 0, value;

for ( int i = 0; i < 5; i++ ) // Notice no semicolon
{
    cout << "Enter value " << i + 1 << ": ";
    cin >> value;

    sum += value;
}
```

```
cout << "The sum of the five values is: " << sum << endl;

// Example Output
// Ex. 1      // Ex. 2      // Ex. 3
0             0 5          Enter value 1: 4
1             1 4          Enter value 2: 7
2             2 3          Enter value 3: 3
3             3 2          Enter value 4: 12
4             4 1          Enter value 5: 99
                          The sum of the five values is: 125
```

Notice the use of both accumulators and counters in Example 8.4.2. The expression `i++` is representative of a counter, whereas the expression `sum += value` is an example of an accumulator. Remember to initialize the variables associated with each of these expressions to zero.

STYLE NOTE   In Example 8.4.1, notice that although the control variable, `i`, could be initialized to any value, it is initialized to zero. This may seem unnatural at first because most of us are used to starting counting at one. However, since future concepts will require the programmer to start counting at zero, it is good practice to initialize the control variables of loops to zero.

Notice also in Example 8.4.1 that the condition of the loop is `i < 5`. Although it would have worked just as well to have `i <= 4`, using the condition `i < 5` provides an extra visual clue to the programmer to show how many times—5—the loop will execute. The condition is also easier to comprehend because of the relational operators used. The `<` operator is simpler to understand and debug than the `<=` operator.

8.4.1 Nested `for` loops

Like other loops, `for` loops can be nested. This technique is commonly used in conjunction with other concepts discussed later in the text. To help visualize a nested `for` loop, we've provided you with the example flowchart shown in Figure 8.4.2. Please take a few minutes and carefully review this graphical representation illustrating a nested `for` loop. The code for this loop is shown as the first example in Example 8.4.3.

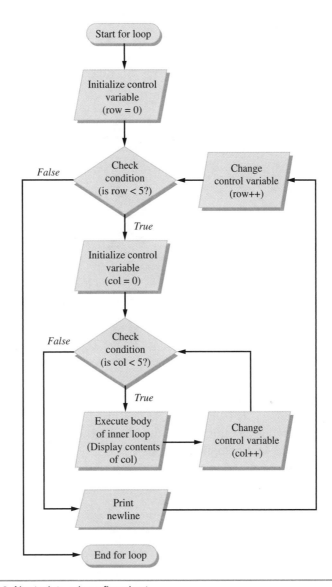

Figure 8.4.2 Nested for loop flowchart

Example 8.4.3 Nested for loops

```
// Example 1
for ( int row = 0; row < 5; row++ )
{
    for ( int col = 0; col < 5; col++ )
        cout << col << ' ';
```

```
        cout << endl;
}

// Example 2
for ( int row = 0; row < 5; row++ )
{
    for ( int col = row; col < 5; col++ )
        cout << col << ' ';

    cout << endl;
}

// Example Output
// Ex. 1      // Ex. 2
0 1 2 3 4    0 1 2 3 4
0 1 2 3 4    1 2 3 4
0 1 2 3 4    2 3 4
0 1 2 3 4    3 4
0 1 2 3 4    4
```

Section 8.4 Exercises

For each of the following code fragments, indicate if there are any errors. If there is an error, identify what type of error it is (syntactical, logical, runtime) and how you would fix it. If the code fragment would compile and run, what would be the output? If you are unsure or would like to see the proof, type it into your compiler and run it.

1. ```
for (int count = 0, count < 10, count++)
{
    cout << count << endl;
}
```

2. ```
for ( int count = 0; count < 10; ++count );
{
    cout << count << endl;
}
```

3. ```
int count = 0;
for (;count < 10;)
{
    cout << count << " ";
}
```

4. ```
for ( int count = 10; count < 15; count-- )
    cout << count << " ";
```

5.
```
int count = 0;
for ( ; ; )
    cout << count++ << " ";
```

Convert the following while loop to a `for` loop.

6.
```
int i = 0, j = 10;
while ( i <= 10 )
    cout << i++ << ' ' << j-- << endl;
```

What is the output from the following code fragment?

7.
```
for ( int count = 0; count < 5; count++ )
{
    for ( int  indx = 0; indx <= count; indx++ )
        cout << indx << ' ';

    cout << endl;
}
```

Section 8.4 Learn by Doing Exercises

1. Write a program that prompts the user for the number of assignments in a specific class. Then using a `for` loop, prompt for each score. Use an accumulator to store the sum of the assignments, and then calculate the average score for the assignments.

2. Write a program that displays an upside-down right triangle made of asterisks for a user-specified base length. The triangle shown here is created for the input of four.

```
* * * *

* * *

* *

*
```

8.5 Breakpoints and Loops

When we discussed debugging tools in Chapter 5, we covered breakpoints and showed how important they were to have available. We also said there were some added features in breakpoints that wouldn't be useful until later. Well, it's later!

As you start developing more complicated programs that make extensive use of loops, you will find it time consuming and annoying to step through the loop when you already know the program doesn't break until the 10,000th iteration. Breakpoints have the added functionality to break, or stop, execution, either dependent on a condition or after a line of code has been encountered a certain number of times.

```
1 ⊟ #include <iostream>
2 │ using std::cout;
3 │ using std::endl;
4 │ └
5 ⊟ int main( )
6 │ {
7 │     for (int i = 0; i < 1000000; i++)
8 │         cout << i << endl;
```

Delete Breakpoint
Disable Breakpoint   0;
Location...
Condition...
Hit Count...
Filter...
When Hit...

Figure 8.5.1 Breakpoint pop-up

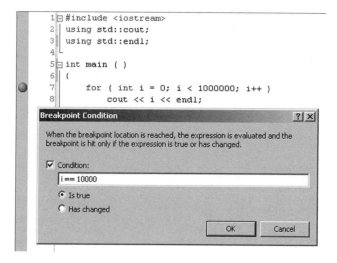

```
1 ⊟ #include <iostream>
2 │ using std::cout;
3 │ using std::endl;
4 │ └
5 ⊟ int main ( )
6 │ {
7 │     for ( int i = 0; i < 1000000; i++ )
8 │         cout << i << endl;
```

Breakpoint Condition   ? X

When the breakpoint location is reached, the expression is evaluated and the
breakpoint is hit only if the expression is true or has changed.

☑ Condition:

    i == 10000

○ Is true
○ Has changed

                                OK   Cancel

Figure 8.5.2 Breakpoint Condition

In Visual Studio, it is very easy to set these conditions on breakpoints. Place
a breakpoint anywhere in the body of a loop and then right-click on the red dot
that designates a breakpoint. A pop-up menu is displayed that provides a number of options, as shown in Figure 8.5.1.

The two options that are the most useful are Condition and Hit Count. After
choosing the Condition option, a new window will appear. This will allow you
to enter a condition that will cause the execution of the program to stop based
on the evaluation of that condition. This window is shown in Figure 8.5.2.

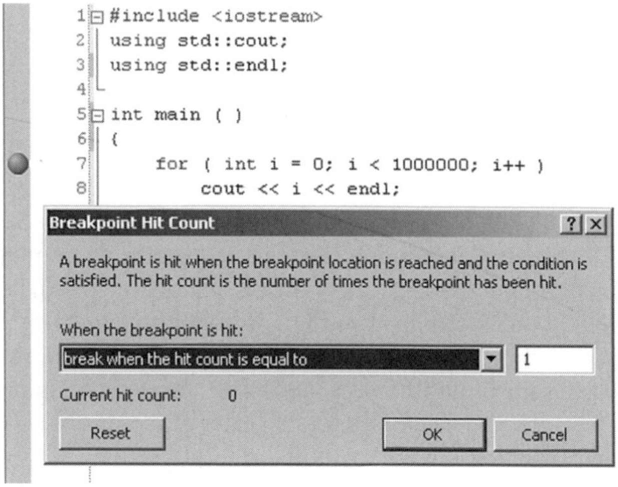

```
1 ☐ #include <iostream>
2   using std::cout;
3   using std::endl;
4 └
5 ☐ int main ( )
6   {
7       for ( int i = 0; i < 1000000; i++ )
8           cout << i << endl;
```

Breakpoint Hit Count   ? ✕

A breakpoint is hit when the breakpoint location is reached and the condition is
satisfied. The hit count is the number of times the breakpoint has been hit.

When the breakpoint is hit:

break when the hit count is equal to   ▼   1

Current hit count: 0

Reset   OK   Cancel

Figure 8.5.3 Breakpoint Hit Count

Once the condition is set, the execution of the program will stop as soon as the variable i reaches 10,000.

The Hit Count option performs much in the same way as the Condition option. This window is shown in Figure 8.5.3.

Once the breakpoint options have been selected, the red dot will change to include a white + inside the dot to show that the breakpoint has a condition attached.

Like other debugging tools, this will take some time to get familiar with. Please take this opportunity to experiment with these breakpoint options. Although there are other breakpoint options available, they won't be discussed in this text. Don't worry, however; there will be other debugging tools introduced throughout the book.

8.6 Problem Solving Applied

Updated problem statement: In the last chapter you got a part-time job working for one of your teachers on campus. She was happy with your work and would like you to expand the program. The problem now includes all the requested material from Chapter 7 plus two additional aspects:

1. The teacher would like the ability to use the program to do the calculations for the approximately 20 students in her class entering each student's information until she indicates she is finished.

2. After all of the students' information has been entered and printed, the program will need to calculate and print the total number of students in the class and the overall class average.

To save you a bit of time, we have provided you with the information from the previous chapter.

Previous information: The teacher you work for has asked for your help in writing a program that can be used to determine the grade assigned to an individual student based on the results of his or her three exam scores. You will need to ask the user for his or her student ID—a 5-digit number created by the school—and scores on each of the three exams. Once you have all the necessary input, please calculate the individual student's overall average and letter grade. The cutoffs for the letter grades are shown here:

```
A >= 92.0   B >= 84.0   C >= 75.0   D >= 65.0   F < 65.0
```

Requirement Specification:

Input(s):

Input Type	Data	Source
Integer	student_id	Keyboard
Decimal	exam_1	Keyboard
Decimal	exam_2	Keyboard
Decimal	exam_3	Keyboard

Output(s):

Output Type	Data	Destination
Integer	student_id	Screen
Decimal	exam_1	Screen
Decimal	exam_2	Screen
Decimal	exam_3	Screen
Decimal	overall_average	Screen
Character	letter_grade	Screen
Integer	number_of_students	Screen
Decimal	overall_class_average	Screen

Constants:

Type	Data	Value
Decimal	A_GRADE	92.0
Decimal	B_GRADE	84.0
Decimal	C_GRADE	75.0
Decimal	D_GRADE	65.0

Design:

Original Pseudocode

C++ Source Code

```cpp
// #include
...
const float A_GRADE = 92.0F;
const float B_GRADE = 84.0F;
const float C_GRADE = 75.0F;
const float D_GRADE = 65.0F;

int main()
{
    double exam_1, exam_2, exam_3,
        overall_average;
    char letter_grade;

    // variables related to counting number of
    // students and accumulating overall class
    // scores and calculating overall class avg
    int number_of_students = 0;
    float total_of_students_averages = 0;
    float overall_class_average;
    char again = 'Y';
```

NEW CONCEPTS FROM THIS CHAPTER

```cpp
    // Input
    ...
```

Ask user if they want to enter students
Read users response (again)

```cpp
    cout << "\nEnter student data (y/n)? ";
    cin  >> again;
```

While (again is equal to 'Y')
Begin loop
    Prompt "Enter in student id"

    ...

```cpp
    // Processing
    while ( again == 'y'||again == 'Y' )
    {
        cout << "Enter in student id: ";

        ...
```

    Calculate overall_average =
    (exam_1 + exam_2 + exam_3) / 3

```cpp
        overall_average = (exam_1 + exam_2 +
                            exam_3) / 3;
```

    Add overall_average to
    total_of_students_averages
    accumulator

```cpp
        total_of_students_averages +=
                            overall_average;
```

    Add 1 to the number_of_students
    counter
    ...

```cpp
        ++number_of_students;

        cout << "Student ID: " << student_id;
        cout << "Exam 1: " << exam_1;

        ...
```

    Ask user if they want to enter
      more students
    Read users response (again)
End loop
Calculate overall_class_average =
  total_of_students_averages /
  number_of_students

...

```cpp
        cout << "\nDo another: (y/n)? ";

        cin  >> again;
    }
    overall_class_average =
                total_of_students_averages /
                number_of_students;
    ...
```

// Output final values/averages

```cpp
    return 0;
}
```

8.7 C—The Differences

The only difference between C and C++ related to loops is that it used to be illegal to declare a variable in the initialization section of the `for` loop within C. This is because all variables in C were to be declared at the beginning of a block, right after an opening curly brace. The current version of ANSI C no longer has this limitation. Example 8.7.1 shows a legal C `for` loop.

Example 8.7.1 C/C++ for loops

```c
#include <stdio.h>
int main()
{
    //Legal in both C++ and C:
    int count;
    for ( count = 0; count < 5; count++ )
        printf( "%d\n", count );

    // Legal in C++ but not in C:
    // for ( int i = 0; i < 5; i++ )
    //     cout << i << endl;

    return 0;
}
```

8.8 SUMMARY

This chapter examined the three major types of C++ loops. It also showed how to combine conditional expressions with various looping structures to repeat a group of statements based on a specific condition.

The first loop discussed was the pre-test `while`. As noted, if the pre-test condition fails, the loop body will never be executed, and control will flow to the statement following the action. The second structure was the `do-while`, which is based on the post-test condition, meaning it is guaranteed to do the action once before the condition is even checked. The last structure presented was the `for` loop, along with the three major components required: `init-expr; condition; post-loop-expr`.

You were also provided with some general guidelines for deciding which loop to use for a given task. The `for` loop should be used when there are a specific, known number of iterations. The `do-while` is a good loop to use for menus because the menu will be displayed at least once. In this way, the user can choose to quit the program through a menu item. The `while` loop is used when the body of the loop may not be executed at all, depending on the condition.

The chapter also tried to make you aware of various errors made by beginning programming students (and experienced ones, too), such as including a semicolon after the parenthesis of the `for` statement, which signifies an empty action body.

You are now familiar with a number of extremely powerful programming constructs that you will use in a variety of future programming activities. Make sure you feel comfortable with the material presented in this chapter before moving on.

8.9 Debugging Exercise

Download the following file from this book's website and run the program following the instructions noted in the code.

```
/********************************************************************
* File: Chap_8_Debugging.cpp
*
* General Instructions: Complete each step before proceeding to the
* next.
*
* Debugging Exercise 1
*
* 1) Insert a breakpoint on the lines indicated in the code.
* 2) Run to Breakpoint 1.
* 3) Place a watch on i.
* 4) Execute the while statement by doing a "Step Into".
* 5) The execution continues to the cout statement as expected.
* 6) Step over the cout statement.
* 7) Why didn't the flow of the program return back to the while
*    statement?
* 8) Fix this problem by removing the ; after the while statement.
* 9) Stop debugging and repeat Steps 2 - 5 to verify that the correction
*    worked.
* 10) Stop debugging.
*
* Debugging Exercise 2
*
* 1) Run to Breakpoint 1.
* 2) Step into the while loop.
* 3) Why did the cout not execute?
* 4) Check the value of i, now check the condition; does the
*    condition evaluate to true?
* 5) Change the "< 0" to a "< 10".
* 6) Stop debugging and repeat Steps 1 - 4 to verify that the correction
*    worked.
* 7) Stop debugging.
*
* Debugging Exercise 3
*
* 1) Run the program without debugging.
```

```
 * 2) What is happening now is an infinite loop.
 * 3) End your program by holding down the Ctrl key and pressing C.
 * 4) Fix the problem by adding a "++" after the i in the cout
 *    statement.
 * 5) Run the program to Breakpoint 2 and verify that the output
 *    displayed on the screen is 0 - 9.
 *
 * Debugging Exercise 4
 *
 * 1) Run to Breakpoint 2.
 * 2) Add a watch to the variable count.
 * 3) Verify that the contents of count is garbage.
 * 4) Step into the loop.
 * 5) What is the value stored in count now?
 * 6) Where was 10 assigned to count?
 * 7) Fix the problem and re-run to verify.
 *********************************************************************/
#include <iostream>
using std::cout;
using std::endl;

int main()
{
      int i = 0;
      int count;

      // Breakpoint 1
      // Put a breakpoint on the following line
      while ( i < 0 );
            cout << i << endl;
      // Breakpoint 2
      // Put a breakpoint on the following line
      for ( count = 0; count < 10; count++ );
            cout << count << endl;

      return 0;
}
```

8.10 Programming Exercises

The following programming exercises are to be developed using all phases of the development method. Be sure to make use of good programming practices and style, such as constants, whitespace, indentation, naming conventions, and commenting. Make sure all input prompts are clear and descriptive and that your output is well formatted and looks professional.

1. Write a program to calculate the sum of $.01 a day, doubled for *n* number of days. For example, on the first day you would receive $.01; on the second day you would receive $.02, for a total of $.03. On the third day you would receive $.04, for a total of $.07. Get the input for the number of days from the user, but make sure it is between 1 and 30 days. Display the number of cents accumulated, along with the number of days entered by the user.

2. Write a program that calculates the factorial of a user-defined number. For example, 5! = 1 * 2 * 3 * 4 * 5 = 120. The "!" is the mathematical notation for factorial. Because factorials get very large very quickly, limit the input to a maximum of 25 and a minimum of 2.

3. Write a program to generate a Fibonacci sequence up to a user-specified ending number. For example, if the user entered 25, the Fibonacci sequence would be:

   1, 1, 2, 3, 5, 8, 13, 21

   Notice that after the initial two numbers, each new number is generated by adding the previous two numbers.

4. Write a program that takes input from the user that represents a numerator and a denominator of a fraction. Then reduce the fraction to its lowest terms and display it to the screen. If appropriate, display the fraction as a mixed number (3 1/2).

   To reduce a fraction to its lowest terms, divide both the numerator and the denominator by the greatest common denominator. The GCD can be calculated by using Euclid's algorithm. Euclid's algorithm states: Let *m* represent the numerator and *n* represent the denominator of a fraction. Divide *m* by *n*. Save the divisor in *m* and save the remainder in *n*. If *n* is 0, then stop: *m* contains the GCD. Otherwise, repeat the process.

   Be sure to display the fraction in a well-formed manner. If the denominator is a one, display the fraction as a whole number. If the denominator is a zero, display a message that the fraction is undefined. A fraction will never be displayed with a negative denominator.

5. Write a program that displays the ASCII chart. Display numeric values as well as characters so that there are four columns and as many rows as it takes. For an extra challenge, display the chart so that its outside borders are made up of double line ASCII characters, and separate each column with a single vertical ASCII character.

6. Write a program that draws a rectangle on the screen using ASCII characters. The program will prompt the user for the height and width, specified in characters, of the rectangle. Use the following ASCII values for the box characters: 218 upper left-hand corner, 217 lower right-hand corner, 196 top and bottom, 192 lower left-hand corner, 191 upper right-hand corner, and 179 left and right sides.

8.11 Team Programming Exercise

Marcus's children really liked what you did for them in Chapter 7's Team Programming Exercise. Marcus would like you to expand what you did to include the following functionality.

- The children got a little tired of having to rerun the program each time to try another menu item. Add a loop to the program that continues until an Exit menu option has been chosen.

- Marcus noticed that if his children accidentally entered a wrong number for the menu choice, they were a little confused when the program abruptly ended. Add functionality to the `switch` statement that checks the menu choice and displays an error message if an incorrect value is entered.

- Good news: Marcus got his promotion and so will be programming even less. He is, however, taking his kids to Disneyland with his raise. Unfortunately, he doesn't have enough cash to take you.

- Add a few additional menu options.

  - The first new menu option displays the number of digits in the number. **Hint:** Repeatedly divide the number by 10, keeping track of the number of times you divide.

  - Another new menu item is similar to the last except that Marcus wants you to find the digit at a specific position in the number. For example, if the number entered is 98765, Marcus wants you to display "8" if the user specifies the fourth digit.

  - Display an addition table for all numbers up to 12.

  - Display a multiplication table for all numbers up to 12.

Don't forget to perform all phases of the development process on each new additional piece, including pseudocode, for all the new functionality. Don't forget to verify your results. It would be very embarrassing if Marcus's 4-year old caught you on an error.

8.12 Answers to Chapter Exercises

Section 8.2

1. **Error:** Logic

   Fix/Explanation: Remove the semicolon after the `while`. This semicolon indicates that the loop contains an empty action; it has no body. Since the control variable is not manipulated in the loop, this loop becomes an infinite loop.

   Output: None

2. **Error:** Logic

   Fix/Explanation: Change the "count + 1" in the `cout` statement to a "count++". Although it might appear that the control variable is being changed in the body of the loop, it really isn't.

The statement "count + 1" does *not* change the actual contents or value of the variable count. Therefore, this is another infinite loop.

Output: 1 1 1 1 1 1 1 . . .

3. **Error:** Logic

   Fix/Explanation: Because the control variable is initialized to zero, the condition states that the loop will continue while the control variable is less than five, and since the control variable is decremented, this results in, for all practical purposes, an infinite loop. The reason it is not a full infinite loop is that as the variable is decremented, the number gets more and more negative. Once the variable is decremented far enough, the sign bit of the integer will get set to a zero. This makes the integer a positive number greater than five, which stops the loop. Even though this is technically not an infinite loop, it is considered an error.

   Output: $0 -1 -2 -3 -4 \ldots -2147483648$

4. **Error:** Syntax

   Fix/Explanation: The "W" in the `while` reserved word needs to be lowercase. Remember, all the keywords in C++ begin either with a lowercase letter or an underscore.

   Output: None; won't compile

5. **Error:** Logic

   Fix/Explanation: The loop will never execute because the condition is initially false. Change the condition or the initialization.

   Output: Hello World

Section 8.3

1. **Error:** Syntax

   Fix/Explanation: The conditional expression belongs with the `while` part of the `do-while` loop.

   Output: None; won't compile

2. **Error:** Syntax

   Fix/Explanation: Place a semicolon behind the condition associated with the `while`.

   Output: None; won't compile

3. **Error:** Logic

   Fix/Explanation: The body of the loop will only execute once even though the condition is initially false. Because the `do-while` is a post-test loop, the condition is not evaluated until the body of the loop is executed at least once.

   Output: 0

4. **Error:** Logic and Syntax

   Fix/Explanation: Logic error: Since the control variable is not manipulated in the loop, the loop becomes an infinite loop.

   Fix/Explanation: Syntax error: Place a semicolon behind the condition associated with the `while`.

   Output: None; won't compile

5. **Error:** Logic

   Fix/Explanation: Since there is no control variable in the conditional, the loop becomes an infinite loop. Avoid writing this type of conditional statement! There is no way out of the loop as shown. Always include a variable inside your conditional expression so that it can be altered during program execution.

   Output: 0 1 2 3 4 5 . . .

Section 8.4

1. **Error:** Syntax

   Fix/Explanation: The commas between each section of the `for` loop need to be replaced with semicolons.

   Output: None; won't compile

2. **Error:** Logic

   Fix/Explanation: The `for` loop doesn't need the semicolon at the end. Because the semicolon acts as the body or action of the loop, all the loop accomplishes is to increment the control variable. Therefore, after the condition becomes false, the next line—the `cout` statement—is executed. Notice that the value of the control variable is 10, proving exactly what you would (hopefully) have thought.

   Output: 10

3. **Error:** Logic

   Fix/Explanation: The statement is syntactically correct; however, the control variable is not changed, making this an infinite loop.

   Output: 0 0 0 0 0 . . .

4. **Error:** Logic

   Fix/Explanation: The control variable is initialized to 10. The condition states that the loop will continue as long as the control variable is less than 15. However, the control variable is decremented, which makes the value move even farther away from the terminating condition, resulting in—for all practical purposes—an infinite loop. The reason it is not a full infinite loop is that as the variable is decremented, the number gets more and more negative. Once the variable is decremented far enough, the sign bit of the integer will get set to a zero. This makes the integer a positive number greater than 15, which would finally terminate the loop.

Output: 10 9 8 7 6 . . . −2147483648

5. **Error:** Logic

   Fix/Explanation: Infinite loop. No condition section of the `for` loop. Note: to be clear and readable, avoid writing `for` loops without all three of the components we discussed.

   Output: 0 1 2 3 4 5 . . .

6.
```
for ( int i = 0, j = 10; i <= 10; i++, j--)
   cout << i << ' ' << j << endl;
```

7. 0

   0 1

   0 1 2

   0 1 2 3

   0 1 2 3 4

Functions

Chapter Objectives

By the end of the chapter, readers will be able to:

- Understand the concept of a function.
- Understand the advantages and disadvantages of functions.
- Develop programmer-defined functions.
- Pass parameters by value and reference.
- Return values from a function.
- Understand the issues regarding variable scope.
- Distinguish between formal and actual parameters.
- Call functions and pass arguments.
- Declare functions with default arguments.
- Use various character functions.
- Use and develop structure charts.

Introduction

In Chapter 6, we introduced some of the predefined mathematical functions available in C++. These functions became an important component in developing the more complicated program solutions required in the exercises. It was very convenient to just call the appropriate function with the proper information and get back the result without having to write the code for each of these mathematical functions.

This chapter focuses on developing the skills necessary to write your own functions—probably one of the most important aspects in programming. Very few programs are ever written without the extensive use of functions.

For many of you, the term *function* may have been introduced in the area of mathematics. For others, the idea of the programming concepts associated with functions may have been presented in terms of methods, subroutines, or even procedures. Regardless of what you call them, you will find functions powerful and extremely helpful in developing your programming skills.

9.1 What Are Functions?

Functions are a group of related statements that together perform a specific task or job. We have already used predefined functions, such as `pow`, `sqrt`, and `abs`. Because our programs required `main`, we have already written a function definition.

We also know some of the terminology associated with functions.

- **Function header:** The start of the function.

- **Function call:** The act of invoking the function.

- **Parameters:** Variables that provide information to a function.

- **Return:** A function sending back a value.

Another aspect of a function is that it allows us to treat its role in our programs as a *black box*. The concept of a black box implies that we can regard the function as a stand-alone unit. We supply, or pass in, values and it produces, or returns, a specific output to us. For example, a manufacturing plant takes in raw goods—sugar and food coloring—and creates jelly beans. We

Figure 9.1.1 Black box magic

really don't need to understand the process; we can just enjoy what it produces. Figure 9.1.1 illustrates the black box philosophy.

Although there is a lot more to the concept of functions, the previous discussion should help get us started.

9.1.1 Advantages and Disadvantages of Functions

There are many advantages to using subroutines or functions. The first advantage is that the modularization of functions aids in the process of stepwise refinement. In Chapter 2 we discovered that stepwise refinement is the process of breaking a program into smaller, more manageable, and detailed pieces, each of which can then be designed, implemented, and tested. As you can probably see, partitioning your program into functions facilitates this process.

A second advantage is that by breaking our code into individual components, the program becomes easier both to maintain and for others to understand. Along the same lines, functions enable us to focus our debugging energies in one specific area, resulting in a shorter error-correction time.

Another distinct advantage is that once we have written a function, if we need to use that code again, all we have to do is call it. This code reuse is extremely important. In fact, it is what you did each time you called any of the predefined mathematical functions. The code was already developed and tested by somebody else, and all you had to do was call the function.

In the computer industry—as in many other industries—working in teams is crucial to the success of almost any project. Having multiple programmers concurrently writing key functions and then integrating those functions into a working and cohesive project is essential. Although there are other forms of modularization, which we will discover later in the text, they all build off the concept of functions.

So are there any disadvantages to using functions? Yes. Every time a function is called, there is a slight performance cost involved. When a function is called, the flow of the program is transferred to that function. When the function has completed its task, control returns to where the function was originally called. How does the computer know where to go back to? How does the computer maintain the state of all of the variables when the function was called?

All of this information is saved prior to the flow of the program being transferred to the function and then restored when control is returned to the calling function.

Because of this overhead, it is important that you not write functions that are one or two lines long unless that function is going to be used repeatedly. If the function is short and is not going to be called again, the overhead would be detrimental to the performance of your program. While there is some cost associated with using functions, the expense is relatively minor when compared to the benefits they provide in saving the developer time in debugging, maintaining, and extending the code.

9.1.2 What about `main`?

Every program still needs to have `main`, but `main` will now take on a special role as the director. The `main` function will control the flow of the program but should do very little else. Remember, no matter how many functions are in your program, `main` will always be the entry point.

Your `main` function might have a conditional, a loop, and function calls, but that is about it. There should be a minimum of processing going on in `main`, which simply acts as a driver for the rest of your code. Because of its importance, we suggest you physically place `main` as the first function within your source code.

Section 9.1 Exercises

Please identify the best responses for each of the following questions:

1. Which of the following terms is not another name for functions?

   a. methods   b. subroutines   c. labels   d. procedures

2. When you execute a C++ program, what function is executed first?

   a. `Main`   b. `main`   c. `return`   d. `void`

3. Which of the following is an advantage of using functions?

   a. Facilitates code reuse.

   b. Often makes debugging your program easier.

   c. Aids in the process of stepwise refinement.

   d. All of the above are advantages.

9.2 Function Components

There are three components to every function: declaration, definition, and call. So is this different from predefined functions? Nope! It's just that two of the components—the declaration and the definition—are hidden from you. The declaration exists in the header files, and the definition in the C++ library. The third component, the call, is provided by the programmer to invoke the function.

9.2.1 Function Declaration

As previously learned, all variables must be declared before they are used. Functions are no different. The programmer must provide the *function declaration* so that when the compiler encounters the function call, it can verify the existence of the function name and the required parameters. At this point, all function declarations should be placed above `main`, making them global. This provides each function within your program the ability to call any other function.

The terms **function prototype** and **function declaration** are often used interchangeably in C++.

There are three parts to every function declaration, as shown in the following syntax diagram:

```
<return-type> <function-name> ( <parameter-list> );
```

The `<return-type>` specifies the data type of any value returned from the function. As you might suspect from this statement, a function is able to return a maximum of one value. The data type of the value returned and the return type of the function must match. If the function does not return a value, the return type of the function must be specified as `void`.

The term **void** in C and C++ literally means "nothing". Therefore, if a function has a `void` return type, that function will return nothing.

The `<function-name>` represents a valid identifier name. The name must adhere to the same naming rules for variables, as was discussed in Chapter 4.

Although not a rule, some programmers feel that the function name should begin with a strong verb to signify what task the function will perform.

The `<parameter-list>` represents a comma-delimited list of the variables that will be passed to the function. If there are to be no parameters passed to the function, it is acceptable to place the `void` keyword in the parentheses or to leave the parentheses empty. Example 9.2.1 shows several function declarations.

Example 9.2.1 Function declarations

```
// Returns nothing, is passed nothing
void DisplayMenu();

// Returns nothing, is passed nothing
void PrintInstructions( void );

// Returns an integer and is passed nothing
int ReadData();

// Returns an integer and is passed two integers
int FindMaximum( int value1, int value2 );

// Returns nothing and is passed a float, a double, and a bool
void DisplayResults( float, double, bool );
```

Although all of the examples in Example 9.2.1 are legal, the last example is not as readable as it could be. It is acceptable in the parameter list to have only the data types of the parameters; however, if the names of the parameters are specified, it would give a more meaningful clue as to what the parameters are used for.

Within this text we make it a point to include the names of all the parameters when declaring functions because of the improved readability of the code. We would strongly urge you to follow a similar style.

9.2.2 Function Definition

The *function definition* is just what it sounds like; it defines what the function does. In your previous programs, all you did was define `main`. There are actually two parts to the function definition. The function definition starts with the *function header*. The function header will look exactly like the declaration except that it doesn't have a semicolon. Also, the names of all the parameters in the function header are required.

The other part of the function definition is the *function body*, which must be enclosed in curly braces. Just like the body of a loop, the body of a function defines what the function will do when it is invoked. Once the function has done its job, the flow of the program returns to where the function was invoked. A complete function definition is shown in Example 9.2.2.

Example 9.2.2 Function definition

```
// Returns nothing, is passed nothing
void PrintInstructions() // Function header - notice no ';'
{      // Beginning of function body
    cout << "Staple all 3 pages of your loan application.\n";
    cout << "In addition, date and sign your form!\n\n";
    cout << "\t\t\t ***** Have a great day ****";
}      // End of function body
```

One big difference from other statements we have seen is that the function definition *must* be placed outside of any other function. It is syntactically incorrect to define a function within another function.

STYLE NOTE ▶ Because of the declarations, it is legal to place your function definitions above or below `main`. We suggest that you physically place `main` as the first function definition in your source code file, since `main` is always the first function to execute.

Another term used by some programmers is *signature*. The signature refers to the function declaration or prototype minus the return type. A teammate might refer to *FunctionA* as having a different signature than *FunctionB*. This means that the two functions have different parameters as well as a different function name. We will have more to say about function signatures when we get into the subject of classes later in the text, but a signature basically includes the function name, and the type and number of parameters it takes.

Finally, as previously discussed, we strongly suggest that you take the time to carefully align the { } and indent the function body. You will find that it greatly improves both the readability and the maintainability of your code.

A **function signature** is a method for identifying a specific function based on its name, and the type and number of parameters it takes.

9.2.3 Function Call

The last piece of the function puzzle is the *function call*. The function call tells the function that it is time to do its job. The control of the program is transferred to the function definition, and the body of the function is executed. Although we have already said this, it is crucial for you to understand that when the function has finished its job, the flow or control of the program goes back to where it was called.

A **function call** transfers the control of the program to a specific function or method.

Before moving on, we need to make one additional comment about the call and return statements. If you return a value from a function, you must immediately assign that return value to a variable or in some other way use it in an expression. If you don't use or store the value that is returned, it will indeed be lost. Example 9.2.3 shows several function calls, including functions that return a value.

Example 9.2.3 Function calls

```
// Example 1 - function returns no value
PrintInstructions();

// Example 2 - function returns an integer
cout << "Maximum number is: " << FindMaximum( val_1, val_2 );

// Example 3 - function returns an integer
int max_value = FindMaximum( val_1, val_2 );

// Example 4 - function returns an integer but value is never used
FindMaximum( val_1, val_2 );
```

Notice that all of the function calls in Example 9.2.3 don't have data types associated with the parameters. It would be syntactically incorrect to do so. In the first statement in Example 9.2.3, we simply call the `PrintInstructions` function. No values are passed into the function, and nothing is returned.

In the second example, the value returned from the `FindMaximum` function is immediately printed. When the function was called, two values, or arguments, were passed. When the function exits, it returns a value back to the point where it was called, thus allowing the ability to display the value in the `cout` statement.

In Example 3, we assigned the value returned from the `FindMaximum` function to another variable. Remember, the return type must match, or be automatically converted to, the type of the variable used in the assignment.

Notice in the final example, however, that the called function would have again returned a value as required because of the function's signature. Unfortunately, this time we did not use the value once it was returned to us, so the value is lost forever. Rarely will we ignore a return value from a user-defined function. Doing so is one of the more common errors made by our beginning students.

Section 9.2 Exercises

Please identify the best response for each of the following questions:

1. When used with functions, the term `void` means:

   a. Nothing is returned from a function or passed to a function.

   b. Anything can be passed to the function or returned from a function.

   c. The function does not use `cout` within its body or action.

   d. The function returns an integer value.

Please use the following prototype for the next three questions:

```
int CantTouchThis( double time, char code );
```

2. Which of the following statements is the correct way to call the preceding function?

   a. `int hammer = CantTouchThis();`

   b. `int hammer = CantTouchThis;`

   c. `int hammer = CantTouchThis( 11.4, 'A' );`

   d. `int hammer = CantTouchThis( 11.4, "A" );`

   e. `int hammer = CantTouchThis( double 11.4, char 'A' );`

3. What is the data type returned from the preceding function?

    a. `void`

    b. `int`

    c. `double`

    d. `char`

    e. `indeterminate`

4. How many parameters are passed into the preceding function?

    a. none

    b. one

    c. two

    d. three

Section 9.2 Learn by Doing Exercise

1. Write a program that has a function, in addition to `main`, that displays your name. This function will return no values and will be passed no parameters.

9.3 Return

In all of the predefined mathematical functions we have used, when the function finished its calculations, it gave a value back so that it could be stored in a variable. In other words, the function *returned* a value. As we saw in both the function header and the declaration, a return type other than `void` specifies that the function will return a value.

So how does the function return a value? Well, you have been returning a value from a function from the very first program you wrote. In `main`, the last statement in all of our examples has been `return 0;`. This statement returns the numeric literal 0 to where `main` was called. Since `main` is called by the operating system, this is where the value is returned. Typically, a return value of 0 from `main` indicates normal termination of your program. A value other than 0 indicates that an error has occurred. Also notice that the return type of `main` is an `int`, which matches the data type of the value returned.

When a return statement is encountered, the execution of the function immediately stops and control returns to the point of the call. Any value specified in the `return` statement is returned at that point. If there are additional statements after the `return` statement, they will *not* be executed, as shown in Example 9.3.1. Take note, though: No errors or warnings will be generated from the compilation of this code.

Example 9.3.1 Unreachable code

```cpp
bool DisplayLogoffMsg( bool done )
{
    cout << "Staple all 3 pages of your loan application.\n";
    cout << "In addition, date and sign your form!\n\n";

    if ( done )
        return true;
    else
        return false;

    cout << "\t\t * Have a great day *\n\n" ;   // Unreachable code!
    cout << "\t\t\t\t ** Logged off **";         // Unreachable code!
}
```

Although it is legal to have multiple return statements in a function, such as in the action of an if statement, it is important to remember that all paths through the function must have a return statement. Executing Example 9.3.2 would generate the following warning: not all control paths return a value.

Example 9.3.2 Not all control paths return a value

```cpp
bool DetermineHonorRollStatus()
{
    double gpa = 2.4;
    if ( gpa > 3.50 )
    {
        cout << "Excellent Work" << endl;
        return true;
    }
    else if ( gpa >= 3.0 )
    {
        cout << "Nice Job"  << endl;
    }
    else
    {
        cout << "Keep Trying" << endl;
        return false;
    }
}
```

Even though multiple `return` statements are acceptable, you are still returning only one value per function execution. This is worth repeating: A function can return *only* one value.

There are a couple of issues concerning `return` statements you should avoid. While it is legal to have a `return` statement in the body of a loop, it is considered poor programming. The only way a loop should terminate is through its condition. Also, you can use a `return` statement without actually returning a value to immediately end the function. Both of these tactics are unacceptable in the courses we teach. There are better, more elegant, alternatives. Example 9.3.3 illustrates a function containing a simple loop construct and the proper approach to return a value.

Example 9.3.3 Proper return usage

```
int SumTheValues()
{
    int sum = 0, value = 0;
    for ( int i = 0; i < 5; i++ )
    {
        cout << "Enter value " << i + 1 << ": ";
        cin  >> value;

        sum += value;
    }
    return sum;
}
```

Remember, it is not necessary to return a value from a function. Without a `return` statement, the function will end. The flow will then transfer back to where it was called from when the last statement in the body of the function has executed. You must remember that the signature of this type of function will have `void` as its return type.

STYLE NOTE Some programmers feel there should be only one entry point and one exit point in any function. It is our personal programming style to avoid multiple returns in a function.

Section 9.3 Exercises

1. For each of the following code fragments, indicate if there are any errors. If there is an error, identify what type of error it is (syntactical, logical, runtime) and how you would fix it. If you are unsure or would like to see the proof, type it into your compiler and run it.

a. `return (void);`

b. `int return;`

c. `return var_a;`

d. `return(var_a, var_b, var_c);`

e. `return(var_a + var_b);`

f. `return;`

g. `return(true);`

h. `return('A', 'B');`

2. Indicate whether each of the following statements is true or false:

a. A function can return more than one value.

b. It is legal for a function to contain more than one `return` statement. T

c. Every function must contain a `return` statement.

d. The function `main` should return an `int`.

Section 9.3 Learn by Doing Exercise

1. Write a program that has a function that prompts for three values. The function will then return the average of those values to `main`. The returned value will then be displayed to the screen.

9.4 Passing Parameters

All of the mathematical functions we learned in Chapter 6 required us to provide a value, or values, to the function. This is called *passing* a value or parameter. The calling function provides information for the called function to work with. The value to be sent to the function is placed within the function call's parentheses.

Example 9.4.1 shows how we pass the required two `double` values to the `pow` function. The first value passed into the `pow` function will be the contents of `var_x`, and the second value passed will be the contents of `var_y`. Note also how we assign the value returned from the `pow` function to `var_z`.

Example 9.4.1 Passing parameters

```
double var_x = 3.0, var_y = 4.0, var_z;
...
var_z = pow( var_x, var_y );  // Calling the pow function
```

For every value in the call, there must be a corresponding value in the function header and declaration. The first parameter from the call is caught in the first parameter in the header. The second parameter in the call is caught in the second parameter, and so on. The data types of the parameters must *all* match. Notice that it is the order of the parameters that determines where the values go, not the name of the individual parameters. For example, you could call a function named `foo` and pass it the values `a`, `b`, and `c`. However, in the function header, you could catch those three ordered values as `x`, `y`, and `z`, respectively. While we don't usually alter the names to that extent, it is important that you know that it is indeed legal to do.

Example 9.4.2 calls the function `CalculateBoxVolume` from `main` and passes it three values: the contents of the variable `length`, the contents of the variable `width`, and the value 2, which represents the `height`.

Example 9.4.2 Passing parameters

```
// Declaration/Prototype
int CalculateBoxVolume( int length, int width, int height );

int main()
{
    int length = 3, width = 4;
    ...
    // Call
    int box_volume = CalculateBoxVolume( length, width, 2 );
    ...
    return 0;
}
// Definition
int CalculateBoxVolume( int len, int width, int height )
{
        return len * width * height;
}
```

Remember: The function declaration doesn't require the parameter names, only the data types. That is why we can get away with having different parameter names between the declaration and the header in Example 9.4.2.

What a function can do with the parameter depends on how the parameter is passed. Although there are several different modes in which we can pass parameters, this chapter focuses on passing by value and passing by reference.

9.4.1 Formal and Actual Parameters

Before discussing the modes of passing values, we need to present some terminology. The terms *formal* and *actual parameters* refer to the parameters in the function header and those in the call. Formal parameters are found in the function definition, and actual parameters appear in the function call. This terminology becomes very important when we start to encounter compilation errors that deal with functions. If you don't have matching data types for all the pieces of your functions, you will receive a compilation error or warning.

Remember: The names of the variables in the function call do not have to match the names in the function prototype or the function header, but the data types should match.

9.4.2 Scope

We have already discussed the concept of *scope*. Variables declared within curly braces are available only within that code block. Variables declared within functions—called *local* variables—are no different. Because the variables can only be seen within the scope of the function, you can use the same variable names within different functions without any problem.

Another thing to be aware of is that all formal parameters are treated as local variables. Therefore, all variables associated with the function, including all formal parameters, are destroyed when that function is finished.

Local variables are variables declared within the body of a specific function. Their visibility is only within that particular function, and their lifetime is limited to that function only.

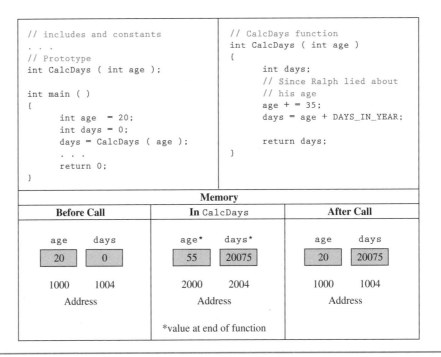

Figure 9.4.1 Passing by value

9.4.3 Passing by Value

In *passing by value*, a copy of the value is made and passed to the function. The function, therefore, manipulates the copy and not the original. When the called function is done, the function's actual parameter—the variable in the call—retains its original value. Again, it is important to remember that a copy of the value is made. The diagram in Figure 9.4.1 demonstrates this process.

Notice in Figure 9.4.1 that the variables `age` and `days` are declared within the body of `main`. At that point, each variable is created in a specific location in memory. For our illustration, we assume the value of `age` is at address 1000 and the variable `days` is physically located at address 1004. When the function `CalcDays` is called, we pass it the contents, or value, of the variable `age`, in this case 20. In order to use this value and make it available within the `CalcDays` function itself, we catch the contents of the variable `age` declared in `main` and store the value in a new variable, again called `age`.

As you can see, this `age` variable has its own physical location at address 2000. When the function exits, any local variables, in this case `age` and `days`, will be destroyed. The bottom line is that these variables are physically stored in two distinct locations, each having only function scope. If you make a change to one of these formal parameters in the called function, it will not impact the values of the actual parameters in the calling function.

To further illustrate the syntax of passing by value, Example 9.4.3 contains several additional function declarations that have parameters passed in this manner.

Example 9.4.3 Passing by value function declarations

```
double CalcAverage( double first_val, double second_val );

int FindTestTotal( int test1, int test2, int test3 );

char FindLetterGrade( int overall_score );
```

9.4.4 Passing by Reference

Instead of passing a copy of the value, *passing by reference* passes an alias that directly references the variable. This means that any changes made to the formal parameter are reflected in the actual parameter when the function is done. To pass by reference, you must place an ampersand after the formal parameter's data type. Figure 9.4.2 shows the impact of passing by reference on variables.

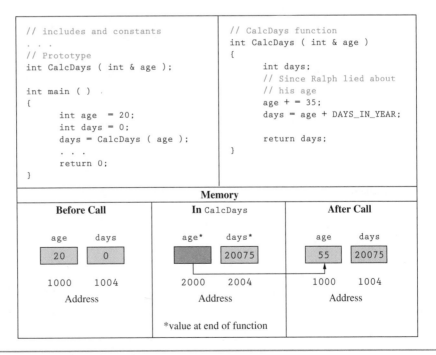

Figure 9.4.2 Passing by reference

Notice in Figure 9.4.2, the `age` in `CalcDays` doesn't really contain a value but refers to the actual parameter in `main`. Therefore, any changes to the reference in `CalcDays` are reflected in `main`. Example 9.4.4 shows function declarations that indicate that its parameters are passed by reference.

Example 9.4.4 Passing by reference function declarations

```
// Example 1
void Swap( int &a, int &b );

// Example 2
void FindAverage( double a, double b, double &average );

// Example 3
int EnterData( int &id, char &code );
```

In the first example, two variables are passed by reference. Changes made within this function to either of these two variables will be reflected in the calling function.

In the second example, variables `a` and `b` are both passed by value while `average` is passed into the function by reference. The `EnterData` function receives two values, both by reference.

Passing by reference should only be used if the original value needs to be changed. Use passing by value for all other occasions.

One final point needs to be made in relation to passing by value or reference: Regardless of how you decide to pass the arguments into the function, the call statement remains the same.

Section 9.4 Exercises

Please identify the best response for each of the following questions:

1. In the following function, how many parameters will be passed into the function?

```
void  SumThem( int a, int b, int c );
```

    a. one   b. two   c. three   d. four   e. five

2. In passing by _____, a copy of the value is made and passed to the function.

    a. void   b. const   c. reference   d. value   e. alias

3. In passing by _____, you pass an alias or reference to a variable instead of the value.

    a. void   b. const   c. reference   d. value   e. *r*-value

4. For each of the following code fragments, indicate if there are any errors. If there is an error, identify what type of error it is (syntactical, logical, runtime) and how you would fix it. If you are unsure or would like to see the proof, type it into your compiler and run it.

  a. `// Function prototype - var_a by value and var_b by reference`
    `void PartA(int var_a, int var_b&);`

  b. `// Function prototype - all variables by value (x and y - ints - // z - double`
    `int PartB(int x, y, double z);`

  c. `// Function prototype -  var_a and var_b by reference, var_c by`
    `// value - all variables type int`
    `char LetterGrade(& var_a, &var_b, var_c);`

Section 9.4 Learn by Doing Exercise

1. Write a program that asks for an employee's salary and years of service. Use the following functions to manipulate the information as described, as well as the included function signatures.

    `void GetInput( float & salary, int & years_service );`

    This function prompts for and reads the required salary and years of service.

    `void CalcRaise( float & salary, int years_service );`

    This function changes the salary depending on the years of service. If the employee has greater than 10 years of service, he or she will receive a 10% raise. Between 5 and 10 years, the raise is 5%. Everybody else will receive a 2% raise.

    `int CalcBonus( int years_service );`

    This function calculates and returns the employee's bonus for the year. An employee will receive $500 for every 2 years of service.

    `void PrintCalculations( int years_service, float salary, int bonus );`

    This function will display in a clear and professional manner all of the calculated information.

9.5 Default Arguments

Another powerful feature used with functions is called *default arguments*. A default argument is simply a value the programmer provides in the function declaration that will automatically be inserted if no value is provided in the function call.

There are two types of arguments or parameters: mandatory and default. Obviously, it is a requirement that all mandatory arguments be specified in the function call. As a result, all mandatory arguments must come before any default arguments in the parameter list.

Default arguments, however, are optionally specified. When omitting arguments in your call statement, you must omit the arguments from the right end of the parameter list. This would require you to have already specified the necessary default values in the function declaration.

When setting default arguments in your function declarations, remember that the defaults must be provided starting with the right-most variable(s) in your parameter list. The default values can continue from right to left, but once you stop providing specific default values, you cannot start providing them again.

The final thing to note when using default arguments is that you can only put the default values in the function declaration or prototype; you cannot include them in the function header.

Fortunately for you, all of this sounds much more confusing than it really is. Example 9.5.1 will quickly show you how easy default arguments are to use.

Example 9.5.1 Default arguments

```
// Example 1 - Function prototype
void DisplayMenu( int times = 1 );

// Example 2 - Function prototype
void PrintInstructions( int length, int height = 7 );

// Example 3 - Function prototype
int ReadData( int &records, double units = 45.5, int size = 11 );

// Examples of different calling options
DisplayMenu( times );
DisplayMenu();
DisplayMenu( 3 );
PrintInstructions( 5, 10 );
PrintInstructions( 7 );
ReadData( records );
ReadData( records, 50.5 );
ReadData( records, 50.2, 11 );
```

Section 9.5 Exercises

1. In the following function prototype, how many default arguments exist?

```
void  SumThem( int a, int b = 3, int c = 5 );
```

   a. one   b. two   c. three   d. four   e. five

2. Using the following prototype, please indicate which of the call statements would be valid. If the statement is invalid, please state why.

```
int records = 0;

void ReadData( int & records,   int size = 11 );
```

a. `ReadData( records );`

b. `ReadData( 7.45 );`

c. `ReadData();`

d. `ReadData( records, 10, 3 );`

e. `ReadData( records, 50.5 );`

3. For each of the following, specify whether the function declaration is valid. If it is not valid, please indicate why.

a. `void PrintInstructions( int len = 1, int page, int height = 7 );`

b. `void PrintWelcomeMessage( int len = 2, int height );`

c. `void MaxValue( int val_a = 1, int val_b = 2, int & val_c = 3 );`

d. `void FindIt( int val_a, int val_b = 2 );`

Section 9.5 Learn by Doing Exercise

1. Write a program that uses a function to read three values representing hours, minutes, and seconds. Pass these three values to another function that will display the time in an appropriate style. A fourth optional argument to the display function specifies whether to display the time in 24-hour notation, military time, or standard format. Both of these functions are to be called from `main`. Be sure to call the display function using three arguments as well as four arguments.

9.6 Putting It All Together

Now that all the fundamental aspects associated with functions have been covered, it will be extremely beneficial to review a more complete and comprehensive program. Example 9.6.1 incorporates many of the topics discussed in this chapter. Please take some time to carefully review the code listing and the output it generated. Make sure you fully understand each line of code, focusing especially on the sections associated with passing by value and passing by reference. To check your understanding of functions and the passing of parameters, try to determine the output of the program. Use the output provided with the example to validate your results.

After you have walked through the code in the text, we would strongly urge you to copy the code from the book's website and use the debugger to step into the various functions and watch the contents of the variables as the program executes.

Example 9.6.1 Passing by value and passing by reference—complete example

```cpp
// Chapter 9 - Section 9.6
// Filename:   Example9_6_1
#include <iostream>
#include <cmath>
using std::cout;
using std::endl;

int Fun1( int a, int b );
void Fun2( int & a, int b );
void Fun3( int & c, int & d );
void PrintOutput( int a, int b );

int main()
{
    int a = 2, b = 10;

    PrintOutput( a, b );

    a = Fun1( a, b );

    cout << a << "\t" << b << endl;

    Fun2( a, b );
    PrintOutput( a, b );

    return 0;
}
// PrintOutput
void PrintOutput( int a, int b )
{
    cout << a << "\t" << b << endl;
}
// Output
2       10
3       9       12
12      10
```

```cpp
// Fun1
int Fun1( int a, int b )
{
    int c;

    c = a + b;
    a++;
    --b;

    cout << a << "\t" << b << "\t" << c << endl;

    return c;
}
// Fun2
void Fun2( int & a, int b )
{
    a += 5;
    double temp = pow(static_cast<double>(a), 2);
    b = static_cast<int>( temp );

    PrintOutput( a, b );
    Fun3( a, b );
    PrintOutput( a, b );
}
// Fun3
void Fun3( int & c, int & d )
{
    c = 25;
    d = 10;

    PrintOutput( c, d );
}
```

17	289
25	10
25	10
25	10

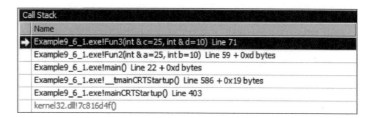

Figure 9.7.1 Call stack window

9.7 Debugging—Call Stack

As they have become relevant, we have tried to introduce new debugging tools and techniques. Now that you are becoming more familiar with functions, it is important to be introduced to the Call Stack window. The Call Stack allows us to view where in the hierarchy of our function calls the current line of execution is located.

By default, the Call Stack window in Visual Studio is not displayed. To show this window, click on the Debug menu while debugging. The top menu option is the Windows option, which has a submenu containing the item Call Stack. This can also be accessed from the hot key Ctrl+Alt+C. Figure 9.7.1 shows the Call Stack window from the execution of Example 9.6.1.

Notice that the Call Stack window shows the name of the program with the currently executing function at the top. Also shown is the data type of each parameter as well as the value. You can also see from the window that `Fun3` was called from `Fun2`, which was called from `main`. Typically, this is as far as we need to look at the contents of the window. As you can see, though, there are other functions that called `main`. These functions are responsible for displaying the console window as well as loading the program into memory.

9.8 More Predefined Functions

In Chapter 6 we discussed some of the predefined mathematical functions. Now that you are more familiar with functions, let's explore some additional ones. All of the functions in this section manipulate individual characters.

9.8.1 Character Case

There are two functions that allow us to change the case of a single character. Since you know about function signatures and declarations, it will be good practice to learn about these functions, starting with the following declarations:

```
int toupper ( int c );
int tolower ( int c );
```

As you can see, these functions are passed an integer by value and return an integer. But wait! We just said these were character functions—and besides, how can you change the case of a number? Don't forget about ASCII values. You can pass a character and catch it as an integer because this would be a widening conversion, no type casting is needed.

> ⚠ **Remember:** Every value can be stored in any variable with a larger data type. This is called a **widening conversion**. To be safe, however, only use widening conversion on similar data types. In other words, don't mix floating-point and integral values.

In order to use these two functions, you will need to include the header file `<cctype>`. Example 9.8.1 demonstrates the use of these functions.

Example 9.8.1 Character case functions

```
#include <cctype>
...
char again;

cout << "\nDo you wish to multiply two numbers (y/n)? ";
cin  >> again;

// Notice the function call
while( toupper ( again ) == 'Y' )
{
    ...
    cout << "\nDo you wish to multiply two more numbers (y/n)? ";
    cin  >> again;
}
```

Function	Description
isalnum	Is the character alphanumeric? (A–Z, a–z, 0–9)
isalpha	Is the character a letter? (A–Z, a–z)
iscntrl	Is the character a control character? (ASCII values 0–31 and 127)
isdigit	Is the character a digit? (0–9)
ispunct	Is the character punctuation?
isspace	Is the character whitespace? (ASCII values 9–13 and 32)

Table 9.8.1 Some "is" functions

Because the toupper function returns the character stored in the variable again converted to uppercase, we only need to check the uppercase version of the character 'Y'. If the actual parameter contains an uppercase letter or a character that is not a letter, no conversion will be performed. Therefore, the original character is returned. The tolower function is used in exactly the same manner.

Notice that a using statement was not used in Example 9.8.1. This is because the functions in this section are not contained within a namespace.

9.8.2 The "is" Functions

There is a group of functions that help us test characters to determine what classification the character fits into. For example, we can use one of these functions, ispunct, to determine if the character is punctuation. All of these functions have the following syntax:

```
int <is-function> ( int c );
```

Several of these functions are shown in Table 9.8.1. Just like toupper and tolower, to use the "is" functions, the <cctype> header file is required.

All of the functions in Table 9.8.1 return a nonzero value if the character meets the criteria and zero if the character fails to meet the criteria. Just like toupper and tolower, these functions are also C functions. Remember, C doesn't have a Boolean data type; therefore, 0 is always treated as false and nonzero as true. Example 9.8.2 shows a specific example of how to use these functions; however, the same technique can be applied to all of the "is" functions.

Example 9.8.2 The `isalpha` function

```
// Example 1
if ( isalpha( grade ) == 0 )
{
    cout << "Error: Not a letter grade!";
}
// Example 2
if ( !isalpha( grade ) )
{
    cout << "Error: Not a letter grade!";
}
```

The second example in Example 9.8.2 demonstrates a shorthand version using the logical NOT operator, which is commonly encountered. Both methods are equally effective.

Section 9.8 Exercises

1. The functions `toupper`, `tolower`, `isalpha`, and `isdigit` all work on:

   a. a number

   b. a character

   c. any data type

   d. void data types

2. Which of the following functions would test the value in a specific variable to determine if it is either a number or a letter?

   a. `isalpha`

   b. `isnumeric`

   c. `iseither`

   d. `isalnum`

   e. `isany`

3. What is the name of the header file you must include when using functions like `toupper`, `tolower`, `isspace`, or `isdigit`?

a. `<iostream>`

b. `<cmath>`

c. `<cctype>`

d. `<iomanip>`

9.9 Structure Charts

Recall that in Chapter 2 the concept of a flowchart was introduced as a graphical approach for representing an algorithm. Another tool used to help us better visualize the organization of our solution or program is called a *structure chart*. Like a flowchart, a structure chart uses symbols and connectors, as we have previously seen. However, while a flowchart helps us outline the specific details associated with a solution, a structure chart takes a much higher-level approach, graphically showing the various tasks or functions needed as well as the relationship of these tasks to each other.

Structure charts work well in the area of procedural programming to represent functions and their relationships to each other. We have chosen to use them within the text as simply another tool to help in designing and visualizing programming solutions. Figure 9.9.1 illustrates the use of a structure chart to represent the organization of the program provided in Example 9.6.1.

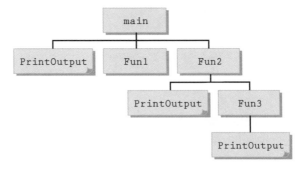

Figure 9.9.1 Structure chart

Notice that the structure chart resembles a hierarchy chart and that it is organized from top to bottom and from left to right. In the structure chart shown in Figure 9.9.1, the functions `PrintOutput`, `Fun1`, and `Fun2` are all called from `main`. Likewise, `PrintOutput` and `Fun3` were called from `Fun2`. `Fun3` also calls `PrintOutput`. We have chosen the symbol with the folded corner to represent a common function that is called from more than one place.

We suggest you draw your structure chart first, either by hand or by using tools such as Microsoft's Visio, Word, or PowerPoint. Notice that the only text appearing within the individual boxes is the exact name of your functions. Once you have given some thought to the overall organization of your program and drawn the structure chart, you can easily focus on the individual functions that you have identified. You can now break these individual functions into more detailed tasks or statements by writing the specific pseudocode for each respective function.

9.10 Problem Solving Applied

We will now begin to incorporate this new technique into our program development to help organize the required functions, demonstrating the use of the structure chart as an aid in developing our solution.

Since this section uses the previous chapter's Problem Solving Applied solution, please refer to Section 8.6 for problem specifications.

Structure Chart:

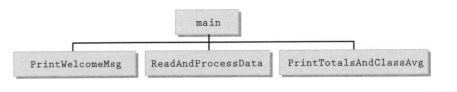

Figure 9.10.1 Structure chart

Now that the structure chart shown in Figure 9.10.1 has been created, use this diagram to help develop the pseudocode, as shown in the Design phase.

Design:

Pseudocode

```
/*********************************
* Name: main
*********************************/
Call PrintWelcomeMsg

class average = Call ReadAndProcessData

Call PrintTotalsAndClassAvg


/*********************************
* Name: PrintWelcomeMsg
* Parameters: none
* Return: none
* Purpose: Display a message to the user to
* welcome him or her to the program.
*********************************/
Print "Welcome Message"
Print "Name of program"


/*********************************
* Name: PrintTotalsAndClassAverage
* Parameters: The number of students. By Val.
*          The class average. By Val.
* Return: none
* Purpose: Display the number of students and
* the class average.
*********************************/
Display "Number of students: "
        number_of_students
Display "Class average: "
      overall_class_average
```

```
/*********************************
* Name: ReadAndProcessData
* Parameters: The number of students. By Ref.
* Return: The class average
* Purpose: Read and process all of the
* student data and calculate the class
* average.
*********************************/
While (again is equal to 'Y')
Begin loop
    Prompt "Enter in student id"
      ...

    Calculate overall average =
      (exam 1 + exam 2 + exam 3) / 3

    Add overall average to
        total of students averages
        accumulator

    Add 1 to the number of students
End loop
  ...

Calculate overall class average =
      total of students averages /
      number of students

Return the overall class average
```

Like always, this pseudocode is now translated into C++ source code. Notice that we have added function descriptions in our pseudocode, which will be placed in the C++ source code as comments. These comments serve as documentation not only for you but for other programmers who may be involved in the modification or maintenance of your code.

C++ Source Code

```cpp
// Function Prototypes

int main()
{
    // Local variables
    // Function Calls
    PrintWelcomeMsg();
    class_average = ReadAndProcessData( number_of_students );
    PrintTotalsAndClassAverage( number_of_students, class_average );
     . . .
    return 0;
}


/***************************************************************
* Name: PrintWelcomeMsg
* Parameters: none
* Return: none
* Purpose: Display a message to the user to welcome him or her to the
* program.
***************************************************************/
void PrintWelcomeMsg()
{
    cout  << "\t\t ** Welcome ** \n";
}


/***************************************************************
* Name: ReadAndProcessData
* Parameters: The number of students. By Ref.
* Return: The class average
* Purpose: Read and process all of the student data and calculate
* the class average.
***************************************************************/
double ReadAndProcessData( int &number_of_students )
{
    // Local variables
    . . .
    cout << "\nEnter student data (y/n)? ";
    cin  >> again;
    // Processing
    while ( again == 'y'||again == 'Y' )
    {
```

```
        cout << "Enter in student id: ";
        cin >> id;
        . . .
        ++number_of_students;

        cout << "\n\nStudent ID: " << id;
        . . .
    }
    overall_class_average = total_of_students_averages / number_of_students;

    return overall_class_average;
}
/*****************************************************************
* Name: PrintTotalsAndClassAverage
* Parameters: The number of students. By Val.
*             The class average. By Val.
* Return: none
* Purpose: Display the number of students and the class average.
*****************************************************************/
void PrintTotalsAndClassAverage( int number_of_students, double class_average )
{
    cout << "\n\n\t * Number of Students: "
         << number_of_students
         << " Overall Class Average:   "
         << class_average << endl << endl;
}
```

9.11 C—The Differences

There are only a few differences between C++ and C in relation to the material presented in this chapter. A couple of these differences are minor, while one is major. One of the minor differences is that in C, there is a distinction between a function that specifies a `void` parameter list and one that has an empty parameter. A `void` parameter list specifies that no parameters will be passed to the function; an empty parameter list means that there are an indeterminate number of parameters. Example 9.11.1 illustrates both of these options.

Example 9.11.1 C prototypes

```
// Prototypes
// Example 1
void DisplayTitle( void );      // no parameters will be passed

// Example 2
void DisplayColumnHeadings(); // indeterminate number of parameters
```

The major difference is that passing by reference in C is done in an entirely different way. C accomplishes the same functionality as passing by reference by using something called *passing by pointer*. Because you can also pass by pointer in C++, we have devoted almost an entire chapter to passing by pointer and pointers in general. Please see Chapter 12 for more on passing by pointer.

> ⚠ **Remember:** In the C programming language, passing variables by pointer is often referred to as passing by reference.

Finally, it is important to note that using default arguments in the C programming language is not allowed.

9.12 SUMMARY

In this chapter, we explored the powerful concept and components associated with functions. Functions are simply a group of related statements that are assembled together to carry out a specific task. The numerous advantages that functions offer to programmers—including the ability to break a problem down into smaller, more manageable, and maintainable components—were also discussed. Code reuse is another huge advantage in using functions.

We followed up with a discussion of the three main components required in every function: the declaration, the definition, and the call. To help reinforce your understanding of these various components, we related programmer-defined functions to your existing background with predefined math functions, presented earlier in the text.

One of the additional strengths of functions is that they can both receive values and send results back to the place from which they were called. We explored two methods for sending data or values into a function: passing by value and passing by reference. In relation to passing by value, it was noted that the called function receives only a copy of the variable's contents. Since it has only a copy of the data, any changes made to the copy will have no impact on the actual parameter located in the function call. In discussing passing by reference, we noted how formal parameters that use the ampersand allow changing the contents of the original or actual parameter, making the modifications permanent.

We also discussed the value and functionality of the `return` statement, noting that when a `return` statement is executed, control immediately returns to the point of the call. We also stressed that a `return` can send only one value back to the calling function.

We also revisited the previously introduced topic of scope. Within this chapter, we expanded this concept to include local variables, and mentioned that all formal function parameters are indeed treated as local variables. As a result, upon exiting the function, all of the local variables are destroyed.

Finally, we provided a complete example to help reinforce the various concepts presented. Hopefully you are feeling very comfortable with functions and their overall usage. As you will soon see, they will act as a fundamental cornerstone to the programs developed in the remainder of the text.

9.13 Debugging Exercise

Download the following file from this book's website and run the program following the instructions noted in the code.

```
/***********************************************************************
 * File: Chap_9_Debugging.cpp
 *
 * General Instructions: Complete each step before proceeding to the
 * next.
 *
 * Debugging Exercise 1
 *
 * 1) Insert a breakpoint on the lines indicated in the code.
 * 2) Run to Breakpoint 1.
 * 3) Place a watch on age and days.
 * 4) Add another watch using &age for the name. This will display
 *    the address of age.
 * 5) Write down the address of age.
 * 6) Step into the code for the function GetAge.
 * 7) The execution continues to the function header for GetAge.
 * 8) Step into one more time.
 * 9) Why did the address of age and value change?
 * 10) Step over the cout and cin statements.
 * 11) Verify that the value entered is stored properly in age.
 * 12) Step into until the flow returns to main.
 * 13) Step over one more time.
 * 14) Why didn't the value entered get transferred back to main?
 * 15) Stop debugging and fix the error.
 * 16) Run to Breakpoint 1.
```

```
* 17) Step over the function call to GetAge.
* 18) Verify that the value entered was returned and stored
*     correctly from GetAge.
* 19) Stop debugging.
*
* Debugging Exercise 2
*
* 1) Run to Breakpoint 1.
* 2) Step over the call to GetAge.
* 3) Step into CalcDays.
* 4) Step into one more time so that the current line is the
*    calculation.
* 5) Why is age grayed out in your watch window?
* 6) Stop debugging.
*
* Debugging Exercise 3
*
* 1) Run to Breakpoint 2.
* 2) When asked, enter the value of 20 for your age.
* 3) Verify that the variable age is 20 and the variable days
*    is 7300.
* 4) Step into the PrintResults function.
* 5) Age is 7300? Not even Ralph is that old.
* 6) Why did the values for both variables change?
* 7) Stop debugging and fix the error.
*
* Debugging Exercise 4
*
* 1) Run to Breakpoint 2.
* 2) Display your Call Stack window.
* 3) View the contents of the window and notice that the top
*    function on the stack is main.
* 4) Step into the PrintResults function.
* 5) Notice that the call stack now shows PrintResults on top of
*    the stack.
*********************************************************************/
#include <iostream>
using std::cout;
using std::cin;
using std::endl;

const int DAYS_PER_YEAR = 365;

int GetAge();
int CalcDays( int age );
void PrintResults( int age, int days );

int main()
{
    int age = 0;
    int days = 0;
```

```
    // Breakpoint 1
    // Put breakpoint on the following line
    GetAge();
    days = CalcDays( age );

    // Breakpoint 2
    // Put breakpoint on the following line
    PrintResults( age, days );

    return 0;
}
int GetAge()
{
    int age;

    cout << "Please enter your age: ";
    cin >> age;

    return age;
}
int CalcDays( int years )
{
    int days;

    days = years * DAYS_PER_YEAR;

    return days;
}
void PrintResults( int days, int age )
{
    cout << age << "! Boy are you old!\n";
    cout << "Did you know that you are at least "
        << days << " days old?\n\n";
}
```

9.14 Programming Exercises

The following programming exercises are to be developed using all phases of the development method. Be sure to make use of good programming practices and style, such as constants, white-space, indentation, naming conventions, and commenting. Make sure all input prompts are clear and descriptive and that your output is well formatted and looks professional. Although some of these exercises are from previous chapters, rewrite them so they now include appropriate function modularization.

1. Write a program that draws a rectangle on the screen using ASCII characters. The program will prompt the user for the height and width, specified in characters, of the rectangle. Use the following ASCII values for the box characters: 218 upper left-hand corner, 217 lower right-hand corner, 196 top and bottom, 192 lower left-hand corner, 191 upper right-hand corner, and 179 left and right sides.

2. Write a program that takes input from the user that represents a numerator and a denominator of a fraction. Then reduce the fraction to its lowest terms and display it to the screen. If appropriate, display the fraction as a mixed number (3 1/2).

   To reduce a fraction to its lowest terms, divide both the numerator and the denominator by the greatest common divisor (GCD). The GCD can be calculated by using Euclid's algorithm. Euclid's algorithm states: Let m represent the numerator and n represent the denominator of a fraction. Divide m by n. Save the divisor in m and save the remainder in n. If n is 0, then stop: m contains the GCD. Otherwise, repeat the process.

   Be sure to display the fraction in a well-formed manner. If the denominator is a one, display the fraction as a whole number. If the denominator is a zero, display a message that the fraction is undefined. A fraction will never be displayed with a negative denominator.

3. Display a menu to the user that has the following options:

   — Main Menu —
   1.   Calculate Area
   2.   Calculate Volume

   Write a `switch` statement that handles the user's choice. For each of the main menu options, display a submenu that has the following options:

— Area Menu —	— Volume Menu —
a. Rectangle	a. Cylinder
b. Circle	b. Sphere
c. Right Triangle	

   Write nested `switch` statements to handle each of the submenus. For all of the `switch` statements, use the default case to handle any incorrect menu options. If you are unsure of the correct formulas, research them on the Internet or in your math books. Display the results of each of the calculations based on the appropriate user input.

4. The "`is`" functions `toupper` and `tolower` are all C functions. Rewrite these functions so that they are more C++ like. Use Boolean return types and use the `char` data type for parameters instead of `int`. Make sure you write a program that tests the functionality of these new functions.

9.15 Team Programming Exercise

As you have probably noticed, your source code for Marcus from Chapters 7 and 8 is getting more than a little messy. Break the solution you previously created into the following functions:

- Name: `GetData`
  - Parameters: none
  - Return: The integer number entered by the user

- Purpose: This function will allow the user to enter the number to be tested. Marcus would like you to limit the input from negative one million to positive one million. If the number entered is out of bounds, display an error message and have the user reenter the value
- Name: `DisplayMenu`
  - Parameters: The variable that holds the menu choice, passing by reference
  - Return: none
  - Purpose: This function displays the menu to the user
- Name: `ProcessMenuChoice`
  - Parameters: The variable that holds the menu choice, passing by value
    The variable that holds the number entered, passing by reference
  - Return: none
  - Purpose: This function will call the appropriate function based on the menu choice that is passed in
- Name: `IsPosNeg`
  - Parameters: The variable that holds the number entered, passing by value
  - Return: none
  - Purpose: This function tests the number that is passed to determine whether it is positive, negative, or zero. The function displays an appropriate message based on the results of the test
- Name: `IsOddEven`
  - Parameters: The variable that holds the number entered, passing by value
  - Return: none
  - Purpose: This function tests the number that is passed to determine whether it is odd, even, or zero. The function displays an appropriate message based on the results of the test
- Name: `FindNumDigits`
  - Parameters: The variable that holds the number entered, passing by value
  - Return: The number of digits
  - Purpose: This function determines the number of digits in the number that is passed in
- Name: `FindDigitAtPosition`
  - Parameters: The variable that holds the number entered, passing by value
    The variable that contains the digit's position, passing by value
  - Return: The digit at the specified position
  - Purpose: This function determines what digit is at a specific position in the number
- Name: `DisplayAdditionTable`
  - Parameters: none
  - Return: none
  - Purpose: This function displays the addition table

- Name: `DisplayMultiplicationTable`
  - Parameters: none
  - Return: none
  - Purpose: This function displays the multiplication table

Both the `FindNumDigits` and `FindDigitAtPosition` functions return a value, which is then displayed in the `ProcessMenuChoice` function.

Marcus has supplied you with a structure chart shown in Figure 9.15.1 that he thinks will help develop your program. Although it seems that all of the functions are accounted for, use a drawing program like Microsoft Visio to clean this up. Make sure all of the boxes are the same style and size and that it is indeed an appropriate structure chart.

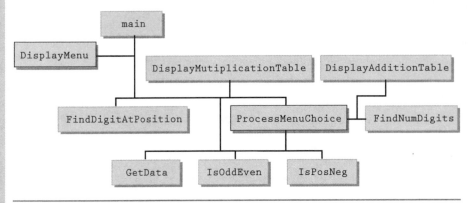

Figure 9.15.1 Team programming structure chart

9.16 Answers to Chapter Exercises

Section 9.1

1. c. labels

2. b. `main`

3. d. All of the above are advantages.

Section 9.2

1. a. Nothing is returned from a function or passed to a function.

2. c. `int hammer = CantTouchThis( 11.4, 'A' );`

3. b. `int`

4. c. two

Section 9.3

1. a. Syntactical—no data type in a return statement.

   b. Syntactical—can't declare a variable using a reserved word.

   c. Valid.

   d. Syntactical—can only return one value.

   e. Valid.

   f. Valid, although not a very good approach.

   g. Valid.

   h. Syntactical—can only return one value.

2. a. False—only one value can be returned from a function.

   b. True—but we suggest you have only one return in your function.

   c. False—a function will automatically exit when it is at its end.

   d. True—`main` should always return an integer value.

Section 9.4

1. c. three

2. d. value

3. c. reference

4. a. Syntactical—the ampersand must come before the variable name.

   ```
   void PartA(int var_a, int &var_b);
   ```

   b. Syntactical—need the data type for the second parameter.

   ```
   int PartB(int x, int y, double z);
   ```

   c. Syntactical—need the data type for each of the parameters.

   ```
   char LetterGrade(int & var_a, int &var_b, int var_c);
   ```

Section 9.5

1. b. two

2. a. Valid.

   b. Invalid—the first argument passed to the function must be a variable, not a numeric literal. You cannot pass a literal by reference.

   c. Invalid—the call requires at least one argument.

    d. Invalid—only one or two arguments can be passed to the function.

    e. Invalid—data types don't match.

3. a. Invalid—default arguments must be continuously supplied from right to left.

   b. Invalid—default arguments must be supplied starting at the right-most position.

   c. Invalid—you cannot initialize a reference to a literal.

   d. Valid.

Section 9.8

1. b. a character

2. d. `isalnum`

3. c. `<cctype>`

CHAPTER 10

Arrays and cStrings

Chapter Objectives

By the end of the chapter, readers will be able to:

- Explain in a language-independent fashion the concepts of single and multidimensional arrays.
- Illustrate the layout of arrays in memory.
- Declare and initialize both single and multidimensional arrays.
- Apply both single and multidimensional arrays to programming solutions.
- Demonstrate the characteristics and application of cStrings.
- Use a variety of predefined cString functions.
- Explain the concepts of parallel arrays.

Introduction

As the text has progressed, our programs have become more and more complex. However, the amount of data required for these programs has remained relatively small. The reason for not requiring large amounts of data lies in the difficulty associated with storing that much information. Multiple variables could have been used, but that would have been very challenging and time consuming to manage. For example, using the variables assign1, assign2, assign3, . . ., assign100 would be awkward. Also, you have probably noticed that we have not asked you to enter strings from the keyboard. All of these issues can be addressed and programs made more efficient by using arrays. This chapter is dedicated to the language-independent theory behind arrays as well as their C++ implementation.

10.1 What Are Arrays?

Arrays allow us to associate multiple pieces of data with one variable name. Let's examine the definition of an array in greater detail.

An **array** is a collection of two or more contiguous memory cells of a homogenous data type.

There are three key points in this definition. The first is the phrase "two or more . . . memory cells." This alludes to the fact that we never want to declare an array that holds a single piece of data, often called an *element*. If you need to have a single-element array, use a regular variable instead.

The second point relates to the phrase "contiguous memory cells." This means that each element of the array is physically adjacent to each other in memory.

An area within the block of memory where one piece of data will be stored is referred to as an **element**.

The third key point in the array definition is "homogenous data type." This means that an array can only contain data of a single type. Although this data type can be any of the types we have discussed, you can't mix data types within the same array.

The definition of arrays just discussed can be applied to any programming language. One key point we have not examined is how arrays are implemented specifically in C++. The variable name associated with an array refers to an address, not the actual data.

 Remember: The name of an array refers to its starting address.

Even more importantly, the address is a constant address, meaning that an array can never be placed on the left side of an assignment operator. Therefore, an array is not an appropriate *l*-value.

Now you know the fundamentals associated with arrays, but you still may not understand when arrays would be useful in your algorithm development. To help illustrate the usefulness of arrays, assume we need to store the test scores for 25 students. We could declare an array that contains 25 elements. Each element, or cell, would represent a score for one student. Before continuing our discussions, the next section provides a quick summary of the pros and cons associated with arrays.

10.1.1 Advantages and Disadvantages of Arrays

Arrays offer a number of advantages, including providing the opportunity to declare a number of related elements, all of the same type, quickly. In addition, arrays can be used with any of the data types we have already discussed. Likewise, arrays are useful tools when needing to sort or search for information, as you will see in Chapter 11. Finally, when using the various looping structures presented in previous chapters, arrays provide a fast and easy method for accessing a potentially large amount of data.

On the other hand, arrays can create additional costs or potential disadvantages as well. For example, if we declare an array to hold 100 elements, but end up needing and using only 10 elements, we have unnecessarily wasted our computer's resources. Likewise, if while accessing our arrays we go outside the block of memory allocated, we have just created one of the more difficult programming errors to find and correct.

10.2 Declaring Arrays

The syntax for an array declaration is as follows:

    <data-type> <array-name> [<number-elements>];

The data type and the naming rules and conventions remain the same as they were for ordinary variables. The `<number-elements>` must be an integer constant or a literal that specifies the total number of elements. It is syntactically incorrect to use a variable to represent the number of elements in the array declaration. Example 10.2.1 contains several array declarations.

Example 10.2.1 Array declarations

```
// Example 1
char first_name[20];

// Example 2
const int LEN = 20;
char last_name[LEN];

// Example 3
int test_scores[5];

// Example 4
int lab_scores[4], assignment_scores[4];
```

Example 10.2.1 shows a number of different arrays being declared. Example 1 declares a character array called `first_name` with 20 elements. In the second example, `last_name` is declared with the number of elements established by the use of a constant called `LEN`. Example 3 creates an array made up of five individual integer elements. The final example creates two different arrays of integers, the first called `lab_scores` and the second `assignment_scores`, both of which contain four elements.

Each element in an array can hold exactly one value of the specified type, even though the value could physically occupy more than one byte. This means that if we have an array of 10 `floats`, the array will occupy 40 bytes of memory. The memory required for the array is calculated by multiplying the number of elements by the size of the data type.

Since arrays are a fixed size, care needs to be taken when the array is declared to make sure the size is appropriate for your data. For example, assume that at the beginning of the term a class might have 30 students, but toward the end of the term only about 20 students may remain. You would still need to allocate room for 30 students because that is your maximum limit, or size. Sometimes determining the maximum size is a difficult decision. You really need to know a lot about your data and have a thorough understanding of the problem you are trying to solve.

If you make an error in judging the size of your array, make sure you have made it a bit larger than required by your data rather than making it too small. It is better to waste a little memory than take the chance of going out of bounds of the array.

> *i* The term **going out of bounds** of an array refers to accessing an element, or memory cell, that does not belong to the array.

STYLE NOTE Use constants to specify the number of elements in an array. Constants not only make your code more readable but also make your code easier to modify. If the size of the array needs to change, you need only change the value of the constant and recompile. To gain the biggest advantage, use the constant whenever referencing the array bounds.

Section 10.2 Exercises

Please respond to each of the following questions.

1. The _____ of an array actually refers to an address.

   a. size   b. dimensions   c. name   d. data type

2. Based on the following line of code, how many different elements would the array `test` hold?

   ```
   int test[5];
   ```

   a. 4   b. 5   c. 6   d. unknown

3. How many values can each element in an array hold?

   a. 0   b. 1   c. 2   d. unknown

4. Indicate whether each of the following statements is true or false.

   a. An array is a group of three or more contiguous memory locations composed of the same data type.

   b. While syntactically possible, we would not declare an array with only one element.

   c. When possible, we will use literals to indicate the size of an array.

5. It is best to use a _____ to indicate the number of elements in an array and when referencing the array bounds.

   a. variable   b. literal   c. constant   d. type

10.3 Using Arrays

To access a specific element in an array, you must use brackets ([ ]), also called the *subscript operator*. The subscript operator actually specifies the `offset` from the beginning address. Therefore, to access the first element, you need to specify an offset of 0; to access the second element, an offset of 1, and so on. This process is illustrated in Figure 10.3.1.

Figure 10.3.1 simulates how the array `test_scores` might appear in memory. While we have indeed made up the first or beginning address location, 1000, a number of important points are worth noting. As previously mentioned, the first element of the array has an offset of 0; the second element, an offset of 1. Second, notice that each individual element of the array is the same size, or four bytes, representing the size of an integer. Finally, observe that the individual elements are contiguous, or physically located one after another.

The number within the brackets in the declaration of an array specifies the total number of elements. The number in the subscript operator specifies the offset from the beginning address. Example 10.3.1 shows the various uses of the brackets.

Example 10.3.1 Bracket usage

```
int offset = 2;
int test_scores[5];          // 5 elements referenced 0 - 4
test_scores[0] = 94;         // 0 offset or first array element
test_scores[1] = 89;         // 1 offset or second array element
test_scores[offset] = 65;    // 2 offset or third array element
```

Array Declaration: `int test_scores[5];`

	OFFSET	0	1	2	3	4
	test_scores					
MEMORY ADDRESSES		1000	1004	1008	1012	1016

Figure 10.3.1 Memory layout of an array

In Example 10.3.1, the number placed within the brackets in the second line declares that the array will have five elements. In the case of our variable `test_scores`, we have now indicated that we need an array big enough to hold five different test scores. These five elements will be referenced with an offset from zero to four.

In the third line, the 0 represents the offset from the start of the array. In this case, the value 94 is being assigned into the contents of the first element of `test_scores`, which is at offset 0. Likewise, in the next line the value 89 is being assigned to the variable `test_scores` at offset, or sub, 1. The term *sub* is shorthand for *subscript*, which programmers often use in place of *element*. For example, the statement `test_scores[3]` is often read as "test_scores sub three." In the last line of Example 10.3.1, a variable is used to access an element of the array. Although a constant or literal must be used in the brackets when the array is declared, variables can be used within the subscript operator to access a specific element.

When referencing a specific element, be careful not to go beyond the bounds of the array. There is nothing to stop you from doing so; however, you *will not* like the resulting problems. A few of the problems associated with going out of bounds follow.

1. Incorrect data can occur—not just in the array but in other variables.

2. The program could immediately terminate or crash with a runtime error.

3. The program could crash upon exiting.

The first problem can occur because two variables for your program could happen to reside next to each other. If you go out of bounds of your array, you would overwrite the next memory location, thus changing the other variable. This is an extremely tough error to find, and it should be avoided at all costs. If it does happen, however, use your debugger to help find the error. Figure 10.3.2 shows how the array `test_scores` and the variable `var_a` might look in memory.

Notice that all subscripts are within the appropriate range, 0–4, in Figure 10.3.2. In Figure 10.3.3, however, we have made the mistake of accidentally overwriting one of our variables by referencing an element outside the bounds of the array.

In Figure 10.3.3, notice that `test_scores[5]` is out of bounds. The actual contents are indeterminate, and the execution of this statement will *sometimes* cause the following runtime error to be displayed:

```
Run-Time Check Failure #2 - Stack around the variable
'test_scores' was corrupted.
```

```
int test_scores[5];   // 5 elements (0 - 4)
int var_a = 10;

test_scores[0] = 94;  // 0 offset or array element
test_scores[1] = 89;  // 1 offset or array element
```

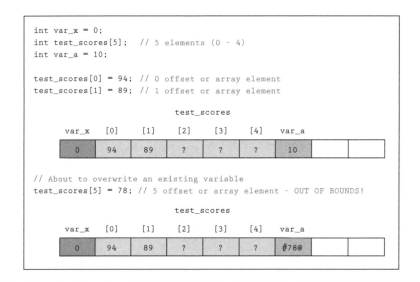

Figure 10.3.2 Memory layout of an array and a single variable

```
int var_x = 0;
int test_scores[5];   // 5 elements (0 - 4)
int var_a = 10;

test_scores[0] = 94;  // 0 offset or array element
test_scores[1] = 89;  // 1 offset or array element
```

```
// About to overwrite an existing variable
test_scores[5] = 78;  // 5 offset or array element - OUT OF BOUNDS!
```

Figure 10.3.3 Memory layout of an array that goes out of bounds

Both C and C++ were designed to be used by experienced programmers. As a result, the compiler assumes the programmer knows what he or she is doing, even if a mistake is sometimes made. The compiler will not provide a warning that you are about to create your own problem. As you can see in Figure 10.3.3, by taking a quick peek under the hood, we can see—and avoid—a potentially dangerous situation.

 Remember: Be very careful that you do not go outside the bounds of your array.

When your program executes and is placed in memory, it is given a specific area in memory for its use. Going outside this area demonstrates the second problem and causes your program to immediately crash with a runtime error. This type of error isn't too difficult to find. Simply step through the program until it crashes, stop debugging, and then run to the place where it crashed and examine all variables around that section of code.

The third error is probably one of the most difficult runtime errors to find. This happens when you go out of bounds of your array but it lands in an area of memory not used at this time. When the program exits, the area around your program is checked for integrity. If you have written into this unused area, the program will crash. The reason this is such a difficult error to find is that there can be a significant distance, in both time and space, between the introduction of the error and when we become aware of the error. If your program behaves in this manner, use the debugger to check each of your array subscripts to make sure they aren't out of bounds. As should be clear by now, a little extra time ensuring you don't go out of bounds of your arrays can save a lot of frustration and a considerable amount of time debugging.

Section 10.3 Exercises

Please respond to each of the following questions.

1. To access a specific element in an array, you must use the _____ operator.

   a. subscript   b. offset   c. dimension   d. modules

2. The beginning element of an array is at offset _____.

   a. 0   b. 1   c. 2   d. unknown

Based on the following array declaration, please respond to questions 3–6:

```
int sample[5];
```

3. What would be the largest subscript you should use when referencing an element of the array `sample`?

   a. 0   b. 1   c. 4   d. 5

4. What would be the smallest subscript you should use when referencing an element of the array `sample`?

   a. 0   b. 1   c. 4   d. 5

5. How many different integers can be held in `sample`?

   a. 0   b. 1   c. 4   d. 5

6. Indicate whether each of the following statements is logically valid or invalid based on our previous declaration of `sample`.

   a. `sample[0] = 1;`

   b. `sample[1] = 2;`

   c. `sample[5] = 3;`

   d. `const int r = 4;`
      `sample[r] = 0;`

7. Indicate whether each of the following statements is true or false.

   a. An expression can be used as a subscript.

   b. The last element you should reference in an array is the same value used to declare the array.

   c. Making a reference to an element outside the bounds of an array is likely to cause the programmer a great deal of time and perhaps frustration.

   d. All of the elements contained within an individual array have the same physical size.

10.4 Initialization

Like any other variable, arrays can be initialized. The syntax of array initialization is as follows.

```
1. <data-type> <name> [ <number-elements> ] = { val1, val2,
   ... };
2. <data-type> <name> [ ] = { val1, val2, ... };
```

In the first syntax diagram, you can specify up to `<number-elements>` number of values. If you provide fewer values than the number of elements, remaining elements will be allocated but the values will be unknown or garbage. Some compilers, such as Visual Studio, may initialize the rest of the elements to 0; however, you should not depend on this happening. The second syntax uses the actual number of values in the braces to determine the size of the array. If there are 10 values, there will be 10 elements allocated for the array. Example 10.4.1 demonstrates how to initialize arrays.

Example 10.4.1 Initializing arrays

```
int nums[5] = {0, 1, 2, 3, 4};
float reaction_times[] = {0.005F, 0.001F};
char grades[5] = {'A', 'B', 'C', 'D', 'F'};
int frequency_counts[5] = {1};
```

Notice the declaration of `frequency_counts` only uses a single value for initialization. The first element will be initialized to 1, but in some environments, the rest of the elements will be initialized to 0.

STYLE NOTE ▶ The initialization method in which we explicitly specify the number of elements is the preferred approach, which makes it easy to determine the total number of elements allocated for the array. Calculating the number of elements when not explicitly specified requires you to either count the values or perform the calculation shown in Example 10.4.2.

Example 10.4.2 Determining the number of elements in an array at runtime

```
int test_scores[] = {85, 92, 83};// No value specified for array size

int num_elements = sizeof( test_scores ) / sizeof( int );

cout << "num_elements = " << num_elements;

// Output
num_elements = 3
```

Section 10.4 Exercises

Please respond to each of the following questions.

1. What would be the value in `numA[1]` based on the following declaration?

   ```
   int numA[5] = {0, 1, 2, 3, 4};
   ```

   a. unknown   b. 0   c. 1   d. 4

2. Write a `for` loop to find the average of all the elements in the array `numA` in Exercise 1.

3. What would be the value in `numB[2]` based on the following declaration?

   ```
   int numB[5] = {0};
   ```

   a. unknown   b. 0   c. 1   d. 4

4. What would be the value in `numC[3]` based on the following declaration?

   ```
   int numC[5] = {0, 1, 2};
   ```

   a. unknown   b. 0   c. 1   d. 4

5. What would be the value in `num_elements` based on the following code fragment?

   ```
   char letter_grades[6] = { 'A', 'B', 'C', 'D', 'F' };

   int num_elements = sizeof( letter_grades ) / sizeof( char );
   ```

   a. unknown   b. 4   c. 5   d. 6

6. Write the necessary statement to create an array to hold the days in each of the 12 months of the year and to initialize each element with the correct number of days for each respective month (assuming a non–leap year).

10.5 Array Manipulation

With one exception, which we will discuss later in this chapter, you must read and write arrays one element at a time. As a result, the use of loops becomes a crucial tool in performing operations, especially those involving input and output. As illustrated in Example 10.5.1, `for` loops are a natural choice when manipulating arrays because they are generally used for specific numbers of iterations.

Example 10.5.1 Using a `for` loop with arrays

```
const int NUMBER_STUDENTS = 25;
int test_scores[NUMBER_STUDENTS];
```

```
for ( int i = 0; i < NUMBER_STUDENTS; i++ )
{
    cout << "Enter Test Score #" << i + 1 << ": ";
    cin >> test_scores[i];
}
```

As you can see in Example 10.5.1, using a constant for the number of elements has become even more important. If the array was declared using a literal instead of a constant and you modified the array bounds, you would need to change each loop that is used to access the array. By declaring a global constant and using that constant in the condition of the loop, all you would need to do is change the constant declaration and recompile.

> **Remember:** A `for` loop is generally used when you need to repeat statements a specific number of times.

Another thing to notice in Example 10.5.1 is that this loop requires you to enter 25 test scores. However, many situations do not require the use of all the elements. Example 10.5.2 shows a solution to this problem.

Example 10.5.2 Using a portion of an array's elements

```
int values[MAX_VALUES] = {0};
int num_values = 0;
char enter_another = 'n';
do
{
    cout << "Enter a value: ";
    cin >> values[num_values++];

    cout << "Enter another value (y/n)? ";
    cin >> enter_another;

} while ( toupper( enter_another ) == 'Y' && num_values < MAX_VALUES );
```

In Example 10.5.2, the loop terminates either when the maximum number of values is entered or when the user chooses to quit. Regardless of which portion of the condition causes the loop to terminate, the variable `num_values` will hold the number of elements used in the array. Therefore, the variable containing the actual number of elements must be used when accessing the array, as shown in Example 10.5.3.

Example 10.5.3 Accessing a portion of an array's elements

```
for ( int i = 0; i < num_values; i++ )
    sum += values[i];
```

Section 10.5 Exercises

Please respond to each of the following questions.

1. What would be displayed based on the following section of code?

```
char letters[] = {'A', 'B', 'C', 'D', 'E', 'F', 'G'};
for ( int i = 0; i < 3; i++ )
    cout << " " << letters[i];
```

2. What would be displayed based on the following section of code?

```
const int SIZE = 3;
int nums[SIZE] = {1, 10, 20};

for ( int i = 0; i < SIZE; i++ )
    nums[i] = nums[i] * nums[i];

cout << " " << nums[1];
```

Section 10.5 Learn by Doing Exercise

1. Write a program that uses an array to store 10 elements, representing 10 students' test scores that will be entered from the keyboard. Given the following grading scale, iterate through the array, determine the letter grade each score will receive, and store the grade in a corresponding character array.

   A >= 92.0   B >= 84.0   C >= 75.0   D >= 65.0   F < 65.0

Display the numeric score and the corresponding letter grade. Also calculate and display the class average as well as the number of students that receive each letter grade. For the purposes of this exercise, everything should be done from `main`.

10.6 Passing Arrays to Functions

Like any other variable, arrays can be passed to functions. But are they passed by value and reference like any other variable? Afraid not. Since the name of an array is associated with its beginning address, arrays are actually *passed by pointer*. Passing by pointer is very similar to passing by reference. The nuances between the two forms will not be discussed at this point, but Chapter 12 should clear up any issues regarding passing by pointer.

At this time all you really need to be concerned with is the fact that any changes made to the array inside the function are permanent and thus retained when the function ends. This is because you have the address of the array. A rule in C and C++ programming is that if you have access to the address of a memory location, you have the capability to change what is stored at that address. Since we pass the address of an array, the function can change any values in the array.

There is a very good reason why both C and C++ pass arrays by pointer. Think about how much overhead it would take to make a copy of a very large array. You would need to make a copy, which would not only take time but also double the memory usage. With passing by pointer, however, you only need to pass the address, which is four bytes. The problem with passing by pointer is that it becomes a little less safe. Functions could change the array when you really wouldn't want them to have that capability. Fortunately, as you will soon see, there is a way around this pitfall. Example 10.6.1 shows how arrays are passed to functions.

Example 10.6.1 Function declarations and calls

```
// Function declarations
int GetValues( int values[] );
float CalculateMean( int values[], int num_values );
int FindMode( int values[], int num_values );

// Function calls passing arrays
num_values = GetValues( values );
mean = CalculateMean( values, num_values );
mode = FindMode( values, num_values );
```

In Example 10.6.1, the brackets in the function declarations are empty. Although it is legal to specify the number of elements in the array, it usually isn't done. If you do specify the number of elements in the brackets, all references to the array size must match. Although it doesn't change the performance of your program, it is stylistically better not to include the array size in the header and declaration.

All of the functions in Example 10.6.1 are passed the beginning address of the array. However, what if you only wanted to pass one element of the array? This process is shown in Example 10.6.2.

Example 10.6.2 Passing an element of an array

```
// Function declarations
void Fun1( int element_by_value );
void Fun2( int & element_by_reference );

// Function calls passing (by reference) arrays
Fun1( values[0] );
Fun2( values[1] );
```

Notice that the actual parameters are not arrays but one element in the array. Since each element in the array is an integer, passing a specific element of this array requires you to catch an integer. In Example 10.6.2, we passed the element by value to `Fun1`, but we could just as easily have passed the element by reference, as we did in `Fun2`. One common mistake is to place empty brackets in the call when passing arrays. This is syntactically incorrect; the only time brackets should be present in the call is when you are passing an element of the array.

To further demonstrate the process of passing arrays, we have provided a complete program in Examples 10.6.3 and 10.6.4.

Example 10.6.3 Putting it all together (Part 1)

```
#include <iostream>
using std::cout;
using std::cin;
using std::endl;

const int MAX_VALUES = 25;

int GetValues( int values[] );
float CalculateMean( int values[], int num_values );
int FindMode( int values[], int num_values );

int main()
{
```

```
    int values[MAX_VALUES] = {0}, num_values = 0, mode = 0;
    float mean = 0;

    num_values = GetValues( values );
    mean = CalculateMean( values, num_values );
    mode = FindMode( values, num_values );

    cout << "Mean = " << mean << endl;
    cout << "Mode = " << mode << endl;

    return 0;
}
```

Example 10.6.4 Putting it all together (Part 2)

```
int GetValues( int values[] )
{
    int num_values = 0;
    char enter_more = 'n';

    do
    {
        cout << "Enter a value: ";
        cin >> values[num_values++];

        cout << "Enter another value (y/n)? ";
        cin >> enter_more;

    } while ( toupper( enter_more ) == 'Y' &&
            num_values < MAX_VALUES );

    return num_values;
}

int FindMode( int values[], int num_values )
{
    int mode;
    int count, oldcount = 0;

    // Searching through the array for the most
    // commonly used number
    for ( int i = 0; i < num_values; i++ )
    {
        count = 1;
```

```
        for ( int j = i + 1; j < num_values; j++ )
        {
            if ( values[i] == values[j] )
                count++;
        }
        if ( count > oldcount )
        {
            mode = values[i];
            oldcount = count;
        }
    }
    return mode;
}

float CalculateMean( int values[], int num_values )
{
    float sum = 0;

    for ( int i = 0; i < num_values; i++ )
        sum += values[i];

    return sum / num_values;
}
```

Please spend some time examining the code in Examples 10.6.3 and 10.6.4. The code pulls all of the pieces from the previous sections into a fairly cohesive program.

One final point we need to make in relation to passing arrays to functions involves the use of the reserved word `const`. As discussed in Chapter 4, prefacing a variable with the word `const` indicates that once it is initialized, its value cannot be changed. When used with a formal parameter that is an array, `const` provides us with a method that prevents the body of the function from changing or altering the contents of our array. In essence, we have now achieved both the efficiency associated with passing our array by pointer and the safety of passing our array by value. Example 10.6.5 shows how we can make our array unchangeable by including the word `const` in both the function declaration and the function header.

Example 10.6.5 Using `const` **with arrays**

```
// Function Call
DisplayValues( values, num_values );
```

```
// Function Definition
void DisplayValues( const int values[], int num_values )
{
    for ( int i = 0; i < num_values; i++ )
        cout << values[i] << ' ';

    // The following line of code is invalid because
    // the array cannot be changed
    // values[0] = 99;
}
```

In Example 10.6.5 it is invalid to try to change the array because it is caught as a `const`, which is slightly different than passing by value. Passing a variable by value allows you to make as many changes as necessary to the formal parameter—changes that just go away when the function ends. By catching the array with `const`, no changes can be made at all.

Another thing to be aware of is that it is illegal to return an array from a function. This makes a lot of sense if you remember that arrays can't appear on the left side of an assignment operator. Even if you could return an array, how would you catch it?

Section 10.6 Exercises

Please respond to each of the following questions.

1. By default, an array is passed by _____.

    a. value   b. reference   c. constant   d. pointer

2. Which of the following would be the correct way to pass an array declared as `int ids[10];` to the function `Sample`?

    a. `Sample( ids );`   b. `Sample(ids[] );`

    c. `Sample( int ids[10] );`   d. `Sample( int ids );`

3. What would be the correct way to write the declaration for a function called `Sample` that returns no value and receives an array of 10 integers called `ids`?

    a. `void Sample( ids );`   b. `void Sample( ids[] );`

    c. `void Sample( int ids[] );`   d. `void Sample( int ids );`

4. Indicate whether each of the following statements is true or false.

    a. If an array is passed to a function, any changes or alterations made to the array within the body of the function are permanent and remain even after you leave the function.

    b. It is not possible to pass only one specific value or element of an array to a function.

    c. If you pass an array of integers to a function, you must catch an array of integers.

5. Assuming we declared an array as `int ages[5]`, explain what is happening in the following function call.

```
Sample( ages[2] );
```

6. Based on the information provided in the previous question and assuming that the function returns no value, please write the function declaration for `Sample`.

7. Explain the purpose of using the reserved word `const` in front of an identifier contained within a function declaration and header.

Section 10.6 Learn by Doing Exercise

1. Rewrite the program in the Learn by Doing Exercise in Section 10.5. Break the program into functions so that it adheres to a good modular design.

10.7 Special Case: cStrings

Up to this point we haven't discussed how to read or store strings or how to write strings other than string literals, placing an obvious limit on what we've been able to do with our programs.

In order to add the functionality of strings to our programs, we will use a special form of a character array called a *cString*. A cString is a null-terminated character array that can be used to store strings. As we mentioned in Chapter 4, the null character—ASCII value 0—is represented as '\0'. When this character is placed within a character array, the array becomes a cString. Figure 10.7.1 demonstrates the use of the null character within an array.

Figure 10.7.1 shows how the variable `first_name` might look in memory containing the string "Willy". Notice that `first_name[5]` contains the terminating null character, marking the end of the string.

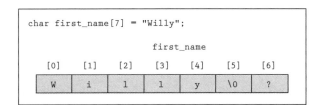

Figure 10.7.1 Memory containing a cString

i

A **cString** is a C-style, null-terminated, character array.

In the C++ world and in this text, the older C-style strings are often referred to as cStrings, since they are the only means by which C is able to use strings. C++ has an additional method, which we will cover later in this text.

When declaring a character array to be used as a cString, you must allocate one extra element to hold the null character. For example, if storing first names with an assumed maximum length of 15 characters, we would need to declare a character array with 16 elements, to allow room for the null character. As you will come to see, cStrings require special care and attention to ensure that there is room for the null. To reemphasize: cStrings require a terminating null character, but all other types of arrays—including character arrays not used as cStrings—*do not* have this requirement.

10.7.1 cString Initialization

At this point you could probably initialize a cString with the knowledge you have gained in the previous sections. A good guess might be what is shown in Figure 10.7.2; notice the inclusion of the terminating null character.

Although the method demonstrated in Figure 10.7.2 would work, it would be much better to initialize the array as shown in Figure 10.7.3. Notice that the memory used in storing our cString would be exactly the same, regardless of the method chosen.

!

Remember: A string literal can only be used to initialize a cString. A cString can never appear on the left of an assignment operator, therefore it is illegal to assign a string literal to a cString.

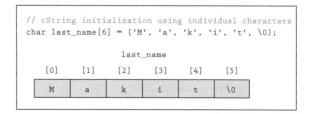

Figure 10.7.2 Initializing a cString character by character

```
// cString initialization using a string literal
char last_name[6] = "Makit";

                    last_name
        [0]   [1]   [2]   [3]   [4]   [5]
       | M  |  a  |  k  |  i  |  t  | \0 |
```

Figure 10.7.3 Initializing a cString using a string literal

10.7.2 I/O with cStrings

Fortunately, `cin` and `cout` work seamlessly with cStrings. On the surface, there isn't really much difference in how `cin` and `cout` deal with cStrings. Underneath the hood, however, these I/O routines behave a little differently, as shown in Example 10.7.1.

Example 10.7.1 Using `cin` and `cout` with cStrings

```
// Room for 15 characters + null character
char last_name[16];

cout << "Please enter the last name: ";
cin >> last_name;

cout << "Last Name: " << last_name << endl;

// Output
Please enter the last name: Makit
Last Name: Makit
```

When used with cStrings, `cout` takes the address given and prints to the output buffer, character by character, until the null character is encountered. This is one reason why it is critical that the null character always be present in any cString. If there isn't a null character in the cString, `cout` will continue to print until you stop the program, the program crashes, or `cout` just happens to find a null character. Any of these situations is obviously undesirable.

The `cin` statement reads from the input buffer one character at a time, storing each in the cString variable. This continues until a whitespace character is read. The `cin` then places a null character at the next character location, terminating the cString.

One problem using `cin` is that it uses whitespace to delimit the input, therefore making it impossible to read a space from the keyboard. Another problem arises when the user enters too many characters at the keyboard. The `cin` statement will still read all of the characters up to the first whitespace, even if it means going out of bounds of your array. As discussed earlier, this is a highly undesirable situation.

There is another form of input that doesn't have the limitations of `cin`. This form allows you to specify the maximum number of characters to be read and also stops reading from the input buffer when the newline character is encountered or the maximum length, minus 1, is reached. This new form of reading input is shown in Example 10.7.2.

Example 10.7.2 Using `.getline` to read a group of characters

```
// Room for up to 80 characters + null character
char whole_name[81];

cout << "Please enter your whole name: ";
cin.getline( whole_name, 81 );   // getline with 2 parameters

cout << "Here is the whole name: " <<  whole_name << endl;

// Output
Please enter your whole name: I. M. Sample
Here is the whole name: I. M. Sample
```

As you probably noticed in Example 10.7.2, `.getline` is a member function of `cin`, just as `.width` and `.precision` are member functions of `cout`. The `.getline` method reads from the input buffer until the carriage return is encountered or until the maximum number of characters, minus 1, is reached.

An optional form of `.getline` allows you to change the default delimiter from the carriage return to a programmer-specified character. This form is shown in Example 10.7.3.

Example 10.7.3 Using `.getline` with a programmer-specified delimiter

```
// Room for up to 80 characters + null character
char whole_name[81];
```

```
cout << "Please enter your whole name: ";
cin.getline( whole_name, 81, '-' );  // getline with 3 parameters

cout << "Here is the whole name: " <<  whole_name << endl;

// Output
Please enter your whole name: Lori Murray-Smith
Here is the whole name: Lori Murray
```

In Example 10.7.3, an additional parameter has been added to the `.getline` member function. This parameter, `'-'`, changes the character that terminates the input from the default carriage return to the dash. Notice how this change affects the processing of the input. Reading from the input buffer stops as soon as the dash is encountered. Therefore, everything before the dash is stored in the cString `whole_name`, while the rest of the input is left in the buffer.

One potential problem with `.getline` is what happens if there is already a carriage return in the input buffer. The `.getline` function will read the carriage return, assume its job is done, and then continue on without the user being able to enter anything at the keyboard. So where could that carriage return come from? Many places, but the most common is from other `cin` statements. For example, if your program asks for your age, and you enter 20 and press the enter key to signify that you are done, all three keys that you pressed go into the input buffer. The 2 and the 0 are read from the input buffer and stored in your variable, but because `cin` is whitespace delimited, the enter key is left in the input buffer. Therefore, when `.getline` is executed, the enter key is the first character waiting in the buffer.

Another problem is created if the user typed too many characters at the keyboard the last time a `.getline` function executed. The maximum number of characters specified in the function call are read and stored in the cString variable while the rest of the characters are left in the buffer. Therefore, when the next `.getline` function executes, the user, once again, doesn't get to enter anything from the keyboard because `.getline` reads all of the existing information from the input buffer.

Is there a way to flush the input buffer like we saw with the output buffer in Chapter 5 in relation to the `.flush` member function or the `flush` manipulator? Yes, but unfortunately not nearly as simple. The code in Example 10.7.4 will flush the input buffer before and after the `.getline` function call.

Example 10.7.4 Flushing the input buffer with the `.ignore` function

```
char whole_name[81];

cout << "Please enter your whole name: ";
```

```
cin.ignore( cin.rdbuf()->in_avail() );  // Flush input buffer
cin.getline( whole_name, 81 );
cin.clear();
cin.ignore( cin.rdbuf()->in_avail() );  // Flush input buffer

cout << "Here is the whole name: " <<  whole_name << endl;
```

In Example 10.7.4, we flush the buffer before and after our call to `.get-line`. The first `.ignore` cleans the buffer prior to the `.getline` call. The second flush is used to clean any remaining characters in the buffer after the `.getline` function has executed. What exactly is that nasty looking line of code doing? Unfortunately, any detailed explanation at this point would probably be meaningless. The simple explanation is that the line of code flushes the input buffer. A little more detailed explanation is that the `.ignore` member function removes a certain number of characters from the keyboard buffer. Everything in the parentheses for the `.ignore` function call allows us to find the number of characters currently in the keyboard buffer. Although not intuitive, `.getline` sets a flag if it reads the maximum number of characters. If this happens, the `.clear` function call is required to reset any flags that may have been set by the `.getline` function.

Based on the previous discussion, it may appear that `.getline` is more trouble than it's worth. In reality, however, `.getline` is *much* safer for reading cStrings from the keyboard than `cin` is.

> **Remember:** Using `cin` allows us to read one word at a time. The `.getline` method allows us to read a sentence.

10.7.3 cStrings and the "address-of" Operator

When explaining how `cout` worked with cStrings, we stated that `cout` takes the address given, prints one character at a time starting from that address, and continues until the null character is encountered. Therefore, if we could get the address of one of the elements other than the first, we could print a portion of the cString. The operator used to do this is called the *address-of operator* and is represented by a single ampersand (&).

Don't confuse the address-of operator and the reference operator. The address-of operator returns an address of its operand, which, by the way, can be any identifier. The reference operator is usually associated with passing arguments to functions and makes an alias to another variable. At this point, a reference operator will only appear in the header or declaration of a function.

Example 10.7.5 illustrates how to use the address-of operator to print a portion of a cString.

Example 10.7.5 Using the address-of operator with cStrings

```
char first_name[7] = "Alexis";

for ( int i = 0; i < 7; i++ )
    cout << &first_name[i] << endl;

cout << "End Sample" << endl;

// Output
Alexis
lexis
exis
xis
is
s

End Sample
```

Section 10.7 Exercises

Please respond to each of the following questions.

1. A null-terminated character array is referred to as a _____.

   a. variable   b. cString   c. vector   d. problem

2. Assuming you wanted to create a cString to hold a maximum of 15 characters for an ID, how big would you need to declare your array?

   a. 14   b. 15   c. 16   d. unknown

3. Which of the following statements would correctly declare and initialize our cString array called `name`?

   a. `char name[5] = {'s', 'a', 'l', 'l', 'y'};`

   b. `char name[] = "Sally";`

   c. `char name[6] = "Sally";`

   d. `char name[] = {'s', 'a', 'l', 'l', 'y', '\0'};`

   e. `char name[5] = "Sally";`

4. Indicate whether each of the following statements is true or false.

   a. The `cin` statement reads from the input buffer one character at a time until a whitespace character is encountered or read.

   b. When reading data from the keyboard, `cin` places a null character immediately after the last character read, thus terminating the cString.

   c. Assuming that both `name1` and `name2` are declared as cStrings of equal length, the following statement would copy the contents from `name2` to `name1`.

   ```
   name1 = name2;
   ```

   d. Assuming you declared a cString called `name1`, the following statement is valid.

   ```
   name1 = "Jamie";
   ```

   e. One of the most important things you must remember is not to reference an element of an array outside the bounds of the array.

5. When using `cout` with cStrings, the output buffer is printed character-by-character until _____ is reached.

   a. the end of the array
   b. a space character
   c. a period character
   d. the null character

6. What is the name of the method for reading characters from the input buffer until either a carriage return is encountered or the maximum number of characters, minus one, is achieved?

   a. `cin`
   b. `cout`
   c. `.getline`
   d. `.ignore`

7. What is the overall purpose of the rather complex line of code that follows?

   ```
   cin.ignore( cin.rdbuf()->in_avail() );
   ```

   a. flush the input buffer
   b. flush the output buffer
   c. clear out a cString array
   d. impress your friends

8. Declare a cString called `first_name`, one called `last_name`, and another called `temp_name`. Make sure they can each hold up to 15 individual characters. Initialize `first_name` to your first name and the other two cStrings to 0.

Section 10.7 Learn by Doing Exercises

1. Write a program that prompts for the user's first and last names. Use the `toupper` function to ensure that the first character of each name is uppercase. Then display a cordial greeting including their whole name.

2. Write a program that prompts for the user's first and last names. Declare a third array that will hold the user's last name and first name, separated by a comma and a space. Use loops to iterate through the names one character at a time, storing them into the full name array. Don't forget about the terminating character.

3. Modify the Learn by Doing Exercises from Sections 10.5 and 10.6. Add a function that prompts for the course number (e.g., CST 116) and your professor's name (e.g., Dr. Sherry Yang). When the results of the program are displayed, use the new information as part of the report's title.

10.8 cString Functions

There are some limitations as to what we can do with cStrings because of the way they are implemented in C++. As discussed earlier, it is syntactically incorrect to place a cString on the left side of an assignment operator. So how do we place strings into cString variables other than through initialization? There are many predefined cString functions accessible through the <cstring> header file that perform some of these basic manipulations. These functions all expect at least one cString parameter. The following sections discuss some of the more popular cString functions available. Check your online help for more functions.

> **Remember:** The cString functions manipulate arrays of characters terminated by the null character.

In the previous discussion, we stated that there was some limitation as to what we can do with cStrings and operators. These limitations arise because the name of an array references its beginning address. Example 10.8.1 illustrates the incorrect method of comparing two strings using the relation equality operator.

Example 10.8.1 Incorrect comparison

```
char str1[15] = "Troy";
char str2[15] = "Troy";
```

```
if ( str1 == str2 ) // DON'T DO THIS
    cout << "Your name is Troy.";
else
    cout << "Your name is Mud.";

// Output
Your name is Mud.
```

Even though the two string values are the same, the relational operator compares the two addresses, not the strings. Since the arrays will *never* have the same address, this statement will always be false.

10.8.1 Copying

As already stated, we can't assign a cString or string literal to another cString. We can, however, use a couple of predefined functions to accomplish this task. The basic syntax follows:

```
strcpy ( <destination>, <source> );
strncpy ( <destination>, <source>, <number-characters> );
```

Both functions copy up to and including the null character from the source to the destination. The destination must be a cString variable, but the source can be either a cString or a string literal. The second function differs from the first in that it needs a third parameter—an integer value specifying how many characters to copy from the source to the destination. Example 10.8.2 illustrates both the `strcpy` and the `strncpy` functions.

Example 10.8.2 Using `strcpy` **and** `strncpy`

```
char holder_1[10] = {0}; // initializing all elements to 0 (null)
char holder_2[10] = {0}; // initializing all elements to 0 (null)
char part_1[10] = "Hello ";
char part_2[10] = "World";

// Example 1 - strcpy
strcpy( holder_1, part_1 );
cout << "holder_1 is: " << holder_1
     << " and part_1 is: " << part_1 << endl;

// Example 2 - strncpy
strncpy( holder_2, part_2, 3 );
```

```
cout << "holder_2 is: " << holder_2
     << " and part_2 is: " << part_2 << endl;

// Output
holder_1 is: Hello  and part_1 is: Hello
holder_2 is: Wor and part_2 is: World
```

10.8.2 Appending

We can also use a couple of functions to append one cString or string literal to another cString.

```
strcat ( <destination>, <source> );
strncat ( <destination>, <source>, <number-characters> );
```

These functions behave in much the same manner as the copy functions. The only difference is that these functions concatenate, or append, the source onto the end of the destination. Remember: the second function will only append the number of characters specified from the beginning of the source onto the end of the destination. Example 10.8.3 uses strcat to append one cString onto another.

> **Remember:** Make sure the destination cString has the necessary room to hold all the characters from both cString parameters and the required terminating null.

Example 10.8.3 Using strcpy and strcat

```
// Room for 15 characters + null character
char last_name[16];
char first_name[16];
char whole_name[32];   // make sure you have enough room

cout << "Please enter the first name: ";
cin >> first_name;

cout << "Please enter the last name: ";
cin >> last_name;

strcpy( whole_name, first_name );
strcat( whole_name, " " );  // adding a space after the first name
strcat( whole_name, last_name );

cout << "The whole name is: " << whole_name << endl;
```

```
// Output
Please enter the first name: Willy
Please enter the last name: Makit
The whole name is: Willy Makit
```

10.8.3 Comparing

If we used relational operators to compare two cStrings, all it would do is compare the addresses of the two operands. Typically, it is necessary to compare the contents of two cStrings or string literals, not the addresses. Four functions can be used to accomplish this, the syntax of which follows:

```
<int-var> = strcmp ( <str1>, <str2> );
<int-var> = strncmp ( <str1>, <str2>, <number-characters> );
<int-var> = stricmp ( <str1>, <str2> );
<int-var> = strnicmp ( <str1>, <str2>, <number-characters> );
```

All of these functions return one of three different values, as shown in Table 10.8.1.

So how can one cString be less than another? By comparing ASCII values. These functions compare character by character until they encounter a difference between two characters. The functions then compare the ASCII values of the two characters. That is how the results of the table are computed.

i Character-by-character comparison is often called **lexical analysis**.

The *i* in the `stricmp` and `strnicmp` functions means to *i*gnore the case while doing the comparisons. The following examples illustrate the use of the compare functions. Please review each of the examples and the related output. Example 10.8.4 demonstrates the `strcmp` function.

Return Value	Relationship of str1 to str2
< 0	str1 less than str2
0	str1 equals str2
> 0	str1 greater than str2

Table 10.8.1 Return values from compare functions

Example 10.8.4 The `strcmp` **function**

```
// Holds return value from string compare functions
int result;

char string_1[] = "Jamie";
char string_2[] = "Jaime";

cout << "\nComparing: \t" << string_1
     << "\nwith: \t\t" << string_2 << "\n\n";

result = strcmp( string_1, string_2 );

if ( result > 0 )
    cout << "string_1 is greater than string_2 above\n";
else if ( result < 0 )
    cout << "string_2 is greater than string_1 above\n";
else
    cout << "string_1 is identical to string_2 above\n";

// Output
Comparing:      Jamie
with:           Jaime

string_1 is greater than string_2 above
```

Example 10.8.4 demonstrates that the two names are not equal. Furthermore, since the two names differ at the third character, the *m* has a greater ASCII value than the *i*. Therefore, `string_1` is greater than `string_2`. Example 10.8.5 demonstrates the `strncmp` function.

Example 10.8.5 The `strncmp` **function**

```
int result;
char string_1[] = "Jamie";

cout << "\nComparing: \t" << string_1
     << "\nwith: \t\tJames\n\n";

result = strncmp( string_1, "James", 3 );
```

```
if ( result > 0 )
    cout << "string_1 is greater than James above\n";
else if (result < 0)
    cout << "James is greater than string_1 above\n";
else
    cout << "string_1 is identical to string literal James\n";

// Output
Comparing:      Jamie
with:           James

string_1 is identical to string literal James
```

In Example 10.8.5, the output specifies that the two strings are identical. This is because we only compared the first three characters. If we had used strcmp, string_1 would have been greater than James. Example 10.8.6 shows how the case of the characters is related to the ASCII chart.

Example 10.8.6 Case-sensitive comparison

```
int result;
char upper_string[] = "MARIE";
char lower_string[] = "marie";

cout << "\nComparing: \t" << upper_string
     << "\nwith: \t\t" << lower_string << "\n\n";

result = strcmp( upper_string, lower_string );

if ( result > 0 )
    cout << "upper_string is greater than lower_string above\n";
else if ( result < 0 )
    cout << "lower_string is greater than upper_string above\n";
else
    cout << "upper_string is identical to lower_string above\n";

// Output
Comparing:      MARIE
with:           marie

lower_string is greater than upper_string above
```

The results in Example 10.8.6 may not be what you expected. We tend to think of uppercase characters as being bigger than lowercase characters. Remember, however, that one of the oddities of the ASCII table is that upper-case letters come before lowercase letters. Therefore, a lowercase *m* has a greater value than an uppercase *M*. Example 10.8.7 shows how to accomplish a case-insensitive comparison.

Example 10.8.7 Case-insensitive comparison

```
int result;
char upper_string[] = "MARIE";
char lower_string[] = "marie";

cout << "\nComparing: \t" << upper_string
     << "\nwith: \t\t" << lower_string << "\n\n";

result = stricmp( upper_string, lower_string );

if ( result > 0 )
    cout << "upper_string is greater than lower_string above\n";
else if ( result < 0 )
    cout << "lower_string is greater than upper_string above\n";
else
    cout << "upper_string is identical to lower_string above\n";

// Output
Comparing:      MARIE
with:           marie

upper_string is identical to lower_string above
```

Example 10.8.7 uses the stricmp function to achieve a case-insensitive comparison. All of these comparison examples show the nuances involved in comparing strings. These functions will become valuable tools for you in the near future.

10.8.4 Finding the Length

Another useful function is `strlen`, which returns the number of characters preceding the null character. The syntax of the `strlen` function is:

```
<size_t-variable> = strlen ( <cString> );
```

The return type of the `strlen` function is a variable of type `size_t`. This data type equates to an `unsigned int`, which makes sense because we can never have a negative length. Example 10.8.8 shows a couple of different uses associated with the `strlen` function.

Example 10.8.8 Using `strlen`

```
// Example 1
size_t len;
char string_1[] = "Hello World";
len = strlen( string_1 );
cout << "The string \"" << string_1
    << "\" is " << len << " characters\n\n";

// Example 2
cout << "The length of the string literal Rock and Roll is "
    << strlen( "Rock and Roll" ) << " characters\n";

//Output
The string "Hello World" is 11 characters

The length of the string literal Rock and Roll is 13 characters
```

10.8.5 Changing the Case

We introduced a couple of functions, `toupper` and `tolower`, in Chapter 9 that allow you to change the case of a single character. There are a couple of functions that perform the same task but on an entire cString. The syntax of these functions is as follows:

```
strupr ( <cString> );
strlwr ( <cString> );
```

Notice that unlike `toupper` and `tolower`, these functions permanently change the parameter itself. Example 10.8.9 demonstrates both the `strupr` and the `strlwr` functions.

Example 10.8.9 Using `strupr` **and** `strlwr`

```
char first_name[] = "maRie";
char last_name[] = "MUrrAY";

cout << "Original value in first_name: " << first_name << endl;
strupr( first_name );
cout << "Converted value in first_name: " << first_name << endl;

cout << "\nOriginal value in last_name: " << last_name << endl;
strlwr( last_name );
cout << "Converted value in last_name: " << last_name << endl;

//Output
Original value in first_name: maRie
Converted value in first_name: MARIE

Original value in last_name: MUrrAY
Converted value in last_name: murray
```

10.8.6 Reversing

Another function that is sometimes useful is the `strrev` function. This function reverses the cString and has the following syntax:

```
strrev ( <cString> );
```

Like `strupr` and `strlwr`, `strrev` permanently changes the actual parameter. Therefore, the actual parameter must be a cString—not a string literal. Example 10.8.10 uses several cString functions, including `strrev`, to determine whether a string is a palindrome—spelled the same forward as backward.

Example 10.8.10 Using `strrev`

```
bool Palindrome( const char str1[] )
{
    char temp[25];
    bool palindrome = false;

    strcpy( temp, str1 );
    strrev( temp );

    if ( stricmp( str1, temp ) == 0 )
```

```
        palindrome = true;

    return palindrome;
}
```

10.8.7 Converting cStrings to Numbers

Other often-used functions allow you to convert strings to numbers. The three functions are shown here:

```
<double-var> = atof ( <cString> );
<long-var> = atol ( <cString> );
<int-var> = atoi ( <cString> );
```

These functions convert the parameter until they reach a character that is not valid for the return type. Example 10.8.11 uses atof as a model to illustrate the use of the previous three functions. Notice the impact of the comma used within string_3.

Example 10.8.11 Using atof

```
char string_1[] = "12345";
char string_2[] = "1234.567";
char string_3[] = "123,456";

double double_value;

double_value = atof( string_1 );
cout << "Original cString value: " << string_1
     << " after conversion: " << double_value << endl;

double_value = atof( string_2 );
cout << "Original cString value: " << string_2
     << " after conversion: "
     << fixed << setprecision(3) << double_value << endl;

double_value = atof( string_3 );
cout << "Original cString value: " << string_3
     << " after conversion: " << double_value << endl;

//Output
Original cString value: 12345 after conversion: 12345
Original cString value: 1234.567 after conversion: 1234.567
Original cString value: 123,456 after conversion: 123
```

The third conversion in Example 10.8.11 stops when the process reaches the comma. The computer considers the comma an invalid character, which stops the conversion. The comma separator in numbers is for human readability and is not necessary, or desirable, for the computer. Although we only demonstrated the use of one conversion function, all of the others work the same way.

10.8.8 Converting Numbers to cStrings

Two functions that perform the opposite of `atof`, `atol`, and `atoi` are the `ltoa` and `itoa` functions. These functions convert numbers to cStrings and have the following syntax:

```
ltoa ( <long-var>, <cString>, <radix> );
itoa ( <int-var>, <cString>, <radix> );
```

The parameters passed to these functions should be fairly obvious, except for `<radix>`. This parameter indicates to which base the number should be converted. For example, the value 16 for the radix converts the number to a hexadecimal value. The radix can be any value from 2 to 36. As discussed in Chapter 1, hexadecimal values use the characters 0–9 and A–F to implement a base 16 number. Base 36 extends this concept to include 0–9 and A–Z to represent numbers. Example 10.8.12 demonstrates the use of the `itoa` function to convert a number to a cString.

Example 10.8.12 Converting integers to cStrings

```
char converted_value[25];
int var_i;

cout << "Please enter an integer: ";
cin >> var_i;

itoa( var_i, converted_value, 10 );
cout << "Decimal value: " << converted_value << endl;

itoa( var_i, converted_value, 16 );
cout << "Hexadecimal value: " << converted_value << endl;

itoa( var_i, converted_value, 2 );
cout << "Binary value: " << converted_value << endl;

//Output
Please enter an integer: 1205
```

```
Decimal value: 1205
Hexadecimal value: 4b5
Binary value: 10010110101
```

Notice that there isn't a function to convert a `float` or a `double` to a cString. You will have to write your own!

10.8.9 Summary of cString Functions

In the previous eight sections we presented a variety of very powerful functions for manipulating cStrings, although there are a few additional functions we didn't cover. Table 10.8.2 is designed to act as a quick reference, summarizing the string-related functions as discussed.

Function	Purpose
`strcpy ( <dest>, <source> );`	Copies source to dest
`strncpy ( <dest>, <source>, <n> );`	Copies n characters from source to dest
`strcat ( <dest>, <source> );`	Appends source onto dest
`strncat ( <dest>, <source>, <n> );`	Appends n characters from source onto dest
`<int> = strcmp ( <str1>, <str2> );`	Compares str1 to str2
`<int> = strncmp ( <str1>, <str2>, <n> );`	Compares first n characters from str1 to str2
`<int> = stricmp ( <str1>, <str2> );`	Compares str1 to str2 with case insensitivity
`<int> = strnicmp ( <str1>, <str2>, <n> );`	Compares first n characters from str1 to str2 with case insensitivity
`<size_t> = strlen ( <cString> );`	Returns length of cString
`strupr ( <cString> );`	Converts all characters to uppercase
`strlwr ( <cString> );`	Converts all characters to lowercase
`strrev ( <cString> );`	Reverses the characters
`<double> = atof ( <cString> );`	Converts characters to a double
`<long> = atol ( <cString> );`	Converts characters to a long
`<int> = atoi ( <cString> );`	Converts characters to an integer
`ltoa ( <long_var>, <cString>, <radix> );`	Converts long integer to cString using radix (base of long_var)
`itoa ( <int_var>, <cString>, <radix> );`	Converts integer to cString using radix (base of int_var)

Table 10.8.2 cString functions

Section 10.8 Exercises

Please respond to each of the following questions.

1. To access the various predefined functions for manipulating cStrings, include the _____ header file.

   a. ⟨cstring⟩   b. ⟨iostream⟩   c. ⟨string⟩   d. ⟨manip⟩

2. We refer to the process of doing a character-by-character comparison as _____.

   a. dangerous   b. lexical analysis   c. sorting   d. examination

3. Appending one string onto another is called _____.

   a. dangerous   b. concatenation   c. adding   d. extending

4. Whenever you copy one string to another, it is imperative that the _____ cString has the room needed to hold all the characters and the required null terminating character.

   a. starting   b. source   c. destination   d. base

5. Use the appropriate function to find the length of `tester` and assign that value into the variable `length`.

```
char tester[] = "C++ Rules";
size_t length;
```

6. Use the appropriate function to copy all of the contents of the cString variable `string_1` to the variable `temp_first`.

```
char string_1[] = "Frank";
char temp_first[11];
```

7. Write the necessary section of code to compare the first six characters of `string_1` to `string_2`. If the strings are the same, simply display 'Same'; otherwise, display 'Different'.

```
char string_1[] = "Frank";
char string_2[] = "Franklyn";
```

8. Use the appropriate function to convert all the letters in `last_name` to uppercase.

```
char last_name[] = "Smith";
```

9. Use the appropriate function to convert the contents of the variable `a_grade` to a double, assigning the results to `grade_holder`.

```
char a_grade[] = "92.0";
double grade_holder;
```

10. Use the appropriate function to reverse all the characters in the variable `palindrome`.

```
char palindrome[] = "Can I attain a C";
```

11. Use the appropriate function to convert `var_a` into hexadecimal, placing the results in `hex_value`.

```
int var_a = 1950;
char hex_value[20];
```

10.9 cString Function Standards

Many of the functions discussed in Section 10.8 are not ANSI standard functions. Functions such as `strlwr`, `strupr`, and `stricmp` are very useful functions provided by Microsoft with its Visual Studio compiler. If you are developing with a different IDE, you may or may not have these functions available to you. If you don't, it might be a good idea to write your own versions.

Another issue that already occurs in Microsoft Visual Studio is that many of the string functions are flagged as deprecated. A deprecated function is one that has a newer function to take its place. For example, Microsoft would rather you use the `strcpy_s` function than the older `strcpy` function. The newer function has a different syntax that provides a more secure functionality. This has been done to alleviate the problems with buffer overrun errors and attacks.

The current ISO standard does not contain definitions for these more secure versions of the cString functions, but the ISO is working on including these newer functions for future standardization. It is our belief that the older functions are still a valuable part of any new C or C++ programmer's repertoire of routines. There are many millions of lines of code in existence that use the older functions. These programs will still need to be maintained and upgraded, so knowledge of these older functions will not be wasted. Also, once you understand the functions listed in this chapter, it is a relatively easy task to learn the newer functions.

Those of you using the Microsoft compiler will receive a warning anytime one of these deprecated functions is used. To use the older functions without receiving a warning, include the following line of code at the beginning of your source code.

```
#define _CRT_SECURE_NO_DEPRECATE
```

Some functions—such as `strrev` and `stricmp`—may have newer implementations that can be accessed by placing an underscore at the beginning of the function. For example, `strrev` would become `_strrev`. Except for the underscore, the syntax and capabilities of these functions are exactly the same.

As you can see, the status of these functions is in a state of flux. However, you shouldn't be discouraged or disappointed about this; the functions discussed in this chapter are still widely used.

10.10 Multidimensional Arrays

At this point, many of our students ask, "Can you have an array of arrays?" Yes. "Can you have an array of arrays of arrays?" Yes. "Can you have an array of arrays of arrays of arrays . . .?" Yes! In C and C++, this is how multidimensional arrays are implemented.

C and C++ allow you to have as many dimensions as you want. However, after three or four dimensions, the ability to visualize the array becomes rather stretched and often its usefulness is replaced with utter confusion. It is easy to visualize a two-dimensional array as a simple grid made up of rows and columns. Figure 10.10.1 shows one method of visualizing a two-dimensional array.

In Figure 10.10.1, the array called `last_name` is made up of 3 rows and 6 columns, for a total of 18 elements. The upper left element would be referred to as `last_name[0][0]`, while the shaded section is located at `last_name[1][2]`.

Since this is indeed an array of arrays, if we access a row of a two-dimensional array, we are accessing an address. This is a key point to remember, especially when we start demonstrating how to create an array of cStrings.

> ⚠ **Remember:** When referencing the elements in a two-dimensional array, use the first subscript to represent the row and the second subscript, the column (i.e., last_name[row][column]).

Three-dimensional arrays are also easy to visualize, this time as a cube, with the added dimension supplying the depth of the cube. The fourth dimen-

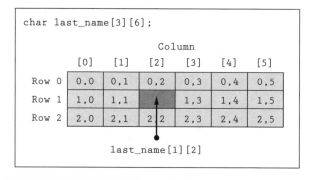

Figure 10.10.1 Visualizing a two-dimensional array

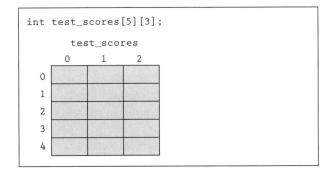

Figure 10.10.2 Another example of visualizing a two-dimensional array

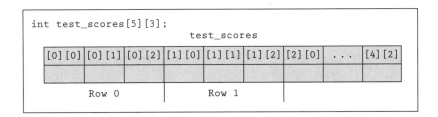

Figure 10.10.3 Memory layout of a two-dimensional array

sion is harder to visualize and often deals with time. We will leave the visualization of a four-dimensional array as an exercise for you!

We have presented one approach to visualizing multidimensional arrays; however, this is not how they are stored in memory. Multidimensional arrays are stored as a contiguous block of memory, as stated by the definition of an array. Therefore, there needs to be an algorithm to figure out how the arrays are stored in memory. Picture a two-dimensional array, as shown in Figure 10.10.2.

This method of visualizing an array is similar to what you have previously seen. In this case, we are creating an array called `test_scores` made up of five rows, referenced 0–4, and three columns, referenced 0–2.

C and C++ store arrays in what is called *row-major order*. This means the first row is stored in memory, then the next, and so on. Figure 10.10.3 shows the array from Figure 10.10.2 as it might appear in memory. Notice how the memory associated with the entire array is contiguous, similar to the memory for a one-dimensional array. In this example, the array `test_scores` has enough room for five students with three test scores each.

Using the array in Figure 10.10.3, we can extrapolate the following formula to find a specific element.

```
[desired_row * total_columns + desired_column]
```

Therefore, if we wanted to find `test_scores[2][1]`, it would be similar to `test_scores[2 * 3 + 1]`, or `test_scores[7]`. Logically we can now see that the desired element is the eighth element. However, it is important to always use two sets of brackets when accessing a specific element in a two-dimensional array.

Not all languages store their arrays in row-major order; some use *column-major order* instead. In column-major order, an entire column would be stored before storing the next.

So in what type of scenario could we use these multidimensional arrays? As we saw in previous sections, we can hold one string in a single-dimensional array—for example, the last name of one student. With a two-dimensional array, we could hold the last names of all the students in one course. A three-dimensional array could hold the last names of all the students in all the courses taught by a single professor. A four-dimensional array could hold the last names of all the students in all the courses taught by a single professor for all terms in an academic year.

Although multidimensional arrays can be used in this way, there are better tools to accomplish these tasks. This text, therefore, will focus on single- and two-dimensional arrays.

10.10.1 Declaration

To declare a two-dimensional array, you need to simply specify the number of rows needed for the array via another set of brackets. The syntax of the declaration of a two-dimensional array follows:

```
<data-type> <array-name> [ <rows> ] [ <columns> ];
```

Even though we said we would focus on two-dimensional arrays, it is easy to extend this syntax to declare a three-dimensional array:

```
<data-type> <array-name> [ <depth> ] [ <rows> ] [ <columns> ];
```

Example 10.10.1 shows a variety of multidimensional array declarations.

Example 10.10.1 Multidimensional array declarations

```
// Example 1
char last_name[20][16];
int test_scores[20][3];
int parents_age[20][2];

// Example 2
char salesmen_id[20][5];
int monthly_sales_per_region[2][20][12];
```

In Example 10.10.1, the first example declares three separate two-dimensional arrays for a group of 20 different students. In the second example, we create an array large enough to hold the 12 monthly sales for two different regions for 20 different salesmen.

> **Remember:** When determining the amount of room you need to hold an array of cStrings, you must add room for the null or terminating character in each respective row. Numeric arrays do not have this requirement.

10.10.2 Initialization

Initialization is accomplished in much the same manner as with a single-dimensional array, but with a few more curly braces. This process is demonstrated in Example 10.10.2.

Example 10.10.2 Initializing multidimensional arrays

```
int parents_age[20][2] = {0};      // initializes all elements to 0
char game_board[2][2]  = { {'x', 'o'}, {'o', 'x'} };

char last_name[5][16] = { "Jamie", "Jody", "Linda",
                          "Robert", "Troy" };
int test_scores[5][3] = { {90, 88, 91}, {80, 80, 85}, {91, 90, 94},
                          {76, 61, 84}, {79, 85, 88} };
```

If you do not initialize any of the elements in the array, all of the elements will be garbage. Figure 10.10.4 shows the contents from the Watch window of the uninitialized version of the array `parents_age`.

10.10.3 Multidimensional Array I/O

In a previous section, we demonstrated how a loop is often used in reading, manipulating, or displaying the contents of arrays. You've probably already guessed that in order to fill or print a multidimensional array you need to use nested loops. This technique is demonstrated in Example 10.10.3.

	parents_age	0x0012ff44	int [4][2]
[0]	0x0012ff44	int [2]	
	[0]	-858993460	int
	[1]	-858993460	int
[1]	0x0012ff4c	int [2]	
	[0]	-858993460	int
	[1]	-858993460	int
[2]	0x0012ff54	int [2]	
	[0]	-858993460	int
	[1]	-858993460	int
[3]	0x0012ff5c	int [2]	
	[0]	-858993460	int
	[1]	-858993460	int

Figure 10.10.4 Uninitialized array elements

Example 10.10.3 Using nested `for` loops to enter and print data

```
// Example 1 - Entering data into a 2-dimensional array
int parents_age[4][2];
for ( int r = 0; r < 4; r++ )
{
    cout << "Enter the 2 parents ages (i.e., 45 48): ";
    for ( int c = 0; c < 2; c++ )
        cin >> parents_age[r][c];
}
// Another way to accomplish the above task
for ( int r = 0; r < 4; r++ )
{
    cout << "Enter the 2 parents ages (i.e., 45 48): ";
    cin >> parents_age[r][0]
        >> parents_age[r][1];
}


// Example 2 - initializing the array
int test_scores[5][3] = { {90, 88, 91},{80, 80, 85},
                    {91, 90, 94}, {76, 61, 84},
                    {79, 85, 88} };
// Printing the data
for ( int r = 0; r < 5; r++ )
{
    cout << "Student: " << r + 1 << endl;
    for ( int c = 0; c < 3; c++ )
```

```
            cout << " Score " << c + 1
                << " equals " << test_scores[r][c];
    cout << endl;
}
```

Multidimensional arrays of cStrings are a little easier to manipulate because they do not require the use of nested loops, as shown in Example 10.10.4.

Remember: When reading or printing arrays of cStrings, you are accessing one row of the two-dimensional array. All other two-dimensional arrays must use two sets of brackets to access a specific element.

Example 10.10.4 Reading arrays of cStrings

```
char first_name[4][16]; // To hold data for 4 students
// Reading the name into our array
for ( int r = 0; r < 4; r++ )
{
    cout << "Enter the student's first name: ";
    cin >> first_name[r];
}
// Another method
for ( int r = 0; r < 4; r++ )
{
    cout << "Enter the student's first name: ";
    cin.ignore( cin.rdbuf()->in_avail() );  // Flush input buffer
    cin.getline( first_name[r], 16 );
    cin.clear();
    cin.ignore( cin.rdbuf()->in_avail() );  // Flush input buffer
}
// Printing the names from our array
for ( int r = 0; r < 4; r++ )
{
    cout << "First name is: " << first_name[r] << endl;
}
```

10.10.4 Passing Multidimensional Arrays

Passing multidimensional arrays is nothing more than an extension of what we've already learned about passing arrays. The difference is that only one set of brackets can be left empty. In a two-dimensional array, the rows can be left empty but the number of columns must be specified. When passing arrays, only the first set of brackets can be empty; all other sets must contain values. This is because all that the functions really receive is the beginning address. Requiring us to specify the number of columns in a two-dimensional array allows the function to determine the beginning of each row. That way we can use the double subscript operator to access the elements of the array. This is demonstrated in Example 10.10.5.

Example 10.10.5 Passing multidimensional arrays

```
// Function declarations
void PlayGame( char game_board[][2] );
void GetData( char last_name[][16], int age[], int sales[][12] );
void PrintStudent( char last_name[], float avg, char grade );

// Function calls
PlayGame( game_board );
GetData( last_name, age, sales );

// Pass one student
PrintStudent( last_name[r], avg[r], grade[r] );
```

Section 10.10 Exercises

Please respond to each of the following questions.

1. Indicate whether each of the following statements is true or false.

   a. In C and C++, you can have a maximum of three dimensions in an array.

   b. When trying to visualize a two-dimensional array of integers, it is best to picture a grid made up of rows and columns.

   c. Similar to single-dimension arrays, multidimensional arrays are physically stored internally in a contiguous block of memory.

   d. Similar to single-dimension arrays, multidimensional arrays by default are passed to functions by value.

2. When we reference an individual element within a two-dimensional array, we use the first subscript to represent the _____ and the second subscript for the _____.

   a. row / column   b. column / row   c. index / minor   d. row / minor

3. If an array of integers or doubles has three dimensions, how many subscripts are needed to reference an individual element?

    a. 2   b. 3   c. 4   d. unknown

4. Declare a two-dimensional array called `l_name` that can hold the last names of 10 students, each having a maximum length of 12 characters.

5. Declare an array called `sales` that contains a company's unit sales for the past twelve months. There are 30 salespeople in the company.

6. How many elements are contained within the following array declaration?

    ```
    int check_it[10][21];
    ```

7. Write the necessary statements to declare a two-dimensional array called `names` and initialize the first row to Sue and the second row to Marie. Assume that the longest name will be 15 characters and that we will not have more than 10 names.

8. Write one statement to print out both the first and the second person's name in the array `names` created in the previous question.

9. Write the necessary statements to create an array to hold three different integers representing quiz scores for a class of 25 students. Initialize each element of the array to 0.

10. Using the array you created in the previous question, assign the first quiz score for the second person in the array the value 91. Assign the third quiz for the fourth person the score of 88.

11. Assume the following variables have been declared and the `siblings` array has been populated with the appropriate data.

    ```
    // column 0 = sisters, column 1 = brothers
    int siblings[20][2];
    int ind_siblings_total[20] = { 0 };
    int total_sisters = 0;
    int total_brothers = 0;
    ```

    a. Write two separate and unique `for` loops to:

    i. Add up the values of all the elements contained in the first column, putting the results in the `total_sisters` variable.

    ii. Add up the number of siblings each person has, putting each individual's result into the array called `ind_siblings_total`.

    b. Write the necessary statement to pass the array called `siblings` to a `void` function called `Foo`.

    c. Write the function declaration for `Foo`.

d. Write a `for` loop (or loops) to neatly print out all the elements of the array called `siblings`. Make sure you include some space between each value and print each individual's data or record on its own line.

10.11 Parallel Arrays

Up to this point we have helped foster your understanding of arrays by illustrating different methods you could use to visualize how arrays might look, at least from a conceptual point of view. One additional concept we need to introduce is called *parallel arrays*.

Within our programs we often use a number of separate but related arrays for holding data. Suppose for example that there is a need to hold the information for five students. It would be necessary to have an array for holding the student ID, an array for the last name, another for the age of each student, and one last one for each student's gender. If you think of these four arrays as being related, then the first element of each of the arrays would be the data for a specific student. Likewise, the second element of each array would contain the information for a different student. These four separate but related arrays are often referred to as parallel arrays, as illustrated in Figure 10.11.1.

If you are referencing the student with the ID of 1010 in Figure 10.11.1, he is a 21-year-old male with the last name of Jones, based on the relationship of the first array to the other three. While C++ does not provide any built-in functionality for working with parallel arrays, it is relatively easy for the programmer to manually synchronize the subscript between the different arrays.

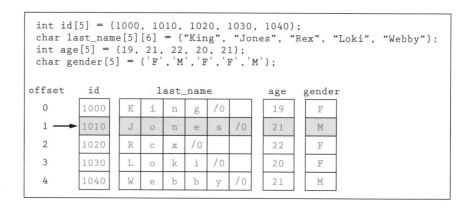

Figure 10.11.1 Parallel arrays

Remember: All information belonging to a specific entity is called a **record**.

Section 10.11 Exercises

Please respond to each of the following questions.

1. Based on the data in the parallel arrays contained within Figure 10.11.1, what is the last name, age, and gender of the individual with the ID of 1040?

2. A record is made up of one or more related fields and contains all of the data associated with a specific entity.

   True   False

Section 10.11 Learn by Doing Exercise

1. Write a complete modular program that accepts the following information from the keyboard:

Student Club	President	Number of Students
Computer Systems Society	Kim Cares	49
Society of Women Engineers	Jeanie Queen	51
Sigma Tau Gamma	Storm Drain	241
Trekkies	C. Kirk	230
Home Brewers	Ross Coe	15
High Altitude Ballooning	Justin Time	19
Rugby	Ryan Johns	25
IEEE	Marc Bansmere	36
International Club	Kong Mbenkum	102
Dance Club	Will Shaver	64

Table 10.11.1 Sample data

Also, the university gives each club $75 for every student in the club. Create another array to hold the amount of money received from the school. Please display all of the information in a neat, tabular format. Don't forget the column headings as well as appropriate formatting for the data.

10.12 Problem Solving Applied

Our objective is to write a program to read and store a group of student records, process the data, and print the results. This is fundamentally the same problem we used in the past couple of chapters, but now we employ arrays to help us in our solution. If necessary, please refer to Section 8.6 and Section 9.10 to review the problem specifications.

In earlier chapters we introduced and discussed the concept of I(nput) → P(rocess) → O(utput). Based on our years of teaching, we have found that this model often works well when used by beginning programming students in designing the overall flow or structure of their programs. It is especially useful when the solutions involve the use of arrays.

Employing this technique in the design of our current project and the related use of arrays causes us to make some slight modifications to the previous structure chart, as shown in Figure 10.12.1. Although main continues to act as a driver for the overall flow of our program, the major functions are clearly broken up into three main categories: input, process, and output. Within the input phase, we will focus on reading or entering the data into our arrays. Once we have loaded or entered all of the data, we will move into the second major phase, processing. Finally, when all of the necessary processing is complete, we will iterate through our arrays to print the necessary data and information, thus completing the output phase.

Using this approach allows us to isolate the various components of the programming problem into three main sections. By focusing on only one specific section, or even a subsection, at a time, we can more easily identify the specific functionality needed to solve the problem.

During the design of the individual components, make sure to focus only on the task or function at hand and not the entire problem. Indeed, the ability to isolate and break down the major tasks and concentrate on the related details is one of the real advantages to using this model. This technique, as you may remember, is also the key to incremental programming.

Notice how each of the three sections act as individual drivers for their own respective and related tasks. Control is transferred into each of these sections from main, so it will later become imperative that you give some careful thought to where you define your variables to provide the appropriate levels of access. The reorganization of the overall functionality of our program was done in an effort to make it easier to visualize, identify, and develop the specific tasks we need to accomplish.

Structure Chart:

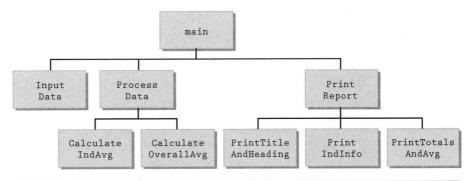

Figure 10.12.1 Structure chart

Now that the structure chart has been created, we will use this diagram to help develop the pseudocode shown in the design phase.

Design:

Pseudocode

```
/*********************************************************************************
* Name: main
*********************************************************************************/
Call InputData
Call ProcessData
Call PrintReport
/*********************************************************************************
* Name: InputData
* Parameters: Student info/arrays including ID and each of three exam scores.
*              Student counter. By ref.
* Return: none
* Purpose: Read all of the student data from the keyboard
*********************************************************************************/
While ( again equals 'Y' and student counter < MAX_STUDENTS )
Begin loop
   Prompt "Enter in student ID: "
   Read id[student_counter];
   Prompt "Enter 3 exam scores: "
   Read test_scores[student_counter][0]
      test_scores[student_counter][1]
      test_scores[student_counter][2]
   Add 1 to student_counter
   Prompt to determine if loop is to continue
End loop
/*********************************************************************************
* Name: ProcessData
* Parameters: Student info including the arrays holding the three exam scores,
```

```
*              individual average to hold each student's exam average, and an
*              array to hold each student's grade.
*                  Student counter and overall_class_average. By ref.
* Return: none
* Purpose: Act as a driver for all processing and calculations
***************************************************************************/
call CalculateIndAvg
call CalculateOverallAvg


/**************************************************************************
* Name: CalculateIndAvg
* Parameters: Student info including the array holding the three exam scores and the array to
*                  hold each student's overall exam average and letter grade.
*                  Student counter. By val.
* Return: none
* Purpose: Calculate the average score and letter grade for each student
***************************************************************************/
For each student
Begin loop
   Calculate inds_average[r] = (test scores[r][0] + test scores[r][1]
                  + test scores[r][2]) / 3

   if(inds_average[r] >= A cutoff)
     assign letter_grade[r] = 'A'
   else if (inds_average[r] >= B cutoff)
     assign letter_grade[r] = 'B'
   else if (inds_average[r] >= C cutoff)
     assign letter_grade[r] = 'C'
   else if (inds_average[r] >= D cutoff)
     assign letter_grade[r] = 'D'
   else
     assign letter_grade[r] = 'F'
End loop
/**************************************************************************
* Name: CalculateOverallAvg
* Parameters: Array holding the inds_average of three exam scores.
*                  Student counter. By val.
*                  Overall class average.  By ref.
* Return: none
* Purpose: Calculate the overall class average
***************************************************************************/
For each student
Begin loop
   Calculate the total_of_averages = inds_average[r] + total_of_averages
End loop
Calculate overall_class_average = total_of_averages / number_of_students


/**************************************************************************
* Name: PrintReport
* Parameters: Student info/arrays including ID, age, gender, each of three exam
*                  scores, and individual average.
*                  Student counter and overall class average. By ref.
* Return: none
```

```
* Purpose:  To act as a driver for printing all the necessary components of the
*                report
*********************************************************************************/
Call PrintTitleAndHeading
Call PrintIndInfo
Call PrintTotalsAndClassAvg


/********************************************************************************
* Name: PrintTitleAndHeading
* Parameters: none
* Return: none
* Purpose: Display welcome message and column headings
*********************************************************************************/
Print "* Welcome to the Grader Program *"
Print column headings for "ID  Quiz 1  Quiz 2  Quiz 3  Average  Grade"


/********************************************************************************
* Name: PrintIndInfo
* Parameters: Student info/arrays including ID, each of three exam scores, average,
*                 and letter grade.
*                 Student counter. By val.
* Return: none
* Purpose:  Display to the screen all the data for each student, including their
*              individual average on the three exams
*********************************************************************************/
For each student
Begin loop
   Print id[r]
   Print test_scores[r][0], test_scores[r][1], test_scores[r][2]
   Print inds_average[r]
   Print letter_grade[r]
End Loop
/********************************************************************************
* Name: PrintTotalsAndClassAvg
* Parameters: Student counter and overall class average for all students in the class. By val.
* Return: none
* Purpose:  Display the total number of students processed along with overall
*              class average
*********************************************************************************/
Print Total number of students processed
Print Overall class average
```

Some programmers would argue that the functions `ProcessData` and `PrintReport` are unnecessary because the function calls that make the body of these functions could be placed in `main`. While this would be even more efficient, it is our belief that the current structure clearly identifies each phase of the IPO model and allows for more extensible code if we need to add other calculations or reports.

Like always, this pseudocode can now be translated into C++ source code. In Section 10.17, our colleague Troy will provide us with some start-up code that will basically implement the preceding algorithm.

One additional feature you may have already discovered within the Microsoft IDE is the small box on the left side of the area where you type your code. Within this box you will find either a '+' or a '–' symbol. Clicking on the symbol will either collapse or show the body of the function or comment. This can be especially helpful when you have a function you know is working and you no longer need to continue scrolling through the listing. If you want to see the contents of the function or comment, you can either click the box or maneuver your cursor over the grayed-out section to the right that contains the ellipses (...). If you have not explored this feature, please make it a point to do so now.

10.13 C—The Differences

Although there is a lot of information in this chapter, there aren't very many differences between C and C++. In C, cStrings are just called strings, and you need to include `<string.h>` in order to use the functions from Section 10.8.

As always, input and output between C and C++ is radically different. Therefore, you are not able to use `cin.getline` in a C program. Also, since `scanf` is our primary input function, we need to discuss how to use this function to read strings.

Remember, `scanf` requires any variable to be passed by pointer. In other words, `scanf` requires the address of the variable to store the information. With regular variables, you are required to use the address-of operator to send the address to `scanf`. However, since the name of the array is already an address, the address-of operator is not needed when reading strings. Also the format specifier for a string is the `%s`, as we saw in Chapter 5. Example 10.13.1 shows a couple of examples of reading strings from the keyboard.

Example 10.13.1 Using `scanf` **to read strings**

```
/* Example 1 */
char fname[15];

printf( "What's your name? " );
scanf( "%s", fname );

/* Example 2 */
```

```
char lnames[5][15];
int i = 0;

for ( i = 0; i < 5; i++ )
{
    printf( "Enter name %d: ", i + 1 );
    scanf( "%s", lnames[i] );
}
printf( "Names entered:\n" );
for ( i = 0; i < 5; i++ )
{
    printf( "%c%s\n", toupper( lnames[i][0] ),
                    strlwr( &lnames[i][1] ) );
}
```

The problem with `scanf`, as with `cin`, is that you can't have strings with spaces as input. However, there is a counterpart to `cin.getline` called `gets`. The major difference between the two routines is that `gets` does not specify the number of characters to be read. The good news is that the routine to flush the buffer is much simpler. The `gets` and `flush` routines are shown in Example 10.13.2.

Example 10.13.2 Using `gets` to read strings

```
char lnames[5][15];
int i = 0;

for ( i = 0; i < 5; i++ )
{
    printf( "Enter name %d: ", i + 1 );
    flushall();
    gets( lnames[i] );
}
```

1 0 . 1 4   S U M M A R Y

This chapter has been devoted to the exciting and powerful concept of arrays. We first examined how, through the use of arrays, we can relate or connect numerous pieces of data with one specific variable name. These arrays hold a set of contiguous elements, or pieces—all of which are the same data type and are referenced by the array's name, which is also its beginning address. Because of this organization, we can easily and quickly manipulate arrays.

To gain access to a specific element in our arrays, we examined the subscript operator. The subscript value can be any integer variable, constant, or literal, and allows us to specify an offset from the beginning of the array, with the starting element being 0. Be sure to avoid going out of bounds of any array. We will have more to say about this in Chapter 12, but for now just remember that the individual elements in an array are physically located next to each other in memory.

When passing arrays, keep in mind that arrays are passed by pointer. Therefore, the function can change the original data, similar to passing by reference. If necessary, you can use the reserved word `const` to stop the array from being altered from within a specific function.

Another important concept introduced in this chapter revolved around a special form of character arrays called cStrings. As you may recall, cStrings must be null terminated and have some unique requirements and functions for using and manipulating their contents. Functions such as `strcpy`, `strcat`, `strcmp`, `strupr`, and `strlwr` are all available to provide some significant functionality when working with cStrings.

After your understanding of one-dimensional arrays became more solidified, you had the necessary foundation required to extend that concept and discovered the power and application of multidimensional arrays. We ended our discussion by presenting the topic of parallel arrays and how they aid in coordinating and visualizing data.

10.15 Debugging Exercise

Download the following file from this book's website and run the program following the instructions noted in the code.

```
/*************************************************************
* File: Chap_10_Debugging.cpp
*
* General Instructions: Complete each step before proceeding to the
* next.
*
* Debugging Exercise 1
*
* 1) Build and run the program.
* 2) Examine the code and the output and notice the use of
*    parallel arrays.
* 3) Insert breakpoints at Breakpoint 1, Breakpoint 2, and Breakpoint
*    3.
```

```
*  4)   Run to Breakpoint 1.
*  5)   Place a watch on varX, varY, and varZ. Click on the '+' in the
*       Watch window to see the individual elements associated with each
*       of the arrays.
*  6)   Continue running your program to Breakpoint 2.
*  7)   Add a watch on the array called name. Again, click on the '+'
*       symbol. Notice how a multidimensional array is shown in the
*       debugger, the null terminating character's location, and how a
*       character is represented within each element of the array.
*  8)   Continue running the program to Breakpoint 3.
*  9)   Notice the contents of varX and varY now that you are back in the
*       main function.
* 10)   Clear all the breakpoints.
* 11)   Stop debugging.
*
* Debugging Exercise 2
*
*  1)   Change the constant SIZE from 5 to 10.
*  2)   Change any literal containing a 5 to the constant SIZE.
*       Notice the usefulness of the constant when changes need
*       to be made to your code.
*  3)   Set a breakpoint at Breakpoint 4. Now
*       set the necessary condition on this breakpoint so that the loop breaks
*       when x hits 8.
*       (Hint: If you need help setting breakpoints based on a
*       condition, refer to Chapter 8.)
*  4)   Run to Breakpoint 4.
*  5)   Continue stepping into the remainder of the for loop until the
*       flow returns back to main.
*  6)   Make sure your Watch window is visible, and notice the contents
*       of varY and varZ now that you are back in main.
*  7)   Stop debugging.
*  8)   Disable all breakpoints.
*  9)   Rebuild and execute the program and verify the results.
*
* Debugging Exercise 3
*
*  1)   Just before the call to the PrintFunction in main, add an
*       assignment statement to change the first element in the
*       array varZ to -99.
*  2)   Build and execute your code, verifying that the calculations
*       are correct in relation to element 0 of varZ.
*  3)   Add a line to assign the contents of the second element of
*       varX to 99 in FunctionTwo.
*  4)   Rebuild your program.
*  5)   Obviously there is a problem. Remove the const from the
*       function declaration and header for varX.
*  6)   Now you should be able to build and execute your code. Do it.
*  7)   Set a breakpoint on Breakpoint 2.
```

```
* 8)   Re-enable Breakpoint 2.
* 9)   Run to Breakpoint 2 and make sure you have a watch on the
*      variable name.
* 10)  Click on the '+'. Once you see all the elements
*      within the array, change the 'Value' (in the Value field)
*      for the first element of the array directly within the Watch
*      window to the character 'Z'.  Notice how the value is updated
*      by displaying the new ASCII value too.
* 11)  Stop debugging.
* 12)  Disable all breakpoints.
*
*************************************************************************/
#include <iostream>
#include <iomanip>
using std::cin;
using std::cout;
using std::endl;
using std::setw;

void GetAndDisplayWelcomeInfo();
void FunctionOne( int varX[], int varY[] );
void FunctionTwo( const int varX[], const int varY[], int varZ[] );
void PrintFunction( const int varX[], const int varY[],
                    const int varZ[] );

const int SIZE = 5;

int main()
{
      int varX[5];
      int varY[SIZE];
      int varZ[SIZE];   // Notice how we used the const here!

      // Breakpoint 1
      // Put breakpoint on the following line
      GetAndDisplayWelcomeInfo();
      FunctionOne( varX, varY );

      // Breakpoint 3
      // Put breakpoint on the following line
      FunctionTwo( varX, varY, varZ );
      PrintFunction( varX, varY, varZ );
      return 0;
}
void GetAndDisplayWelcomeInfo()
{
      char name[2][20]; // First name in row 0, last name in row 1

      cout << "Please enter your first name: ";
      cin >> name[0];
```

```
        cout << "\nPlease enter your last name: ";
        cin >> name[1];

        // Breakpoint 2
        // Put breakpoint on the following line
        cout  << "\n\n\tWelcome " << name[0] << " " << name[1]
              << "!\n\t   Hope all is well \n\n";
}
void FunctionOne( int varX[], int varY[] )
{
        for ( int x = 0; x < SIZE; x++ )// Notice '<' not <=
              // Breakpoint 4
              // Put breakpoint on the following line
              varX[x] = x;

        for ( int x = 0; x < 5; x++ )
              varY[x] = x + 100;
}
void FunctionTwo( const int varX[], const int varY[], int varZ[] )
{
        for ( int x = 0; x < SIZE; x++ )
              varZ[x] = varX[x] + varY[x];
}
void PrintFunction( const int varX[20], const int varY[20],
                    const int varZ[20] )
{
        int x;

        cout << " \t  x \t  y  \t  z\n\n";

        for ( x = 0; x < SIZE; x++ )
           cout << "\t"  << setw(3) << varX[x]
                << "\t " << varY[x]
                << "\t " << varZ[x] << endl;
}
```

10.16 Programming Exercises

The following programming exercises are to be developed using all phases of the development method. Be sure to make use of good programming practices and style, such as constants, white-space, indentation, naming conventions, and commenting. Make sure all input prompts are clear and descriptive and that your output is well formatted and looks professional.

1. Write a program that includes the following three functions, making sure each is clearly exercised within your program:

   a. IsPalindrome: This function returns true if the cString parameter is a palindrome, false if it is not. As you have seen, a palindrome is any group of characters (i.e., a word) that appears the same when written forward and backward.

   b. `IsAlphaStr`: A function that returns true if the cString you pass it contains all alphabetic characters. If the parameter does not contain all alpha characters, the function returns false. Feel free to use the `isalpha` function we discussed earlier.

   c. `CountChar`: A function to simply count and return the number of times a specific character occurs in a cString. This function will take two parameters: the cString to check and the specific character you are looking for.

2. For this exercise, you will write a program to convert numbers to different bases. For example:

$$FF_{16} = 255_{10} = 377_8 = 11111111_2 = C3_{21} = 73_{36}$$

Your program will prompt the user to enter a number and the base of the number. It will then ask what base to convert the number to. Your program will handle bases 2–36.

Your program should include the following features:

- If the user enters a base outside the range, display an error message and make the user reenter the base.
- If the number doesn't match the base the user typed in (i.e., the character A is invalid for a base 10 number), display an error message and have the user reenter all of the information again.
- The number displayed to the user should be displayed in uppercase.
- Be sure your output is self-documenting. For example:
  FF (base 16) = 255 (base 10).

Hints:

- The maximum digit that can be in a number is one less than its base. For example, 7 is the maximum digit in a base 8 number, and 1 is the maximum digit in a base 2 number.
- Convert all numbers to base 10 first and then convert them to the desired base.
- Since the number is entered into a character array, each digit is a character. You must convert this ASCII value to the appropriate value for that base. For example, A is value 10, B is value 11; to calculate these values, use the ASCII value for the alphabetic character and subtract 55. This works because A is ASCII value 65, B is ASCII value 66. If the character in the array happens to be a digit (i.e., numeral), use the same philosophy but subtract 48.

If you are unsure how to change bases, please review Chapter 1.

3. Assume you are employed by a small company to help track the sales for four salespeople, each of whom sells three different products. Along with the salesperson's ID, you will ask the user to enter the dollar sales for each of the three products sold last week. Once the user has entered the data for all four salespeople, your program should generate a table that prints out the salesperson's ID, his or her individual sales for each product, and the individual's overall sales. In addition, the program should print the overall percentage of the total sales that each

individual's total sales represent and, at the end of your report, print the total sales for each respective product and the overall sales total. An example report format follows:

ID	Prod1	Prod2	Prod3	Total	Percent
1234	10.23	15.37	20.50	46.10	xx.xx%

...

...

_____

Totals	xx.xx	xx.xx	xx.xx	xx.xx

Use a two-dimensional array to hold the sales information.

4. Design and implement a menu-driven program that will take two two-dimensional arrays, or matrices, of floating-point numbers and perform mathematical operations on them. The matrices will all be 3 × 3. The operations will be selected from a menu with the following options:

■ Get new matrices

■ Multiply matrices

■ Add matrices

■ Exit

Make sure the output is readable and self-documenting. The examples that follow provide patterns for your output.

Matrix addition can only be performed if the dimensions of the matrices are the same. This is not a concern since we are assuming all of the matrices are the same size. An example of matrix addition follows:

$$\begin{bmatrix} 1 & 2 & 3 \\ 4 & 5 & 6 \\ 7 & 8 & 9 \end{bmatrix} + \begin{bmatrix} 4 & 5 & 3 \\ 2 & 7 & 9 \\ 2 & 6 & 0 \end{bmatrix} = \begin{bmatrix} (1+4) & (2+5) & (3+3) \\ (4+2) & (5+7) & (6+9) \\ (7+2) & (8+6) & (9+0) \end{bmatrix} = \begin{bmatrix} 5 & 7 & 9 \\ 6 & 12 & 15 \\ 9 & 14 & 9 \end{bmatrix}$$

Matrix multiplication is much more complicated. An example of matrix multiplication follows:

The formula $c_{ij} = a_{i1}b_{1j} + a_{i2}b_{2j} + a_{i3}b_{3j}$ creates a resulting matrix in which a and b are matrices, i is the row number, and j is the column number.

$C_{11} = (3)(1) + (0)(4) + (-1)(0) = 3$

$C_{12} = (3)(-5) + (0)(1) + (-1)(-1) = -14$

$C_{13} = (3)(0) + (0)(-2) + (-1)(3) = -3$

$C_{21} = (0)(1) + (4)(4) + (2)(0) = 16$

$C_{22} = (0)(-5) + (4)(1) + (2)(-1) = 2$

$C_{23} = (0)(0) + (4)(-2) + (2)(3) = -2$

$C_{31} = (5)(1) + (-3)(4) + (1)(0) = -7$

$C_{32} = (5)(-5) + (-3)(1) + (1)(-1) = -29$

$C_{33} = (5)(0) + (-3)(-2) + (1)(3) = 9$

$$\begin{bmatrix} 3 & 0 & -1 \\ 0 & 4 & 2 \\ 5 & -3 & 1 \end{bmatrix} \begin{bmatrix} 1 & -5 & 0 \\ 4 & 1 & -2 \\ 0 & -1 & 3 \end{bmatrix} = \begin{bmatrix} 3 & -14 & -3 \\ 16 & 2 & -2 \\ -7 & -29 & 9 \end{bmatrix}$$

Although there are many opportunities to do so in this program, be careful not to introduce redundant code. If you want to copy and paste a section of code, think about making it a function.

5. Write a program that creates and displays Pascal's triangle. Pascal's triangle is used in the manipulation of polynomials. A basic Pascal's triangle is shown here:

```
                    1
                1       1
            1       2       1
        1       3       3       1
    1       4       6       4       1
```

As you can see, the outside edges are always 1. The inside numbers are computed by adding the two numbers from the row above.

Pascal's triangle is used is calculating the coefficients of the x terms in a polynomial. For example, if we have the following mathematical expression: $(x + 1)^3$, the resulting polynomial would be: $x^3 + 3x^2 + 3x + 1$. Notice the coefficients of the x terms are: 1, 3, 3, 1, which are also the same values in the fourth row of Pascal's triangle.

Create a program that asks for a maximum value from the user. Then calculate and display the resulting triangle. Note: The preceding triangle was created for the user input of the fourth power.

10.17 Team Programming Exercise

Do you remember good old Troy from earlier chapters—the guy who recently joined your development team? Well Troy has once again started a project that you will need to finish. The code that follows is his first attempt at extending the solution to the problem presented in Section 10.12. Basically, you now need to make sure the code can be built and executed. Unfortunately, there appear to be some problems with it as it now stands. After you get the code working, you will need to add two additional functions and of course pass in the necessary arrays. The first function simply iterates through the array of individual averages and counts the number of A's, B's, C's, and so on. Remember: This function should be called from the `ProcessData` method provided.

After you have printed the totals on the report, call the other new function you wrote that will generate a graph showing the frequency of the individual letter grades (A–F) for the class.

Your graph should look somewhat like the following:

Grade Frequency Graph

```
A    ***
B    ****
C    *******
D    ***
F    **
```

Before you get too carried away, get the code to compile. Make sure you carefully review and correct any errors before adding the additional functionality. In your review you will notice that Troy has put some comments within the code, asking for an additional feature or two. Please make it a point to implement those as well. Also, Troy wasn't consistent in his formatting. Correct the formatting so it is consistent and conforms to an appropriate style. Once you have the code compiling, we suggest you develop the relatively short pseudocode for each of the two new functions. Once you have the pseudocode, you should find it relatively straightforward to write and implement the new functions.

And one last thing: Troy said he should probably print the graph as shown here. If time permits, write the code to generate the new style report. Provide the option to display the graph in either of the two formats.

Grade Frequency Graph

```
        *
        *
        *
    *   *
*   *   *   *
*   *   *   *   *
*   *   *   *   *
A   B   C   D   F
```

```cpp
// Chap_10_Team.cpp - Team Programming
//
// This code is NOT complete - there are a few areas that need to be
// corrected. It is almost done except for a few logic and syntax errors
// and the additional features that still need to be added.   TROY

#include <iostream>
#include <iomanip>
#include <cmath>
#include <cctype>

using std::cout;
using std::endl;
using std::cin;
using std::setprecision;

const float A_GRADE = 92.0F;
const float B_GRADE = 84.0F;
const float C_GRADE = 75.0F;
const float D_GRADE = 65.0F;
const int MAX_STUDENTS = 20;

// Function Prototypes
void InputData(int id[ ], float test_scores[ ][3], int & student_counter);

void ProcessData(float test_scores[ ][3], float inds_average[ ],
            char letter_grade[], int student_counter,
            float & overall_class_average);

void CalculateIndAvg(float test_scores[][3], float inds_average[],
               char letter_grade[], int counter);

void CalculateOverallAvg(float inds_average[], int student_counter,
                  float & overall_class_average);

void PrintReport(int id[ ], float test_scores[ ][3], float inds_average[ ],
            char letter_grade[], float class_average,
            int number_of_students);
```

```
void PrintTitleAndHeading();

void PrintIndInfo(int id[ ], float test_scores[ ][3], float inds_average[ ],
                  char letter_grade[], int number_of_students);

void PrintTotalsAndClassAvg(int number_of_students, floats class_average);

int main( )
{
        int ids[MAX_STUDENTS];
        float test_scores[MAX_STUDENT][3];
        float inds_average[MAX_STUDENTS];
        char letter_grade[MAX_STUDENTS];
        float class_average
        int student_counter = 0;

        InputData(id, test_scores, student_counter);

        ProcessData(test_scores, inds_average, letter_grade, student_counter,
                    class_average);

        PrintReport(id, test_scores, inds_average, letter_grade, class_average,
                    student_counter);
    return 0;
}
/*****************************************************************************
 * Name: InputData
 * Parameters: Student info/arrays including ID and each of three exam scores.
 *             Student counter. By reference.
 * Return: none
 * Purpose: Read all of the student data from the keyboard
 *
 * Seems to be a problem with the loop or something - TROY
 *****************************************************************************/
void InputData(int id[ ], float test_scores[ ][2],int student_counter)
{
    char again = 'Y';
    cout << "\nEnter student data (y/n)? ";
    cin >> again;
    again = toupper(again);
    // Notice guarding against letting the arrays get out of bounds
    while ( again = 'Y' && student_counter < MAX_STUDENTS )
    {
        cout << "\n Enter in student ID: ";
        cin >> id[student_counter];

        cout << "\n Enter 3 exam scores: ";
        cin >> test_scores[student_counter][0]
            >> test_scores[student_counter][1]
            >> test_scores[student_counter][2];

        student_counters++;
```

```
                cout << "\nDo another: (y/n)? ";
                cin  >> again;
                again = tolower(again);
        }
}


/********************************************************************************
* Name: ProcessData
* Parameters: Student info including the arrays holding the three exam
* scores, inds_average to hold each student's exam average, and an array to
· hold each student's grade.
*              Student counter and overall_class_average. By reference.
* Return: none
* Purpose: Act as a driver for all processing and calculations
********************************************************************************/
void ProcessData(float test_scores[ ][3], float inds_average[ ],
                char letter_grade[], int student_counter,
                float & overall_class_average)
{
        CalculateIndAvg(test_scores, inds_average, letter_grade,
                        student_counter);
        CalculateOverallAvg(inds_average, student_counter,
                        overall_class_average);


/********************************************************************************
* Name: CalculateIndAvg
* Parameters: Student info including the array holding the three exam
* scores and the array to hold each student's overall exam average and letter
* grade.
*              Student counter. By val.
* Return: none
* Purpose: Calculate the average score and letter grade for each student
********************************************************************************/
void CalculateIndAvg(float test_scores[][3], float inds_average[],
                char letter_grade[], int student_counter)
{
        for(int r = 0; r < student_counter + 1; r++)
        {       inds_average[r] = (test_scores[r][0] +
                                test_scores[r][1] +
                                test_scores[r][2]) / 3;
                if(inds_average[r] >= A_GRADE)
                        letter_grade[r] = 'A';
                else if (inds_average[r] >= B_GRADE)
                        letter_grade[r] = 'B';
                else if (inds_average[r] >= C_GRADE)
                        letter_grade[r] = 'C';
                else if (inds_average[r] >= D_GRADE)
                        letter_grade[r] = 'D';
                else if
                        letter_grade[r] = 'F';
        }
}
```

```
/*****************************************************************************
* Name: CalculateOverallAvg
* Parameters: Array holding the inds_average of three exam scores.
*             Student counter. By val.
*             Overall class average.  By ref.
* Return: none
* Purpose: Calculate the overall class average
*****************************************************************************/
void CalculateOverallAvg(float inds_average[],int student_counter,
                         float & overall_class_average)
{
    float total_averages = 0;

    for(int r = 0; r <= student_counter; r++)
        total_averages += inds_average[r];

    overall_class_average =  total_averages / student_counter;
}


/*****************************************************************************
* Name: PrintReport
* Parameters: Student info/arrays including ID, age, gender, each of three
* exam scores, and individual average.
*             Student counter and overall class average. By reference.
* Return: none
* Purpose: To act as a driver for printing all the necessary components of
*          the report
*
* Not sure exactly what the problem is below... -  TROY
*****************************************************************************/
void PrintReport(int id[ ], float test_scores[ ][3], float inds_average[ ],
                 char letter_grade[], float class_average,
                 int number_of_students)
{
        PrintTitleAndHeading()
        PrintIndInfo(id, test_scores, inds_average, letter_grade,
                     number_of_students);
        PrintTotalsAndClassAverages(number_of_students, class_average);
}


/*****************************************************************************
* Name: PrintTitleAndHeading
* Parameters: none
* Return: none
* Purpose: Display welcome message and column headings
*****************************************************************************/
void PrintTitleAndHeading( )
{
        cout << "\t\t ** Welcome to the Grader Program ** \n";
        cout << " ID  \tQuiz 1\tQuiz 2\tQuiz 3\t  Average \t Grade \n\n";
}
```

```
/****************************************************************************
 * Name: PrintIndInfo
 * Parameters: Student info/arrays including ID, each of three exam scores,
 * average, and letter grade.
 *              Student counter. By val.
 * Return: none
 * Purpose: Display to the screen all the data for each student, including
 * their individual average on the three exams
 *
 * Please update to always print one decimal point for the average - TROY
 ****************************************************************************/
void PrintIndInfo(int id[],float test_scores[][3],
                  float inds_average[], char letter_grade[], int counter)
{
     cout << setprecision(3);
     for(int r = 0; r < counter ; r++)
          cout << "\n" << id[r] << "\t " << test_scores[r][0] << "\t "
               << test_scores[r][1] << "\t " << test_scores[r][3]  << "\t "
               << setw(2) << inds_average[r] << "\t  "
                  letter_grade[r] << endl;
}


/****************************************************************************
 * Name: PrintTotalsAndClassAvg
 * Parameters: Student counter and overall class average for all students in
 * the class. By val.
 * Return: none
 * Purpose: Display the total number of students processed along with the overall
 *          class average
 ****************************************************************************/
void PrintTotalsAndClassAvg(int number_of_students, float class_average)
{        cout << "\n\n\t ** Number of Students: " << number_of_students
             << " Overall Class Average:  " << classAverage << " **/n";
}
```

10.18 Answers to Chapter Exercises

Section 10.2

1. c. name

2. b. 5

3. b. 1

4. a. false

   b. true

   c. false

5. c. constant

Section 10.3

1. a. subscript

2. a. 0

3. c. 4

4. a. 0

5. d. 5

6. a. valid

   b. valid

   c. invalid—out of bounds

   d. valid

7. a. true

   b. false

   c. true

   d. true

Section 10.4

1. c. 1

2.
```
int sum = 0;
for ( int i = 0; i < 5; i++ )
    sum += numA[i];
float average = sum / 5.0F;
```

3. b. 0

4. b. 0

5. d. 6

6. `int days_in_month[] = {31, 28, 31, 30, 31, 30, 31, 31, 30, 31, 30, 31};`

Section 10.5

1. A B C

2. 100

Section 10.6

1. d. pointer

2. a. `Sample( ids );`

3. c. `void Sample( int ids[] );`

4. a. true

   b. false

   c. true

5. We are passing only one individual element of the array *ages* to the function called `Sample`.

6. `void Sample( int age );`

7. The word `const` in front of the identifier prevents the body of the function from altering or changing the contents within the function.

Section 10.7

1. b. cString

2. c. 16

3. b. `char name[] = "Sally";`

   c. `char name[6] = "Sally";`

   d. `char name[] = {'S', 'a', 'l', 'l', 'y', '\0'};`

4. a. true

   b. true

   c. false

   d. false

   e. true

5. d. the null character

6. c. `.getline`

7. a. flush the input buffer

8. `char first_name[16] =  "yourFirstName";`
   `char last_name[16] = {0};`
   `char temp_name[16] = {0};`

Section 10.8

1. a. `<cstring>`

2. b. lexical analysis

3. b. concatenation

4. c. destination

5. `length = strlen( tester );`

6. `strcpy( temp_first, string_1 );`

7. ```
if (strncmp(string_1, string_2, 6) == 0)
      cout << "Same";
  else
      cout << "Different";
```

8. `strupr( last_name );`

9. `grade_holder = atof( a_grade );`

10. `strrev( palindrome );`

11. `itoa( var_a, hex_value, 16 );`

## Section 10.10

1. a. false

   b. true

   c. true

   d. false

2. a. row / column

3. b. 3

4. `char l_name[10][13];  // 12 + 1 for null character`

5. `float sales[30][12];`

6. 210 elements

7. `char names[10][16] = {"Sue", "Marie"};`

8. `cout <<  names[0] << " " << names[1];`

9. `int quizzes[25][3] = {0} ;`

10. ```
quizzes[1][0] = 91;
  quizzes[3][2] = 88;
```

11. a. i. ```
for (int r = 0; r < 20; r++)
             total_sisters += siblings[r][0];
```

   ii. ```
for ( int r = 0; r < 20; r++ )
             ind_siblings_total[r] = siblings[r][0] +
                              siblings[r][1];
```

```
// OR


for ( int r = 0; r < 20; r++ )
{
    for ( int c = 0 ; c < 2; c++ )
        ind_siblings_total[r] += siblings [r][c];


}
```

b. Foo(siblings);

c. void Foo(int siblings[][2]);

d. ```
for (int r = 0; r < 20; r++)
    cout << siblings[r][0] << " " << siblings[r][1] << endl;

// OR

for (int r = 0; r < 20; r++)
{
    for (int c = 0 ; c < 2; c++)
        cout << " " << siblings[r][c];
    cout << "\n";
}
```

## Section 10.11

1.  Webby, 21, Male

2.  True
```

File I/O and Data Manipulation

Chapter Objectives

By the end of the chapter, readers will be able to:

- Explain the characteristics of data files and report files.
- Discuss the advantages associated with writing and reading data to various forms of storage mediums.
- Apply predefined stream classes `ifstream` and `ofstream` to create stream variables.
- Discuss the purpose of the file position marker (FPM).
- Explain the options available for opening files, checking for successfully opening files, and closing files.
- Demonstrate programmatically reading and writing data to files.
- Understand the basic concepts associated with sorting and searching.

Introduction

In the last chapter, we discussed how to create and manipulate arrays. Unfortunately, filling those arrays involved a lot of typing at the keyboard every time our programs were run. In this chapter, the concepts of data files and the statements necessary to read from and write to these text files are introduced. This will allow us to store the information in a file and access it as needed without retyping the data. As you will quickly see, the use of data files will make debugging and testing your code easier and will provide yet another powerful tool to use in writing your programs.

11.1 Data Files

There is a difference between a report and a data file. A *report* is always generated by a computer program for human consumption and usually includes title information, column headings, and other formatting. In essence, we have been creating reports throughout the book, but now instead of just being displayed on the screen, they will be written to a file for storage. This storage can be on any device accessible by your computer. This includes the hard drive, network drives, and even USB flash drives.

A *data file* must be written with data only and created following a consistent layout for each record in the file. A data file will generally be used as input for our programs. Because of their ease of use, the tendency is to write, and read, space-delimited files. An example of a space-delimited file is shown in Figure 11.1.1.

Although these do work in a wide variety of situations, if your data includes multiword strings, space-delimited data files won't work. Another common format for data files is a comma-delimited layout, in which all strings are enclosed in quotation marks. An example of a comma-delimited file is shown in Figure 11.1.2.

```
Stormy Weather 123-09-8765 9.00 46 F
Willy Makit 432-89-7654 9.50 40 F
Ima Nerd 239-34-3458 11.25 83 F
Fish Gill 762-84-6543 6.50 35 P
```

Figure 11.1.1 Space-delimited file

```
1, "Tim","Wheeler","Physical Plant Director",50000
2, "Mike","Hitson","Small Business Owner",25000
3, "Ralph","Carestia","Summer Term Professor",0
4, "Princess"," ","Game Developer",1
```

Figure 11.1.2 Comma-delimited file

As shown in Figure 11.1.2, all fields must be represented, even if the value is an empty string or zero. Also notice that the format of the file is consistent for each record. To write a program that reads this file, you will need to know the organization of the record as well as what each field represents.

The data files represented in this chapter are text files. To create the initial data file, it is a simple matter to use your favorite text editor, such as Notepad, vi, or Visual Studio. In fact, for simplicity we suggest you use your IDE for creating the data file as well as viewing your output or report file. It is best to use the filename extension of .txt for all of your text files. This is not a necessity but is a common practice. Not all data files will be text files, however; some will be binary. We will discuss binary data files later in the text.

Section 11.1 Exercises

Please respond to each of the following questions.

1. The purpose of generating reports is to provide:

    a. data for our program

    b. data in a human-readable format

    c. electronic digital output

    d. a storage format

2. Indicate whether each of the following statements is true or false.

    a. Within this chapter we will be creating our input, data files, as regular text files.

    b. A report file is used for input, and a data file is used for output.

    c. Data files must be produced following a consistent layout for individual records contained within the file.

    d. Data files often use either a space or a comma to separate or delimit the individual fields within a record.

11.2 File Streams

Up to this point, you have been using `cout` and `cin` so much that you probably don't even give their functionality a second thought. The good news is, much of what you have learned about `cout` and `cin` applies to reading and writing files. The `cout` and `cin` statements are predefined stream objects that are tied to `stdin` (keyboard) and `stdout` (screen). Unfortunately, there aren't any predefined streams associated with files. Therefore, we will have to make our own file streams.

There are two predefined stream *classes* from which we can make our own stream objects. For the purpose of this chapter, think of a class as a very powerful data type. Classes are extremely useful tools we will get to learn more about in later chapters. The related term, *object*, refers to a variable that was created from a class.

Remember: The stream classes are predefined, not primitive, data types.

The two stream classes we will use are `ifstream` and `ofstream`. Both of these classes are found in the `<fstream>` header file.

Remember: The `ifstream` class stands for <u>i</u>nput <u>file</u> <u>stream</u> and `ofstream` stands for <u>o</u>utput <u>file</u> <u>stream</u>.

The `ifstream` class allows us to create an object that provides the functionality to read from a file. The `ofstream` class allows us to create objects so that we can write to files. Example 11.2.1 demonstrates how to use these classes and shows the necessary `#include` and `using` statements.

Example 11.2.1 File stream objects

```
#include <fstream>
using std::ifstream;
using std::ofstream;
```

```
int main()
{
    ifstream fin;
    ofstream fout;

    return 0;
}
```

As demonstrated in Example 11.2.1, it is important to remember that these objects, `fin` and `fout`, are just variables. Many students use `fin` and `fout` exclusively as counterparts to `cin` and `cout`. This is not necessary or desirable. Like any other variable name, stream objects should be descriptive of their purpose.

Another form of declaring stream objects allows us to pass the name of the file to the object during its declaration. In Example 11.2.2, we use both a string literal and a constant to represent our filenames.

Example 11.2.2 File stream objects with filenames

```
const char FILENAME[] = "file.txt";

ifstream input( "filename.txt" );
ofstream output( FILENAME );
```

One last option available allows us to create a file stream object specifying that data will be appended to an existing file. Therefore, any new information will be added to the end of the file. This technique is shown in Example 11.2.3.

Example 11.2.3 Append mode

```
#include <fstream>
using std::ofstream;
using std::ios;

int main()
{
    ofstream report( "c:\\code\\data.txt", ios::app );

    return 0;
}
```

In Example 11.2.3, the declaration of the `report` stream object includes the `ios::app` parameter, which allows us to append data to an existing file. Also notice that the string literal representing the complete path and filename uses the '\\' escape sequence, which is only required with string literals to represent a single backslash.

Be aware that if you supply a filename in the declaration of any stream object, that file will be opened, or at least an attempt will be made to open that file. More information on opening files will be discussed in the next section.

Section 11.2 Exercises

Please respond to each of the following questions.

1. When using the two stream classes, `ifstream` and `ofstream`, we need to include the header file _____.

   a. `<iostream>`   b. `<streams>`   c. `<fstream>`   d. `<iomanip>`

2. Which of the following methods illustrate how we can pass the name of our file to the object at the time it is being declared?

   a. `ifstream fin;`

   b. `ofstream fout;`

   c. `ifstream input( "filename.txt" );`

   d. that is not possible

3. Indicate whether each of the following statements is true or false.

   a. It is possible to open a file in append mode, thus allowing additional data to be added to the end of an existing file.

   b. Both the `ifstream` and the `ofstream` classes allow us to create objects so that we can write data to the files.

   c. The `ifstream` and `ofstream` classes are predefined data types.

   d. When using a string literal to represent the complete path and filename, use the '\\' escape sequence.

   e. Stream variables must be named `fin`, for input files, and `fout`, for output files.

11.3 Opening Files

Before manipulating the information stored in a file, we need to open it from within our program. As discussed in the last section, if we supply a filename during the declaration of a stream object, an attempt to open that file will be made. This attempt may fail for various reasons, such as if the name is misspelled or the path is incorrect.

There is another method of opening a file that utilizes a member function available through the use of stream objects. The syntax is as follows:

```
stream.open ( filename );
```

Just like with the report shown in Example 11.2.3, you can open a file in append mode by passing the ios::app flag to the .open member function. The three modes in which you can open a file are read, write, and append. The read mode is accomplished by using the ifstream class. The other two modes are accomplished using the ofstream class. Example 11.3.1 demonstrates these methods of opening a file.

Example 11.3.1 Opening files

```
// *************** Read mode ***************
//          -- Method 1 --
ifstream input( "filename.txt" );
//          -- Method 2 --
ifstream fin;
fin.open( filename );

// *************** Write mode ***************
//          -- Method 1 --
ofstream output( filename );
//          -- Method 2 --
ofstream fout;
fout.open( "filename.txt" );

// *************** Append mode ***************
//          -- Method 1 --
ofstream datafile( "c:\\code\\data.txt", ios::app );
//          -- Method 2 --
ofstream fout;
fout.open( filename, ios::app );
```

When a file is opened, the current position is indicated by something we call a file position marker (FPM). When the file is opened in read and write mode, the FPM is placed at the beginning of the file. If the file is opened in append mode, the FPM is placed at the end of the file.

> ! **Remember:** Our term, "file position marker (FPM)," is often referred to by other names, such as file pointer or cursor. Regardless of what you call it, the functionality remains the same.

Be aware that opening a file in write mode destroys any existing information in that file. Be absolutely certain you are referencing the correct file. A former student of ours made the mistake of opening her source code file in write mode from within her program. This caused more than a little grief when she learned she needed to rewrite her entire program.

Both write and append modes will attempt to create the file if the one specified doesn't exist. The opening process would still fail if the file could not be created. Many things could cause the file not to be created, such as specifying an incorrect directory, not having write permissions to that location, or the drive not being ready, maybe due to a pen drive not being plugged in. Opening a file in read mode will immediately fail if the file doesn't exist, and the file will not be created under any circumstance.

Section 11.3 Exercises

Please respond to each of the following questions.

1. What are the three different modes for opening a file?

    a. in, out, erase

    b. in, mod, out

    c. read, write, add

    d. read, write, append

2. The current position within a file is noted by the file pointer, or something we call the

    a. file indicator (FI)

    b. pointer

    c. file position marker (FPM)

    d. file locator

3. If you try to open a file in read mode that does not exist, what happens?

   a. The request fails and the file will not be created.

   b. The file is created.

   c. The file is created but you cannot read from it.

   d. The file will be created but only on an external drive or device.

4. Explain why it is so important to be very careful when opening a file that already exists in write mode.

11.4 Checking for Successful Opening

If your request to open a file is denied, the program will continue executing unless an attempt is made to access the file. At this point your program will crash. For this reason, you *always* need to check to determine if the file-open request is granted.

There are two member functions associated with file stream objects that check to see if the files are open. The .fail function returns true if the file did not open and returns false if it did. The .is_open member function returns the opposite values of .fail: true if open, false if not. Example 11.4.1 demonstrates the use of these functions.

Example 11.4.1 Checking for an open file

```
if ( fout.is_open() )
    // File is open
else
    // File is not open

if ( fout.fail() )
    // File is not open
else
    // File is open
```

STYLE NOTE It is our preference to use the .is_open member function. We find it is more intuitive for our students than .fail, because the name of the function is more indicative of what we are trying to accomplish.

Remember: Always check the file to see if it was opened before trying to access it.

Section 11.4 Exercises

Please respond to each of the following questions.

1. After attempting to open a file, always make it a point to _____.

   a. read the data it contains

   b. write your new data to it as soon as possible

   c. release it when done

   d. make sure the file opened successfully

2. Which of the following member functions check to make sure the file is open?

   a. `.is_ok`

   b. `.is_working`

   c. `.is_open`

   d. `.is_up`

3. While not our preferred option, the _____ method can also be used to see if a file is open.

   a. `.is_up`

   b. `.fail`

   c. `is_trouble`

   d. `.trouble`

11.5 Closing Files

If you open a file, make sure you close it. However, only attempt to close the file when you are sure that the file was open. Closing a file informs the operating system that you are finished with that resource. Example 11.5.1 shows how to use the `.close` member function to close a file if it was open.

Example 11.5.1 Closing an open file

```
if ( fout.is_open() )
{
    // Perform file operations
    fout.close();
}
else
    // File is not open
```

STYLE NOTE ▶ Not only should you close a file if you open it, but you should close it as soon as you are finished using the file. Always free any resources tied up by your program as soon as possible. This allows the operating system to manage your computer's limited resources more efficiently.

Section 11.5 Learn by Doing Exercise

1. Create a text file in your IDE. Place the text, "Sample text." in the file. Save the file in a new directory on your hard drive, called Sample, as Sample.txt.

   Write a program that opens the file in read mode. If the file is opened correctly, display the text, "File opened!" to the screen. Otherwise, print, "File was not opened!". Don't forget to close the file if it was opened successfully. Compile and run your program.

   Now modify the program so that you open the same file in append mode. Again, compile and rerun the program. Open the data file from within your IDE and verify that the contents are still correct.

   Lastly, open the same file in write mode. Compile and rerun the program. Open the data file from within your IDE to see if the contents of the file still exist.

11.6 Writing to Files

Now that we understand the opening and closing of files, we can start to use files to store data or other information. Fortunately, an `ofstream` object allows us to use all of the same functionality as `cout` to write to a file. Example 11.6.1 illustrates how to generate a report that is written to a file.

Example 11.6.1 Writing a file

```
void PrintReport( char lname[][NAME_LENGTH], int salary[],
                  int num_records )
{
    // Open file
    ofstream report( "report.txt" );

    // Check to see if file is open
    if ( report.is_open() )
    {
        // Print header and title information
        PrintHeader( report );

        // Write the information to the file
        for ( int i = 0; i < num_records; i++ )
        {
            report << left << setw(NAME_LENGTH + 1) << lname[i]
                   << right << setw(8) << salary[i] << endl;
        }
        // Close the file
        report.close();
    }
    else
    {
        cout << "Error: Unable to open report file." << endl;
    }
}
```

Example 11.6.1 uses some familiar formatting commands presented in Chapter 5. Notice that the `report` stream object is passed to the function `PrintHeader`. Anytime a stream object is passed, it must be passed by reference to avoid crashing your program. It may not be intuitive, but inserting into or extracting information from the stream changes the state of the stream. Therefore, always pass these stream objects by reference. The function declaration of `PrintHeader` is shown in Example 11.6.2.

Example 11.6.2 Passing streams by reference

```
void PrintHeader( ofstream & report );
```

Section 11.6 Exercises

Please respond to each of the following questions.

1. If you open a file, you need to make sure you _____ it.

   a. read

   b. write

   c. append

   d. close

2. What object allows us to write data to a file?

   a. `instream`

   b. `ofstream`

   c. `outstreamer`

   d. `consolestream`

3. Always make it a point to pass stream objects to functions by _____.

   a. value

   b. constant

   c. pointer

   d. reference

Assume the following:

```
ofstream out( "filename.txt" );
```

4. Write the necessary statements to do the following:

   a. Check to make sure the file is open; if not, display a message to the console

   b. Write your first name and last name, separated by a space, into the file

   c. Close the file

11.7 Reading from Files

As discussed earlier, an `ofstream` object can be used to write to a file, but we must use an `ifstream` object to read from a file. An `ifstream` object can be used exactly like `cin`, including the `.getline` member function.

    It is unlikely that we would know how much data exists in any given data file. Therefore, we typically want to read every piece of data until the end of the file has been reached. In every file there is an end-of-file (EOF) marker placed at the end. Although a simple concept, it is important to realize that the marker is automatically placed by the operating system immediately after the last piece of information. Example 11.7.1 shows how to read from a data file until the EOF marker has been reached.

Example 11.7.1 Reading from a file

```cpp
int ReadData( char lname[][NAME_LENGTH], int salary[] )
{
    int num_records = 0;

    // Open file
    ifstream data_file( "data.txt" );

    // Check to see if file is open
    if ( data_file.is_open() )
    {
        // Priming read
        data_file >> lname[num_records]
                  >> salary[num_records];

        // Read until end of file is reached
        while( !data_file.eof() )
        {
            num_records++;

            data_file >> lname[num_records]
                      >> salary[num_records];
        }
        data_file.close();
    }
    else
    {
        cout << "Error: Unable to open data file." << endl;
    }
    return num_records;
```

In Example 11.7.1, the `.eof` member function returns true if the EOF marker has been read, false if not. Therefore, we want to continue to read as long as the EOF marker has not been encountered.

The `ReadData` function returns the number of records read from the file. This value would be used to inform other functions in our program how many records are stored in our arrays. Also, we implemented a *priming read* to ensure that we read the correct number of records, as discussed in Chapter 8. The priming read in our example ensures that if the file exists but is empty, the number of records returned from the function would remain zero.

File access is fairly slow, especially if you are using an older floppy drive. Therefore, we suggest you keep the number of file accesses to a bare minimum. Since the data is stored in memory, it will always be faster to access this data than the data in the file.

Section 11.7 Exercises

Please respond to each of the following questions.

1. What object allows us to read data from a file?

   a. `mystream`

   b. `ofstream`

   c. `ifstream`

   d. `consstream`

2. What does EOF represent?

   a. educational opportunity fund

   b. end of format

   c. end of file

   d. end of fun

3. When using stream objects, we use a(n) _____ object when writing to files and a(n) _____ object for reading files.

   a. `fout` / `fin`

   b. `ofstream` / `ifstream`

   c. `outfile` / `infile`

   d. `in` / `out`

4. How long do we continue to try to read an input file?

   a. until the EOF marker is encountered

   b. until a compiler warning is received

   c. until a complete record is processed

   d. until an exception is thrown

Assume the following:

```
ifstream input_file ( "sample.txt" );
char lname[21], id[5];
int age;
```

5. Write the necessary statements to do the following:

   a. Check to make sure the file is open

   b. Read and display all the information contained within the space-delimited file; include a priming read and assume that each record in the file contains the following three fields: lname, id, and age

   c. Close the file when you have processed all the records

6. Indicate whether each of the following statements is true or false.

   a. It is faster to read data from a storage device, like a floppy disk or a USB drive, than accessing data directly from RAM.

   b. The exact number of records contained within a data file is usually not known ahead of time.

   c. A data file will usually only be completely read once during the execution of an individual application.

   d. When reading data from an input file, it is imperative to count the number of records processed.

   e. The EOF marker is automatically placed at the end of a text file.

11.8 Searching

Now that we have the capability to easily store large amounts of data in memory, one of the more common capabilities required of any program is the ability to search for a specific piece of information. For example, if a program holds information on employees, the capability of finding a single employee's information would be a necessity.

The easiest method is to start at the first record, comparing a value from within our arrays to a user-specified target. If the value matches the target record, process the information; otherwise, move to the next record. If the search examines all records without finding a match, obviously the record

```
/***********************************************
 * Name: LinearSearch
 * Parameters: The data array. (Pass by Const Pointer)
 *             The number of records. (Pass by Value)
 *             The target. (Pass by Value)
 * Return: none
 * Purpose: Display the target information or
 * a message stating the record could not be found
 ***********************************************/
found = false

Loop number of record times or until found
      If array (loop counter) equals target
            Display information
            found = ture
      Increment loop counter
End loop
If not found
      Display "The value you are searching for doesn't exist"
```

Figure 11.8.1 Linear search algorithm

didn't exist, and appropriate action should be taken. A simple error message displayed to the screen might suffice.

This method is called a *linear* or *sequential search*. Although simple to understand and implement, let's see how efficient it is. In the best-case scenario, the record is found after the first comparison. The worst case would be if the desired record did not exist in our arrays. The average number of iterations would be $n/2$, where n is the number of elements in the array. Figure 11.8.1 shows an algorithm for a linear search.

Another method is called a *binary search* and is, on average, much more efficient. The one requirement for a binary search to work is that the data must be ordered by the *key value*. In other words, if we are searching by an employee's last name, the data must be arranged (i.e., sorted) in order by the last name field. In this case, the last name becomes our key value. Sorting will be covered in the next section.

The premise behind the binary search is to logically cut the array in half. Then a comparison is made to see which half the target would be located in, and it too is logically cut in half. This process continues until the target is located. Although much more complicated, this algorithm requires many less iterations on average. The number of iterations for a binary search to find its target is roughly the number of times we can divide the array in half, or $1 + \log_2 n$. Table 11.8.1 evaluates the number of iterations for the linear and binary search, dependent on the number of elements.

As you can see in Table 11.8.1, the number of comparisons required of a binary search is much less than that of a linear search. An algorithm for a binary search is shown in Figure 11.8.2.

Notice that the last two lines in Figure 11.8.2 handle the situation in which the item to be found doesn't exist in the array. If the loop terminates and the variable found is still false, the element was not found and an appropriate message will be displayed. We only show the pseudocode for the searches dis-

| | Worst Case Number of Iterations | |
Number of Elements	Linear Search	Binary Search
100	100	8
1000	1000	11
10,000	10,000	15
100,000	100,000	18
1,000,000	1,000,000	21

Table 11.8.1 Linear versus binary searches

```
/*********************************************
* Name: BinarySearch
* Parameters: The data array. (Pass by Const Pointer)
*             The number of records. (Pass by Value)
*             The target. (Pass by Value)
* Return: none
* Purpose: Display the target information or
* a message stating the data could not be found
*********************************************/
found = false
left = 0
right = number of records

Loop while left is less than or equal to right and found not equal to true
    mid = (left + right) / 2

    If the target equals array(mid)
        Display information
        found = ture
    Else if the target is greater than array(mid)
        left = mid + 1
    Else
        right = mid - 1
End loop
If not found
    Display "The value you are searching for doesn't exist"
```

Figure 11.8.2 Binary search algorithm

cussed in this section because the best way to fully understand these search algorithms is for you to implement them.

Section 11.8 Exercises

Please respond to each of the following questions.

1. To do a binary search, the data we are searching must have the following characteristics:

   a. Be in order

   b. Contain at least three or more characters

   c. Be in all uppercase

   d. Be used only on alphabetic characters

2. Doing a search that starts with the first record in our list and compares each successive record's key until either a match is found or we have reached the end of the list is called a _____ search.

   a. selection

   b. binary

   c. linear (or sequential)

   d. object

3. Indicate whether each of the following statements is true or false.

   a. On the average, a linear or sequential search would be faster than a binary search.

   b. A binary search requires that the list be in order.

   c. A sequential search requires that the list be in order.

   d. Cutting a list of values in half as we search for a specific target value is the basic idea behind the linear search.

   e. You can search a list for either numeric or alphabetic characters.

11.9 Sorting

There are many sorting algorithms, ranging from the simple to the extremely complicated. As you might suspect, the simple algorithms are usually the least efficient. Although the focus of this text is not on sorting algorithms, being able to sort your information is a valuable skill to have in your toolbox. In this section, we present one of the slowest but easiest algorithms to implement: the *bubble sort*.

Just as a bubble floats to the surface of a pond, the bubble sort "bubbles" the largest element to the end of the array. Once one element is in place, the process restarts at the beginning of the array to bubble the next largest value to its place within the array. Each pass consists of comparing two elements, and if the first element is greater than the second, the elements are swapped. This continues until the end of the array is encountered. Figure 11.9.1 shows how the first pass would place the largest element at the end of the array.

As you can see from Figure 11.9.1, the largest element is now at the end of the array. All we need to do is repeat the process four more times and the array will be sorted. The bubble-sort algorithm is shown in Figure 11.9.2.

While the algorithm shown in Figure 11.9.2 works correctly, we can make the bubble-sort algorithm a little more efficient by making a couple of observations. First of all, each pass places one more element in the correct location. Therefore, we don't need to compare the element just placed in the correct

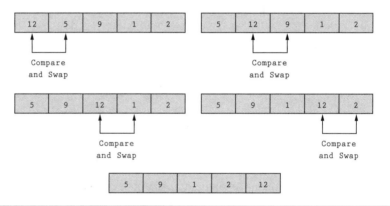

Figure 11.9.1 First pass of the bubble sort

```
/*********************************************
* Name: BubbleSort
* Parameters: The data array. (Pass by Pointer)
*             The number of records. (Pass by Value)
* Return: none
* Purpose: Sort an array using the bubble-sort
* algorithm
*********************************************/
Loop number of records times (loop counter: pass)
        Loop number of records - 1 times (loop counter: i)
                If array(i) > array(i +1)
                        temp = array(i)
                        array(i) = array(i + 1)
                        array(i + 1) = temp
                End if
        End Loop
End Loop
```

Figure 11.9.2 Bubble-sort algorithm

position in any future passes. This means that each pass now requires one less comparison. The change to the algorithm is displayed in blue in Figure 11.9.3.

Another thing to notice is that even if the array is sorted, the process continues. We can use the concept of a flag to stop the processing once we are guaranteed that the array is in order. If we make a complete pass without having to swap an element, we know that the array is ordered. Therefore, if after the first pass we can determine that the array is already sorted, all unnecessary future passes would be circumvented. This change to the algorithm is often called a *flagged bubble sort* and is shown in Figure 11.9.4.

```
/***********************************************
* Name: BubbleSort
* Parameters: The data array. (Pass by Pointer)
*             The number of records. (Pass by Value)
* Return: none
* Purpose: Sort an array using the bubble-sort
* algorithm
***********************************************
Loop number of records times (loop counter: pass)
        Loop number of records - pass - 1 times (loop counter: i)
                If array(i) > array(i + 1)
                        temp = array(i)
                        array(i) = array(i + 1)
                        array(i + 1) = temp
                End If
        End Loop
End Loop
```

Figure 11.9.3 Bubble-sort algorithm, more efficient approach

```
/***********************************************
* Name: BubbleSort
* Parameters: The data array. (Pass by Pointer)
*             The number of records. (Pass by Value)
* Return: none
* Purpose: Sort an array using the bubble-sort
* algorithm
***********************************************
sorted = false
Loop number of records times (loop counter: pass) or until sorted
        sorted = true
        Loop number of records - pass - 1 times (loop counter: i)
                If array(i) > array(i + 1)
                        sorted = false
                        temp = array(i)
                        array(i) = array(i + 1)
                        array(i + 1) = temp
                End If
        End Loop
End Loop
```

Figure 11.9.4 Flagged bubble sort

Figure 11.9.4 shows the use of the `sorted` variable as a flag to help determine when the array is ordered. As you can see, with very minor changes we can greatly increase the performance and efficiency of the bubble sort.

Section 11.9 Exercises

Please respond to each of the following questions.

1. Which popular sorting method floats the largest element in an array to the end?

   a. merge sort

   b. selection sort

   c. heap sort

   d. bubble sort

2. Indicate whether each of the following statements is true or false.

   a. To potentially improve the efficiency of the bubble-sort method, the use of a flag was introduced to act as a signal when the array is in the desired order and no additional comparisons need to be made.

   b. There are a number of popular sort methods available.

   c. The bubble sort is not very efficient.

   d. The bubble sort basically involves comparing each item in the array or list with the item next to it and, if needed, swapping them.

Section 11.9 Learn by Doing Exercise

1. Using Examples 10.6.3 and 10.6.4 as a guide, write a function that finds the median of the list of values.

11.10 Problem Solving Applied

In this section we make the final addition to the problem associated with the class management program discussed in the past few chapters. The fundamental aspects of the project are the same as they have been in the past, but now we will use external files for reading and writing data and reports. Once the program has read the data from an external file into a series of parallel arrays, we process it and write the results to a report file instead of the console. If you need a bit of a refresher on the overall project, please refer to Section 8.6, Section 9.10, and Section 10.12 for the problem specifications.

As was done in the previous chapter, we continue to incorporate the use of the I → P → O model to help guide us in the design associated with the required updates for our program. As you will quickly see, both the Input and the Output components of the model lend themselves well to reading and writing data from external sources or files.

Using file streams along with arrays from the last chapter will really help make your job easier in the long run. From a design and programming point of view, the fact that we are now employing external streams versus the console provides only a few additional concerns.

As in the past, `main` continues to act as the driver for the overall program. As needed, calls are made to deal with each of the three main components of the I $\rightarrow$ P $\rightarrow$ O model. In relation to the input phase, we now acquire and read our data from an external storage device. Because the device is a separate entity of the computer, there are additional conditions that could arise, which we will need to be concerned with from a programming perspective. For example, the device could be full or not in a ready state when we attempt to read the input data. Likewise, where in the past the output phase directed the related output information to the console, we must now concern ourselves with some potential issues, such as a device that's not ready. Fortunately, the ability to use and validate these different forms of input and output streams is relatively easy when we write the actual code.

One final point you need to remember in terms of file streams versus the keyboard or console for I/O is that the role of the programmer is in no way reduced or diminished. For example, it is imperative that you always check to make sure that all records are read from the input file and that all records or information is written to any output-related devices or files. Missing the last, or first, record in the input file has no doubt caused many students and professionals a great deal of embarrassment, humiliation, and frustration. Please make it a point to always double-check both your inputs and outputs.

Figure 11.10.1 shows the structure chart used in the previous chapter with only two small modifications. The label for `InputData` has now been changed to `ReadData`, reflecting the fact that the data will be coming from a file stream

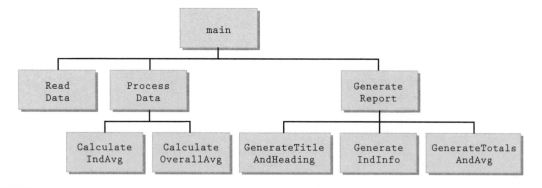

Figure 11.10.1 Structure chart

versus the keyboard. Likewise, the previous output components called `Print` have been replaced by the word `Generate` to help avoid any potential confusion.

Now that the minor updates to the structure chart have been made, we can show the corresponding rough draft of the pseudocode, with only limited changes relating specifically to input and output activities.

Design:

Pseudocode

```
/*********************************************************************************
* Name: main
*********************************************************************************/
trouble_with_file = Call ReadData
If ( trouble_with_file equals False )
    Call ProcessData
    Call GenerateReport
End If


/*********************************************************************************
* Name: ReadData
* Parameters: Student info/arrays including ID and each of three exam scores.
*                     student_counter. By ref.
* Return: bool - trouble_with_file
* Purpose: Read all of the student data from the keyboard
*********************************************************************************/
Open student_data_file
Check for successful open
If (student_data_file opened successfully)
    Read id[student_counter],score[student_counter][0],
        test_scores[student_counter][1], test_scores[student_counter][2]

    While not EOF of studentDataFile
        Add 1 to student_counter
        Read id[student_counter],score[student_counter][0],
            test_scores[student_counter][1], test_scores[student_counter][2]
    End loop

    Close student_data_file
    Set trouble_with_file = False
Else
    Display "Trouble with student_data_file"
    Set trouble_with_file = True
End If

Return trouble_with_file


/*********************************************************************************
* Name: ProcessData
```

```
* Parameters: Student info including arrays holding the three exam scores,
*                 individual's average to hold each student's exam average, and
*                 an array to hold each student's grade.
*                 student_counter and overallClassAverage. By ref.
* Return: none
* Purpose: Act as a driver for all processing and calculations
*********************************************************************************/
Call ProcessData
Call CalculateIndAvg
Call CalculateOverallAvg


/*******************************************************************************
* Name: CalculateIndAvg
* Parameters: Student info including array holding three exam scores and the array
*                 to hold each student's overall exam average and letter grade.
*                 student_counter. By val.
* Return: none
* Purpose: Calculate average score and letter grade for each student
*********************************************************************************/
For each student
Begin loop
   Calculate inds_average[r] = (test_scores[r][O] + test_scores[r][1]
                 + test_scores[r][2]) / 3
   . . .
End Loop


/*******************************************************************************
* Name: CalculateOverallAvg
* Parameters: Array holding inds_average of three test scores.
*                 student_counter. By val.
*                 overall_class_average. By ref.
* Return: none
* Purpose: Calculate overall_class_average
*********************************************************************************/
For each student
Begin loop
   Calculate the total_averages = inds_average[r] + total_averages
End loop
Calculate overall_class_average = total_averages / student_counter


/*******************************************************************************
* Name: GenerateReport
* Parameters: Student info/arrays including ID, age, gender, each of three exam
*                 scores, and individual average.
*                 student_counter and overall_class_average. By ref.
* Return: none
* Purpose: Act as a driver for generating all the necessary components of the
*          report
*********************************************************************************/
```

```
Open report_file
Check for successful open
If (report_file opened successfully)
    Call GenerateTitleAndHeadings
    Call GenerateIndInfo
    Call GenerateTotalsAndClassAvg
    Close report_file
Else
    Display "Trouble with student_data_file"
End If


/*******************************************************************************
* Name: GenerateTitleAndHeadings
* Parameters: report_file – by ref.
* Return: none
* Purpose: Display welcome message and column headings
*******************************************************************************/
Print "* Welcome to the Grader Program * "
. . .


/*******************************************************************************
* Name: GenerateIndInfo
* Parameters: Student info/arrays including ID, each of three exam scores, average,
*             and letter grade.
*             student_count. By val.
*             report_file. By ref.
* Return: none
* Purpose: Display to the screen all the data for each student, including his or her
*          individual average on the three exams
*******************************************************************************/
For each student
Begin loop
  . . .
End Loop


/*******************************************************************************
* Name: GenerateTotalsAndClassAvg
* Parameters: student_counter
*             overall_class_average for all students in class. By val.
*             report_file. By ref.
* Return: none
* Purpose: Display the student_counter along with overall class average
*******************************************************************************/
Print "Total number of students processed: " student_counter
Print overall_class_average
```

It is now time to double-check your pseudocode. Make any needed corrections or additions. Once you have proven that your algorithm works, the next step requires translating the pseudocode into C++ source code.

After you have created your Visual Studio Project and written the source code, be sure to add both the input and the output files to your project. This will save time in validating and examining the data and the associated results without ever having to leave the IDE.

11.11 C—The Differences

As we learned in Chapter 5, C accomplishes keyboard and console I/O in a totally different manner from C++, and the same goes for file I/O—no stream classes or objects are used. However, just as `cin` and `cout` were similar to the way we read and write files in C++, `printf` and `scanf` are very closely related to the way we read and write text files in C.

11.11.1 File Pointer

Instead of file streams, C uses something commonly called a *file pointer*—a variable that holds the address of a `FILE` structure. This pointer is what we will use to access the file once it has been opened. A *structure* is another data type similar to what we saw with classes. We will have much more to say about structures in Chapter 13. Example 11.11.1 demonstrates how to declare a file pointer.

Example 11.11.1 Declaration of file pointers

```
FILE * fptr;
FILE * report;
FILE * data_file;
FILE * input;
FILE * output;
```

Notice that a file pointer can be used to access both input and output files. To use the `FILE` structure, you need to include `<stdio.h>`, the same header file we used for `printf` and `scanf`.

11.11.2 Opening Files

Since `FILE` pointers are used for both reading and writing, C provides six modes that can be specified when opening a file. Three of these modes are listed and explained in Table 11.11.1. The other modes will be discussed in Chapter 17.

Mode	Explanation
r	Read mode. Open fails if file doesn't exist.
w	Write mode. Will create file if possible. Existing data is destroyed.
a	Append mode. Opens the file so data can be appended. Will create file.

Table 11.11.1 File modes

The `fopen` function opens a file in the specified mode and then returns the file pointer used to access the file. The basic `fopen` syntax follows:

```
<file-pointer> = fopen ( <filename>, <mode> );
```

The `<filename>` and `<mode>` are either cStrings or string literals. The `<mode>` is usually a string literal specifying one of the three modes in Table 11.11.1. Example 11.11.2 shows how to use the `fopen` function.

Example 11.11.2 The `fopen` function

```
FILE * input;

input = fopen( "data.txt", "r" );
```

Even though Example 11.11.2 opens a file for reading, other modes are accomplished in the same way.

11.11.3 Checking for a Successful Open

The `fopen` function returns either an address, if the file was opened correctly, or `NULL`, if the file opening failed. As a result, all you need to do is check to see if the file pointer is `NULL`, as shown in Example 11.11.3.

Example 11.11.3 Checking for correct opening

```
FILE * input;
input = fopen( "data.txt", "r" );
```

```
if ( input != NULL )
    printf( "File was opened." );
else
    printf( "File was not opened." );
```

Just as in C++, *always* check to see if the file was successfully opened before trying to access it.

11.11.4 Closing Files

There are a couple of ways to close files in C. The first method uses the `fclose` function. This is the preferred method, but you can also use the `fcloseall` function. The `fclose` function prototype follows:

```
int fclose ( FILE * fptr );
```

The `fclose` function returns a 0 if the file was closed. Be careful, though; if the file pointer is NULL when the `fclose` function is executed, your program will crash. Therefore, ensure that you only attempt to close a file if it was opened successfully.

The `fcloseall` function closes all files except for stdin, stdout, and stderr. The function prototype for `fcloseall` follows:

```
int fcloseall ( );
```

The `fcloseall` function returns an integer representing the number of files that were successfully closed. Example 11.11.4 demonstrates how to use these functions.

Example 11.11.4 Closing a file

```
FILE * input;
int num_files;

input = fopen( "data.txt", "r" );

/* Example 1 */
if ( input != NULL )
    if ( fclose(input) != 0 )
        printf( "File was not closed correctly." );

/* Example 2 */
num_files = fcloseall();
printf( "There were %d files closed.", num_files );
```

The reason `fclose` is preferred over `fcloseall` is that it is more precise. It forces you to specify the exact file to close, guaranteeing that you will not accidentally close something you shouldn't.

11.11.5 Writing to a File

Wouldn't it be nice if we could use `printf` to write to a file? Well, we can't—but we *can* use `fprintf`. The only difference between the two functions is that the first parameter in a call to `fprintf` is a file pointer. Everything else is exactly the same. Example 11.11.5 shows how to write to a file. Notice that even the output formatting used with `printf` remains the same for `fprintf`.

Example 11.11.5 Writing a file

```
void PrintReport( char lname[][NAME_LENGTH], int salary[],
                int num_records )
{
    FILE * report;
    // Open file
    report = fopen( "report.txt", "w" );

    // Check to see if file is open
    if ( report != NULL )
    {
        // Printer header and title information
        PrintHeader( report );

        // Write the information to the file
        for ( int i = 0; i < num_records; i++ )
        {
            fprintf( report, "%-25s %8d\n", lname[i], salary[i] );
        }
        // Close the file
        if ( fclose( report ) != 0 )
            printf( "Error: Can't close output file." );
    }
    else
    {
        printf( "Error: Unable to open report file." );
    }
}
```

11.11.6 Reading from a File

You might suspect that since there is a function called `fprintf`, there probably is a function called `fscanf`. You are absolutely correct! Except for the file pointer, the syntax is exactly the same as for `scanf`. You can also read until the end of the file by using the `feof` function. Both of these functions are shown in Example 11.11.6.

Example 11.11.6 Reading from a file

```c
int ReadData( char lname[][NAME_LENGTH], int salary[] )
{
    FILE * data_file;
    int num_records = 0;

    // Open file
    data_file = fopen( "data.txt" );

    // Check to see if file is open
    if ( data_file != NULL )
    {
        // Priming read
        fscanf( data_file, "%s %d", lname[num_records],
                                    &salary[num_records] );
        // Read until end of file is reached
        while ( !feof(data_file) )
        {
            num_records++;

            fscanf( data_file, "%s %d", lname[num_records],
                                        &salary[num_records] );
        }

        if ( fclose( data_file ) != 0 )
            printf( "Error: Can't close data file." );
    }
    else
    {
        printf( "Error: Unable to open data file." );
    }
    return num_records;
}
```

Now you should be able to perform file input and output routines using either C++ or C.

1 1 . 1 2   S U M M A R Y

Over the past few years, the cost-associated with various external storage devices, such as pen drives and hard drives, have continued to drop dramatically. This chapter examined the value and use of these types of external devices for holding files made up of both input data and reports.

Since you have already been exposed to the use of streams via `cin` and `cout`, much of the material associated with getting information from a stream or sending information into a stream hopefully made sense rather quickly. Early on we showed how to associate a file located on an external device to an object or variable within a program. Once it was decided what to call a particular file, we established in what mode we wanted to open the file. The available modes presented included opening a file for reading, writing, or appending. Because there may indeed be a problem with locating a file, we illustrated how important it is that a check always be made to indicate that a file was successfully opened. Once the file is known to be open, we were ready to read or write data to the external device. Once access to the file is no longer needed, we discussed the need to close the file and release the resource back to the operating system.

The final two sections of the chapter introduced the concepts of sorting and searching data. Sorting involves placing the data contained within our arrays into an established order, while searching provides the facility to locate a specific key from within a list of data. While a thorough discussion of these two topics is beyond the scope of this text, this brief overview introduced two powerful activities often associated with handling or manipulating data.

11.13 Debugging Exercise

Download the following file from this book's website and run the program following the instructions noted in the code.

```
/**********************************************************************
* File: Chap_11_Debugging.cpp
*
* General Instructions: Complete each step before proceeding to the
* next.
*
* Debugging Exercise 1
*
* 1) Copy the file Chap_11_data.txt to a directory you create on
*    your drive.
* 2) Under the Project menu, select Add Existing Item and
*    add the input file you just placed on your drive to your
*    current project. Make sure your Solution Explorer window
*    is visible. If not, you can display it by selecting Solution
*    Explorer (or Ctrl+Alt+L).
* 3) Open the input file by simply double-clicking the name of the
```

```
*      file in your Solution Explorer.
* 4) Build and execute the program.
* 5) Update the file paths that follow to correctly represent the path you
*      created.
* 6) Rebuild and execute the program.
* 7) Examine the code and the output and notice the use of
*      parallel arrays.
* 8) Add the output file created via the execution of
*      your program to your project. Execute your program again
*      and notice how Visual Studio has rewritten your output file
*      and asks if you would like to reload the file (select Yes).
* 9) Examine the contents of both the input and the output file.
* 10) Fix all the problems in your code that exist in relation to
*       the output. Verify that your output is appropriate for your
*       input file.
* 11) Build and execute your code until you have all errors
*       removed and all the output is correct.
*
* Debugging Exercise 2
*
* 1) Replace the double slashes (\\) in the input file open statement
*      with only a single slash
*      (i.e., inFile.open("C:\TEMP\Chap_11_data.txt").
* 2) Build your code, noticing the impact of the invalid path you
*      created in the previous step.
* 3) Replace the slashes as they were.
* 4) Change both the input and the output filenames so that they are
*      invalid.
* 5) Update the file-related error messages within the code
*      to also provide the specific name of the file that is having a
*      problem.
* 6) Rebuild and execute your program to verify that your messages
*      are correct.
* 7) Correct the path names.
* 8) Build and execute your code and carefully check your
*      output both on the console and in the output file.
*
**************************************************************************/
#include <iostream>
#include <fstream>       // For the files!!!!
#include <iomanip>
using std::cin;
using std::cout;
using std::endl;
using std::setw;
using std::ios;

using std::ifstream;
using std::ofstream;
```

```
const int EMPLOYEES = 20;
const int MAX = 21;

int ReadData( ifstream &inFile, ofstream &outFile, char name[] [MAX],
              int age[] );
void WriteOutputFile( ofstream &outFile, char name[] [MAX], int age[],
                      int counter );
void PrintTotalsAndSummary( ofstream &out, int totalRecords ) ;

int main()
{
     char name[EMPLOYEES] [MAX];
     int age[EMPLOYEES];
     int record_counter(0);

     ifstream inFile;

     // Notice how this automatically opens the file
     ofstream outFile( "C:\\TEMP\\Chap_11_Report.txt" );

     inFile.open( "C:\\TEMP\\Chap_11_data.txt" );

     if ( inFile.is_open() )
     {
          record_counter = ReadData( inFile, outFile, name, age );
          inFile.close();

          if ( outFile.is_open() )
          {
               WriteOutputFile( outFile, name, age, record_counter );
               PrintTotalsAndSummary( outFile, record_counter );
               outFile.close();
          }
          else
          {
               cout << "Trouble Opening File";
               cout << "\n\n\t\t ** About to EXIT NOW! ** ";
          }
     }
     else
     {
          cout << "Trouble Opening File";
          cout << "\n\n\t\t ** About to EXIT NOW! ** ";
     }
     return 0;
}
int ReadData( ifstream & inFile, ofstream & outFile, char name[] [MAX],
              int age[] )
{
     int counter = 0;
```

```
    inFile >> name[counter] >> age[counter]; // Priming Read

    while( !inFile.eof () )
    {
         cout << setiosflags(ios::left) << setw(25)
              <<  name[counter] << resetiosflags(ios::left)
              << setw(4) << age [counter] << endl;
         counter++;
         inFile >> name[counter] >> age[counter];
    }

    return counter;
}

void WriteOutputFile( ofstream &outFile, char name[] [MAX], int age[],
                      int counter )
{
    outFile << "   Here is the Output File" << endl;
    for ( int r = 0; r <= counter ; r++ )
    {
       outFile << setiosflags(ios::left) << setw(25)
               << name[r] << setw(4)
               << resetiosflags(ios::left) << age[r]
               << endl;
    }
}

void PrintTotalsAndSummary ( ofstream &outFile, int totalRecords )
{
    // To screen
    cout  << "\n\n\t** Total Records: " << totalRecords << " **\n"
          << "\t\t The End \n";

    // To file
    outFile << "\n\n\t** Total Records: " << totalRecords << " **\n"
            << "\t\t The End \n";

}
```

11.14 Programming Exercises

The following programming exercises are to be developed using all phases of the development method. Be sure to make use of good programming practices and style, such as constants, white-space, indentation, naming conventions, and commenting. Make sure all input prompts are clear and descriptive and that your output is well formatted and looks professional.

1. For this exercise, read from a file a person's name, Social Security number, and wage; the number of hours worked in a week; and his or her status. For full-time employees, $5.00 is

deducted from wages for union fees. A person is full time if he or she has an F as the status. Time and a half is paid for any time worked over 40 hours in a week. For the output, you must display the person's name, Social Security number, wage, number of hours, straight time pay, overtime pay, employee status, and net pay. Make sure the output is formatted into **rows and columns** and includes the appropriate titles and column headings.

Data: Use the following information as data for your data file:

John Smith 123-09-8765 9.00 46 F
Molly Brown 432-89-7654 9.50 40 F
Tim Wheeler 239-34-3458 11.25 83 F
Keil Wader 762-84-6543 6.50 35 P
Trish Dish 798-65-9844 7.52 40 P
Anthony Lei 934-43-9843 9.50 56 F
Kevin Ashes 765-94-7343 4.50 30 P
Cheryl Prince 983-54-9000 4.65 45 F
Kim Cares 343-11-2222 10.00 52 F
Dave Cockroach 356-98-1236 5.75 48 F
Will Kusick 232-45-2322 15.00 45 P

2. For this exercise, you will write a program to perform two main tasks. The first task simply asks the user to enter the name of a data file containing a list of 10 integers, each separated by a space or a line feed. After you have made sure that the file opened successfully and the data loaded into an array, display the smallest and the largest integer to the console. Once the smallest and largest integers have been printed, sort the entire list in ascending order and display each of the elements in the sorted list. Please use the following integers to test your program: 120 234 33 2021 44 23 530 567 340 501.

3. For this project, your supervisor wants you to write a program that starts by asking the user to enter the name of a text file that contains a number of sentences or lines. For each line you read, display a line number followed by a space and the line of text from the file. At the end of each line, display the number of characters in the line.

4. This program involves developing a menu-driven database application. You need to accept as input from a file a person's first name, last name, phone number, and birth date. This program will be menu driven with the following options:

   1. Find a person's information
   2. Add a person to the database
   3. Edit a person's information
   4. Display all records to the screen
   5. Quit

- Option 1 allows the user to enter a name, after which the program will search for and display the person's information. Use the binary-search algorithm discussed in this chapter.

- Option 2 allows the user to add a person to the database.

- Option 3 allows the user to change any information related to a specific individual. Be aware that if the user changes the last name of the person, the arrays will need to be resorted.

- Option 4 displays to the screen all of the records sorted by last name in the database.

- Option 5 will end the program.

The data will be read from the file only once, and will only update the file after the person has chosen Option 5 from the menu. All other modifications to the data are performed on the arrays storing the information. Create your own data file using realistic personal data to exercise all of the options in the program.

11.15 Team Programming Exercise

Do you remember Marcus, the developer turned manager we introduced a few chapters back? Well Marcus recently started another relatively short project but unfortunately didn't have the time to finish it. He asked Troy to complete it, but regrettably Troy was only able to spend a little time on the code before he too was called away to work on another project. As luck would have it, you have been asked to work through the code and get it functioning, even though it is in a pretty rough state.

Basically the program is to read from an external data file the first name, last name, extension number, and department for each of the employees of a small company. Once all the information has been placed into a series of arrays, the program should generate two separate output files. The first file, Employee Report, should be nicely formatted and contain the employee's name (i.e., last name, first name), extension number, and department. The second file, Telephone Guide, should contain only the name (first name followed by last name) and the extension number. Include titles and column headings for both reports.

Following is some additional information provided by Marcus and Troy:

1. The company has approximately 10 employees.

2. The name fields and the department field are limited to 15 characters.

3. There was some confusion on the naming convention to use within the source code. Make sure all your variables and constants are consistently named.

4. Either copy the input file from the website or create your own input file called Chap_11_employee_data.txt with the following data:

Alexis Blough 1-1921 CEO
Bill Pay 1-7711 Accounting
Willy Makit 4-1595 Sales
Marie Murray 1-4986 MIS
Cal Caldwellowinski 5-0911 MIS
Jamie Johanasola 5-9999 Marketing

5. Do *not* make the scope of the file streams global. Pass them to the appropriate function as needed.

6. Fix any of the "small" problems Marcus and Troy indicated were still in the source code—and make sure you close all the files.

7. Have fun and make sure you deal with all the necessary records and components being asked for.

8. Clean up Troy's code so that it follows a consistent style.

```cpp
/*****************************************************************
 * Filename:  Chap_11_Team.cpp
 * This is a draft of the code started by Marcus and Troy - please
 * clean it up and make sure it works correctly and that it is easy to
 * maintain and modify. Unfortunately they did NOT have time to fix
 * a number of errors and omissions contained within the file.
 *****************************************************************/
#include <iostream>
#include <fstream>
using std::cout;
using std::endl;

using std::ifstream;
using std::ofstream;

const int EMPLOYEES = 16;
const int MAX = 14;
const int EXTENSION = 7; // Telephone length-6 char's plus 1 for null

int ReadEmpData(char first_name[][MAX], char last_name[][MAX],
                char phone_ext[][EXTENSION], char department[][MAX]);
void WriteEmpReport(char first_name[][MAX], char last_name[][MAX],
                    char phone_ext[][EXTENSION], char department[][MAX],
                    int record_counter);
void WriteEmpPhoneGuide(char first_name[][MAX], char last_name[][MAX],
                        char phone_ext[][EXTENSION]) ;

ifstream emp_data("Chap_11_employee_data.txt");
ofstream empReport("EmployeeReport.txt");
```

```cpp
ofstream phone_report("PhoneReport.txt");

int main()
{
        char first_name[EMPLOYEES][MAX], last_name[EMPLOYEES][MAX];
        char  phone_ext[EMPLOYEES][EXTENSION], department[EMPLOYEES][MAX];
        int record_counter(0);
        if ( emp_data.is_open() )
        {
                record_counter = ReadEmpData(first_name, last_name, phone_ext,
                                    department);

                // Also check Phone Report file status too - TROY
                if( empReport.is_open() )
                {
                        WriteEmpReport(first_name, last_name, phone_ext,
                                    department, record_counter);

                        WriteEmpPhoneGuide(first_name, last_name, phone_ext) ;
                }
                else
                {
                        cout << "Trouble Opening Employee Report File";
                        cout << "\n\n\t\t ** About to EXIT NOW! ** ";
                }
        }
        else
        {
                cout << "Trouble Opening File";
                cout << "\n\n\t\t ** About to EXIT NOW! ** ";
        }
        emp_data.close();
        empReport.close();
        phone_report.close();
        return 0;
}
int ReadEmpData(char first_name[][MAX], char last_name[][MAX],
                                    char phone_ext[][EXTENSION],
                                    char department[][MAX])
{
        int counter = 0;
        emp_data >> first_name[counter] >> last_name[counter]
                >> phone_ext[counter] >> department[counter];
        while (!emp_data.eof())
        {
                cout << last_name[counter] << endl;
                counter++;
                emp_data >> first_name[counter] >> last_name[counter]
                        >> phone_ext[counter] >> department[counter];
        }
        return counter;
}
```

```
// Remember the output/reports are to go to separate files - TROY
void WriteEmpReport(char first_name[][MAX], char last_name[][MAX],
                    char phone_ext[][EXTENSION], char department[][MAX],
                    int count)
{
        cout << "\n\t\t   EMPLOYEE REPORT\n\n";
        // Think we might have a problem somewhere in here - MARCUS
        cout << "First \t    Last   \tTelephone    \t Department\n";
        for(int r = 0; r <= count; r++)
                empReport  << first_name[r] << "\t   " << last_name[r]
                           << "\t   " << phone_ext[r] << "\t    "
                           << department[r] << endl;
}
// Got it almost done - just finish up the rest for us - TROY
void WriteEmpPhoneGuide(char first_name[][MAX], char last_name[][MAX],
                        char phone_ext[][EXTENSION])
{
        cout << "\n\nHere is in Phone Guide";


}
```

11.16 Answers to Chapter Exercises

Section 11.1

1. b.   data in a human-readable format

2. a.   true

   b.   false

   c.   true

   d.   true

Section 11.2

1. c.   `<fstream>`

2. c.   `ifstream input( "filename.txt" );`

3. a.   true

   b.   false

   c.   true

   d.   true

   e.   false

Section 11.3

1. d. read, write, append

2. c. file position marker (FPM)

3. a. The request fails and the file will not be created.

4. You need to be careful because if the file does exist and you open it in write mode, you will be overwriting (i.e., destroying) any data previously contained within the file.

Section 11.4

1. d. make sure the file opened successfully

2. c. `.is_open`

3. b. `.fail`

Section 11.6

1. d. close

2. b. `ofstream`

3. d. reference

4. a.
```
        if ( out.is_open() )
            cout << "File opened successfully";
        else
            cout << "Trouble opening file!";
```
   b. `out << "yourFirstName " << "yourLastName\n";`

   c. `out.close();`

Section 11.7

1. c. `ifstream`

2. c. end of file

3. b. `ofstream` / `ifstream`

4. a. until the EOF marker is encountered

5. a.
```
    if ( input_file.is_open() )
        cout << "Input file opened successfully";
    else
        cout << "Trouble opening input file!";
```

b. ```
input_file >> lname >> id >> age;
while (!input_file.eof())
{
    num_records++;
    cout << lname << " " << id << " " << age << endl;
    input_file >> lname >> id >> age;
}
```

c. ```
if ( input_file.is_open() )
    input_file.close();
```

6. a. false

   b. true

   c. true

   d. true

   e. true

Section 11.8

1. a. Be in order

2. c. linear (or sequential)

3. a. false

   b. true

   c. false

   d. false

   e. true

Section 11.9

1. d. bubble sort

2. a. true

   b. true

   c. true

   d. true

Pointers and Dynamic Memory Allocation

Chapter Objectives

By the end of the chapter, readers will be able to:

- Explain the concepts of pointers.
- Explain and use indirect addressing.
- Declare, initialize, and use pointers, with up to three levels of indirection.
- Pass parameters by pointer.
- Use pointer arithmetic in the manipulation of pointers.
- Use various predefined cString functions.
- Perform dynamic memory allocation and deallocation.
- Define and use ragged arrays.
- Use dynamic single- and two-dimensional arrays.
- Use memory-leak detection tools.
- Define, use, and initialize function pointers.

Introduction

This chapter explores one of the most powerful tools in C and C++ programming. Unfortunately, it is also one of the more difficult topics to master. Pointers allow us to increase the complexity of our solutions unlike anything we have discussed up till now. It is especially important that you read this chapter's text carefully and do all of the exercises.

12.1 Definition

A *pointer* is a variable that holds an address. Although we learned in Chapter 10 that the name of an array references the array's beginning address, array names are not pointers. The address referenced by the name of an array is a constant and therefore can't be changed. Bottom line, a pointer is a *variable* that holds an address. Therefore, four bytes of memory is allocated for the pointer, assuming a 32-bit operating system. This is because addresses are always four bytes regardless of what they point to.

It may not be clear at this point why pointers are so powerful. However, pointers play an extremely important role in increasing the efficiency of our programs in many different ways. Arrays become more flexible, memory access is enhanced and expanded, and the creation of dynamic data structures becomes a possibility through the use of pointers.

Before we get to the more powerful aspects of pointers, we need to discuss the details of how pointers work.

Section 12.1 Exercises

1. A pointer:

    a. increases the efficiency of our programs.

    b. is a variable.

    c. holds an address.

    d. all of the above.

2. True or false: The name of an array is a pointer.

12.2 Declaration

Like any other variable, pointers need to be declared. The basic syntax is as follows:

`<target-type>` * `<variable-name>`;

The target type in the above syntax is any data type. The asterisk indicates that the variable will hold an address of the specified target type. Example 12.2.1 shows several pointer declarations.

Example 12.2.1 Pointer declarations

```
char * ptr;
int * int_ptr;
double * dbl_ptr = 0;
```

The third declaration in Example 12.2.1 initializes the pointer to zero. The value 0 in this context is commonly referred to as *null*. This is done to give the pointer a known starting value. Otherwise, the address in the pointer will be unknown and more than likely invalid. From our discussion of cStrings you learned that there is an ASCII value 0 that is referred to as the null character ('\0'). Make sure you use the null character to terminate cStrings and the null pointer to initialize pointers. There is a third method you may encounter that is used to initialize a pointer. This involves using a predefined value, NULL, that is a holdover from C and should never be used in C++. This incorrect C++ initialization of pointers is shown in Example 12.2.2.

Example 12.2.2 Incorrect C++ pointer initialization

```
char * ptr = NULL;
```

There is a proposal put forth by Bjarne Stroustrup—the father of C++—and Herb Sutter—chair of the ISO C++ Standards Committee—to replace the value 0 for the initialization of pointers with the reserved word nullptr. Although most compilers don't currently support this, be aware that this may be available, and may perhaps be the standard, in the near future. As the authors of this text, as well as professors, we heartily embrace this proposed addition to the C++ language. The proposed syntax is shown in Example 12.2.3.

Example 12.2.3 Proposed C++ addition

```
char * ptr = nullptr;
```

Declaring more than one pointer in the same line of code often causes some confusion, as shown in Example 12.2.4.

Example 12.2.4 Pointer declarations

```
char * str1 = 0, str2;
```

Example 12.2.4 does not declare two pointers. Instead, we have declared a character pointer called `str1` and a character variable called `str2`. This is more than a little misleading for many students. Example 12.2.5 shows the correct method of declaring two pointers in the same statement.

Example 12.2.5 Pointer declarations

```
char * str1 = 0, * str2;
```

Even though we can now declare pointers, we still can't do much with them. We can't store data in them because they hold addresses, not data. Somehow we need to get a valid address into the pointer.

At this point there are two ways to assign addresses to a pointer. The first is to assign something that is already an address to the pointer. We know from previous chapters that the name of an array references the array's beginning address. Therefore, we can assign that address to a pointer, as shown in Example 12.2.6.

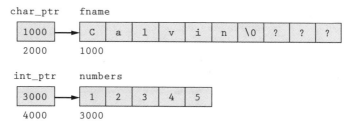

Figure 12.2.1 Memory layout of pointers

Example 12.2.6 Pointers to arrays

```
char fname[10] = "Calvin";
char * char_ptr = fname;

int numbers[5] = {1, 2, 3, 4, 5};
int * int_ptr = numbers;
```

Figure 12.2.1 shows the memory layout after the declaration of these variables. As you can see, the pointers hold the addresses of the first elements of the arrays. You can also see how pointers get their name. They *point* to, or reference, another piece of memory.

Remember: The target type of the pointer must match the data type of the value stored at that address.

The second way to retrieve an address to store in a pointer is by using the *address-of operator* (&). The address-of operator returns the address of its operand, which can be stored in a pointer, as shown in Example 12.2.7.

Example 12.2.7 Pointers and the address-of operator

```
char ch = 'A';
char * ch_ptr = &ch;
```

```
float average = 0.0F;
float * flt_ptr = &average;

int numbers[5] = {1, 2, 3, 4, 5};
int * int_ptr = &numbers[0];
```

The third pointer declaration in Example 12.2.7, demonstrates another way to retrieve the beginning address of an array. Since `numbers[0]` is the first element of the array, the address of operator returns the address-of this element.

STYLE NOTE▶   The spacing between the asterisk and the data type and pointer name is often debated. Some programmers believe that the asterisk should be next to the pointer name, as follows:

```
int *ptr;
```

However, other programmers feel strongly that the asterisk should be next to the data type:

```
int* ptr;
```

It is our preferred style to put a space on either side of the asterisk to ensure that it stands out from both the data type and the pointer name. Whatever your preference, choose a style and stick with it; consistency is what's important. In addition, don't forget to check the style guidelines for your company or school and conform to their standards.

Section 12.2 Exercises

1. The _____ of the pointer must match the _____ of the value stored at that address.

2. Explain the following statement:

   ```
   double * ptr = 0;
   ```

3. Please declare two integer pointers with appropriate initialization in the same statement.

4. Please indicate whether the following statements are valid or invalid. If a statement is invalid, please state why and correct the errors.

   ```
   a. int num = 0;
      int * ptr = num;
   ```

b. `int num = 0;`
   `int ptr = &num;`

c. `char ch = 'A';`
   `int * ptr = &ch;`

d. `char ray[15] = "Ray";`
   `char * ptr = &ray;`

5. With reference to the following statement, explain the statements that follow:

`char fname[15] = "Phong";`

a. `char * ch_ptr = fname;`

b. `char * ch_ptr = &fname[0];`

12.3 Advanced Pointer Declarations

Since we can have a pointer to any data type, we can have a pointer that contains the address of yet another pointer. Now the fun starts! (Of course our students have always thought we had a warped definition of fun.) Example 12.3.1 demonstrates the declaration and initialization of a pointer to a pointer.

Example 12.3.1 Pointers to pointers

```
float average = 0.0F;
float * flt_ptr = &average;
float ** flt_ptr_ptr = &flt_ptr;
```

Typically, programmers will call this a *two-star pointer*. The variable `flt_ptr_ptr` will hold the address of an address that contains a float. Figure 12.3.1 illustrates the memory layout corresponding to Example 12.3.1.

You can have as many stars, or *levels of indirection*, as needed. It is likely that the most levels of indirection you will ever see, or use, are three- or four-star pointers—and even those very rarely and in very special situations.

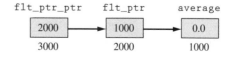

Figure 12.3.1 Memory layout of a pointer to a pointer

Indirection is a method of referencing a variable in a roundabout way, rather than directly accessing the variable by its name. Accessing a variable's value via its memory address rather than its name is an example of indirection.

Although it seems logical that we can assign the address of a two-dimensional array to a pointer, it is syntactically incorrect. Remember that a two-dimensional array is an array of arrays, therefore, a single-star pointer will not work. However, a two-star pointer will not work either, even though it may seem like it should. Example 12.3.2 shows some invalid and valid pointer assignments.

Example 12.3.2 Invalid and valid pointers

```
int nums[3][5] = { {0, 1, 2, 3, 4},
                   {0, 1, 2, 3, 4},
                   {0, 1, 2, 3, 4} };
// Example 1 - Invalid
int * ptr = nums;
// Example 2 - Invalid
int ** ptr = nums;
// Example 3 - Valid
int * ptr = nums[1];
```

Notice that the third example in Example 12.3.2 is valid because we are accessing a row in the two-dimensional array. Since the row references an address of an integer, we can store that address in a pointer.

So now we have an address stored in the pointer. We still can't do much, but hang in there—we still have more to learn.

12.4 Indirection Operator

If we use a pointer on the left side of an assignment operator, we change the address stored in the pointer. To retrieve or alter the value that the pointer is pointing to, we use the *indirection operator* (*). The indirection operator removes one level of indirection. Using the indirection operator to acquire the

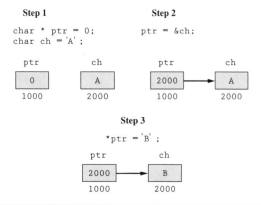

Figure 12.4.1 Dereferencing

value being referred to by the pointer is called *dereferencing*. This process is illustrated in Figure 12.4.1.

In Figure 12.4.1, the first step declares a pointer and a character variable. As shown, the character pointer, `ptr`, is initialized to null, and the character variable, `ch`, to `'A'`. The second step uses the address-of operator to assign the address of `ch`, replacing the contents of the pointer `ptr`. Step 3 demonstrates the process of dereferencing the pointer. Once dereferenced, we replace the value `'A'` with the character `'B'`. Example 12.4.1 also demonstrates the use and effect of the indirection operator.

Example 12.4.1 Indirection operator

```
float average = 0.0F;
float * flt_ptr = &average;

cout << "-Before-";
cout << "\n&average: " << &average
     << "\naverage:  " << average
     << "\nflt_ptr:  " << flt_ptr
     << "\n*flt_ptr: " << *flt_ptr << endl;

*flt_ptr = 5.0F;

cout << "\n-After-";
cout << "\n&average: " << &average
     << "\naverage:  " << average
     << "\nflt_ptr:  " << flt_ptr
     << "\n*flt_ptr: " << *flt_ptr << endl;
```

```
// Output
-Before-
&average:  0012FF64
average:   0
flt_ptr:   0012FF64
*flt_ptr:  0

-After-
&average:  0012FF64
average:   5
flt_ptr:   0012FF64
*flt_ptr:  5
```

As you can see from Example 12.4.1, it is possible to print addresses. However, there is no good reason to do this except for debugging purposes.

As stated previously, the indirection operator removes one level of indirection. If we have a two-star pointer—that is, two levels of indirection—dereferencing once gets us to the first address and dereferencing a second time allows us to access the value. Example 12.4.2 demonstrates this process.

Example 12.4.2 Two levels of indirection

```
float average = 20.0F;
float * flt_ptr = &average;
float ** flt_ptr_ptr = &flt_ptr;

cout << "average:        " << average;

cout << "\n\nflt_ptr:      " << flt_ptr
     << "\n*flt_ptr:     "   << *flt_ptr;

cout << "\n\nflt_ptr_ptr:  " << flt_ptr_ptr
     << "\n*flt_ptr_ptr: "   << *flt_ptr_ptr
     << "\n**flt_ptr_ptr: "  << **flt_ptr_ptr << endl;

// Output
average:        20

flt_ptr:        0012FF60
*flt_ptr:       20
```

```
flt_ptr_ptr:   0012FF54
*flt_ptr_ptr:  0012FF60
**flt_ptr_ptr: 20
```

We can now declare a pointer, assign an address to a pointer, and even manipulate what the pointer is pointing at. But just you wait—things are about to get a little more interesting.

Section 12.4 Exercises

1. Explain what is meant by a two-star pointer.

2. Explain the term "indirection."

3. What is the indirection operator, and what does it do?

4. Explain what is happening in the following code:

```
char fname[15] = "Randy";
char * ptr = fname;

*ptr = 'M';
```

5. Draw the diagram that represents the memory corresponding to Example 12.4.2.

Section 12.4 Learn by Doing Exercises

1. Use the following code to implement the exercises required in this section. Write a program that includes all of the following statements. Label each part in your output.

```
int numbers[5] = { 99, 34, 1, 88, 100 };
int * int_ptr = numbers;
int ** int_ptr_ptr = &int_ptr;
```

   a. Write the statement that prints the address of the array using the array name.

   b. Write the statement that prints the address of the array using `int_ptr`.

   c. Write the statement that prints the address of the array using `int_ptr_ptr`.

   d. Write the statement that prints the address of `int_ptr` using `int_ptr`.

   e. Write the statement that prints the address of `int_ptr` using `int_ptr_ptr`.

   f. Write the statement that prints the first element of the array using `int_ptr`.

   g. Write the statement that prints the first element of the array using `int_ptr_ptr`.

h. Write the statement that changes `int_ptr` to point to the second element of the array.

i. Write the statement that prints the second element of the array using `int_ptr`.

j. Write the statement that prints the second element of the array using `int_ptr_ptr`.

k. Write the statement that changes the second element of the array to 101 using `int_ptr`.

l. Write the statement that changes the second element of the array to 102 using `int_ptr_ptr`.

m. Change the address in `int_ptr` so that it points to the third element of the array using `int_ptr_ptr`.

n. Write the statement that changes the third element of the array to −1 using `int_ptr`.

o. Write the statement that changes the third element of the array to −2 using `int_ptr_ptr`.

p. Print the contents of the array to the screen to verify that the contents of the array were changed.

12.5 Passing by Pointer

In Chapter 10 we learned that arrays are, by default, passed by pointer. This is because we pass the address of the array. Now we can learn how to pass by pointer variables other than arrays. This topic is especially important for those of us learning C. Passing by pointer is the only way C programmers can pass variables so that they can be permanently changed within a function. In fact, what C++ programmers call passing by pointer, C programmers call passing by reference.

Remember, any time we have the address of a memory location, we can change what is stored at that address. This is the reason passing by pointer allows us to change a value within a function. Example 12.5.1 demonstrates a parameter being passed by pointer.

Example 12.5.1 Passing by pointer

```
int main()
{
    int numer = 0, denom = 0;

    GetFraction( &numer, &denom ); // Pass by pointer

    cout << numer << '/' << denom << endl;

    return 0;
}
```

```
void GetFraction( int * numer, int * denom )
{
    cout << "Enter numerator: ";
    cin >> *numer;

    cout << "Enter denominator: ";
    cin >> *denom;
}

// Output
Enter numerator: 1
Enter denominator: 2
1/2
```

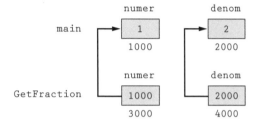

Figure 12.5.1 Memory layout of passing by pointer

The function call in Example 12.5.1 passes the two addresses of integers; therefore, we need to catch these addresses in variables that can hold addresses: pointers. Figure 12.5.1 illustrates what is happening under the hood in Example 12.5.1.

What if we need to pass those pointers to another function from within GetFraction? This is not a problem, but it is an area where many of our students get confused. You do not need to pass the address of the pointers in GetFraction. Since you already have the addresses of the variables declared in main, you are still able to affect these original variables. Example 12.5.2 shows the proper way to manipulate these pointers. As this example is fairly long, make sure to look carefully at the parameter passing. Running this example, more than any others, is crucial in helping you understand the demonstrated process.

Example 12.5.2 More passing by pointer

```
int main()
{
    int numer = 0, denom = 0;
```

```cpp
    GetFraction( &numer, &denom );
    DisplayFraction( numer, denom );

    return 0;
}
void GetFraction( int * numer, int * denom )
{
    cout << "Enter numerator: ";
    cin >> *numer;

    cout << "Enter denominator: ";
    cin >> *denom;

    FormatNegative( numer, denom );      // Passing by pointer
    DisplayFraction( *numer, *denom );   // Passing by value
}
void FormatNegative( int * numer, int * denom )
{
    if ( *numer < 0 && *denom < 0 )
    {
        *numer = abs( *numer );
        *denom = abs( *denom );
    }
    else if ( *denom < 0 )
    {
        *denom = abs( *denom );
        *numer *= -1;
    }
}
void DisplayFraction( int numer, int denom )
{
    cout << numer << '/' << denom << endl;
}
```

Notice the function call to `FormatNegative` in Example 12.5.2 passes only the pointer, not the address of the pointer. Also notice that the call to `DisplayFraction` from within `GetFraction` dereferences both pointers before passing them. Therefore, `DisplayFraction` just catches a copy of the two integers. Figure 12.5.2 graphically illustrates what is happening here.

Figure 12.5.2 shows that the pointers, `numer` and `denom`, in `GetFraction` were actually passed by value to `FormatNegative`. But since the *r*-value of the

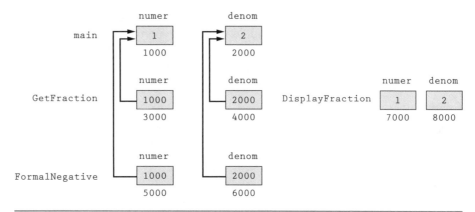

Figure 12.5.2 Memory layout of passing by pointer

parameters are the addresses of the original variables declared in `main`, you can still change these variables from within `FormatNegative`.

By now the C programmers among us are pretty excited about being able to finally pass by reference. However, the C++ programmers are wondering why we took a pretty simple topic and muddied it up. There is, of course, a reason for this, but you will need to wait just a little bit longer to find out what it is.

Section 12.5 Exercises

1. Explain the difference between passing by reference and passing by pointer.

2. True or false: In passing by pointer, you need to place an ampersand in front of the parameter in the call.

Section 12.5 Learn by Doing Exercise

1. Convert the program shown in Example 9.6.1 so that only passing by value and passing by pointer are used.

12.6 Pointer Arithmetic

In all of our examples in this chapter, we obviously made up the addresses. However, our addresses do have one thing in common with the real thing: they're all numbers. The size of an address depends upon the operating system. In a 32-bit operating system, the address is 32 bits.

Since addresses are numbers, we can perform arithmetic operations on them. But why would we want to perform math on pointers? One reason is that if we have a pointer to an array, we can efficiently iterate through the array using the pointer. Example 12.6.1 demonstrates this process.

Example 12.6.1 Pointer math

```
char fname[15] = "Calvin";
char * ptr = fname;

for ( int i = 0; i < 3; i++, ptr++ ) // Notice the pointer math
    cout << *ptr;

// Output
Cal
```

As you can see, the increment operator moves the pointer to the next element. One of the misconceptions is that if we have an array of integers, each of which is four bytes, we would have to increment the pointer four times to make sure we are at the start of the next element. This is unnecessary because pointer arithmetic takes into account the size of the target type of the pointer and increments appropriately. Example 12.6.2 demonstrates this feature of pointers.

Example 12.6.2 Pointer math with integers

```
int nums[10] = {0, 1, 2, 3, 4, 5, 6, 7, 8, 9};
int * ptr = nums;

for ( int i = 0; i < 3; i++, ptr++ )
    cout << *ptr << endl;

// Output
0  1  2
```

We can use any mathematical operators we want; however, you should be careful not to go to the extreme, for you might access memory that you don't have the right to, causing your program to crash. The bottom line is to manage your pointers carefully to ensure that they maintain an appropriate address. Example 12.6.3 shows some additional pointer math.

Example 12.6.3 More pointer math

```
int nums[10] = {0, 1, 2, 3, 4, 5, 6, 7, 8, 9};
int * ptr = nums;

// Example 1
for ( int i = 0; i < 3; i++ )
    cout << *ptr++ << ' ';   // Dereference, print, increment ptr

cout << endl;

// Example 2
for ( int i = 0; i < 3; i++ )
    cout << --*ptr++ << ' ';   // Dereference, decrement value,
                               // print, increment ptr
// Output
0 1 2
2 3 4
```

As you can see from Example 12.6.3, using pointer arithmetic causes the code to become more difficult to read and understand. The first example is fairly straightforward and very commonly used. The indirection operator dereferences the pointer to access the first element, which is then printed. The address in ptr is then incremented to the next element. This process is repeated two more times, as indicated by the loop.

The second example dereferences the pointer, which is currently still pointing at the fourth element, value 3. The value is then decremented from 3 to 2, which is then displayed. Finally, the pointer is incremented to point to the next element. This process continues until the condition of the loop is false. We are not stuck using the increment and decrement operators either. Example 12.6.4 shows some additional pointer manipulations.

Example 12.6.4 Pointers and cStrings

```
char lname[15] = "Metzler";
char * ptr = lname;

// Example 1
```

```
cout << ptr << endl;

// Example 2 after Example 1 was run
cout << *(ptr + 2) << endl;

// Example 3 after Examples 1 and 2 were run
cout << (ptr += 3) << endl;
cout << ptr << endl;

// Output
Metzler
t
zler
zler
```

In the first example, since `ptr` holds the address of a character, `cout` will print from that address and will continue until it reaches a null character. It behaves exactly as if we had supplied the name of the array to `cout`. The second example adds 2 to the beginning address, therefore, `ptr` points to the character "t". This address is dereferenced, so `cout` prints that specific character. The third example changes the pointer to point to the address of the fourth character. The `cout` statement then prints starting from that address until the null character. Notice that the address in `ptr` physically changed, so that when we print once again, we'll get the same output.

One thing that we have not discussed is using the subscript operator (`[]`) with pointers. Both the subscript operator and the indirection operator dereference an address. All four of the `cout` statements in Example 12.6.5 will produce the same output.

Example 12.6.5 Pointers and the subscript operator

```
char lname[15] = "Metzler";
char * ptr = lname;

cout << lname[2] << endl;        // Array notation
cout << *(lname + 2) << endl;    // Pointer notation
cout << *(ptr + 2) << endl;      // Pointer notation
cout << ptr[2] << endl;          // Array notation
```

You can use the subscript operator and the indirection operator interchangeably. Although pointer notation is rarely used with arrays, array notation is often used with pointers.

One last thing regarding pointer arithmetic: Do not try to increment the address of the array. The name of an array references the beginning address of the array; however, the address is a constant address and therefore can't be changed. Attempting to use the increment operator with an array name will result in a syntax error.

Section 12.6 Exercises

1. Given the following code fragments, determine the output.

   a. ```
   char fname[15] = "Alexis";
   char * ptr = fname;

   for (int i = 0; i < 4; i++, ptr++)
       cout << *ptr;
   ```

   b. ```
   char fname[15] = "Alexis";
   char * ptr = fname;

   ptr += 4;
   cout << ptr;
   ```

   c. ```
   float nums[5] = {111.1, 23.23, 45.67, 12.21, 99.99};
   float * ptr = nums;

   for (int i = 0; i < 5; i++)
       cout << *ptr++ << ' ';
   ```

## Section 12.6 Learn by Doing Exercise

1. Write a program that declares a two-dimensional array of integers with four rows and five columns. Initialize the array to any numbers of your choosing. Using a pointer, display the contents of the array.

# 12.7 Pointers Applied

The following examples demonstrate the power and elegance of pointers when applied to real-world situations. We strongly suggest that you examine each function carefully and make appropriate drawings, similar to the figures provided in this chapter, to aid in your understanding. Then run the code using your debugger to confirm your findings. If you don't understand the code, reread the chapter and work through all of the exercises.
   ```

Example 12.7.1 deletes a portion of a string. This function takes a cString (`str`), a starting array index (`start`), and an integer (`num_char`) representing the number of characters to delete from the supplied starting position.

Example 12.7.1 More pointer arithmetic

```
void DeleteString( char * str, int start, int num_char )
{
    strcpy( str + start, str + start + num_char );
}
```

Example 12.7.1 illustrates how using pointers can make your code much more compact. This example makes good use of a predefined function and some simple pointer arithmetic. Example 12.7.2 is probably not as easy to understand in terms of what is happening under the hood, even if the name of the function indicates its purpose.

Example 12.7.2 Pointers and the increment operator

```
void StrCpy( char * dest, char * src )
{
    while ( *dest++ = *src++ );
}
```

Like the predefined `strcpy`, the function in Example 12.7.2 copies the characters from `src` to `dest`. There are a couple of things to point out in the code. Notice the semicolon at the end of the `while` loop. This would usually mean the loop would be infinite; however, because we use the assignment operator within the loop's condition, we are actually changing the control variable within the loop. Since the null character equates to zero, and zero represents false, as soon as the null is copied from `src` to `dest`, the loop ends.

The function in Example 12.7.3 illustrates one way of finding the first instance of the character (`ch`) in the cString (`str`). The function then returns the index of the specified character or -1 if the character is not found.

Example 12.7.3 Subtracting addresses

```
int CharAt( char * str, char ch )
{
    char * cur = str;
```

```
    int return_val = -1;

    while ( *cur != '\0' && *cur != ch )
        cur++;

    if ( *cur != '\0' )
        return_val = static_cast<int> (cur - str);

    return return_val;
}
```

Example 12.7.3 demonstrates one feature of pointers that should be fairly obvious. Since addresses are numbers, we can subtract two addresses. This concept, coupled with the knowledge that arrays are contiguous blocks of memory, is what makes this function work.

As you can see from the previous functions, pointers can make your code fairly efficient, compact, and even elegant. Understanding what is happening at a very low level, or under the hood, is extremely important when using pointers.

Section 12.7 Exercise

1. What is the purpose of the following function?

```
void foo( char * var1, char * var2, int var3 )
{
    char t[255];

    strcpy( t, var1 + var3 );
    *(var1 + var3) = '\0';
    strcat( var1, var2 );
    strcat( var1, t );
}
```

Section 12.7 Learn by Doing Exercise

1. Write a program that includes a function called StrCat, which simulates its predefined namesake. This function receives two values, a pointer to the source (src), and a pointer to the destination (dest) cString. Make sure your destination parameter is large enough to accommodate the additional characters by creating your own version of strlen using pointer notation only.

12.8 More cString Functions

In Chapter 10 we spent a considerable amount of time discussing various pre-defined functions for manipulating cStrings. However, because the concept of pointers had not yet been introduced, we decided to hold off on presenting three additional functions: `strtok`, `strstr`, and `strchr`. Now that you have become familiar with pointers, you should find these functions relatively easy to understand. Note: All three of the functions return a character pointer and require the header file `<cstring>`.

In addition, there are a series of predefined functions, usually considered string handling functions, that actually work with blocks of memory of any type. A function that is representative of these is `memset`. Other related functions are `memcpy`, `memcmp`, `memmove`, and `memchr`. The `memset` function will be used to demonstrate how this category of functions works.

12.8.1 The `strtok` Function

The `strtok` function is used to separate a cString into pieces, or chunks, of information based on a specific delimiter. This process is also referred to as *tokenizing* a string.

The syntax for the `strtok` function is as follows:

```
char * strtok ( const char * str, const char * delimiter );
```

The first parameter is a null-terminated cString containing the token(s). A token is simply a sequence of characters separated by a delimiter. The delimiter represents a set of null-terminated characters containing the desired symbols that separate each of the tokens in the cString.

The return value is a pointer to the next token found in the first parameter. When no more tokens are found, NULL is returned. Be aware that each call to `strtok` modifies `str` by actually substituting a null character for each delimiter encountered. Example 12.8.1 demonstrates how this function can be used.

Example 12.8.1 The `strtok` function

```
void StringTokSample()
{
    char textTitle[] = "C++: An Active Learning Approach";
    char * tokenPtr;

    cout << "Our string to be tokenized is: " << textTitle
         << "\n\nThe tokens/pieces are:\n";

    // Begin tokenization - notice the delimiter is a space
```

```
        tokenPtr = strtok( textTitle, " " );

        // Continue tokenizing until tokenPtr becomes NULL
        while ( tokenPtr != NULL )
        {
            cout << tokenPtr << '\n';

            // Get next token (or NULL)
            tokenPtr = strtok( NULL, " " );
        }
        cout << "\nAfter strtok - textTitle = " << textTitle
            << endl;
    }

// Output
Our string to be tokenized is: C++: An Active Learning Approach

The tokens/pieces are:
C++:
An
Active
Learning
Approach

After strtok - textTitle = C++:
```

In Example 12.8.1, after the first call to strtok, the first parameter is replaced with NULL. This may seem confusing, but it allows strtok to work off of the original cString and be able to keep its position within the string.

12.8.2 The strstr Function

Another cString function we can now discuss is strstr. This function is designed to return a pointer to the first occurrence of a target cString within an existing cString.

Following is the syntax for the strstr function:

```
char * strstr ( const char * str, const char * searchString );
```

The str parameter is the null-terminated string we want to search. The parameter searchString represents the sequence of characters we are looking for.

The value returned by the strstr function is a pointer to the first occurrence of searchString in str, or NULL if searchString is not found. Example

12.8.2 illustrates how the `strstr` function is used to search for "`World`" in `str` and, if found, replace it with "`Earth`".

Example 12.8.2 The `strstr` function

```
void StringStringSample()
{
    char * ptr_ch;
    char str[] = "Hello World!";

    cout << "Original String: " << str;

    ptr_ch = strstr( str, "World" );
    if ( ptr_ch != NULL )
    {
        strncpy( ptr_ch, "Earth", 5 );
        cout << "\nModified cString: " << str << endl;
    }
    else
        cout << "\nThe search string is not in the original!\n";
}
// Output
Original cString: Hello World!
Modified cString: Hello Earth!
```

In Example 12.8.2 we made it a point to check the value returned from the `strstr` function to make sure that the string "`World`" was indeed contained within our cString. Had the value not been found, the function would have returned NULL.

12.8.3 The `strchr` Function

The final cString function we are going to explore is `strchr`. This function locates the first occurrence of an individual character in a cString. If the specified character is not found, the function returns NULL. If the character is found, the function returns a pointer to the first occurrence of the character in our original cString.

Following is the syntax for the `strchr` function:

```
char * strchr ( const char * str, int ch );
```

The `str` parameter is the cString we want to perform the search on, while `ch` represents the individual character we are looking for.

The return value is a pointer to the first occurrence of the character, or `NULL` if the individual character is not found. Example 12.8.3 demonstrates how to find and print the location of all the "n"s in the title of our text, "`C++: An Active Learning Approach`."

Example 12.8.3 The `strchr` **function**

```
void StringCharSample()
{
    char * ptr_ch;
    char str[] = "C++: An Active Learning Approach";

    cout << "Searching for all 'n' characters in "
         << str << '\n';

    // Find first occurrence of 'n'
    ptr_ch = strchr( str, 'n' );
    if ( ptr_ch == NULL )
        cout << "The character is NOT in the string!\n";

    // Find the positions of all remaining occurrences of 'n'
    while ( ptr_ch != NULL )
    {
        // Remember what we had said earlier about doing
        // arithmetic on addresses
        cout << "'n' found at " << ptr_ch - str + 1  << '\n';
        ptr_ch  = strchr( ptr_ch + 1, 'n' );
    }
}

// Output
Searching for all 'n' characters in C++: An Active Learning Approach
'n' found at 7
'n' found at 20
'n' found at 22
```

As we had done in our previous example, we checked the value returned from the `strchr` function call to make sure the character was contained within the cString.

12.8.4 The `memset` Function

The `memset` function is a very useful function that sets a block of memory to a specified value. Although this function is usually thought of as a string-handling function, it actually works with any block of memory. The syntax for `memset` is as follows:

```
void * memset ( void * dest, int c, size_t count );
```

The first parameter is a pointer to the block of memory. The `void` pointer means we are able to pass a pointer to *any* block of memory. The second parameter is the value to be stored in the block of memory, and the third parameter is the number of bytes to set. Example 12.8.4 demonstrates the `memset` function.

Example 12.8.4 The `memset` function

```
char letter_grades[25];
double grades[25];

memset( grades, 0, sizeof(double) * 25 );
memset( letter_grades, 'F', sizeof(char) * 25 );
```

The code shown in Example 12.8.4 demonstrates that `memset` works well with any data type. When the code is done executing, the block of memory represented by "`grades`" will be completely full of zeros. Likewise, the `letter_grades` array will have the character "F" in all of its elements.

As stated before, the other functions in the same category as `memset` work in a similar manner. Now that you've seen how one function works, you should be able to use the other functions without any problem. Look at your help files to read more about these other functions.

Section 12.8 Learn by Doing Exercise

1. Write a function that takes two parameters, a pointer to a cString and a single character, and returns the number of instances of the character found in the cString. Write a program that tests that your function is operational.

12.9 Dynamic Memory Allocation

A disadvantage with arrays is the need to estimate the maximum number of elements when the array is declared, and then live with that estimate throughout the execution of our program. If the estimate should prove to be inaccurate, we've either wasted space or created a situation where there isn't enough room for the data to be stored. Another disadvantage is the need to specify the size of the array during its declaration with a constant or literal rather than a variable. *Dynamic memory allocation* allows us to overcome these disadvantages.

Dynamic memory allocation is the process of requesting memory from the operating system at runtime.

The memory required for your variables is automatically allocated when your program is loaded into memory. This special area within memory is called the *stack*. Each program that is running has its own stack. The memory not taken up by the operating system or running programs is called the *heap*.

The **heap** is memory not currently being used by the operating system or running programs.

Dynamic memory allocation requests a specific amount of memory from the heap. The operating system tries to honor the request and marks the memory as being allocated to your program.

One advantage to using dynamic memory allocation is that we only use as much memory as we need. Dynamic memory allocation is required when the amount of memory needed is unknown until runtime.

One of the disadvantages of dynamic memory allocation is that it will cause a speed degradation in your program. Most of the time, however, you will not notice the difference in speed. Another disadvantage is that if the memory is not released it will cause *memory leaks*.

Memory leaks happen when memory is allocated but is not deallocated. If this situation continues, your computer will eventually run out of memory and will need to be rebooted.

We could also create a situation called a *dangling pointer*, in which a pointer contains an address that is no longer valid. As an example, suppose you have two pointers pointing to the same piece of memory on the heap. If one of the pointers is deallocated, the other pointer now has an address that can no longer be legally accessed. If the second pointer is accessed, your program will crash.

The next two sections demonstrate the C++ techniques needed to allocate and deallocate memory.

12.9.1 The new Operator

The new operator makes a request for memory to the operating system. If the operating system can fulfill the request, the new operator will return a pointer to the newly allocated memory. If there isn't enough memory to satisfy the request, your program will either throw an error or new will return 0, depending on your compiler. The techniques involved in recovering from this error are beyond the scope of this text. The syntax of the new operator is as follows:

```
<target-type> * <ptr-name> = new <target-type>;
```

As you can see from the syntax, the target type of the pointer must match what is specified in the new statement. Example 12.9.1 shows how to use the new operator.

Example 12.9.1 The new operator

```
int * ptr1 = new int;
```

Example 12.9.1 allocates enough room for a single integer and stores the returned address in the pointer ptr1. The allocated memory is not initialized and therefore contains garbage. Example 12.9.2 shows how to use new to initialize the memory.

Example 12.9.2 Initializing new memory

```
char * ch_ptr = new char( 'A' );
double * average = new double();
```

Both statements in Example 12.9.2 allocate enough memory for their respective data types and then initialize the new memory. In the case of the character pointer, we initialize the memory with the character 'A'. In the second example, the empty parentheses specify that the memory is to be initialized with the default value for that data type. This is a shortcut way of initializing the memory to 0.

We can also use `new` to dynamically allocate arrays, as shown in Example 12.9.3.

Example 12.9.3 Dynamically allocating arrays

```
int number_elements = 10;

char * str = new char[number_elements];
char ** star_star = new char * [15];
```

The first `new` statement in Example 12.9.3 demonstrates that we can use a variable to specify the number of elements to allocate. The second example allocates an array of 15 character pointers. Notice that the address returned is an address of an address of a character. Also note that you can't initialize an array in the `new` statement.

Now that the process of allocating memory is known, it is necessary to determine how to deallocate memory so that memory leaks aren't introduced into your program. As we've said before, good programmers clean up after themselves. It is imperative that you free any dynamic memory that has been allocated to your program.

12.9.2 The `delete` Operator

Even though there are many different forms associated with the `new` operator, there are only two forms for the `delete` operator. The syntax for both forms is as follows:

```
delete <ptr-name>;
delete [] <ptr-name>;
```

The first form is used to deallocate a single piece of memory, while the second form deallocates a dynamically allocated array. Example 12.9.4 uses `delete` to deallocate memory.

Example 12.9.4 Deallocation

```
int num_elements = 10;

int * ptr1 = new int;
```

```
char * str = new char[number_elements];

delete ptr1;
delete [] str;
```

Notice the difference between the two forms of the `delete` statement in Example 12.9.4. The second `delete` statement includes empty brackets, which designate that this statement deallocates an array. These brackets will always be empty. The first `delete` statement doesn't include brackets, indicating that it will deallocate only a single piece of memory.

> **!** **Remember:** If you use brackets when allocating memory, be sure to use them when deleting memory.

Another thing to remember is that the address referenced by the pointer must be the same one returned by the `new` operator. In other words, when the array was allocated, the address of the memory was returned and stored in a pointer. If the pointer is later manipulated so that it is pointing to a different element within the array, that pointer can't be used in the `delete` statement without returning it to its original address.

There are a few situations in which the execution of the `delete` statement could cause your program to crash. The first two situations will occur if the address in the pointer is invalid or has already been deallocated by another delete operation. Since it is valid to delete a null pointer, it is good practice to initialize your pointers to null. Be aware, however, that after deallocation, the pointer will still contain the address that was just used to deallocate the memory. Should you attempt to reference or deallocate this pointer again, your program will crash because you no longer own that memory.

Another cause of abnormal program termination is when the deallocation process indicates that the area around the memory to be deallocated has been corrupted. This means that if we go out of bounds of a dynamic array, the program will crash when the delete operation is performed. As you might suspect, this error is extremely difficult to track down, making this another reason why it is important to make sure you do not go out of bounds of any array.

Section 12.9 Exercises

1. Explain the purpose of the `new` operator.

2. Explain each of the following lines of code:

   a. `char * ptrA = new char;`

   b. `int * ptrB =  new int[num_elements];`

3. Write the necessary statements to release or free the memory allocated in Exercise 2.

4. True or false: When you use brackets to allocate memory for an array, you must use brackets when deleting that memory.

5. What is wrong with each of the following code fragments?

   a. `int ptr = new int;`

   b. `int * ptr = new char;`

   c. `char * ptr = new char[];`

   d. `char * ptr = new char[15];`
      `delete ptr;`

   e. `char * ptr = new char * [15];`

   f. `char * ptr = new char[15];`
      `ptr++;`
      `delete [] ptr;`

   g. `char * ptr = new char;`
      `char * ptr2 = new char;`
      `ptr = ptr2;`

   h. `char * ptr = new char;`
      `char * ptr2 = ptr;`
      `delete ptr;`
      `*ptr2 = 'A';`

Section 12.9 Learn by Doing Exercise

1. Write a program that accepts from a professor the number of students in a class. Allocate enough room to store final exam scores for all of the students. Display to the screen all of the scores and the average of the scores.

12.10 Passing Pointers by Reference

In a previous section we learned about passing by pointer. But what if we want to pass the pointer itself, so that it can be changed within a function? We have two options; pass by reference or pass by pointer. Example 12.10.1 demonstrates how to pass a pointer by reference.

Example 12.10.1 Passing a pointer by reference

```
const int BUFFER_LENGTH = 256;

void GetString( char *& str );
int main()
{
    char * str = 0;

    GetString( str );

    cout << '\n' << str << endl;

    delete [] str;

    return 0;
}
void GetString( char *& str )
{
    char buffer[BUFFER_LENGTH];

    cout << "Please enter a string: ";

    cin.ignore( cin.rdbuf()->in_avail() );
    cin.getline( buffer, BUFFER_LENGTH );
    cin.clear();
    cin.ignore( cin.rdbuf()->in_avail() );

    str = new char[strlen( buffer ) + 1];
    strcpy( str, buffer );
}
```

There is a lot going on in Example 12.10.1, so examine it carefully. The first thing to notice is the formal parameter in the function header where the character pointer is passed by reference.

Examining the rest of the GetString function we notice that a temporary local array is created to receive input from the keyboard, followed by the dynamic creation of an array that is exactly big enough for the string that was entered, plus one extra space for the null character. The string is then copied from buffer to the new string.

We didn't assign the address of the array to the pointer because local variables are destroyed when the function ends. If we had done so, when the flow of the program returned to main, the address assigned to the pointer would no longer be valid. Dynamically allocated memory, on the other hand, is only destroyed when it is deleted. Therefore, the address would still be valid even after the function ended.

> **Remember: Never** return the address of a local variable. Also, never assign the address of a local variable to a pointer passed by reference.

The other way to pass a pointer to a function so that it can be changed is by passing by pointer, as demonstrated in Example 12.10.2.

Example 12.10.2 Passing a pointer by pointer

```
const int BUFFER_LENGTH = 256;

void GetString( char ** str );
int main()
{
    char * str = 0;

    GetString( &str ); // Notice the address-of operator

    cout << '\n' << str << endl;

    delete [] str;

    return 0;
}
// Catching the address of an address
void GetString( char ** str )
{
    char buffer[BUFFER_LENGTH];

    cout << "Please enter a string: ";

    cin.ignore( cin.rdbuf()->in_avail() );
    cin.getline( buffer, BUFFER_LENGTH );
    cin.clear();
    cin.ignore( cin.rdbuf()->in_avail() );
```

```
    *str = new char[strlen( buffer ) + 1]; // Dereference
    strcpy( *str, buffer );
}
```

We kept the code the same between Example 12.10.1 and Example 12.10.2 except that the first example passes by reference and the second passes by pointer. Passing by pointer complicates things a little by requiring a few extra asterisks, but even that little inconvenience isn't too bad. For those C programmers among us, you don't have a choice; passing by pointer is the only option.

Section 12.10 Learn by Doing Exercise

1. One of the problems with `strcat` is that if there isn't enough room in the destination cString, there will be problems with your program. Write two versions of `strcat` that ensure that there will always be enough room in the destination cString by dynamically allocating the appropriate memory inside the `strcat` function. One version of the function will be passed the destination by reference, while the other will be passed the destination by pointer.

12.11 Pointers and Strings

In Chapter 10 we learned that an array can never appear on the left side of an assignment operator because the name of an array is a *constant* address. A pointer is a variable and therefore can appear on the left side of an assignment operator. Does that mean we can assign the contents of a cString to a pointer? No, but we can assign a string literal to a pointer—well, sort of. Look at the code in Example 12.11.1.

Example 12.11.1 String literal assignment

```
char * str1 = 0, * str2 = 0;
str1 = "Sherry";
str2 = "Sherry";
```

Example 12.11.1 appears to assign a string literal to the pointer. This is obviously not possible because a pointer only holds an address. What is actually happening is the string literal "Sherry" is stored in memory in a place called the *symbol table*. This table holds all of the literals (symbols) needed for your program. When a string literal is accessed, the address of that literal is returned. Therefore, the two pointers in Example 12.11.1 actually contain the same address.

These pointers can even be compared using relational operators. Be sure to remember, however, that all you are comparing are the addresses stored in the two pointers—not the actual strings. Another thing you shouldn't do is to delete a pointer that contains the address of a string literal. If attempted, your program will crash.

Please note that not all compilers optimize this code the same way. Visual Studio, for example, stores duplicates of the string literals. Therefore, the two pointers in Example 12.11.1 would contain different addresses.

12.12 Ragged Arrays

As stated before, pointers allow us to use only the amount of memory needed. We don't waste memory by declaring an array with a constant size and not using all of the elements. Look at the variables declared in Example 12.12.1.

Example 12.12.1 Variable declarations and strings

```
char name1[10] = "Peggy";
char name2[] = "Peggy";
char * name3 = "Peggy";
```

All three of the variable declarations in Example 12.12.1 accomplish the same thing in three different ways. Figure 12.12.1 graphically illustrates these differences.

As you can see after examining the diagram, the third example uses the least amount of memory. The first example is the worst because of the wasted elements. The second example doesn't seem too bad until you realize the symbol table still contains the string literal and that now there is a copy as well.

We can extend this efficient use of memory philosophy one step further by using an array of pointers to save even more space. This is called a *ragged array*. Example 12.12.2 declares a ragged array.

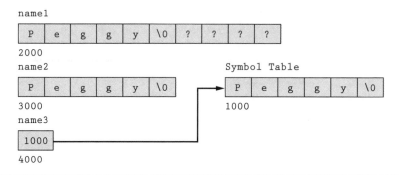

Figure 12.12.1 Differences in string assignments

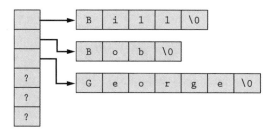

Figure 12.12.2 Ragged array

Example 12.12.2 Ragged array

```
char * names[6] =
{
    "Bill",
    "Bob",
    "George"
};
```

As you can see, an array of six character pointers is declared, the first three of which are initialized to string literals. Figure 12.12.2 is a visual representation of this ragged array.

Notice that the right edges of the literals are not even, hence a ragged array. Ragged arrays are especially useful in the creation of a constant array of string literals, as shown in Example 12.12.3.

Example 12.12.3 Constant ragged array

```
const char * ranks[] = {"Ace", "Deuce", "Trey", "Four", "Five",
                        "Six", "Seven", "Eight", "Nine", "Ten",
                        "Jack", "Queen", "King"};

const char * suits[] = {"Spades", "Diamonds", "Clubs", "Hearts"};
```

As you can see from Example 12.12.3, the two ragged arrays can be used in a variety of programs that use a standard deck of cards. It makes sense to declare them this way because the values will never change and because it takes up the least amount of memory while still keeping all of the values together. We will revisit these ragged arrays in Chapter 13. The next section extends the concept of ragged arrays into the realm of dynamic arrays.

Section 12.12 Exercises

1. What is a ragged array?

2. For each of the following statements, draw a diagram that represents how the data is stored in memory.

   a. `char teams[5][10] = {"Seahawks", "Packers", "Bears"};`

   b. `char teams1[][10] = {"Seahawks", "Packers", "Bears"};`

   c. `char * teams2[5] = {"Seahawks", "Packers", "Bears"};`

   d. `char * teams3[] = {"Seahawks", "Packers", "Bears"};`

12.13 Dynamic Two-Dimensional Arrays

In the last section we learned how to create a ragged array. This section takes the concept one step further by examining how to create a *dynamic ragged array*.

The simplest way to create a dynamic ragged array is by first knowing the number of strings to be stored. If this value is known, we can create a character pointer array of the correct size. Since we are requesting an address of a character pointer, it is necessary to declare a two-star character pointer. The first step in the creation of a dynamic ragged array—the declaration of the pointer and the allocation of the array—is shown in Example 12.13.1.

Example 12.13.1 Step 1: Declaration and allocation

```
char ** names = 0; // Two-star character pointer
char * str = 0;
char buffer[256]; // Will be used in the next step
int num_names = 0;

cout << "How many names will you enter? ";
cin >> num_names;

names = new char * [num_names]; // Notice char * []
```

Now that we have an array of character pointers that was dynamically allocated in the last statement of Example 12.13.1, we can use the technique described earlier in this chapter to create an array of characters that is exactly the needed length. This second step in the process is demonstrated in Example 12.13.2.

Example 12.13.2 Step 2: Dynamic allocation for names

```
for ( int i = 0; i < num_names; ++i )
{
    cout << "Please enter a name: ";
    cin >> buffer;

    str = new char[strlen( buffer ) + 1];
    strcpy( str, buffer );

    names[i] = str; // Assign the address of the cString to an
                    // element in the array of pointers
}
```

In Example 12.13.2, we assigned the address of the dynamic array of characters to an element in the pointer array, which allows us to retain all of the names entered. This technique works fine, but it isn't always feasible to ask the user how many elements are needed. Another approach is presented in Example 12.13.3, which shows changes to the previous method.

Example 12.13.3 Step 1: Variable declarations

```
int num_names = 0;
char ** names = 0;
char ** temp = 0;
char buffer[256];
```

All we did in Example 12.13.3 was add another two-star character pointer. The variable `temp` will contain the address of the array, into which we will copy all of the addresses of the previously entered names.

The next step is to allocate the memory needed for our temporary array and copy all of the addresses associated with any previously entered names into the new array. This is shown in Example 12.13.4.

Example 12.13.4 Step 2: Allocate new array of pointers, and copy previous pointers

```
// Create an array with room for one more pointer
temp = new char * [num_names + 1];
// Copy the addresses of any previously entered names
// to our temporary array. Notice the first time
// the loop will not execute
for ( int i = 0; i < num_names; ++i )
{
    temp[i] = names[i];
}
```

Figure 12.13.1 illustrates how these variables might look in memory, assuming that two names have already been entered.

In Figure 12.13.1, `temp` now points to an array that is one bigger than the array `names` points to. Also, the first two pointers of each array are pointing to the same strings. The names weren't copied; the pointers were just individually assigned from one array to the other.

The next step requires us to read in the new name, allocate the exact amount of memory needed for the name, and store the address of the name at the end of the temporary array. We will then need to copy the name from the buffer into the newly allocated memory. This step is shown in Example 12.13.5.

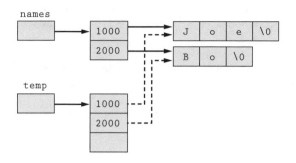

Figure 12.13.1 Step 2 memory layout

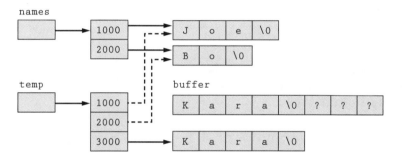

Figure 12.13.2 Step 3 memory layout

Example 12.13.5 Step 3: Read, allocate, and store name

```
// Read name
cout << "Enter name: ";
cin >> buffer;

// Allocate room for the newly entered string
// Store the new address in the last element of the
// temporary array
temp[num_names] = new char[strlen( buffer ) + 1];

// Copy the name from the buffer into the newly
// allocated space
strcpy( temp[num_names], buffer );
```

Figure 12.13.2 illustrates the process presented in Example 12.13.5.

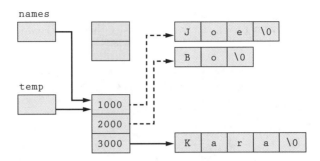

Figure 12.13.3 Step 4 memory layout

The last step is to clean up the old array pointed to by `names`, and make `names` point to the newly generated array pointed to by `temp`. This process is shown in Example 12.13.6.

Example 12.13.6 Step 4: Delete old array and reassign

```
// Delete the old array holding the name pointers
delete [] names;

// Assign the address of the temporary array
// to our original pointer
names = temp;

// Increment the number of names
++num_names;
```

The process involved in Example 12.13.6 is demonstrated in Figure 12.13.3. Notice that only the old array pointed to by `names` is deleted, not the strings themselves.

After this process has been completed, `names` is now pointing to the array that contains pointers to all of the strings. Everything is now set up for the entry of the next name.

The process described in this section can be fairly memory- and processor-intensive, as it requires a lot of memory allocation and deallocation, which has a tendency to decrease your program speed. However, if you understand this process, you have a good understanding of pointers. These dynamic arrays are extremely useful and make good use of available memory.

It is imperative that you don't forget to deallocate all of the memory used in your dynamic arrays. Not doing so will quickly diminish your computer's memory resources because of the numerous memory leaks introduced into your program. This process is shown in Example 12.13.7.

Example 12.13.7 Step 5: Deallocate memory

```
// Delete each name pointed to by the names array
for ( int i = 0; i < num_names; ++i )
    delete [] names[i];

// Delete the array itself
delete [] names;
```

One common mistake that students make is deleting the array without deleting each name pointed to by the elements of the array. This mistake causes major memory leaks. Since memory leaks are a common situation, Visual Studio has included functions to test for them. This process is described in the next section.

Section 12.13 Learn by Doing Exercise

1. Write a program that stores stock symbols into dynamic arrays. The user will enter as many stocks as he or she wishes. The program should display the list of stocks after each one is entered. For an extra challenge, sort the stocks in alphabetical order.

12.14 Testing for Memory Leaks

Visual Studio includes some functions that check for memory leaks during the debugging process. Although in C++ programs you can't tell where your memory leaks have been introduced into your program, you can at least check for their existence. Example 12.14.1 shows a very simple program with a memory leak as well as the code necessary to check for this situation.

Example 12.14.1 Memory leak test

```
#define _CRTDBG_MAP_ALLOC

// Place any other #includes here

#include <crtdbg.h>
```

```
int main()
{
    // Run this program using "Start Debugging"
    _CrtSetDbgFlag( _CRTDBG_ALLOC_MEM_DF | _CRTDBG_LEAK_CHECK_DF );

    int * ptr = new int;

    return 0;
}
```

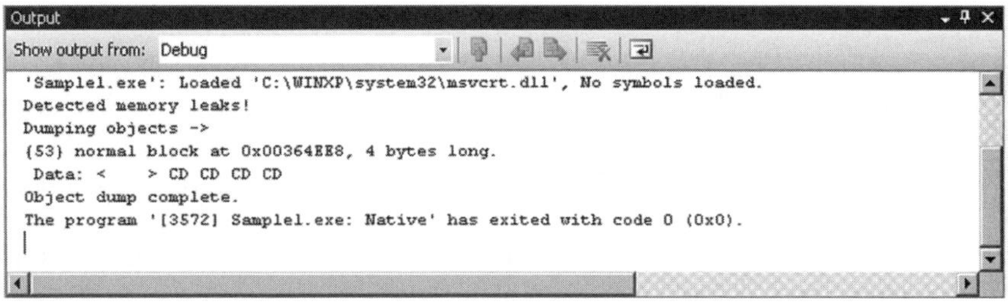

Figure 12.14.1 Output window

The #define should be performed prior to any #includes. Also, the function call to _CrtSetDbgFlag should be the first line of code in main. To test for leaks, run your program using the Start Debug option. When the program exits, the Output window will display the existence of any memory leaks. Figure 12.14.1 shows the Output window after the execution of this program.

Notice that the window displays the message "Detected memory leaks!" The window also shows the beginning address of the memory that was allocated; how many bytes were not deallocated; and the data, displayed in hexadecimal format.

This is an extremely useful debugging tool that should be included during the debugging process for any program using dynamic memory allocation. You should also be aware that there are many third-party software tools that perform memory leak detection. Some of these programs are free of charge while others are very expensive.

Section 12.14 Learn by Doing Exercise

1. Using the program you wrote in Section 12.13 Learn by Doing Exercise, add the code necessary to detect any memory leaks. Run your program, and if you are lucky enough not to have any leaks, comment out the delete statements and rerun the program to see the results of the memory leak testing.

12.15 Function Pointers

When we call a function in our program, the operating system knows what to do and where to get the instruction set for that function. We may not have thought about it before, but it makes sense that the function exists somewhere in memory. Therefore, we can get the address of the function and store that address in a pointer—to be more specific, a *function pointer*. Sounds like fun, doesn't it?

12.15.1 Declaration

When we declared pointers to variables, it made a little sense because we were already familiar with the target types for the pointers. It is difficult to visualize what the target type of a function pointer would look like. The declaration of a function pointer will look similar to the function signature. Therefore, any function whose address is stored in the pointer will have the same signature.

> ⚠️ **Remember:** A function signature is a method for identifying a specific function based on its name, the order and number of parameters it takes, and its return type.

Example 12.15.1 shows various function pointer declarations.

Example 12.15.1 Function pointer declarations

```
// Pointer to a function that returns nothing
// and is passed nothing
void (*fn_ptr1)();

// Pointer to a function that returns an int
// and is passed nothing
int (*fn_ptr2)();

// Pointer to a function that returns an int
// and is passed three parameters
int (*fn_ptr3)( int, double, char [] );
```

The parentheses around the asterisk and the pointer name—(*fn_ptr1)— are required. Without the parentheses, the compiler would interpret the line of code as a function declaration. For example, without the parentheses, the second declaration in Example 12.15.1 would be the declaration of a function that returns an integer pointer and is passed nothing.

As you may have guessed, we can not only dynamically allocate a function pointer but also dynamically allocate an array of function pointers, as shown in Example 12.15.2.

Example 12.15.2 Dynamic allocation of function pointers

```
// Allocate a function pointer
int (**ptr1)() = new( int(*) () );

// Allocate an array of five function pointers
int (**ptr2)() = new( int(*[5]) () );
```

In Example 12.15.2, we do not allocate a function—only function pointers.

12.15.2 Retrieving a Function's Address

Now that we have a function pointer, we need to retrieve a function's address. Just like an array, whose name references the beginning address of the array, a function's name references its beginning address. Example 12.15.3 shows the process of retrieving a function's address.

Example 12.15.3 Retrieving a function's address

```
int GetAge();
int main()
{
    int (*fn_ptr) ();   // Function pointer declaration
    fn_ptr = GetAge;    // Assignment of GetAge's address

    return 0;
}
int GetAge()
{
    int age;

    cout << "Enter age: ";
    cin >> age;

    return age;
}
```

Similar to any other pointer, the target types must match. Therefore, the function signature must match the target type of the pointer.

12.15.3 Indirectly Calling a Function

Now that an address of a function is stored in the pointer, we need to determine how to call the function using the function pointer. One method is to use the function pointer just like we use the name of a function. Since both the pointer and the name are addresses, the syntax is the same. This is one of the two methods to call a function using a function pointer. The other method uses an asterisk to signify that we are using a function pointer. Both methods are shown in Example 12.15.4.

Example 12.15.4 Indirectly calling a function

```
int (*fn_ptr) ();
fn_ptr = GetAge;

// Method 1
int age = fn_ptr();

// Method 2
int age = (*fn_ptr)();
```

STYLE NOTE   Both of the methods shown in Example 12.15.4 accomplish the same task. However, some programmers prefer one method over the other. We actually prefer the second method because it is more visually indicative that a function pointer is being used.

12.15.4 Uses of Function Pointers

We now know *how* to create function pointers, but it is probably unclear *why* we would want to do so. The reasons aren't easy to see at this point. Later in the text we will discuss some of the more advanced concepts of object-oriented programming with C++, such as polymorphism, which make heavy use of function pointers.

A currently relevant example of the use of function pointers is seen in the predefined function `qsort`. This function sorts arrays of any type. How is this possible? To sort something, you need to be able to compare two of the elements to be sorted, yet cStrings and integers are compared differently. So how can the same function sort different types of data? The answer lies in the following function signature of `qsort`:

```
void qsort
(
        void * base,   // Address of array to be sorted
        size_t num,    // The number of elements
        size_t width,  // The size of each element
        int (*compare)( const void *, const void * )
);
```

This example might seem confusing, but we'll try to clarify things a little. First of all, what is a `void` pointer? A `void` pointer is a pointer to anything. The memory pointed to by the `void` pointer is like a lump of clay waiting to be molded into whatever we need. What about `size_t`? As previously discussed, when presenting `strlen`, `size_t` is nothing more than an `unsigned int`. The last parameter is a function pointer that holds the address of a user-defined function, which determines how to compare two of the elements in the array. Example 12.15.5 demonstrates how to use the `qsort` function.

Example 12.15.5 The `qsort` function

```cpp
#include <iostream>
#include <cstdlib>  // Required for qsort
#include <cstring>
using std::cout;
using std::endl;

int compare_strs( const void *arg1, const void *arg2 );
int compare_ints( const void* arg1, const void* arg2 );

int main()
{
    char * shrooms[10] =
    {
        "Matsutake", "Lobster", "Oyster", "King Boletus",
        "Shaggy Mane", "Morel", "Chanterelle", "Calf Brain",
        "Pig's Ear", "Chicken of the Woods"
    };
```

```cpp
    int nums[10] = {99, 43, 23, 100, 66, 12, 0, 125, 76, 2};

    // The address of the array, number of elements
    // the size of each element, the function pointer to
    // compare two of the elements
    qsort( (void *)shrooms, 10, sizeof(char *), compare_strs );
    qsort( (void *)nums, 10, sizeof(int *), compare_ints );

    // Output sorted lists
    for ( int i = 0; i < 10; ++i )
        cout << shrooms[i] << endl;

    for ( int i = 0; i < 10; ++i )
        cout << nums[i] << endl;

    return 0;
}
int compare_ints( const void * arg1, const void * arg2 )
{
    int return_value = 0;

    if ( *(int *)arg1 < *(int *)arg2 )
        return_value = -1;
    else if ( *(int *)arg1 > *(int *)arg2 )
        return_value = 1;

    return return_value;
}
int compare_strs( const void * arg1, const void * arg2 )
{
    return ( stricmp( *(char **) arg1, *(char **) arg2 ) );
}
```

Although there is a lot going on in Example 12.15.5, the thing we want to point out is that the function call to `qsort` accepts as its last parameter the address of the two compare functions. The `qsort` function requires the compare function to have a specific signature. The compare function must return less than 0 if `arg1` is less than `arg2`, 0 if the two arguments are equal, and greater than 0 if `arg1` is greater than `arg2`. If you run the code in Example 12.15.5, the output consists of the two arrays displayed in ascending order.

Another example that uses function pointers is a predefined function called `bsearch`. This function behaves similarly to `qsort`, except that `bsearch` performs a binary search on the array elements. This is the same binary search algorithm we developed in an earlier chapter. Although they might not be an important tool in your toolbox for quite some time, function pointers are a necessary component of C and C++ programming.

Section 12.15 Learn by Doing Exercise

1. Modify the program in Example 12.15.5 so that it sorts in descending order.

12.16 Problem Solving Applied

As stated previously, stepwise refinement is an extremely effective programming technique. Another helpful technique for designing programs that have complicated algorithms or extensive use of pointers is to draw pictures to help you understand and visualize the process. Both of these techniques will be demonstrated as we develop a function to delete a specific stock from the program written for Section 12.13 Learn by Doing Exercise.

The first part of the stepwise refinement process is to develop a very general algorithm for the task we are trying to solve. Don't go into very much detail at this point because the algorithm will be expanded as we proceed. Figure 12.16.1 shows this very high level look at our algorithm.

Once the general algorithm has been developed, expand each step as necessary into appropriate pseudocode. Some pieces of the algorithm may not warrant drawing the diagram before developing the pseudocode. The first step of

```
Step 1: Find index of stock to be deleted
If target is found
        Step 2: Allocate new array or stock pointers
        Step 3: Make new array point to any stocks located before the one to
                delete
        Step 4: Deallocate desired stock
        Step 5: Make new array point to any stocks located after the one
                deleted
        Step 6: Deallocate stock array and assign stock pointer to new array
        Step 7: Decrement number of stocks
Else
        Step 8: Display error message
End If
```

Figure 12.16.1 High-level algorithm to delete a stock

```
found = false

While found_index is less than number of stocks and target not found
        If stocks [found_index] is equal to target
                found = true
        Else
                Increment found_index
        End If
End Loop
```

Figure 12.16.2 Step 1 Pseudocode: Find index of stock to be deleted

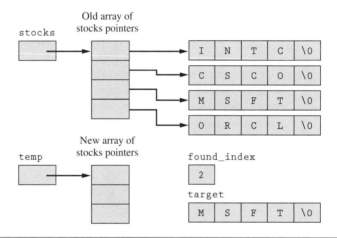

Figure 12.16.3 Step 2 Diagram: Allocate new array of stock pointers

the delete algorithm is a standard sequential search, and is shown in Figure 12.16.2.

As shown in Figure 12.16.2, when this step is finished, the index of the target stock is known.

Since the next step is more complicated and deals directly with pointers, it might be a good idea to draw the diagram of what you are trying to accomplish in relation to Step 2 of the general algorithm. This is shown in Figure 12.16.3.

The pseudocode for the second step shown in Figure 12.16.4 may be fairly trivial, but creating the diagram in Figure 12.16.3 allows us to develop this algorithm in a step-wise manner.

The third step requires us to copy the individual pointers from the old array into the new array. The copying process will stop when the target stock's index is reached. The diagram for the third step is shown in Figure 12.16.5.

The pseudocode for the third step is shown in Figure 12.16.6.

The fourth step requires us to delete the target stock, as shown in the diagram in Figure 12.16.7.

Again, the pseudocode is not very exciting, but it is an extremely important step; it is shown in Figure 12.16.8.

> If target is found
> > Allocate new array of stock pointers one smaller than the current
> > number of stocks

Figure 12.16.4 Step 2 Pseudocode: Allocate new array of stock pointers

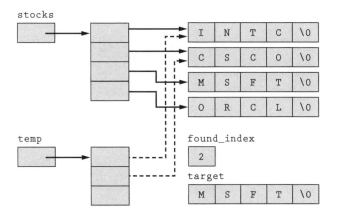

Figure 12.16.5 Step 3 Diagram: Make new array point to any stocks located before the one to delete

> While counter is less than found_index
> > temp [counter] = stocks [counter]
> > Increment counter
> End Loop

Figure 12.16.6 Step 3 Pseudocode: Make new array point to any stocks located before the one to delete

In Step 5, the pointers to the stocks that are located after the deleted stock must be copied into the new array. This process is shown in Figure 12.16.9.

The pseudocode for Step 5 is shown in Figure 12.16.10. Notice the similarities between Step 5 and Step 3.

Now that everything has been copied over into the new array, we need to deallocate the old pointer array and assign the stock pointer to the new array. This process is shown in Figure 12.16.11.

The pseudocode for Step 6 is shown in Figure 12.16.12.

Since the rest of the algorithm is fairly straightforward, no diagrams are necessary. To make it easier to view the entire algorithm, all steps are shown in Figure 12.16.13.

The process in this section may seem like a lot of work. However, it is our experience that programs developed using stepwise refinement and related diagrams are usually developed in less time and have fewer bugs.

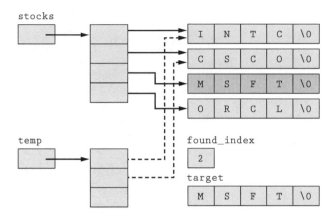

Figure 12.16.7 Step 4 Diagram: Deallocate desired stock

Deallocate stocks [counter] which points to the target stock

Figure 12.16.8 Step 4 Pseudocode: Deallocate desired stock

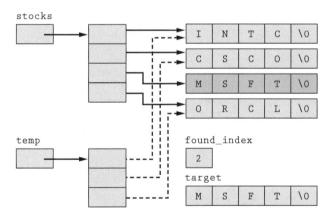

Figure 12.16.9 Step 5 Diagram: Make new array point to any stocks located after the one deleted

While counter is less than number of stocks
        temp [counter] = stocks [counter + 1]
        Increment counter
End Loop

Figure 12.16.10 Step 5 Pseudocode: Make new array point to any stocks located after the one deleted

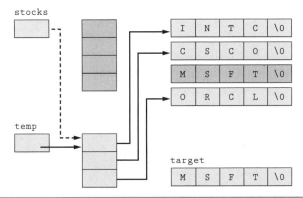

Figure 12.16.11 Step 6 Diagram: Deallocate stock array and assign stock pointer to new array

> Deallocate old array
> Make stocks pointer to new array

Figure 12.16.12 Step 6 Pseudocode: Deallocate stock array and assign stock pointer to new array

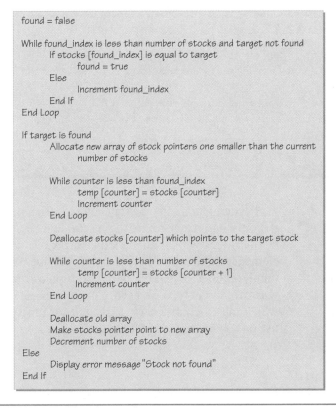

```
found = false

While found_index is less than number of stocks and target not found
        If stocks [found_index] is equal to target
                found = true
        Else
                Increment found_index
        End If
End Loop

If target is found
        Allocate new array of stock pointers one smaller than the current
                number of stocks

        While counter is less than found_index
                temp [counter] = stocks [counter]
                Increment counter
        End Loop

        Deallocate stocks [counter] which points to the target stock

        While counter is less than number of stocks
                temp [counter] = stocks [counter + 1]
                Increment counter
        End Loop

        Deallocate old array
        Make stocks pointer point to new array
        Decrement number of stocks
Else
        Display error message "Stock not found"
End If
```

Figure 12.16.13 Delete algorithm pseudocode

12.17 C—The Differences

There are a few differences between C and C++ in terms of the processes in this chapter. One of the basic differences is that C uses a predefined constant, NULL, to initialize pointers. Although using 0 would still work, its use is discouraged in some C programming circles. Since NULL is predefined but not a reserved word, its definition is located in a header file. Many of the C header files, including <stdio.h>, have a definition for NULL.

12.17.1 Dynamic Memory Allocation

In C++ we learned about the new operator for dynamic memory allocation. This operator is not available in C. C programmers must use the malloc function to dynamically allocate memory. Actually, C++ programmers do this as well—they just don't realize it. The new operator is nothing more than a wrapper or shell around the malloc function. Example 12.17.1 illustrates C++ dynamic memory allocations and the corresponding C statements.

Example 12.17.1 The malloc function

```
int * ptr1 = new int; // C++
int * ptr1 = (int *)malloc( sizeof(int) ); /* C */

char * str = new char[num_elements]; // C++
char * str = (char *)malloc( sizeof(char) * num_elements ); /* C */

char ** star_star = new char * [15]; // C++
char ** star_star = (char **)malloc( sizeof(char *) * 15 ); /* C */
```

If you examine the C statements in Example 12.17.1, you'll notice that the only parameter to malloc is the number of bytes to be allocated. This demonstrates why, if allocating an array, we need to specify the size of each element and then multiply it by the number of desired elements. The other thing to notice is that the pointer returned from malloc must be typecast to whatever target type we need. This is because malloc returns a void pointer, which must be molded or converted for our specific use by typecasting. To use malloc, you must include <malloc.h> or <stdlib.h>.

Initialization of the memory is not as robust as in C++. A C function called `calloc` allows you to initialize the memory, but only to all zeros, you cannot specify the value with which to initialize the memory. Another powerful function available to only C programmers is called `realloc`. This function allows you to change the size of an allocated block of memory.

12.17.2 Dynamic Memory Deallocation

Fortunately, deallocating memory is simpler in C than allocating memory. The `free` function deallocates any memory allocated with `malloc`. One big difference between `free` and `delete` is that some older specifications for `free` state that the program will crash if the pointer is null when an attempt to deallocate the memory is made. Newer versions of `free` don't have this limitation, but this is something important to be aware of. Example 12.17.2 demonstrates the `free` function.

Example 12.17.2 The `free` function

```
if ( ptr != NULL )
    free( ptr );
```

⚠ **Remember: Never** mix language memory allocation and deallocation. If you are writing a C program, use `malloc` and `free`. If you are writing a C++ program, use `new` and `delete`.

12.17.3 Memory Leak Detection

Usually C programmers don't have all of the nice tools and programming constructs that C++ programmers do. So why should memory leak detection be any different? Surprise—it *is* different, and it's much better.

We stated in Section 12.14 that the leak detection function couldn't determine where in your code the memory was originally allocated. This is because `malloc` is what actually requests the memory from the operating system. Therefore, because the `new` operator is a wrapper around `malloc`, all memory leaks in C++ are started from the call to `malloc`. When using C++, double-clicking on the memory-leak error message in the Output window will always transfer you to the code for the `new` operator. However, in C you will be transferred to the actual `malloc` call within your code whose memory didn't get freed. You don't need to do anything different to use this feature of the leak-detection routine.

12.18 SUMMARY

As you almost certainly determined, this chapter has to rate as the most demanding, challenging, mentally stimulating, and exciting chapters so far. It introduced a number of very powerful concepts, all centered around pointers and memory. We began by discussing the fundamental idea of holding an address in a pointer. From there, we covered the concept of what pointers are, examined how they are declared, and illustrated some of their possible uses. During the discussion of using pointers, the indirection operator was introduced as a means to retrieve or access the value that a pointer is pointing to.

Once we presented the fundamental theory associated with pointers, we introduced the idea of passing variables by pointer—which was hopefully made easy by our past presentation of passing by reference. As a result, once the syntactical details were provided and discussed, you had another powerful option for passing data into functions in order to manipulate or alter it.

Another of the fundamental aspects associated with pointers covered was the topic of pointer arithmetic. Having the ability to perform arithmetic on pointers offered some additional methods for accessing or manipulating data, including providing an alternative to use in efficiently iterating through an array.

A few chapters ago we introduced a number of predefined functions available for manipulating cStrings. After presenting the fundamental aspects associated with pointers, this chapter discussed some additional cString functions, including `strtok`, `strstr`, and `strchr`. In addition, the ability to set an entire block of memory to a specific value via the function `memset` was also illustrated.

Another exciting concept dealt with dynamic memory allocation, in which the programmer makes a request via the `new` operator for a specific amount of memory from the operating system at runtime. Along with this capability came some additional programmer responsibility—for example, the need to make it a point to always deallocate, or `delete` any memory. To help the programmer make sure that all memory allocated has been returned to the operating system, we provided a short discussion illustrating some of the functions provided by Visual Studio for checking for memory leaks during the debugging process.

Finally, two additional concepts were presented: ragged arrays and function pointers. The idea of using an array of pointers, or ragged arrays, was presented as a more memory-efficient alternative to two-dimensional arrays. Function pointers were discussed in terms of their ability to store the address of a function and indirectly call the function. In conjunction with function pointers, we presented the predefined function `qsort`.

While you no doubt had to expend some additional energy studying the material presented in this chapter, we believe you will find this knowledge extremely valuable in a wide range of programming settings. Knowing some of the characteristics associated with pointers will likely serve you well as you continue to expand your programming knowledge and gain additional experience.

12.19 Debugging Exercise

Download the following file from this book's website and run the program following the instructions noted in the code.

```
/************************************************************
 * File: Chap_12_Debugging.cpp
 *
 * General Instructions: Complete each step before proceeding to the
 * next.
 *
 * Debugging Exercise 1
 *
 * 1) Create Breakpoint 1 where indicated in the code.
 * 2) Run the program using the Start Without Debugging option. Ignore
 *    any warnings that your compiler may identify.
 * 3) Your program should produce a runtime error.
 * 4) Click on the Abort button of the runtime error notification
 *    dialog box.
 * 5) Run to Breakpoint 1.
 * 6) Place a watch on the variable int_ptr.
 * 7) Look at the address in int_ptr. Since the pointer wasn't
 *    initialized, the address is invalid (garbage).
 * 8) Step over the delete statement to verify that this is the line
 *    causing the problem.
 * 9) Close the runtime error dialog box.
 * 10) Initialize the pointer to 0.
 * 11) Run the program using the Start Without Debugging option.
 * 12) Notice that the runtime error no longer appears.
 * 13) Disable Breakpoint 1.
 *
 * Debugging Exercise 2
 *
 * 1) Run the program using the Start Debugging option.
 * 2) When the program is finished executing, inspect the Output
 *    window (not the console window) in the compiler.
 * 3) Notice that there are memory leaks identified in the Output
 *    window.
 * 4) Inspect the information displayed in the Output window. Notice
 *    the number of bytes left allocated to the program. Also notice
 *    the hexadecimal display of the data.
```

```
 * 5) Plug the leaks! Uncomment the delete statements located just
 *    above the return statement.
 * 6) Rerun the program using the Start Debugging option.
 * 7) You broke it! Create Breakpoint 2 as indicated in the code.
 * 8) Run to Breakpoint 2.
 * 9) Put watches on both double pointers. Notice that they have the
 *    same address. Deleting the first pointer releases the memory.
 *    Deleting the second pointer will most likely produce an
 *    error because the memory has already been released.
 * 10) Step over until your program once again crashes.
 * 11) Notice that there are 40 bytes of memory still
 *     allocated when the program crashes. This is because dbl_ptr1
 *     now has the address of dbl_ptr2, not the original memory
 *     allocated when dbl_ptr1 was declared. The memory originally
 *     allocated will not be able to be recovered because there
 *     isn't a pointer to that address anymore.
 * 12) Comment out the following line of code in the program:
 *         dbl_ptr1 = dbl_ptr2;
 * 13) Run to Breakpoint 2.
 * 14) Step over the delete statement.
 * 15) You broke it again! Now it is broken on the delete statement
 *     for dbl_ptr1.
 * 16) Look at the for loop. Notice that it is going out of bounds of
 *     the dynamic array. Remember, when dynamic memory is
 *     deallocated, the heap is inspected in the general area of the
 *     deallocated memory. If it has been disturbed, the program
 *     will crash.
 * 17) Fix the condition so that it stays within the bounds of the
 *     array.
 * 18) Rerun the program to Breakpoint 2 and step over the delete
 *     statement.
 * 19) Notice that there is still an error on the delete statement.
 *
 * Debugging Exercise 3
 *
 * 1) Create Breakpoint 3 as indicated in the code.
 * 2) Run to Breakpoint 3.
 * 3) Write down the address currently stored in dbl_ptr1.
 * 4) Run to Breakpoint 2.
 * 5) What address is currently stored in dbl_ptr1? Notice the
 *    difference? Remember, you must delete using the address
 *    returned by new.
 * 6) Stop debugging.
 * 7) Uncomment the following lines of code in the program:
 *         double * dbl_ptr3 = dbl_ptr1;
 *         dbl_ptr1 = dbl_ptr3;
 * 8) Disable all breakpoints.
 * 9) Run your program using the Start Debugging option.
 * 10) Verify that there are no memory leaks and that the program
 *     doesn't crash.
 *
 ****************************************************************************/
```

```
#define _CRTDBG_MAP_ALLOC

#include <iostream>
using namespace std;

#include <crtdbg.h>

int main()
{
    _CrtSetDbgFlag( _CRTDBG_ALLOC_MEM_DF | _CRTDBG_LEAK_CHECK_DF );

    int * int_ptr;
    char * ch_ptr = new char();
    double * dbl_ptr1 = new double[5];
    double * dbl_ptr2 = new double[10];
    //double * dbl_ptr3 = dbl_ptr1;

    // Breakpoint 3
    // Put a breakpoint on the following line
    for ( int i = 0; i <= 5; i++, dbl_ptr1++ )
        *dbl_ptr1 = i;

    dbl_ptr1 = dbl_ptr2;

    //dbl_ptr1 = dbl_ptr3;

    // Breakpoint 1
    // Put a breakpoint on the following line
    delete int_ptr;

    // delete ch_ptr;

    // Breakpoint 2
    // Put a breakpoint on the following line
    // delete [] dbl_ptr1;
    // delete [] dbl_ptr2;

    return 0;
}
```

12.20 Programming Exercises

The following programming exercises are to be developed using all phases of the development method. Be sure to make use of good programming practices and style, such as constants, whitespace, indentation, naming conventions, and commenting. Make sure all input prompts are clear and descriptive and that your output is well formatted and looks professional. Also, if available, make sure to use memory leak detection in all programs.

1. Write a program that includes a user-defined function that emulates the predefined `strcmp` function. Within the body of your compare function, use only pointer notation to manipulate the cStrings. Make sure to introduce into your program the code necessary to appropriately test your function. Exercise all possible control paths within your function, and clearly print out both strings and the results of each of your comparisons.

2. Write a program that reads in a text file one word at a time. Store a word into a dynamically created array when it is first encountered. Create a parallel integer array to hold a count of the number of times that each particular word appears in the text file. If the word appears in the text file multiple times, do not add it into your dynamic array, but make sure to increment the corresponding word frequency counter in the parallel integer array. Remove any trailing punctuation from all words before doing any comparisons.

   Create and use the following text file containing a quote from Bill Cosby to test your program.

   I don't know the key to success, but the key to failure is trying to please everybody.

   At the end of your program, generate a report that prints the contents of your two arrays in a format similar to the following:

   Word Frequency Analysis

Word	Frequency
I	1
don't	1
know	1
the	2
key	2
...	

3. Write a program that implements all of the sections (Section 12.13 Learn by Doing and 12.16 Problem Solving Applied) previously discussed relating to a stock tracking program. Your menu-based program should include the following options:

   a. *Add a new stock.*

      Include room for the stock symbol, the name of the stock, and the current price.

   b. *Edit a stock.*

      Provide the ability to locate a stock based on its respective symbol and change the current price.

c. *Delete a stock.*

Offer the user the opportunity to enter a stock symbol and, if found, to delete the stock. If the particular stock symbol is not found, simply display an informative message to the user.

d. *Display all stocks.*

Display a list of all the current stocks stored in your array.

4. Write a program that allows Marcia, an avid cook, to keep an inventory of her spices and herbs. These ingredients will be stored in a text file called `pantry.txt`. When your program is executed, the ingredients from the data file will be stored in a dynamic array. A menu with the following options will then be displayed.

Menu Option	Description
Add Ingredient	Prompt for and add an ingredient to the dynamic array.
Remove Ingredient	Remove a specific ingredient from the dynamic array.
Search for Ingredient	Search for the existence of a specific ingredient.
Edit Ingredient	Search for an ingredient and allow the user to change the spelling of a specific ingredient.
Save Ingredients to File	Write the dynamic array to `pantry.txt`, saving any changes.
Display Ingredients	Display all of the ingredients to the screen.
Check Recipe for Ingredients	Prompt for the filename of a recipe text file. Read the contents of the recipe file a line at a time and store it into a dynamic array. Then search for the existence of the spices and herbs that are currently stored in the dynamic arrays in the recipe. The ingredients in the recipe file are guaranteed to be surrounded by < >. Display any ingredients that are in the recipe file that aren't found in the pantry.
Exit	Exit the program and save the changes to the pantry file.

Table 12.20.1 Menu options

A sample `pantry.txt` file is shown here.

Basil

Flat Leaf Parsley

Thyme

Sage

Cumin

Steak Seasoning

Mace

Garlic Powder

Table 12.20.2 Pantry file

Search the Internet for appropriate recipes. Modify the recipes to surround spices and herbs with ⟨ ⟩. For example, a recipe using basil will need to be modified so it appears as ⟨Basil⟩.

12.21 Team Programming Exercise

Bruce, a senior software engineer, has given you a function to write. He is insistent that your function have a very specific signature, which he has provided. The function is to take a cString and convert it to an array of cStrings based on a delimiter that is passed to the function. The function is to return the number of cStrings in the dynamic array. The function signature, as well as some preliminary documentation Bruce has given you, is found below. Bruce has informed you that under no circumstances should you change the function signature.

```
/ * * * * * * * * * * * * * * * * * * * * * * * * * * * * * * * * * * * * * * * * * * * * * * * * * * * * * * * * * * * * *
* Name: StrToArray
* Parameters: The pointer that will point to the array of
*                cStrings. By Ref.
*             A pointer to the string to be tokenized. By Val.
*             A character that represents the delimiter. By Val.
*
* Return: The number of cStrings in the array.
*
* Pre-Conditions: The pointer to the array will be null.
*                 The cString will be null terminated.
*                 The delimiter will be a valid character but
*                     is not guaranteed to be in the cString.
*
* Post-Conditions: The pointer to the array will either be a
```

```
*                      valid address or null if there were no
*                      instances of the delimiter found.
*              If there aren't any instances of the delimiter
*                      found, the function will return 0, otherwise
*                      the number of cStrings in the array.
*
* Purpose: This function creates a dynamic ragged array of
*              strings as determined by the delimiter. For
*              example, the cString "C++: Learn by Doing" will
*              produce an array of four strings if the delimiter
*              is a space.
********************************************************************/
int StrToArray( char **& str_array, char * str, char delimiter );
```

Bruce, an ex-Marine, is known to be a person who is pretty tough to please. He will want a program that exercises the function to prove that it works under a wide variety of circumstances. You also know that memory leaks will not be tolerated.

12.22 Answers to Chapter Exercises

Section 12.1

1. d. all of the above.

2. false

Section 12.2

1. target type, data type

2. This is a pointer declaration of a variable called `ptr` with the target type of `double`. The pointer is initialized to null.

3. `int * ptr1 = 0, * ptr2 = 0;`

4. a. invalid—missing address of operator

   ```
   int num = 0;
   int * ptr = &num;
   ```

   b. invalid—missing asterisk

   ```
   int num = 0;
   int * ptr = &num;
   ```

   c. invalid—target type and data type don't match

   ```
   char ch = 'A';
   ```

```
char * ptr = &ch;
```

   d. invalid—doesn't need the address-of operator because `ray` already refers to an address

```
char  ray[15] = "Ray";
char * ptr = ray;
```

5. a. declaring a pointer and initializing it to the beginning address of the array

   b. declaring a pointer and initializing it to the beginning address of the array

Section 12.4

1. A two-star pointer is a pointer that has two levels of indirection. This means that the pointer will hold the address of an address.

2. Indirection is a method of referencing a variable in a roundabout way, rather than directly accessing the variable by its name. Accessing a variable's value via its memory address rather than its name is an example of indirection.

3. The indirection operator is the asterisk (*). It removes one level of indirection.

4. A cString is declared and initialized to the string literal "Randy". A character pointer is declared and initialized to the address of the cString. The pointer is then dereferenced and the character `'M'` is assigned to where the pointer is pointing, thus changing the cString to `"Mandy"`.

5.

Section 12.5

1. In passing by reference, an alias, or reference, is created. This is nothing more than a wrapper around a pointer. However, the reference allows us to use the variable like any other variable without any additional syntax. Passing by pointer requires the programmer to handle all of the extra syntax required of pointers.

2. False, because the parameter may already hold an address. If the parameter is already an address, placing an ampersand in front of the parameter will pass the address of an address.

Section 12.6

1. a. Alex

   b. is

   c. 111.1 23.23 45.67 12.21 99.99

Section 12.7

1. The purpose of this function is to test your knowledge of pointers. This function inserts a string into the middle of another string. What follows is a brief explanation for each of the respective lines of code.

```
// Creates a temporary character array
char t[255];

// Adds the integer value in var3 to the beginning address of
// var1 and copies that cString starting at that address
// into the temporary array t
strcpy( t, var1 + var3 );

// Places the null terminating character into the var1 cString
// at var3 characters from the beginning of the address
*(var1 + var3) = '\0';

// Appends the contents of var2 to the end of var1
strcat( var1, var2 );

// Appends the contents of the variable t to the end of var1
strcat( var1, t );
```

Section 12.9

1. The operator `new` makes a request to the operating system for memory. If there is memory available, `new` returns a pointer to the newly allocated memory.

2. a. A request is being made to the OS for enough memory to hold one character. The address returned will be assigned to the character pointer called `ptrA`.

   b. Enough memory to hold an array of integers is being dynamically requested from the OS. The address returned will be assigned into an integer pointer called `ptrB`.

3. a. `delete ptrA;`

   b. `delete [] ptrB;`

4. true

5. a. Need to declare `ptr` as a pointer.

   Corrected: `int * ptr = new int;`

   b. The target type of the pointer must match the type specified in the new statement.

   Corrected: `char * ptr = new char;`

   c. Must identify how many individual elements are to be dynamically allocated.

   Corrected: `char * ptr = new char[num];`

d. If brackets are used in allocating memory, use brackets when deleting that memory.

Corrected: `delete [] ptr;`

e. The value returned from the `new` operator is an address of an address of a character.

Corrected: `char ** ptr = new char * [15];`

f. In the second line of code, the original address contained in `ptr` has been incremented and no longer points to the original address returned from the `new` operator in the previous line.

Corrected: `delete [] (ptr - 1);`

g. By assigning the contents of `ptr2` to `ptr` in the last line of the code, there is no way of referencing the original address returned from the first `new` statement.

To correct: store the original address in another variable so it can be deleted.

h. In the second line of code, both `ptr2` and `ptr` now refer to the same address. In the third line that address is deleted. The final line attempts to assign the character `'A'` to an area of memory that has technically been deleted.

To correct: Once you delete memory, do not reference it later.

Section 12.12

1. A ragged array attempts to make efficient use of memory by using an array of pointers to point to individual elements. Each of the individual arrays contain only the minimum number of elements needed to hold the respective data.

a. `char teams[5][10] = {"Seahawks", "Packers", "Bears"};`

teams

S	e	a	h	a	w	k	s	\0	?
P	a	c	k	e	r	s	\0	?	?
B	e	a	r	s	\0	?	?	?	?
?	?	?	?	?	?	?	?	?	?
?	?	?	?	?	?	?	?	?	?

b. `char teams1[][10] = {"Seahawks", "Packers", "Bears"};`

teams1

S	e	a	h	a	w	k	s	\0	?
P	a	c	k	e	r	s	\0	?	?
B	e	a	r	s	\0	?	?	?	?

c. `char * teams2[5] = {"Seahawks", "Packers", "Bears"};`

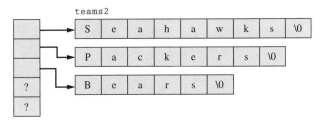

d. `char * teams3[] = {"Seahawks", "Packers", "Bears"};`

CHAPTER 13

User-Defined Types

Chapter Objectives

By the end of the chapter, readers will be able to:

- Distinguish between primitive data types and user-defined types (UDTs).
- Explain and use the `typedef` statement.
- Explain, declare, and apply enumerated data types.
- Define, discuss, and use structures.
- Understand the value of unions and apply them in an application.
- Explain the principles behind a memberwise copy.

Introduction

Up to this point, we've used either primitive data types, such as `int`, `float`, and `char`, or predefined types, such as `ifstream` and `ofstream`. This chapter is dedicated to the methodologies that allow us to create our own data types. For the first time you will be able to extend the C++ language rather than just using what is already available. As you will soon see, each of these user-defined types (UDT) has their own functionality, uses, and advantages. Using UDTs adds readability and another level of modularity to your code.

13.1 The `typedef` Statement

The reserved word `typedef` allows us to create an alternative name or synonym for an existing data type. Although this is the simplest of the methods discussed in this chapter, it is often used to simplify the name of more complicated data types. The syntax for a `typedef` is shown here:

```
typedef <data-type> <synonym>;
```

This is a very straightforward syntax, allowing for the simplification of many variable declarations. Several examples using `typedef` are shown in Example 13.1.1

Example 13.1.1 The `typedef` statement

```
typedef unsigned long ULONG;
typedef unsigned short int USHORT;
typedef char * PCHAR;
```

After examining Example 13.1.1, we can see how `typedef` might make the use of long data types much easier and more readable. Once the synonym has been created, it can be used like any other data type, as demonstrated in Example 13.1.2.

Example 13.1.2 Using typedef **synonyms**

```
ULONG salary = 100000;
USHORT age = 21;
PCHAR str = new char[15]; // Allocate an array of 15 characters

delete [] str;
```

Although the use of typedef can help simplify your code, it has a pretty significant drawback in that it could potentially hide too many details. Notice that the declaration of str in Example 13.1.2 hides the fact that str is a pointer; it would just seem odd to delete a variable that doesn't look like a pointer. To further demonstrate the confusion this can cause, examine Example 13.1.3.

Example 13.1.3 Using typedef **with pointers**

```
typedef char * PCHAR;

PCHAR * str = new PCHAR[15]; // Array of 15 character pointers
    // -- Equivalent to --
char ** str = new char * [15];

delete [] str;
```

Example 13.1.3 fully illustrates that using typedefs with pointers may add more confusion than extra value. Therefore, we suggest that care should be taken when using typedef with pointers.

STYLE NOTE Notice that the synonym examples used in this chapter are all uppercase, similar to constants. This is the generally accepted form for all typedef synonyms.

13.2 Enumerated Data Types

Another method of creating data types allows you to associate a list of identifiers with a type name. Any variable of this newly created type can have only the values you specified in the identifier list. This form of a user-defined type is common throughout many programming languages and is called an *enumerated data type*, or enum. The syntax for creating an enum is shown here:

```
enum <enum-name> {<identifier-list>};
```

The `<enum-name>` in the syntax is any user-specified name that conforms to C++ naming rules. The `<identifier-list>` is a comma-delimited list of finite values that will be considered legal for the data type indicated. Example 13.2.1 creates several data types using an enumerated data type.

Example 13.2.1 Creating an enum

```
enum DaysOfWeek {SUNDAY, MONDAY, TUESDAY, WEDNESDAY,
                 THURSDAY, FRIDAY, SATURDAY};
enum TrafficLightColor {RED, YELLOW, GREEN};
enum ButtonState {OFF, ON};
```

Each identifier in the enum has an underlying integer value that, by default, starts at 0. Every subsequent identifier equates to the next value in sequential order. Therefore, in Example 13.2.1, the identifier OFF equates to 0, and ON equates to 1. These values correspond conceptually to what the identifier represents. In computers, 0 is often used to represent an "off" state, and 1 to represent an "on" state. The power switch on many electronic devices uses 0 and 1 to represent on and off. We can choose to either use the default values or change them, as shown in Example 13.2.2.

Example 13.2.2 Specifying values for enum **identifiers**

```
enum CardRanks {ACE = 1, DEUCE, TREY, FOUR, FIVE, SIX,
                SEVEN, EIGHT, NINE, TEN, JACK, QUEEN, KING};
enum Coins {PENNY = 1, NICKEL = 5, DIME = 10, QUARTER = 25};
```

In Example 13.2.2, the CardRanks type specifies the identifier ACE to correspond with the value 1. All subsequent identifiers correspond to sequential values based on the last specified value, 1. You can also specify a value for each individual identifier, as shown in the `Coins` type.

Once the type is constructed, you can create variables just like you would with any other data type, as shown in Example 13.2.3.

Example 13.2.3 Using an `enum` **to declare variables**

```
DaysOfWeek today;
DaysOfWeek week[7] = {SUNDAY, MONDAY, TUESDAY, WEDNESDAY, THURSDAY,
                      FRIDAY, SATURDAY};
DaysOfWeek * new_day = new DaysOfWeek;
DaysOfWeek best_day = SATURDAY;
```

It is possible to print any of these variables, although you are not going to get what you probably expect. Displaying an `enum` variable is shown in Example 13.2.4.

Example 13.2.4 Printing an `enum`

```
DaysOfWeek best_day = SATURDAY;
cout << best_day << endl;

// Output
6
```

As you can see from Example 13.2.4, printing an `enum` identifier displays the underlying value, not the identifier itself. Although this capability of printing the identifier is not built into C++ as it is in some other languages, we can use a little ingenuity to display the appropriate text, as demonstrated in Example 13.2.5.

Example 13.2.5 Printing the identifier text

```
enum DaysOfWeek {SUNDAY, MONDAY, TUESDAY, WEDNESDAY,
                 THURSDAY, FRIDAY, SATURDAY};
const char * DaysOfWeekText[] = {"Sunday", "Monday",
                                 "Tuesday", "Wednesday",
```

```
                              "Thursday", "Friday",
                              "Saturday"};
DaysOfWeek best_day = SATURDAY;

cout << DaysOfWeekText[best_day] << endl;

// Output
Saturday
```

In Example 13.2.5, we create a constant array of string literals, with each literal matching a corresponding identifier in the enum. Then, instead of printing the enum identifier, we print the text from the array of strings using the identifier as the index into the ragged array.

Using enums adds some safety to your programs because of the extra type checking they provide. Only values specified in the enum declaration can be used in variables of that type. Although you can typecast an integer to be stored in a variable declared from an enum, you should always ensure that it is an appropriate value for that data type. Typecasting can potentially ruin any advantages gained by using an enum; in essence you are forcing the enum to comply with your value.

The best reason to use an enumerated data type is to increase the readability of your program. One last example of using enums is shown in Example 13.2.6.

Example 13.2.6 Menu manipulation with enums

```
enum MenuItems {ADD = 1, DELETE, EDIT, EXIT};
int menu_choice;
cout << "1) Add a new student\n"
     << "2) Delete a student\n"
     << "3) Edit a student's info\n"
     << "4) Exit\n\n";
cout << "Enter menu choice: ";
cin >> menu_choice;

// Verify correct values
if ( menu_choice >= 1 && menu_choice <= 4 )
{
    // Notice the typecast
    switch ( static_cast<MenuItems> (menu_choice) )
```

```
{
    case ADD:
        // Add routines
        break;
    case DELETE:
        // Delete routines
        break;
    case EDIT:
        // Edit routines
        break;
    case EXIT:
        // Exit routines
        break;
    default:
        // Error routines
}
}
```

In Example 13.2.6, the use of the `enum` adds a lot of readability to the `switch` statement. You no longer need to remember what each menu choice does because the `enum` identifier makes your source code much more self-documenting and maintainable.

STYLE NOTE The identifiers associated with an enumerated data type are usually created using all uppercase letters, as shown in this chapter.

Section 13.2 Exercises

1. Associating a list of identifiers with a type name is called a(n) _____.

a. UDT

b. typedef

c. enumerated data type

d. mistake

2. Each identifier in a list of elements associated with an `enum` has a related integer value that by default begins at ____.

   a. 0

   b. 1

   c. 2

   d. unknown

3. Create an enumerated UDT called `Months`. Populate it with the values of all the individual months in a year; then associate the first month with 1, the second month with 2, and so on.

4. Declare a variable of type `Months` called `turkey` and initialize it to NOVEMBER.

5. Explain whether or not the declaration of `favorite_day` in the following code could be used with this `enum`:

```
enum DaysOfWeek {MONDAY = 1, TUESDAY, WEDNESDAY,
                THURSDAY, FRIDAY, SATURDAY, SUNDAY};

DaysOfWeek favorite_day = PAYDAY;
DaysOfWeek days;
```

6. Based on the declaration of `days` in the code in Exercise 5, what would be displayed by the following statement?

```
cout << WEDNESDAY;
```

7. True or false: The best reason to use `enums` within your program is to help improve the overall performance of your application.

13.3 Structures
. . . .

One of the most powerful means of creating a user-defined type is a *structure*. A structure allows you to encapsulate variables of any type into one UDT. Some languages call this concept a *record* because every variable of this type holds one record. The syntax for creating a structure is shown here:

```
struct <struct-name> { <data-members> };
```

The `<data-members>` in the syntax represents the individual variables that make up the structure. A structure definition is shown in Example 13.3.1.

Example 13.3.1 Structure definition

```
struct Student
{
    int    id;
    char   fname[25];
    char   lname[25];
    char   gender;
    float  gpa;
};
```

In Example 13.3.1, each data member appears to be declared inside the structure. This is not entirely accurate, because until a variable is declared from the structure, no memory is allocated. The definition is the specification of the type, not the request for memory. The data members are merely placeholders until such time that memory is allocated (i.e., variable declaration). Therefore, it is illegal to try to provide an initial value for the data members within the structure definition.

Earlier we stated that you can have data members of any data type; this also includes pointers and other structures. Be careful, however, when using pointer data members though; when a structure variable is destroyed, the dynamic memory allocated to the pointer is not automatically deallocated. You must remember to free the memory before the variable goes out of scope or is destroyed in a `delete` statement.

13.3.1 Nested Structures

Nesting structures is useful for further extending the concept of code reuse. Although we could place the definition of a structure inside another structure, it is better to create two separate structure definitions so that you can reuse the individual structures as needed. The process of structure reuse is demonstrated in Example 13.3.2.

Example 13.3.2 Nested structures

```
struct Date
{
    short month;
    short day;
```

```
    short  year;
};
struct Student
{
    int    id;
    char   fname[25];
    char   lname[25];
    char   gender;
    float  gpa;
    Date   admit_date;     // Nested structure
};
struct Homework
{
    short    hw_id;
    Date     due_date;     // Nested structure
    Student  submitted_by; // Nested structure
    Date     submit_date;  // Nested structure
    short    score;
};
```

Remember, however, that the structure has to be defined before it is used. Therefore, in Example 13.3.2, Date is defined before it is used in Student, and Student is defined before it is used in Homework.

13.3.2 Structure Variables

Now that we understand how to define the structure itself, it's time to declare variables from the structure. By now you've probably guessed that any declaration form can be used. Variable declarations are shown in Example 13.3.3.

Example 13.3.3 Structure variables

```
Student student;
Student cst126[20];
Student * student_ptr = new Student;
Student straight_a = {1, "Ima", "Smarty", 'F', 4.0F, {9, 15, 2007} };
```

The final line of Example 13.3.3 demonstrates how we can initialize a structure variable. The values must be in the order in which the data members were specified in the structure definition. Although the nested curly braces are not necessary, they do give a more visual indication that we are initializing the values in the nested structure.

13.3.3 Accessing the Data Members

Once a variable has been declared, accessing each data member requires using the *dot operator*. We saw the dot operator when we discussed members of stream objects (i.e., `cout.width`). The dot operator specifies that the member on the right of the operator belongs to the structure variable on the left. Example 13.3.4 shows the use of the dot operator to access the data members of the variables declared in Example 13.3.3.

Example 13.3.4 The dot operator

```
// Example 1
student.id = 2;
strcpy( student.fname, "Drew" );

// Example 2
cst126[0].id = 3;
strcpy( cst126[0].fname, "Patty" );
```

Example 13.3.4 demonstrates a couple of important issues related to accessing data members using the dot operator. First, don't forget the data type of the structure member. If the data member is a cString, for example, make sure to use the appropriate functions to manipulate the data. Second, notice the proper use of the subscript operator. It is necessary to specify the offset into the array of structures before referencing the data member.

One thing not shown in Example 13.3.4 is how to access the data members from a pointer. Example 13.3.5 shows an older, deprecated style of accessing data members using the dot operator.

Example 13.3.5 The dot operator and pointers

```
Student * student_ptr = new Student;
(*student_ptr).id = 4;
```

The current standard has been around for decades and uses the *arrow operator* to access the data member. You have already seen the arrow operator in use when we discussed how to flush the input buffer in Chapter 10 (i.e., `cin.rdbuf()->in_avail()`). Example 13.3.6 converts Example 13.3.5 to the appropriate current style.

Example 13.3.6 The arrow operator

```
student_ptr->id = 4;
```

Nested structure data members are accessed just like other structure data members. Example 13.3.7 shows the appropriate procedure to access a nested data member, assuming the structure definition in Example 13.3.2.

Example 13.3.7 Accessing nested data members

```
straight_a.admit_date.year = year;
cst126[0].admit_date.day = 10;
student_ptr->admit_date.month = 9;
```

13.3.4 Structure Variable Manipulation

An important concept to understand with structure variables is that they can be passed by any of the methods we have previously discussed: by value, by reference, or by pointer. This is true even if the structure definition contains an array data member. Normally arrays are always passed by pointer, but once they are encapsulated in a structure, they can, in essence, be passed by value.

Another operation we can perform on structure variables is assignment. There is no problem assigning a structure variable to another variable of the same type. C++ performs a *member-wise copy* that allows us to perform assignment operations.

---

i

A **member-wise copy** duplicates the contents of the data members by performing a bitwise replication of the variable.

You should be aware that you can't use `cout` to print an entire structure at once; you will have to print each member individually. There is a fairly advanced way around this problem, but it won't be covered in this text.

Another method of creating a UDT that's similar to a structure is called a union. In the following chapters, we will build on the concepts discussed in relation to structures to create an even more sophisticated method of creating UDTs.

STYLE NOTE All of our examples specify that each data member of a structure be declared on a separate line. Syntactically you can have multiple member specifications on the same line, but it is considered poor style.

13.3.5 Shallow Copy Versus Deep Copy

Using pointers as data members within a structure can cause some problems because of the member-wise copy. If an assignment is made between two structure variables, the addresses in the pointers are copied. Therefore, two pointers will point to the same piece of memory. This is called a *shallow copy*. Examine the code in Example 13.3.8.

Example 13.3.8 Shallow copy

```
struct Person
{
    int    id;
    char * fname;
};
Person var1, var2;
var1.id = 4;
var1.fname = new char[5];
strcpy( var1.fname, "Mike" );

var2 = var1; // Shallow copy
```

As shown in Example 13.3.8, memory is allocated and stored in the `fname` pointer. When the assignment of `var1` into `var2` is executed, two pointers will point to the same instance of "Mike". This situation is illustrated in Figure 13.3.1.

When the code in Example 13.3.9 is executed, your program will crash.

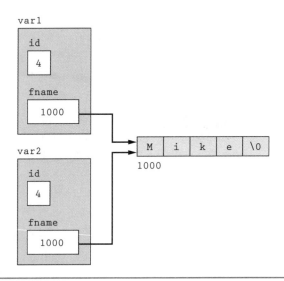

Figure 13.3.1 Shallow copy

Example 13.3.9 Effects of shallow copy

```
delete [] var1.fname;
delete [] var2.fname;
```

The crash will happen when the second statement in Example 13.3.9 is executed because the memory has already been deallocated. The solution to this problem is to create a *deep copy*. A deep copy allocates additional memory for the second variable's pointer and then copies the contents of fname into the newly allocated memory. This process is shown in Example 13.3.10.

Example 13.3.10 Deep copy

```
struct Person
{
    int     id;
    char * fname;
};
Person var1, var2;
var1.id = 4;
var1.fname = new char[5];
strcpy( var1.fname, "Mike" );
```

```
var2 = var1;
var2.fname = new char[strlen( var1.fname ) + 1]; // Deep copy
strcpy( var2.fname, var1.fname );                 // Deep copy
```

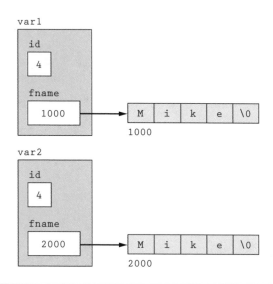

Figure 13.3.2 Deep copy

The deep copy performed in the last two statements of Example 13.3.10 is illustrated in Figure 13.3.2.

As you can see from Figure 13.3.2, there will be no problems when one pointer data member is deallocated.

Section 13.3 Exercises

1. Explain the value of a structure.

2. Some programmers equate the idea of a structure with that of a _____.

   a. byte   b. field   c. record   d. file

3. Using the structure that follows, please respond to each of the following questions:

```
struct Student
{
    int    id;
    char   fname[25];
```

```
char   lname[25];
char   gender;
float  gpa;
};
```

a. How many data members are contained within this structure?

b. Declare a variable called `club_president` of type `Student`.

c. Write the necessary statements to create an array of 20 `Students` in a variable called `club_members`.

d. Write the line of code to assign the `gpa` of the fourth student in your array the value 4.0.

4. Explain what, if anything, is wrong with the following structure definition:

```
struct Employee
{
    int    id;
    char   fname[25];
    char   lname[25];
    char   status = 'F';
};
```

5. Explain what, if anything, is wrong with the following structure definition:

```
struct Player
{
    int    id;
    char   lname[25];
}
```

6. True or false: It is possible to pass a structure by value and by reference.

7. True or false: The definition of a structure acts simply like a model or framework for its respective data members; the definition itself does not take up any memory.

8. True or false: It is possible to have an array of structures and an array within a structure.

9. True or false: Structures can contain other structures.

Section 13.3 Learn by Doing Exercise

1. Write a program that has the following functionality:

a. Define a structure that has a character array for a person's first name, an integer for a person's age, and a character for a person's gender.

b. Create a data file that consists of five records based on the preceding information.

c. Create an array of structures and pass that array to a function called `ReadData`, where the array will be filled by reading from the data file.

d. Create a function called `DisplayOne` that is passed one element of the array by value and is then displayed to the screen.

e. Create a function called `EditRef` that is passed one element of the array by reference. The function will then allow the user to edit the information in the structure.

f. Create another function called `EditPointer` that has the same functionality as `EditRef` except that the structure is passed by pointer.

13.4 Unions

Another method of creating a UDT, called a `union`, is similar to a structure. When created, a `union` defines data members just like a structure. The difference is that a `union` will only store one value in memory, no matter how many members are specified. When a variable is created from a `union`, only enough memory is allocated to hold the largest data member. This is demonstrated in Example 13.4.1.

Example 13.4.1 The size of a union

```
struct SalesPay
{
    float   base;
    float   commission;
    double monthly_sales;
};
struct HourlyPay
{
    float wage;
    float hours;
};
union PayType
{
    double    salary;
    HourlyPay hourly_wage;
    SalesPay  sales;
};
```

Since the structure `SalesPay` in Example 13.4.1 is the largest data type, 16 bytes, it is also the size of the `union`. Storing information into a `union` data member follows the same rules and conventions as a structure and is demonstrated in Example 13.4.2.

Example 13.4.2 Assigning data to a union

```
PayType pay;
pay.hourly_wage.wage = 9.00;
pay.hourly_wage.hours = 80;

cout << "Total pay: "
    << pay.hourly_wage.hours * pay.hourly_wage.wage
    << endl;

// Output
Total pay: 720
```

As you can see, there is no mystery in accessing the members of the union. However, there is a side effect. If a data member other than the one you used to store the data is accessed the results would be indeterminate. Example 13.4.3 demonstrates what happens when the wrong data member in a union is accessed.

Example 13.4.3 Using the incorrect union **data member**

```
PayType pay;
pay.hourly_wage.wage = 9.00;
pay.hourly_wage.hours = 80;

cout << "Base pay: " << pay.sales.base
    << "\nCommission: " << pay.sales.commission
    << endl;

// Output
Base pay: 9
Commission: 80
```

As you can see from Example 13.4.3, the data doesn't make sense. However, this is not the worst of it. If you try to access the monthly_sales data member, you start to have real problems. Unfortunately, it depends on the compiler as to what happens. In Visual Studio, the warning "uninitialized local variable 'pay' used" is displayed by the compiler. Other compilers may show different warnings, or maybe even no warnings whatsoever. Because of this drawback, the use of a `union` is usually paired with a flag that helps the programmer determine which data member of the `union` was used. This technique is demonstrated in Example 13.4.4.

Example 13.4.4 Union with flag

```
enum EmpType
{
      MANAGER, WORKER, SALESPERSON
};
struct Employee
{
      char name[35];
      char ssn[12];
      EmpType flag;      // Enum data type
      PayType wages;     // Union data type
};
```

As you can see in Example 13.4.4, an `enum` is created to differentiate between the three different wage types designated by the `union` created in Example 13.4.1. We can now use this flag to perform the correct operations on the `union`'s members, as shown in Example 13.4.5.

Example 13.4.5 Using the flag

```
Employee sales[15];

cout << "Enter employee type (0 = Manager, 1 = Worker, "
     << "2 = Salesperson): ";
cin >> temp;
sales[i].flag = static_cast<EmpType> (temp);

switch ( sales[i].flag )
{
    case MANAGER:
        cout << "Enter the manager's salary: ";
```

```
            cin >> sales[i].wages.salary;
            break;
        case WORKER:
            cout << "Enter the worker's hourly rate: ";
            cin >> sales[i].wages.hourly_wage.wage;

            cout << "Enter the worker's hours: ";
            cin >> sales[i].wages.hourly_wage.hours;
            break;
        case SALESPERSON:
            cout << "Enter the salesperson's base salary: ";
            cin >> sales[i].wages.sales.base;

            cout << "Enter the salesperson's commission: ";
            cin >> sales[i].wages.sales.commission;

            cout << "Enter the salesperson's monthly sales: ";
            cin >> sales[i].wages.sales.monthly_sales;
            break;
}
```

In Example 13.4.5, we determine the type of employee to be entered and then use a `switch` statement to enter the correct data depending on the specified type. As stated earlier, the pairing of a flag and a `union` is a common practice to help ensure the appropriate use of the `union`'s data members.

STYLE NOTE   Since all UDT definitions must appear prior to their use, they will typically be found directly after any #includes, in the global area of your program. This is because function declarations, which are usually global, require UDTs to specify the types of their parameters. There is a more standard way to include UDT definitions in your program, but this technique will not be discussed until Chapter 15.

Section 13.4 Exercises

1. Assuming a union had four different data members, how many different values can it hold at any one time?

   a. one   b. two   c. four   d. unknown

2. Write the necessary statement to create a union called `Sample` to hold the following three data members: id (an integer), type (a single character), and size (a double).

3. True or false: A union is similar to a structure, except that it can only have one data member.

4. True or false: When creating a union, it is a good idea to also create a flag to help ensure the use of the union's correct data member.

13.5 Problem Solving Applied

This chapter introduced UDTs as a means of creating our own data types. The ability to construct data types is the basis for many of the applications that exist today. This section will walk you through an example designed to extend and apply what was just covered into a real-world application dealing with a couple different forms of media, namely books and audio books.

The problem we are trying to solve deals with how we could best manage a collection of different books, some of which are printed books (i.e., hardcover or paperback) and some of which are audio (i.e., CD or cassette tape).

We know that one of the first steps we must take is to determine how to organize our data in a logical fashion. Establishing the elements contained within our data object is crucial, as it will become the framework for holding, storing, and passing our information. A data object is the information that describes a specific entity. If it is logically organized, it should serve us well in the future in the areas of code reuse, readability, and maintainability.

We begin with the decision on which UDT to use in describing the data object. Data that is common among all instances of the data object should be stored in a structure. In essence, if the description states, "the book has a title *and* an author *and* an ISBN," use a `struct`. If the description uses an *or* instead of an *and*—for example, "the book is either printed or audio"—use a `union`. Lastly, if there is a list of related items, such as genre types, use an `enum`.

Based on our initial review of the problem at hand, the structure describing an instance of a book object is presented here. This layout hopefully includes all the necessary components and information, organized in an efficient and effective manner.

```
enum Genres {HORROR, SCIFI, COMEDY, DRAMA, ACTION};
enum BookTypes {PRINTED, AUDIO};

struct Printed
{
    int num_pages;
    bool paperback;
};
struct Audio
{
    int listening_time;
```

```
        char narrator_name[50];
        bool cd;
};
struct Book
{
        char title[100];
        char author_name[50];
        char isbn[14];
        Genres genre;
        BookTypes book_type;

        union
        {
            Printed hardcopy;
            Audio electronic;

        } media;

};
```

13.6 C—The Differences

C has all of the capabilities to create user-defined types as outlined in this chapter. However, the use of the data types, once created, is a little different. Some versions of C don't allow the name of the data type to be used directly without specifying the form of UDT used to create the data type. This technique is required regardless of the type of UDT—enum, struct, or union—and is shown in Example 13.6.1.

Example 13.6.1 C style structure usage

```
struct Student
{
    int    id;
    char   fname[25];
    char   lname[25];
    char   gender;
    float  gpa;
};
struct Student student;
struct Student cst126[20];
```

Because of the extra work involved in having to specify the type of the UDT in C, `typedefs` are used much more heavily in C than in C++. Example 13.6.2 converts Example 13.6.1 to a more commonly used C style using a `typedef`.

Example 13.6.2 `typedef` **and UDTs**

```
typedef struct Student
{
    int    id;
    char   fname[25];
    char   lname[25];
    char   gender;
    float  gpa;
} STUDENT;
STUDENT student;
STUDENT cst126[20];
```

As you can see in Example 13.6.2, using `typedef` allows us to simulate the functionality of C++ by letting us use the data type directly without having to specify the type of UDT.

13.7 SUMMARY

This chapter discussed the capability to create user-defined types (UDTs). This extremely powerful feature of C++ offers the opportunity to extend the language beyond the primitive data types provided.

We introduced the `typedef` statement, along with a corresponding discussion that examined how it can be used to help improve the overall readability of a program by allowing the programmer to create a shorter, or alternative, name for an existing data type.

Another popular option for creating our own types, called enumerated data types, was also presented. Enumerated data types allow us to specify a comma-delimited list of values that are legal for the specific type. By using `enums`, we help improve the overall readability of our program and add safety to our code by providing further type checking.

The discussion of enumerated data types was followed by an overview of structures. Without a doubt, structures provide the most popular and powerful option for creating user-defined types that we have seen so far. They allow us to easily encapsulate a number of different variables and data types into one package; help us simulate the appearance of a record; and provide another, easy to use, alternative for organizing and passing related information.

One additional point made relating to structures involved a discussion of the characteristics associated with a shallow versus a deep copy. If pointers are contained within a structure, a deep copy needs to be used to allocate additional memory.

The final part of the chapter introduced another technique for creating a UDT called a union. While a union resembles a structure in that it can contain various data members of differing types, it can only store one value in memory at any given time. The memory required to store a union is an amount big enough to hold its largest data member. This ability to save space is one of the major advantages offered by unions.

13.8 Debugging Exercise

Download the following file from this book's website and run the program following the instructions noted in the code.

```
/********************************************************************
 * File: Chap_13_Debugging.cpp
 *
 * General Instructions: Complete each step before proceeding to the
 * next.
 *
 * Debugging Exercise 1
 *
 * 1) Take a few minutes and review the various UDTs provided in the
 *    code below.
 * 2) Create Breakpoint 1 and Breakpoint 2 where indicated.
 * 3) Run the program using the Start Debugging option to Breakpoint 1.
 * 4) Add the variables student_pay, student_hire_date, and summer_hire
 *    to your Watch window.
 * 5) Briefly examine the value and the type associated with each of the
 *    variables.
 * 6) Continue running your program to Breakpoint 2.
 * 7) Inspect the contents of the variable summer_hire. Make it a point
 *    to open up the various members of the structure within the Watch
 *    window (i.e., click on the '+' symbol). Use this feature often to
 *    inspect the contents of your UDT variables.
 * 8) Stop debugging.
 * 9) Disable Breakpoints 1 and 2.
 * 10) Execute your program using the Start Without Debugging option.
 * 11) Notice that there is a problem with the output for the year. Fix the
 *     problem by assigning the current year to the necessary field via
 *     the variable summer_hire.
 * 12) Execute and verify your results.
 * 13) Inspect the output generated by displaying the value associated
 *     with the grade. Notice that it is not very self-documenting.
 * 14) Fix the output by using the PayGradeText ragged array.
 * 15) Execute and verify your results.
 *
 * Debugging Exercise 2
 *
```

```
* 1) Uncomment the following line of code located within the function
*    main:
*        // EditInfo(summer_hire);
* 2) Set Breakpoint 3 where indicated in the code.
* 3) Within the function EditInfo, add the necessary line of code
*    to change the value of the id to 99 and the first name to "Ward".
*    Do not make any modifications to the function signature at this
*    time.
* 4) Within the same function, modify the cout statement to also
*    display the employee last name and hire date (i.e., mm/dd/yyyy).
* 5) Run the program using the Start Debugging option to Breakpoint 3.
* 6) Add the id and fname data members to your Watch window.
* 7) Step over the call to EditInfo and notice the results of
*    the changes you made in the function. Verify that the results
*    produced by the function appear in the console window. Notice that
*    the values return to their original state when the function ends.
* 8) Stop debugging.
* 9) Modify the function EditInfo again so that it receives the Employee by
*    reference.
* 10) Run the program using the Start Debugging option to Breakpoint 3.
* 11) Step over the function call to EditInfo and notice the results of
*     the changes made within the function to the data members.
* 12) Stop debugging.
* 13) Modify the function EditInfo so that it receives an Employee by
*     pointer.
* 14) Update the necessary statements within the function to use
*     pointer notation to access the data members.
* 15) Make sure to change the corresponding calling statement to pass
*     in the address of the variable.
* 16) Run the program using the Start Debugging option to Breakpoint 3.
* 17) Step over the function call to EditInfo and notice that the results
*     of the changes made within the function remain even after the
*     function ends.
* 18) Stop debugging and remove Breakpoint 3.
*
* Debugging Exercise 3
*
* 1) Uncomment the following lines:
*        // Building b1, b2;
*        // b1.security_code = new char [ (strlen ("Classified") + 1) ];
*        // strcpy(b1.security_code, "Classified");
*        // b1.location = 011;
*        // b2 = b1;                    // Shallow copy
*        // cout << "\n\nBuilding b1 Security Code: " << b1.security_code
*        //        << "  B1 location: " << b1.location;
*        // cout << "\nBuilding b2 Security Code: " << b2.security_code
*        //      << "  B2 location: " << b2.location << endl;
* 2) With all Breakpoints removed, run the program using the Start
*    Debugging option and notice the memory leak being reported in
*    your Output window.
* 3) Uncomment the following lines:
*        //delete [] b1.security_code;
```

```
*         //delete [] b2.security_code;
* 4) Create Breakpoint 4.
* 5) Run your program to Breakpoint 4.
* 6) Step over each of the next two lines. Notice that the program
*    crashes on the second delete statement because you are attempting
*    to delete memory that has already been deallocated in the previous
*    line. This happens because of the shallow copy made during the
*    assignment of b1 to b2.
* 7) Comment out the line: b2 = b1;
* 8) Add all the necessary lines of code to perform a deep copy by
*    individually assigning all the data members in the variable
*    b1 to b2.
* 9) Build and execute your code.
* 10) Make sure there are no memory leaks being reported and that your
*     program does not crash.
* ***********************************************************************/

#define _CRT_SECURE_NO_DEPRECATE
#define _CRTDBG_MAP_ALLOC

#include <iostream>
using std::cout;
using std::endl;

#include <cstring>
#include <crtdbg.h>

enum PayGrade {FULL, PART, INT};

const char * PayGradeText[] =
{
    "Full-time",
    "Part-time",
    "Intern"
};
union PayType
{
    int    salary;
    double hourly_wage;
    double intern_wage;
};
struct Date
{
    short month;
    short day;
    short year;
};
struct Employee
{
    int    id;
    char   fname[25];
```

```
    char   lname[25];
    char   gender;
    PayGrade grade;
    Date   start_date;
};
struct Building
{
    char * security_code;
    int location;
};

void EditInfo( Employee e );

int main()
{
    _CrtSetDbgFlag( _CRTDBG_ALLOC_MEM_DF | _CRTDBG_LEAK_CHECK_DF );

    PayType student_pay;
    student_pay.intern_wage = 28000;

    Date student_hire_date;
    student_hire_date.month = 6;
    student_hire_date.day = 15;

    Employee summer_hire;

    // Breakpoint 1
    // Put a breakpoint on the following line
    summer_hire.id = 1019;
    strcpy( summer_hire.fname, "Barbara" );
    strcpy( summer_hire.lname, "Cleaver" );
    summer_hire.gender = 'F';
    summer_hire.grade = INT;
    summer_hire.start_date = student_hire_date;

    // Breakpoint 2
    // Put a breakpoint on the following line
    cout << "\n Here is the summer intern:"
        << "\n\tID:   " << summer_hire.id
        << "\t NAME: " << summer_hire.fname
        << " " << summer_hire.lname
        << "\n\tGENDER: " << summer_hire.gender
        << "\t GRADE: " <<
        << "\t START DATE: " << summer_hire.start_date.month << "/"
                            << summer_hire.start_date.day << "/"
                            << summer_hire.start_date.year << endl;

    // Breakpoint 3
    // Put a breakpoint on the following line
    // EditInfo( summer_hire );
```

```
//Code for Debugging Exercise 3
//Building b1, b2;
//b1.security_code = new char[(strlen( "Classified" ) + 1)];
//strcpy( b1.security_code, "Classified" );
//b1.location = 011;

//b2 = b1;                    // Shallow copy
//cout << "\n\nBuilding b1 Security Code: " << b1.security_code
//      << "  B1 location: " << b1.location;
//cout << "\nBuilding b2 Security Code: " << b2.security_code
//      << "  B2 location: " << b2.location << endl;

// Breakpoint 4
// Put a breakpoint on the following line
//delete [] b1.security_code;
//delete [] b2.security_code;

    return 0;
}

void EditInfo( Employee  e )
{
    cout << "\n\n ** Inside the EditInfo function! **";
    cout << "\nEmployee id: " << e.id
         << "\nFirst name: "  << e.fname
         << endl;

    cout << "\n ** Leaving the EditInfo function! **\n";
}
```

13.9 Programming Exercise

The following programming exercise is to be developed using all phases of the development method. Be sure to make use of good programming practices and style, such as constants, whitespace, indentation, naming conventions, and commenting. Make sure all input prompts are clear and descriptive and that your output is well formatted and looks professional.

For this exercise, you will be modifying a program that originally appeared as Programming Exercise 1 in Section 11.14. In the original exercise, you were asked to do the following:

Read from a file a person's name, Social Security number, wage, hours worked in a week, and status. If a person is a full-time employee, $5.00 is deducted from his or her wages for union fees. A person is full time if he or she has an "F" as the status. Time and a half is paid for any time worked over 40 hours in a week. For the output, you must display the person's name, Social Security number, wage, number of hours, straight time pay, and overtime pay; whether they are a part-time or full-time employee; and their net pay. Make sure the output is formatted into **rows and columns** and includes the appropriate titles and column headings.

Your job is to create a structure called `Employee` that contains the fields identified in the preceding paragraph. Use an array of structures to hold your data. Instead of having to pass all the parallel arrays to the various functions, you can simply pass your array of structures. The following is a copy of the data file used in the exercise in 11.14.

Data: Use the following information as data for your data file:

John Smith 123-09-8765 9.00 46 F
Molly Brown 432-89-7654 9.50 40 F
Tim Wheeler 239-34-3458 11.25 83 F
Keil Wader 762-84-6543 6.50 35 P
Trish Dish 798-65-9844 7.52 40 P
Anthony Lei 934-43-9843 9.50 56 F
Kevin Ashes 765-94-7343 4.50 30 P
Cheryl Prince 983-54-9000 4.65 45 F
Kim Cares 343-11-2222 10.00 52 F
Dave Cockroach 356-98-1236 5.75 48 F
Will Kusick 232-45-2322 15.00 45 P

13.10 Team Programming Exercise

After showing Marcus the convoluted structure created for this chapter's Problem Solving Applied, he immediately thought it would be great to have a program that used that structure. All the members of his family are avid readers, and he would like a program that allows him to keep track of all of their books.

Marcus said he would like to have "standard CRUD" operations available in his program. Unsure what he meant by CRUD, you asked Troy, who thought it was a type of billiards game. Thinking that Troy was wrong once again, you asked Sherry, who told you it was a database term that meant: Create, Retrieve, Update, and Delete. These operations are common among most database applications.

Your job is to write the program for Marcus.

13.11 Answers to Chapter Exercises

Section 13.2

1. c.   enumerated data type

2. a.   0

3. `enum Months {JANUARY = 1, FEBRUARY, MARCH, APRIL, MAY, JUNE, JULY, AUGUST, SEPTEMBER, OCTOBER, NOVEMBER, DECEMBER};`

4. `Months turkey = NOVEMBER;`

5. No; `favorite_day` is trying to be initialized to the identifier `PAYDAY`, a value not contained within the list of items available.

6. 3

7. False—the best reason is to improve readability.

Section 13.3

1. A structure is a powerful UDT that is used to encapsulate variables of any type into a specific type created by the programmer.

2. c. record

3. a. `5`

   b. `Student club_president;`

   c. `Student club_members[20];`

   d. `club_members[3].gpa = 4.0F;`

4. You cannot initialize a data member of a structure within its definition.

5. A semicolon is required at the end of the definition.

6. True, but you can also pass by pointer.

7. True

8. True

9. True

Section 13.4

1. a. one

2.
```
union Sample
{
        int id;
        char type;
        double size;
};
```

3. False

4. True

CHAPTER 14

Introduction to Object-Oriented Programming

Chapter Objectives

By the end of the chapter, readers will be able to:

- Define what is meant by a programming paradigm.
- Explain the overall characteristics associated with object-oriented programming (OOP).
- Identify some of the major components of OOP as well as its major advantages and disadvantages.
- Discuss the characteristics of an object.
- Explain the term "encapsulation."
- Define "information hiding" and discuss its importance.
- Distinguish between the interface and implementation of a class.
- Define "inheritance" and discuss its importance.
- Explain the "has a" and "is a" relationships.
- Briefly discuss the concept of polymorphism.
- Discuss the concept of generic programming.
- Identify the attributes and methods associated with real-world objects.
- Use the string class.
- Model a program using UML class diagrams.

Introduction

In Chapter 2, we discussed the procedural programming paradigm, which is one of the three common paradigms. The other two paradigms are functional and object-oriented. So far throughout this text we have focused on programming using the procedural paradigm. It is our philosophy that the fundamental skills and techniques used in procedural programming are just as important in object-oriented programming (OOP). It was our intent to present problem-solving skills, algorithm development, and the fundamental programming concepts common to most programming languages early in the text. Having now acquired these basic tools and fundamental techniques, you will hopefully find the transition into OOP not only exciting but also relatively painless.

> ⚠️ **Remember:** A **programming paradigm** is a method or approach used to conceptualize how to solve a problem or design and structure a program.

It will soon be time to use these skills in writing object-oriented programs. However, before starting to develop these programs, we will use this chapter to explore the underlying concepts of and philosophy behind this paradigm.

As we begin to make our transition into this new model of programming, remember that at the center of the object-oriented paradigm is the word "object." At first glance, it may not be intuitively obvious what is meant by an object. However, if you look around, everything you see is an object. A textbook, a computer, a car, and even people can be thought of as objects. Many of these objects consist of other objects if you look a little closer. For example, even though a car is an object itself, it is made up of many other objects, such as tires, an engine, and seats. One of the strengths of OOP is that it allows us to easily model, or represent, these real-world entities in a way that makes it simpler to develop, maintain, and expand complex programs.

During previous sections of the text we discussed how C++ is, in many ways, a "better C." Now we will begin to introduce some of the powerful concepts included within C++—mainly classes and inheritance.

14.1 History of Object-Oriented Programming

Programmers have long recognized the power and usefulness of object-oriented programming. Most early languages, however, mainly fell into the realm of procedural languages. Some of the earliest languages that added functionality directly related to enhancing the object-oriented experience are Simula 67, Smalltalk, Ada, and C++.

In the 1990s, much to the credit of C++, object-oriented programming became the predominant programming paradigm. Bjarne Stroustrup, working out of Bell labs, designed C++ to be the next incremental step in the life of the C programming language. The "++", or increment operator, designates that C was raised to the next level to create C++.

Today, many of the more popular languages—such as C# (pronounced C Sharp), Java, and VB .NET—are object oriented. Even scripting languages like JavaScript, Python, and Ruby are object oriented.

14.2 Key Concepts of Object-Oriented Programming

Although there aren't any hard and fast rules regarding the features necessary to be able to classify a language as object oriented, there are some common aspects that most OOP languages include. The following sections discuss these language features and how they pertain to object-oriented programming.

14.2.1 Encapsulation

Encapsulation refers to the ability to enclose the data, or the attributes that describe the object, and the functions that manipulate the data into one container. Collectively these encapsulated components are called a *class*.

As previously noted, the object is at the center of the OOP paradigm. Within programming, objects are usually nouns and are examples of UDTs, characterized by a number of unique elements, including the following:

1. Attributes or properties: These are the data members that make the individual object unique. If we assume a type called Dog, then an object of this type could have attributes including name, breed, and gender.

2. State: This is a description of the data within the object. Assuming we have an object of type Dog, we could assume the dog's name is Webster, his breed is golden retriever, and his gender is male.

3. Behaviors: These describe the activities or functions the object can do and how it can be used. Our dog Webster, for example, could perform such activities as barking, sitting, and fetching.

Just as the individual variables contained within a structure are referred to as data members, so are the variables contained within a class. Data members may also be referred to as *attributes*, or *properties*. The functions that are encapsulated within a class are generally called *member functions* or *methods*. In C++, it is these member functions that provide us a way to manipulate and access the attributes of the class. Taken collectively, a class can be thought of as an abstract entity that is composed of its individual attributes or properties and the things it can do—its behaviors or methods.

Like a structure, a class is just the placeholder for the data and doesn't have any memory allocated until a variable is declared from the class. This process is referred to as *instantiation*, and the resulting variable is called an *object*. A class is very similar to an automobile, a generic category that doesn't have any physical entities or state. The instantiation of a Ford Mustang, with its specific make, model, color, and unique VIN number, would be an example of an object.

To enforce the idea of encapsulation, the data members in a class are often hidden from functions outside of the class. This process of concealing the data members is also called *information hiding*. Information hiding ensures that only the class's methods can change the state of its data members.

Encapsulation also enables an object to stand on its own. Since all of the data and the functions that manipulate the data are tightly bound together, all the user of the class needs to do is call the appropriate methods to manipulate the object.

14.2.2 Interface Versus Implementation

The methods of a class provide the interface through which the functions outside the class manipulate the actual data contained within the object. This interface is all the user needs to know in order to be able to effectively use the class. How the class method or function is actually implemented is usually hidden from the user of the class. This process is often language dependent but is called *implementation hiding*.

For example, when you go out and start your car, you turn on the ignition key, which sends the Start message, and the car starts (hopefully). You may or may not understand all of the processes this simple action initiates, and you really don't need to. You don't have to understand what is taking place under the hood to be able to start your car. The action of turning the key is all you need to know. In other words, turning the key is the interface to the starting process; the implementation details can remain a mystery.

As we continue to move into the area of OOP, you will have to begin to change your way of thinking in relation to the term "user." In all of your previous programs, the user referred to the person who ends up using your program. Now, in many cases, the user will refer to the programmer using the class that you have created. We have found that this change in thinking is very difficult for beginning programmers.

14.2.3 Inheritance

Another extremely important feature associated with object-oriented languages is the ability to take an existing class and extend its functionality to form another class. This process is called *inheritance*. The new class not only has access to the functionality of the parent but can add new attributes and methods as well. This process is key in making your code more reusable.

To continue with our automobile example, we could create a base class that contains the common features of all automobiles. It could have, among other things, attributes that describe the interior and exterior colors, and our Start method discussed earlier. We could then extend the base class to derive or create a Pickup class, an SUV class, and a Hybrid class. These new classes would inherit all of the functionality of the Automobile class, plus add new functionality that more fully describes each of the new classes. For example, we could have an attribute in the Pickup class that specifies the maximum payload for the vehicle. Figure 14.2.1 illustrates this inheritance hierarchy.

Some object-oriented languages even allow you to create a class that inherits from more than one parent class. This feature, called *multiple inheritance*, allows us to create classes like HybridPickup or HybridSUV. Although multiple inheritance is supported by C++, not all languages support it.

Multiple inheritance can cause some implementation problems, especially if the two parents are derived from the same base class. This form of inheritance is called *diamond inheritance* because of the shape of the class diagram, as shown in Figure 14.2.2.

The problem is that since both Hybrid and Pickup objects would be composed of the attributes of the Automobile class, if an object of the HybridPickup class were instantiated, it would contain multiple copies of the attributes of the Automobile. This would cause confusion with the compiler because it wouldn't know which version of the attributes to use to build the HybridPickup object. The solution to this problem depends on the language and will not be discussed at this time.

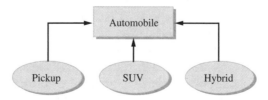

Figure 14.2.1 Inheritance

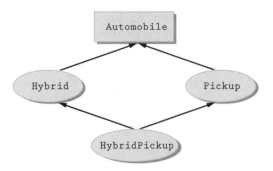

Figure 14.2.2 Diamond inheritance

In OOP, there are two relationships that are crucial in describing the interaction of classes. The first relationship is that of inheritance, sometimes called *specialization*. However, there is a much less formal term to represent this relationship, "*is a*". For example, a Pickup "is a" Automobile, a Duck "is a" bird, and a Student "is a" Person.

The other relationship goes by many formal names, *containment*, *aggregation*, or *composition*. Its informal name, "*has a*", is very descriptive of the relationship. For example, an Automobile "has a" Engine. This means the Automobile class contains an instance of another class called Engine.

> ⚠ **Remember:** A "has a" relationship refers to containment. An "is a" relationship refers to inheritance.

14.2.4 Polymorphism

The formal definition of *polymorphism* is "many forms." However, if you were to give this definition as a description of polymorphism during an interview, you would probably not get the job. A better description would be "the ability of different objects to respond differently to the same message." For example, sending the same *Start* message to a Pickup or Hybrid will start either vehicle even though the starting process under the hood (pun intended) is much different. Starting a gasoline-based internal combustion engine requires a much different process than starting a gas-electric hybrid engine. The valuable thing about polymorphism is that we don't really need to know what type of object we are dealing with. The message, Start, is going to be the same regardless of the type of automobile.

Section 14.2 Exercises

1. Identify the methods and attributes associated with a tire.

2. Identify the methods and attributes associated with a cell phone.

3. Identify the relationship between each of the following entities:

    a. bird – feathers

    b. train – caboose

    c. plant – fern

    d. person – student – Bob

    e. mammal – dog – collar

4. Define each of the following terms:

    a. encapsulation

    b. attribute

    c. method

    d. instantiation

    e. object

    f. information hiding

    g. implementation hiding

    h. inheritance

    i. polymorphism

    j. class

5. Compare and contrast interface versus implementation.

14.3 Advantages and Disadvantages

Remember that OOP is just one of several programming paradigms. Although it is one of the most popular forms of programming in industry, it doesn't mean that the other paradigms are useless or outdated; they have their own place in industry. OOP has several advantages, but these do not come without a price.

14.3.1 Models Real Life

As we've shown in our previous examples, OOP allows us to easily model the real world. Looking at your surroundings, notice that everything you see can be thought of as an object. The coffee cup has attributes that determine its size, shape, color, and contents. The methods associated with the cup could include Fill, Sip, and Guzzle, which might be useful in manipulating the object.

Being able to model the real world is an important advantage of OOP, and many applications use this ability to their advantage. One of the most popular industries to incorporate OOP within their development environment is that of computer gaming. The ability to easily populate a game with a variety of objects is very important for producing games in a timely manner.

14.3.2 Self-Contained

Well-designed objects should be able to manipulate the data or state of the object by passing messages through the object's interface. In other words, the object should be able to stand alone or be *self-contained*.

Another technique or practice that helps an object stand on its own is to always know the state of the object's variables. The methods that manipulate or alter the data members, known as *mutators*, ensure that any data stored in the data members is valid. For example, in our Engine class, the size attribute of an engine should never be negative. It is the responsibility of the mutators to keep this situation from happening.

A **mutator** is a method that changes the state of an object's data members.

Always knowing the state of the object's data members is also accomplished by initializing all data members. Initialization guarantees that the object is originally set to a known state. Each language has different techniques for initializing data members. Regardless of the syntax, however, the reason remains the same: the object should always know the state of its data members.

Controlling the object only through its interface guarantees that it will always behave in a safe manner and have a valid state. The ability of objects to be self-contained has other benefits as well, as discussed in the next section.

14.3.3 Code Reuse

Since objects model real-life things and are intended to be self-contained, it is often possible to reuse them in other applications. For example, if we already have an Engine class that was developed for the Automobile example, the development of a Boat class could use the Engine class for those boats that contain an engine. This stand-alone capability would make the reuse of the Engine class very simple.

In order to take advantage of this ability to seamlessly reuse these classes, care needs to be taken to design and implement classes with reusability in mind. Appropriate methods need to be created to ensure that a flexible interface is provided for the objects. These methods should also establish and maintain the integrity of the data members of the object.

Another way OOP promotes code reuse is through *generic programming*. Although implemented in several different ways, C++ uses *templates*; this feature allows a programmer to specify that a class will contain data members whose data type can change to meet the programmer's needs. For example, we could create a special container of information called a *linked list*. We can create this container so that it can contain any form of data: integers, Automobiles, or Pickups. The container will not need to change to be able to handle all of the different data types.

14.3.4 OOP Overhead

All of the features of OOP do not come without a cost. The extra layer of abstraction often makes program executables developed using object-oriented methodologies bigger. Some environments that have limited resources, such as many embedded systems, may find the overhead of OOP prohibitive.

14.4 String Class

Many of the OOP components discussed in this chapter can be found in the C++ predefined `string` class. This class is very robust and has many member functions that a programmer can use as the interface into the class. The `string` class acts as a wrapper around a dynamic cString. The term "wrapper" implies that the cString is encapsulated within the `string` class. The only way to access the cString is through the interface the `string` class provides.

The following sections introduce some of the more commonly used features of the `string` class. To use the `string` class, the `<string>` header file must be included and namespace rules must be followed.

> ⚠ **Remember:** Use the `<cstring>` header file to access predefined cString functions. The `<string>` header file is only used to access the `string` class.

14.4.1 Instantiation and Initialization

We've already seen the instantiation of objects. In Chapter 11, we showed the instantiation and initialization of `ifstream` and `ofstream` objects. The syntax used to instantiate these objects was exactly the same as that for primitive data types. The `string` class is no different. Example 14.4.1 shows the instantiation of several `string` objects.

Example 14.4.1 Instantiation of `string` objects

```
#include <string>  // Allow access to the string class
using std::string; // Follow namespace rules
. . .

string full_name;
string fname = "Tim";
string lname( "Wheeler" );
string students[25];
```

Remember, encapsulated within the `string` class is a cString data member, which is dynamically allocated and assigned a value during the instantiation process. If the `string` object is not explicitly initialized, the `string` class ensures that its data member is initialized to an empty string. Therefore, printing a noninitialized string will display nothing, rather than the garbage displayed from a noninitialized cString.

14.4.2 Reading and Writing Strings

The `string` class has added functionality to use `cin` and `cout` seamlessly with its objects. This is accomplished by overloading the insertion and extraction operators to work with strings. *Overloading* is the process of providing an alternative definition for a function or, in this case, an operator. Example 14.4.2 demonstrates using I/O streams with strings.

Example 14.4.2 Using `cin` and `cout` with strings

```
cout << "Enter your first name: ";
cin >> fname;

cout << "Enter your last name: ";
cin >> lname;
```

```
cout << "Hello " << fname << " "
     << lname << "!" << endl;
```

Unfortunately, we can't use the `.getline` member function with strings. There is a similar routine that can be used with strings, however, called `get-line`, and it is shown in Example 14.4.3.

Example 14.4.3 Using the `getline` **function with strings**

```
cout << "Enter your full name: ";
cin.ignore( cin.rdbuf()->in_avail() );
getline( cin, full_name );

cout << "Hello " << full_name << endl;
```

In Example 14.4.3, the function `getline` is not a member function of either the `string` or the `stream` class. Instead, it takes as its first parameter the stream to read the data from, and the second parameter is the `string` object. You will need to flush the input buffer just as you would with the `.getline` member function.

14.4.3 Other String Features

Up to this point, you probably haven't seen very many advantages of using the `string` class over that of cStrings. In this section, some of the value of using strings will become apparent.

One advantage of using strings is that we are not required to use any of the cString functions to manipulate the string. The `strcpy`, `strcat`, `strlen`, and `strcmp` functions are all unnecessary because that functionality is encapsulated within the `string` class. Example 14.4.4 illustrates some of the built-in functionality of `string` objects.

Example 14.4.4 Encapsulated string functionality

```
full_name = fname;
full_name += " " + lname;
```

```
if ( full_name == "Tim Wheeler" )
    cout << "Let's go fishing!" << endl;

cout << "There are " << full_name.length()
     << " characters in " << full_name << endl;

// Output
Let's go fishing!
There are 11 characters in Tim Wheeler
```

You can see from Example 14.4.4 that many of the irritating idiosyncrasies of cStrings have been addressed and overcome in the `string` class. The example shows that the assignment operator can be used instead of `strcpy`, the + and += operators replace `strcat`, and even `strcmp` is not necessary because comparison operators can be used with `strings`. The `.length` member function even replaces `strlen`.

There are many other member functions available in the `string` class. Use the help that comes with your IDE to determine what methods are available and their uses.

The `string` class is very powerful because of the object-oriented principles that allow for the encapsulation of data and functions within a class. The only way to manipulate the data stored in the object is through the interface provided by the class. The implementation details can remain a mystery because of the robust interface provided.

Section 14.4 Exercises

1. Which of the following statements are legal? Assume the following declarations.

   ```
   string str1, str2 = "C";
   ```

   a. `string test = 'A';`

   b. `str1 = str2;`

   c. `str2 = "C++";`

   d. `cout << str1[0];`

   e. `cout << strlen( str1 );`

   f. `cin.getline( str1, 80 );`

Section 14.4 Learn by Doing Exercise

1. Rewrite 11.14 Programming Exercise 4 to use strings instead of cStrings.

14.5 UML Introduction

The acronym *UML* stands for Unified Modeling Language and includes standardized symbols for use in developing, documenting, and modeling a software system or application. Like most of the other concepts presented in this chapter, UML is designed to be language-independent.

14.5.1 UML Overview

UML was originally introduced by Grady Booch and Jim Rumbaugh, and first appeared in the mid 1990s. Since its introduction it has continued to evolve, and today it plays a very important role in the development of software.

UML includes a number of types of diagrams for modeling or representing a software system, each providing a different perspective on the system. These diagrams include such tools as use cases, class diagrams, sequence diagrams, and state diagrams. While each of the tools provides valuable information, this section focuses only on a few aspects of class diagrams.

14.5.2 Class Diagrams

Class diagrams illustrate and describe the classes and their relationships within a system. To help represent or characterize a class, we use a box that includes the name of the class in the top section. Below the name, there is an optional compartment containing the attributes of the class. The final section contains the class's operations, or methods. An example of a simple class diagram is shown in Figure 14.5.1.

Figure 14.5.1 shows a diagram for our hypothetical `Dog` class. Class attributes include the name of the dog, its gender, and its breed. The methods include bark, shake, and sit. The combination of the attributes and methods fully describes a class.

Even though developing class diagrams is not always an easy task, this relatively simple diagram allows both the developer and the users of the system to see at a glance the major characteristics associated with a class. UML is an area

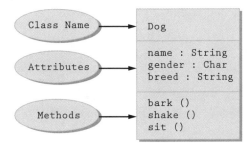

Figure 14.5.1 Class diagram

that continues to gain widespread acceptance within the software development community. In the next chapter we will revisit this topic and introduce some additional characteristics often used with class diagrams to provide even more information.

Section 14.5 Learn by Doing Exercise

1. Create the class diagrams for the classes created for Section 14.2 Exercises 1 and 2.

14.6 Problem Solving Applied

In this section, we will illustrate and reinforce some of the concepts presented in this chapter related to classes and to UML class diagrams. In addition, we will present some extra features that can be included within your class diagrams.

Assume that we have decided to begin the process of creating a database for our movies and music. One of the first steps is to identify the various objects we need to include within our system. After thinking about the problem, we have identified two main objects that will need to be included within our rough design: Music and Movie. After giving the problem some additional thought, we realize that both music CDs and movie DVDs contain some related information. For example, we know that both music and movies can be categorized by a specific genre. Additionally, both a movie and an album have a name and a time length associated with them. Within our example we will call this base or parent class Media.

Even though we only spent a limited amount of time dealing with objects and modeling, we know enough to draw a diagram to help us, and others, visualize some of the aspects of our classes. We begin by drawing the chart shown in Figure 14.6.1 to help visualize the inheritance relationship that exists between our classes.

Notice that both the Movie class and the Music class inherit from the Media class. Likewise, one can see that the Movie class "is a" form of Media and that the Music class "is a" form of Media.

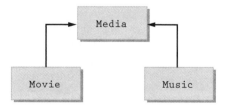

Figure 14.6.1 Inheritance diagram of entertainment media

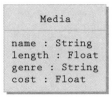

Figure 14.6.2 Media class and related attributes

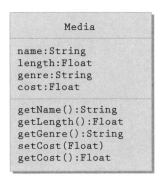

Figure 14.6.3 Media class with attributes and methods

Now that the classes have been identified, we can use a UML class diagram to help us identify and show the various characteristics associated with each respective class. First we add the attributes compartment to our class diagram. Figure 14.6.2 uses a class diagram to illustrate what we know so far about the Media class.

As shown in Figure 14.6.2, the Media class contains four different attributes. Once the attributes of the class are identified, the next step is to determine the various operations required. Figure 14.6.3 shows the next revision of the Media class, along with some of its operations, or methods.

As illustrated within the operations compartment of Figure 14.6.3, the getName method has no parameters and returns a string. The operation setCost receives one value, a float, and does not indicate a return type. If no specific return type is provided within our class diagram, we can assume the method will not return a value.

Remember, both the Movie and Music classes inherit from the Media class, as shown in Figure 14.6.1. As a result, both of these classes will have all of the characteristics associated with the Media class and will also include their own unique attributes and methods.

The diagrams for both the Movie class and the Music class are illustrated in Figure 14.6.4. Remember that each of these classes had extended the functionality originally provided by the Media class.

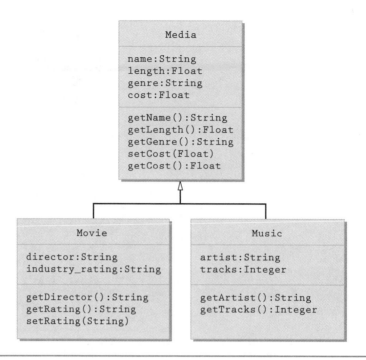

Figure 14.6.4 Media class diagrams

Figure 14.6.4 shows that both the Movie and Music classes inherit from the Media class. This is represented by using a hollow triangle to show specialization.

While there are additional components or options that could be added to the various diagrams presented, it is clear that even these elementary class diagrams present another way of looking at a software system. Remember, there is much more to class diagrams and UML in general than what is presented within this short section. Undoubtedly UML will continue to evolve, and its use will continue to expand within the software industry.

14.7 C—The Differences

This chapter has presented OOP from a broad perspective, without any references to a specific language. However, as previously noted, C++ includes a number of extensions over the C programming language that make it much easier and faster for writing object-oriented programs. If you are doing OOP, you would usually choose C++ over C. We will have a bit more to say about the differences in the next chapter.

1 4 . 8   S U M M A R Y

Within this chapter we introduced a number of fundamental concepts related to the object-oriented programming paradigm. One of the first elements examined was a class. A class usually includes a number of unique features grouped together in one package. These features include attributes, or properties, and related behaviors. Once a class has been defined, we can actually instantiate an instance of a class, resulting in the creation of an object.

We presented the concept of information hiding, which helps ensure that an object is always in a valid and safe state. By using information hiding, we make it a point to protect the data members or attributes from any function outside of our own class. Only methods contained within the class can access or manipulate the class's members, helping us control the object's state. We also discussed two additional terms associated with class methods: "interface" and "implementation." As noted, the interface represents the methods within a class that access or manipulate data. These methods are the only way that functions outside of the class can change an object's state. It is unnecessary to know the specific details behind the implementation of a method to use a class. Concealing the implementation from the user of a class is called implementation hiding.

The next section of the chapter focused on inheritance, or the ability of an object to extend the functionality of an existing class to form another class. This powerful ability greatly improves programmer productivity through an important tool that enables code reuse.

Finally, we discussed the concept of polymorphism. This rather advanced but extremely important component of object-oriented languages contains a number of aspects, including the ability of different objects to react differently to the same message.

To help see the power of OOP and how many of the terms discussed in this chapter are related to real solutions, we introduced the `string` class. This class is a wrapper around a dynamic cString and provides built-in functionality that alleviates some of the problems associated with cString behavior.

To aid us in designing and developing our solutions, we introduced a design tool called UML. While UML includes a number of aspects for modeling software, we focused on class diagrams. A class diagram can be used to illustrate the attributes and the methods of a specific class.

As you discovered, OOP is another powerful paradigm to use in developing software. Like almost everything else, it has both advantages and disadvantages, but we are very likely to see its continual growth and evolution in the foreseeable future.

14.9 Answers to Chapter Exercises

Section 14.2

1. **Class:** Tire
   Attributes:

   > Type: Passenger car, truck/SUV, etc.
   > Diameter: 14, 15, 16, etc.

        Speed Rating: A1, A2, B, C, etc.

        Inflation Pressure: 50, 55, etc.

        Methods: Inflate, Deflate, Check Pressure

2. **Class:** Cell Phone

   Attributes: Dimensions, Brand, Memory, Speaker, Camera, Weight, Bluetooth capable

   Methods: Turn On, Turn Off, Dial, Answer, Hang up, Store Number, Recall Number, Last Number Redial, Activate Speaker, Deactivate Speaker

3. a.   A bird has feathers.

   b.   A train has a caboose.

   c.   A fern is a plant.

   d.   A student is a person. Bob is a student.

   e.   A dog is a mammal. A dog has a collar.

4. a.   Encapsulation:

   The ability to include the attributes that describe the object and the functions that manipulate the data into one container.

   b.   Attribute:

   The data members that make the individual object unique.

   c.   Method:

   Functions that are encapsulated within a class.

   d.   Instantiation:

   Declaring a variable from a specific class, resulting in memory being allocated.

   e.   Object:

   The variable that results from the instantiation or declaration of a variable from a class.

   f.   Information hiding:

   The process of concealing the data members of a class, helping to ensure that only the class's methods can change the state of its data members.

   g.   Implementation hiding:

   Hiding the actual implementation of a function or method from the user of a class.

   h.   Inheritance:

   The ability to take an existing class and extend its functionality to form another class.

i. Polymorphism:

The ability of different objects to respond or act differently to the same message.

j. Class:

Contains the data, or attributes, that describe the object and the functions that manipulate the data into one container.

5. The interface represents the methods of a class through which functions outside the class manipulate the actual data contained within the object. The user need only know the interface to be able to effectively use the class. Implementation relates to how the methods actually perform their respective jobs and is usually hidden from the user of the class.

Section 14.4

1. a. Illegal—must use a `string` or cString

b. Legal

c. Legal

d. Legal

e. Illegal—the `strlen` function expects a cString, not a `string`

f. Illegal—using the wrong `getline`; you need to use:

```
getline( cin, str1 );
```

CHAPTER 15

Introduction to Classes

Chapter Objectives

By the end of the chapter, readers will be able to:

- Define, discuss, and use classes.
- Discuss the difference between public and private access specifiers.
- Distinguish between class data members and class methods.
- Distinguish between a class and an object.
- Explain and demonstrate the concept of instantiation.
- Use the binary scope resolution operator where appropriate.
- Write setter and getter member functions.
- List the four class manager functions.
- Explain and create constructors and destructors.
- Discuss and create overloaded functions.
- Discuss the concept of name mangling and how it relates to function overloading.
- Illustrate how C++ performs implementation hiding.
- Create programmer-defined header files.
- Explain the value of conditional compilation and demonstrate its usage.
- Discuss the use of #pragma once.
- Explain the concept of base member initialization.
- Pass objects by const-ref.
- Explain the importance of const methods and how they apply to const objects.

Introduction

In the last chapter, we presented some of the language-independent philosophies behind object-oriented programming. It is now time to return our focus to C++ and discover how these generic concepts are implemented. Many of these concepts, however, are more advanced than what is appropriate for this chapter, and so we will provide only an introduction to classes as well as some related C++ topics.

15.1 Classes

As discussed in the last chapter, classes form the foundation on which object-oriented languages acquire their capabilities. Classes in C++ are similar in many ways to structures. The following sections illustrate some of the core concepts related to C++ classes.

15.1.1 Definition Syntax

A class definition is similar to a structure definition except that the keyword `class` is used. The syntax for defining a class is as follows:

```
class <class-name>
{
    <methods>
    <data-members>
};
```

In this syntax diagram, the `<methods>` and `<data-members>` can be specified in any order. Remember to include the semicolon at the end of the class definition. Many of our students have forgotten that semicolon, costing them many hours tracking down the error. Unfortunately, the errors that are displayed may not be indicative of the actual cause of the error.

15.1.2 Access Specifiers

As stated earlier, the data members of a class should be sheltered from functions outside the class that attempt to change their values. This is done via *access specifiers*. Think of access specifiers as denoting the level of protection for data members and methods from functions outside the class. There are three access specifiers available: `public`, `private`, and `protected`. The `protected` access specifier is used in conjunction with inheritance and therefore will not be discussed any further in this chapter.

Anything defined in the `public` area of the class is available to any function that has access to an instance of the class. This area is where methods that provide the interface to the class should be defined. Although legal, you should avoid defining data members in this area, as doing so destroys any hope of keeping your data safe.

Members defined in the `private` section can only be accessed by methods that are a part of the class. This is where all data members should be defined, as well as any methods that are not part of the public interface of the class. If no access specifiers are used within the class, everything will default to `private`. This is the opposite level of protection provided by structures, whose default access is `public`.

Adding access specifiers into the syntax diagram shown in the previous section results in the following:

```
class <class-name>
{
public:
      <members>
private:
      <members>
};
```

STYLE NOTE Although it is legal to use one access specifier multiple times within a class definition, it decreases the readability of the class. Placing the private section of the class at the bottom of the class definition is the preferred style.

15.1.3 Data Members

Class data members are defined in exactly the same manner as structure data members. Since data members are just placeholders, they aren't allocated any memory until an object is instantiated; therefore, an initial value cannot be provided in the definition. And stylistically, each data member should be placed on a separate line, as shown in Example 15.1.1.

Example 15.1.1 Class definition with data members

```
enum FuelType {GASOLINE, DIESEL};

class Engine
```

```
{
private:
    unsigned short m_cylinders;
    float m_displacement;
    char m_manufacturer[35];
    FuelType m_fuel;
};
```

STYLE NOTE Notice in Example 15.1.1 that the access specifier violates our style convention of indenting the line following an opening curly brace. The style that is shown is the default style used by Microsoft Visual Studio. However, it is our belief that indenting the access sections improves readability.

Also note that the names of the data members are prefaced with an "m_". This is a common style used to help programmers differentiate between regular variables and class data members.

15.1.4 Member Functions

There are two locations in which a member function for a class can be physically placed. The first places the entire function definition inside the class; it is demonstrated in Example 15.1.2.

Example 15.1.2 Class definition with embedded member function

```
enum FuelType {GASOLINE, DIESEL};

class Engine
{
    public:
        void Start()
        {
            if ( m_fuel == DIESEL )
                HeatGlowPlugs();

            SendPowerToStarter();
        }
    private:
        void HeatGlowPlugs()
        { ... }
        void SendPowerToStarter()
        { ... }
```

```
            unsigned short m_cylinders;
            float m_displacement;
            char m_manufacturer[35];
            FuelType m_fuel;
};
```

As you can see from Example 15.1.2, the class definition can quickly become cluttered. For this reason, the preferred style is to only specify the function declaration within the class definition. The function definition is then supplied elsewhere, as shown in Example 15.1.3.

Example 15.1.3 Class definition with member function declaration

```
enum FuelType {GASOLINE, DIESEL};

class Engine
{
    public:
        void Start();  // Member function declaration

    private:
        void HeatGlowPlugs();
        void SendPowerToStarter();

        unsigned short m_cylinders;
        float m_displacement;
        char m_manufacturer[35];
        FuelType m_fuel;
};

void Engine::Start()  // Member function definition
{
    if ( m_fuel == DIESEL )
        HeatGlowPlugs();

    SendPowerToStarter();
}
```

As you can see from Example 15.1.3, this second location drastically cleans up the class by placing the function definition external to the class, thus making both the class and the function more readable. Notice that the method's definition can be provided immediately after the class definition.

The function header in Example 15.1.3 uses the *binary scope resolution operator* (::) to specify that the Start method belongs to the Engine class.

> **ⓘ** The **binary scope resolution operator** specifies that the identifier on the right belongs to the data type (usually a class) on the left.

Remember, not all methods need to be public. For example, the SendPowerToStarter method does not need to be accessed by any function outside of the class. Therefore, this method should be placed within the private section of the class.

15.1.5 Setters and Getters

There are two types of functions commonly found in classes that provide a way to interface with the data members of a class. A *setter* is a member function that is passed a parameter, which will then be assigned to a specific data member. A *getter* is a member function that returns the value of a specific data member. Setters and getters are added to the Engine class, as shown in Example 15.1.4. For the sake of brevity, the previously shown methods have been removed from the class definition.

Example 15.1.4 Setters and getters

```
enum FuelType {GASOLINE, DIESEL};

class Engine
{
    public:
        void SetCylinders( unsigned short cylinders );
        unsigned short GetCylinders();
    private:
        unsigned short m_cylinders;
        float m_displacement;
        char m_manufacturer[35];
        FuelType m_fuel;
};

void Engine::SetCylinders( unsigned short cylinders )
{
```

```
    m_cylinders = cylinders;
}
unsigned short Engine::GetCylinders()
{
    return m_cylinders;
}
```

The setter and getter shown in Example 15.1.4 are pretty basic. Setters will often provide more error checking to ensure that the data members have valid data. For example, the setter shown in Example 15.1.4 should check the parameter to make sure the user didn't try to set the number of cylinders to a negative number. Getters are almost always like the one in the example; they just return the value of the data member.

It is not appropriate to blindly provide a setter and a getter for every data member. Some attributes, such as pointers, can be dangerous to the integrity of the object if they were to be accessed or changed from outside the class. Therefore, carefully consider all factors before providing a setter or a getter for a data member.

Section 15.1 Exercises

1. Indicate whether each of the following statements is true or false.

   a. A class definition is very similar to a structure definition, except that the keyword `class` is used instead of `struct`.

   b. Within a class, data members must be listed before methods; otherwise, a syntax error will be generated.

   c. A semicolon is required at the end of a class definition.

   d. The default access specifier for a class is public.

   e. When writing your own classes, you are required to include setters and getters for all of your data members.

2. Based on the following class, please complete each of the following tasks:

```
class Sample
{
    public:
        short int GetAge();

    private:
        short int m_age;
        float m_shoe_size;
};
```

a. Write the necessary statement to declare a getter for the shoe size.

b. Declare a setter for the age data member.

c. Write the function defintions for the three methods now contained within your class. Make sure to define the functions external to the class definition.

Section 15.1 Learn by Doing Exercises

1. Write the necessary statements to define a class called `Person`. Within your class, include the following private data members: id (integer) and gender (1 character). Include the setter and getter methods for all of the data members. Make all of your class methods public. Place the entire function definition for each of your methods within the body of the class.

2. Rewrite your class from Learn by Doing Exercise 1, only this time place the definitions for your methods outside of the class.

15.2 Instantiation

Now that we have a basic class definition, we can *instantiate,* or declare an object of the class. Since you have been doing this for quite some time now, Example 15.2.1 should quickly make sense.

Example 15.2.1 Object instantiation

```
Engine V8;
Engine * V6_ptr = new Engine;
Engine assembly_line[35];
```

Once you have instantiated an object, you can call any public method or access any public data member. You can try accessing private members, but your program will not compile. To access public members from outside the class, you must use the arrow or dot operator as appropriate, just as with structures. Example 15.2.2 uses the objects declared in Example 15.2.1 to call the `Start` method.

Example 15.2.2 Calling methods from objects

```
V8.Start();
assembly_line[0].Start();
V6_ptr->Start();
```

Each of these objects has their own copy of the data members specified in the class definition. The methods of the class, however, are shared among all of its objects. The encapsulation of the data members allows you to do anything with these objects that you can with regular variables. Passing by value, passing by reference, passing by pointer, and even assignment operations can all be performed using these objects. However, as soon as you add a pointer data member to the class definition, you will have to be very careful and will have to provide special functions to handle these new data members. These special functions will not be discussed in this chapter because of the advanced techniques they require.

Section 15.2 Exercises

1. Based on the following class, please complete each of the following tasks:

```
class Sample
{
    public:
        short int GetAge();

    private:
        short int m_age;
        float m_shoe_size;
};
```

a. Write the statement to instantiate an object called s1 based on the class Sample.

b. Using the object you just created, write the statement to call the function GetAge and display the value returned.

c. Write the statement to instantiate an array called s2 containing 10 instances of the class Sample.

d. Using the array variable just created, call the function GetAge with the second element and display the returned value.

e. Write the statement to dynamically allocate an instance of the `Sample` class, assigning the pointer into a variable called `s3`.

f. Using the variable `s3`, call the function `GetAge` and display the value returned.

g. Write the statement to delete the memory you dynamically allocated.

15.3 Manager Functions

There are special functions that perform fundamental tasks associated with a class, such as assignment, copy, and initialization. The four *manager functions* are constructor, destructor, copy constructor, and the assignment operator. Anytime you create a class, these manager functions are automatically provided for you. Unfortunately, except for the most trivial classes, these functions will not be robust enough for your class. Therefore, we should provide our own versions of these manager functions.

Copy constructors and overloaded assignment operators are only required once pointers are introduced as data members. These two functions require advanced techniques that will not be discussed in this chapter.

15.3.1 Constructor

A *constructor*, or *ctor*, is a special function that is automatically called anytime an object is instantiated. The job of the constructor is to build, or construct, the object. As stated earlier, even though a *default constructor* is provided for each class, we will often need to write our own.

A **default constructor** is a constructor that can be called without any parameters.

The purpose of a constructor is to provide initial values for the data members and to allocate any resources, such as memory, needed for the class. A constructor is easily recognized in the class definition because it has the same name as the class and has no return type. Example 15.3.1 shows a default constructor for the `Engine` class.

Example 15.3.1 `Engine` **class default constructor**

```
// Public constructor
Engine()
{
```

```
    m_cylinders = 4;
    m_displacement = 2.8F;
    m_manufacturer[0] = '\0';
    m_fuel = GASOLINE;
}
```

Now that we have a constructor that assigns values to our data members, we have effectively accomplished one of the important concepts of OOP: always know the state of your data members. Although important, this type of constructor does not allow for much flexibility. However, we can extend this concept and have multiple constructors for the same class.

In C++ you can have multiple versions of a function with the same name as long as the number and type of parameters are different. This ability is called *function overloading*. Although not limited to being available only within classes, it is important when writing constructors for classes. This topic will be explored in greater detail in a later section.

⚠️ **Remember:** When overloading functions, the number or type of parameters must be different for each version of the function. It is illegal to have multiple functions whose signatures only differ in their return types.

One of the most important uses of constructors is to provide a way for the user of your class to supply initial values for its data members. These values are supplied to the object during its instantiation. Example 15.3.2 demonstrates how to write an overloaded constructor and make the appropriate instantiations.

Example 15.3.2 Overloaded constructor for the `Engine` class

```
Engine( int cyl, float displace, char manf[], FuelType fuel )
{
    m_cylinders = cyl;
    m_displacement = displace;
    strcpy( m_manufacturer, manf );
    m_fuel = fuel;
}

// Instantiation using overloaded constructor
```

```
Engine V8( 8, 5.7F, "Hemi", GASOLINE );
Engine * Tow_Truck_ptr = new Engine( 6, 6.1F, "Cummins", DIESEL );
Engine junker; // Calls default ctor
```

As you can see in Example 15.3.2, the constructor is passed the desired information during the instantiation of the objects. One mistake many of our students make is to use parentheses when instantiating an object using the default constructor. Example 15.3.3 demonstrates this error.

Example 15.3.3 Instantiation error

```
Engine FourBanger(); // Don't do this!
```

Example 15.3.3 may look like it should call the default constructor of the Engine object. However, to the compiler it is a function declaration for a function called FourBanger that is passed nothing and returns an Engine object. Since the syntax is correct for a function declaration, no errors will be generated until you try to access a member of the FourBanger object. The correct syntax is shown in Example 15.3.4.

Example 15.3.4 Instantiation using default constructor

```
Engine FourBanger; // Correct instantiation using default ctor
```

15.3.2 Destructor

Another manager function called a *destructor*, or *dtor*, is automatically invoked when an object is destroyed. Its job is essentially the opposite of a constructor; it frees up any allocated resources. Unlike a constructor, a destructor never takes any parameters and therefore cannot be overloaded.

!

Remember: An object is destroyed when it either goes out of scope or is explicitly deallocated using the delete operator.

A destructor is also easy to recognize. Like a constructor, a destructor's name is the same as the class. However, a destructor's name is always prefaced with a tilde (~) character. Example 15.3.5 demonstrates how to write a destructor.

Example 15.3.5 `Engine` **destructor**

```
~Engine()
{ }
```

Since the `Engine` class doesn't have any explicitly allocated resources, there isn't anything required of the destructor. Therefore, it is acceptable not to explicitly define a destructor for this class.

STYLE NOTE Since a default destructor is provided for you, should you write a destructor even though it is empty? This is another one of those questions about which many programmers disagree. It is our feeling that if there aren't any data members that require dynamic allocation—and, therefore, deallocation—you don't need to write your own destructor.

Section 15.3 Exercises

1. List the four manager functions provided for you every time you create an instance of a class.

2. What is the name of the function that is automatically called whenever an instance of an object is instantiated?

3. What do we call the ctor that is automatically provided for our class, and what are its parameters?

4. Explain the purpose of the constructor.

5. When is a destructor called?

Section 15.3 Learn by Doing Exercise

1. Expand the class specified in Question 1 of Section 15.2 Exercises as indicated in the following:

   a. Write a constructor that assigns age and shoe size the value 0. Within the body of your constructor, display a message indicating that this constructor has been called.

b. Write the destructor for the class and, within its body, display an informative message that indicates that the destructor has been called.

c. Create a `main` function that includes a statement to instantiate an instance of your class that automatically invokes the default constructor.

d. Write another constructor for the `Sample` class that takes two parameters, one for the age and one for the shoe size. Set the shoe size to 8 using a default argument. Within the body of the function, do any necessary assignment statements and display an informative message indicating that this specific ctor was executed.

e. Create another instance of the `Sample` class called `s1`, passing in the initial value of 18 for the age.

f. Exercise your program and note how the various constructors and destructors are being called automatically.

g. Create an array of five `Sample` objects. Execute your program and notice which manager functions get called.

15.4 Implementation Hiding

As discussed in the last chapter, implementation hiding refers to the process of providing an interface to the class without exposing the details of how the member functions were implemented. C++ achieves implementation hiding by placing the class definition in a header file and the associated function definitions in a separate `.cpp` file. Example 15.4.1 shows the files for the `Engine` class.

Example 15.4.1 Implementation hiding

```
// Engine.h
enum FuelType {GASOLINE, DIESEL};

class Engine
{
    public:
        Engine( int cyl, float displace, char manf[], FuelType fuel );
        void SetCylinders( unsigned short cylinders );
        unsigned short GetCylinders();

    private:
        unsigned short m_cylinders;
        float m_displacement;
```

```
        char m_manufacturer[35];
        FuelType m_fuel;
};

// Engine.cpp
#include "Engine.h"
void Engine::SetCylinders( unsigned short cylinders )
{
    m_cylinders = cylinders;
}
unsigned short Engine::GetCylinders()
{
    return m_cylinders;
}
Engine::Engine( int cyl, float displace, char manf[], FuelType fuel )
{
    m_cylinders = cyl;
    m_displacement = displace;
    strcpy( m_manufacturer, manf );
    m_fuel = fuel;
}
```

Notice that the class definition in Example 15.4.1 shows the methods available to manipulate the class as well as what data members are available to store information. The class definition is placed in a header file. The implementation of the methods is placed in the associated .cpp file, which, when compiled, will be translated into an object file. The header file provides the interface that can be used by other programmers, while the implementation details can remain a mystery.

15.4.1 #include "header.h"

In Example 15.4.1, a new form of the #include was demonstrated. If a path is specified in the string literal, the compiler will look in that directory for the header file. If no path is specified, the compiler will look in the current directory. If the header file is not found, the compiler will then look in the standard include file locations. Remember that the < > around the header file's name tells the compiler to look in the include directory, which was created when your compiler was installed. Generally, user-defined header files are included using quotation marks, whereas predefined header files are included using the < >.

The header file itself is required for the .cpp file to correctly compile. The function definitions use the scope resolution operator to specify that the definitions belong to the Engine class. The .cpp file needs to have access to the header file where the class definition is located. When using Visual Studio, it is necessary to incorporate the .cpp file into the project. This allows Visual Studio to compile the source code and then link all object files into an executable.

STYLE NOTE The name of the header file and the associated source code file should have the same name as the class. For example, the Engine class would have the header file engine.h and the source code file engine.cpp. Notice, however, that the filenames are lowercase, which provides some consistency for operating systems that are case sensitive, such as Unix.

Section 15.4 Exercises

1. To help achieve implementation hiding, place the function definition in a _____ file and the class definition in a _____ file.

2. Assume that you wrote a class called Sample. Write the statement to include the header file for this class within the sample.cpp file.

3. Another programmer using your class would be more interested in the _____ it provides than the details of how specific functions are implemented.

Section 15.4 Learn by Doing Exercise

1. Using the class created in Section 15.3 Learn by Doing Exercise, separate the class definition from the function definitions by using the methods shown in this section.

15.5 Conditional Compilation

Separating the interface and the implementation into different files can cause some problems. The header file can be included in multiple .cpp files, causing errors stating that multiple definitions of the class exist. Figure 15.5.1 illustrates this situation.

As you can see from Figure 15.5.1, when the Driver program is compiled, there are multiple definitions of the Engine class. Fortunately, there are a couple of methods for guaranteeing that the class definition is only included once. These are discussed in the next two sections.

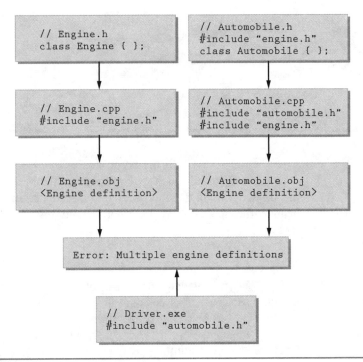

Figure 15.5.1 Class redefinition

15.5.1 #ifndef

Using the #ifndef preprocessor directive is one of several methods for conditionally compiling a section of code. This directive causes the preprocessor to check for the definition of an associated identifier. If the identifier is not defined, the code between the #ifndef and the ending #endif will be compiled.

 Remember: The term #ifndef comes from <u>if</u> <u>n</u>ot <u>def</u>ined.

Example 15.5.1 shows the Engine header file with the appropriate preprocessor directives to perform conditional compilation.

Example 15.5.1 The #ifndef **preprocessor directive**

```
#ifndef ENGINE_H // If not defined
#define ENGINE_H // Define it
```

```
// engine.h
enum FuelType {GASOLINE, DIESEL};

class Engine
{
};
#endif // End of conditional compilation
```

Example 15.5.1 tells the preprocessor that if the identifier, ENGINE_H, is not defined, it should define the identifier and then include the class definition into the object file. If the identifier has already been defined, it means that this header file has already been processed and therefore doesn't need to be included.

STYLE NOTE The identifier associated with the #ifndef can be any unique identifier. However, it is common practice to name the identifier the same as the header file. The only change is to replace the period with an underscore. This is necessary because a period is an invalid character within any C++ identifier. Because it is a constant, the identifier is usually capitalized.

15.5.2 #pragma once

An alternative to using the #ifndef is to use #pragma once. Although not a standard construct, it is supported in many compilers. This directive does not require the use of any other directives and is demonstrated in Example 15.5.2.

Example 15.5.2 The #pragma once directive

```
#pragma once

// engine.h
enum FuelType {GASOLINE, DIESEL};

class Engine
{
};
```

An argument for using #pragma once is that it is usually more optimized and will therefore speed up the compilation process.

> STYLE NOTE Because of the nonstandard nature of #pragma once we suggest that you use the #ifndef method.

Section 15.5 Exercises

1. What is the preprocessor directive that is used to check for the definition of an associated identifier?

2. What is the directive to mark the end of the conditional compilation section?

3. Identify any errors contained within the following code:

```
#ifndef SAMPLE_H // If not defined
define SAMPLE_H // Define it

class Sample
{
    . . .
};

#end // End of conditional compilation
```

Section 15.5 Learn by Doing Exercise

1. Add the appropriate conditional compilation directives to the header file created in Section 15.4 Learn by Doing Exercise.

15.6 Base Member Initialization

Constructors have a feature that is not only beneficial but required in certain circumstances. *Base member initialization*, sometimes called a *colon init list,* provides the only opportunity to initialize the data members of a class. Throughout this book we have stressed the importance of initialization over assignment; therefore, we strongly encourage the use of base member initialization. There are three situations in which base member initialization is required:

1. The class has a constant data member.

2. The class has a reference data member.

3. It is necessary to invoke a base class' constructor other than the default constructor.

Although all three of these situations require other constructs that we are not yet ready to present, it is still important to use base member initialization whenever possible. Example 15.6.1 shows base member initialization used with the `Engine` class constructors.

Example 15.6.1 Base member initialization

```
Engine::Engine( int cyl, float dis, char manf[], FuelType fuel )
  : m_cylinders(cyl), m_displacement(dis), m_fuel(fuel)
{
    strcpy( m_manufacturer, manf );
}
Engine::Engine(): m_cylinders(), m_displacement(), m_fuel(GASOLINE)
{
    m_manufacturer[0] = '\0';
}
```

In Example 15.6.1, the first constructor initializes the data members to the parameters passed into the constructor. There is an obvious anomaly in the initialization process. Arrays cannot be initialized using base member initialization. The default constructor in Example 15.6.1 demonstrates that empty parentheses can be used to initialize the data members to the default value for that data type. This same technique was demonstrated in Chapter 12 to initialize dynamically allocated memory. The data members can be initialized to any value known at the time the constructor is invoked. This is demonstrated in the default constructor when the `m_fuel` data member is initialized to an enum identifier.

Remember: Base member initialization can only be used with constructors.

Section 15.6 Exercises

1. List the three instances when base member initialization is required.

2. True or false: You can use base member initialization with constructors, setters, and getters.

3. Using the following class, write the constructor to initialize `m_age` to 18 and `m_shoe_size` to 0.

```
class Sample
{
      public:
      ...
      private:
            short int m_age;
            float m_shoe_size;
};
```

15.7 Function Overloading

We have seen that a class can have multiple versions of a constructor. This process of overloading functions is in no way limited to classes in C++. Any function can be overloaded as long as the number or type of parameters is different. Function overloading is valuable in that it aids in the readability of your code. Example 15.7.1 shows overloaded functions and how they might be used.

Example 15.7.1 Function overloading

```
int main()
{
    Fraction frac1( 1, 2 ), frac2( 1, 4 );
    double dbl1 = 5.6, dbl2 = 9.9;
    char str1[] = "Test", str2[] = "test";
    if ( GreaterThan( frac1, frac2 ) )
    {
        cout << frac1.getNumer() << '/' << frac1.getDenom()
             << " is greater than "
             << frac2.getNumer() << '/' << frac2.getDenom()
             << endl;
    }
    if ( GreaterThan( dbl1, dbl2 ) )
        cout << dbl1 << " is greater than " << dbl2 << endl;
    else
        cout << dbl1 << " is NOT greater than " << dbl2 << endl;

    if ( GreaterThan( str1, str2 ) )
        cout << str1 << " is greater than " << str2 << endl;
    else
        cout << str1 << " is NOT greater than " << str2 << endl;

    return 0;
```

```
}
bool GreaterThan( Fraction frac1, Fraction frac2 )
{
    bool result = false;

    if ( frac1.getDenom() == frac2.getDenom() &&
         frac1.getNumer() > frac2.getNumer() )
    {
        result = true;
    }
    else if ( frac1.getDenom() < frac2.getDenom() )
        result = true;
    return result;
}
bool GreaterThan( double num1, double num2 )
{
    return (num1 > num2);
}
bool GreaterThan( char str1[], char str2[] )
{
    bool result = false;
    if ( strcmp( str1, str2 ) > 1 )
        result = true;
    return result;
}
```

The next section takes a look under the hood at how functions with the same name can refer to different definitions.

15.7.1 Name Mangling

Name mangling, or *name decoration*, is the process the compiler takes to ensure that each function has a unique name. When a C++ compiler translates a function into object code, the data type of each parameter is used in conjunction with the function name to create a unique identifier. Therefore, to the programmer, functions may have the same name, but under the hood they are quite unique. There isn't any standard specifying how a compiler should mangle names, so different compilers may produce different mangled names. Table 15.7.1 shows the mangled names produced by Microsoft Visual Studio for each of the overloaded functions in Example 15.7.1.

As you can see in Table 15.7.1, the return type does not participate in the name mangling, helping illustrate why functions cannot differ only by their return types.

Function Declaration	Mangled Name
`bool GreaterThan( char str1[], char str2[] );`	`GreaterThan@@YA_NQAD0@Z`
`bool GreaterThan( double num1, double num2 );`	`GreaterThan@@YA_NNN@Z`
`bool GreaterThan( Fraction frac1, Fraction frac2 );`	`GreaterThan@@YA_NVFraction@@0@Z`

Table 15.7.1 Name mangling

15.8 Passing By Const-ref

Since objects may contain data members that need large amounts of memory, passing objects by value and therefore making a copy of the object can be prohibitive, both in the extra amount of memory and in the time it takes to make the copy. The alternatives of passing by reference or pointer are unsafe for those situations that require the object to maintain its original state.

To address these issues, programmers often pass objects in a way that doesn't require a copy to be made but still allows for the object to maintain its original state. This method of passing parameters is called *passing by const-ref*. Passing by const-ref allows a parameter to be passed by reference to avoid the performance cost of making a copy of the object, but still has the safety of passing by value because the object cannot be changed. This method is shown in Example 15.8.1.

Example 15.8.1 Passing By Const-ref

```
bool GreaterThan( const Fraction & frac1, const Fraction & frac2 );
```

> **STYLE NOTE** There is no cost savings, and therefore no advantage, in passing a primitive data type by const-ref. Therefore, use passing by value with primitive data types, and use const-ref for complex data types such as classes and structures.

15.8.1 Const Methods

To ensure that the object retains its original state, calls to methods that change the state of the object's data members are prohibited with constant objects. A new function signature is introduced that guarantees data members will not be changed. Methods that have this signature are often called *const methods*. An example of a const method is shown in Example 15.8.2.

Example 15.8.2 Const method

```
int Fraction::getNumer() const
{
    return numer;
}
```

If an attempt to call a non-const method from a const object is made, the compiler will issue a syntax error.

Remember: Const objects can only call const methods. Non-const objects can call both const methods as well as non-const methods.

Section 15.8 Exercises

1. Explain the value of passing parameters by const-ref.

2. What is the purpose of having const methods?

15.9 Problem Solving Applied

In the last chapter, we introduced the Unified Modeling Language, or UML. As we discussed, the goals of UML include providing some standards we can use to help design, create, and document our software. This section illustrates an example of how we might develop a UML class diagram to help describe one of the classes, Dog, in a hypothetical software system.

We begin our class diagram by simply creating a rectangular box composed of three different sections or components: name of the class, attributes associ-

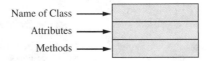

Figure 15.9.1 Components of a class diagram

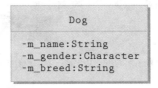

Figure 15.9.2 Components of the Dog class

ated with the class, and the operations or methods the class contains. Figure 15.9.1 illustrates the three sections usually contained within a class diagram.

The first section of the diagram is no doubt the easiest. The name of the class should be descriptive of the entity we are developing. In this example, the ideal name of the class would be Dog, and it is centered within the first section.

The second section contains the attributes, or data members, of the class. Each of these data members has its name, followed by a colon and the type of attribute it is. If the variables have public access, we place a plus symbol on the left side of the variable. If the variable allows only private access, we use the minus symbol.

To determine the attributes of the class, we need to consider the characteristics that describe the entity along with their associated data type. In the Dog class example, it would be useful to include the following data members and their corresponding types: name (string), gender (character), and breed (string). Figure 15.9.2 shows the updated diagram for the Dog class, including the related access specifiers.

The final section of the class diagram contains the various methods the class will need. Each of the methods is listed, followed by the return value. In addition, it is also common to show the data type of any arguments.

Determining the methods associated with the class includes assessing how the outside world will want to interact with objects derived from the class. In the case of our Dog class, we know that there will be a need to retrieve the name, gender, and breed for each respective instance of the class. It was also determined that a one-argument constructor is required to ensure that every instance of Dog has a gender. Consequently, we see the need to include not only a constructor that takes one argument but also two additional methods to set the

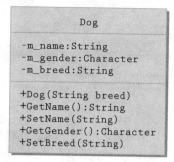

Figure 15.9.3 Completed class diagram

name and the breed. Figure 15.9.3 shows an example of the updated diagram, which includes the methods just mentioned along with the corresponding access privileges.

There are a number of other components associated with UML besides class diagrams. While we have only begun to scratch the surface with this brief introduction of class diagrams, hopefully you can see the value in using diagrams as another tool to help model the various pieces of a software system.

15.10 C—The Differences

Since classes are a C++ construct, some programmers may assume that you can't use the object-oriented paradigm with C; however, this just isn't true. For example, C allows `structs` to contain function pointers, which, when used correctly, can simulate a class. Although advanced features of OOP languages aren't available, such as inheritance, there isn't any reason why programmers can't create objects using `structs`.

15.11 SUMMARY

This chapter focused mainly on classes, one of the cornerstones of object-oriented programming. Syntactically, classes resemble structures, except that classes generally encapsulate both data members, or attributes, and the methods that manipulate the data.

To control the visibility of the attributes and methods, access specifiers are used. Access specifiers allow the developer of the class to determine what can be accessed by functions outside of the class. This ability to safeguard and control access to class members is an important characteristic of classes. To facilitate this safety mechanism, we examined two main specifiers: `public` and `private`. By defining variables within the public section of a class, the attributes and methods can be manipulated by any function. The private area of a class only allows functions that are members of the class to access anything defined in this section.

Within a class, there are several categories of methods. For example, a getter is a member function that returns the value of a specific data member. A setter is a method that is passed a value, which is then assigned to a specific data member. As discussed, there is also a broad group of methods called manager functions. Within this chapter we explored two of the four manager functions that are automatically provided for us: constructors and destructors. The constructor is a function that is automatically called anytime an object is created or instantiated. A destructor, on the other hand, is automatically called whenever an object goes out of scope or is destroyed.

After looking at some of the manager functions, we reviewed the concept of implementation hiding. As you recall, implementation hiding is the practice of supplying a class interface without exposing the details of how an individual member function is written. To actually apply this concept to our source code, we demonstrated how C++ achieves implementation hiding by placing the class definition in a header file and the associated function definitions in a separate `.cpp` file. To help facilitate this approach, we examined a modified version of the `#include` statement, noting how quotation marks are used around the `.h` filename to indicate where the compiler should physically look for the specified file. To further strengthen this process, the concept of conditional compilation was introduced, along with some additional preprocessor directives like `#ifndef` and `#pragma`.

Later in the chapter we revisited the concept of constructors and introduced base member initialization. We stressed how member initialization can only be used with constructors, and noted how it is the only option available for initializing data members.

Next we took a closer look at function overloading, noting how it becomes crucial when we are writing multiple constructors for a class. To help illustrate why a function with the same name must differ by the number or types of parameters, the concept of name mangling was presented.

The chapter concluded by presenting two different methods for passing objects in a way that help protect its data members. The first option centered on passing an object by const-ref, whereby a parameter is passed by reference but still has the safety of being passed by value because the object itself cannot be modified. The second alternative, called a const method, is used to guarantee that the calling object's data members will not be changed.

Obviously there is a lot of information related to object-oriented programming that we didn't present within this chapter. The previous chapter and this chapter were designed simply to introduce you to object-oriented programming and to show how it applies to C++. We chose to defer our discussion of object-oriented programming until these chapters since we felt the reader would now have the tools necessary to understand the building blocks of classes.

15.12 Debugging Exercise

Download the following file from this book's website and run the program following the instructions noted in the code.

```
/**********************************************************************
 * File: Chap_15_Debugging.cpp
 *
 * General Instructions: Complete each step before proceeding to the
 * next.
 *
 * 1) Look at the existing code and identify how many
 *    times you anticipate that the constructor will be called
 *    when the program is executed.
 * 2) Add an informative output message in the constructor
 *    that includes the name of the stock symbol.
 * 3) Build and execute the program and verify that the
 *    constructor was called once for each of the three
 *    objects created.
 * 4) Add a destructor.
 * 5) Set and run your program to Breakpoint 1. Use Step
 *    Into to actually step into the destructor.
 * 6) Stop debugging.
 * 7) Add an informative message in your destructor that
 *    includes the name of the stock symbol.
 * 8) Rebuild and execute the program. Make sure
 *    the dtor is being called for all three of
 *    your Stock objects.
 * 9) If you have not already done so, find and correct
 *    the problem associated with the destructor not
 *    being called for one of your objects.
 *10) Create an array of three Stock objects in main.
 *11) Rebuild and execute the program. Notice that there is a
 *    problem.
 *12) Add the necessary constructor to fix this problem.
 *    Make sure you include a descriptive message noting
 *    that this is the default constructor. Rebuild and
 *    execute the program to make sure that everything is
 *    working.
 *13) Notice the number of times the constructors and the
 *    destructor are being called.
 *14) Try making both of your constructors private.
 *15) Rebuild and execute the program. Notice how this stops
 *    any instance of the object from being created.
 *16) Make your constructors public again.
 *17) Uncomment the following two lines in main:
 *        // Stock s1();
 *        // s1.setPrice ( 12.34 );
 *18) Try rebuilding the program. Notice that there is a problem.
 *19) Look carefully at the first line you uncommented.
 *    This is simply a function declaration; it is not
 *    instantiating an object.
 *20) Remove the ( ), then rebuild and execute the program.
 **********************************************************************/
```

```cpp
// stock.h
#include <string>
using std::string;

class Stock
{
    public:
        Stock( string symbol, int shares, double price = .01 );
        string GetStockSymbol();
        double GetPrice();
        void SetPrice( double price );
        int GetShares();

    private:
        string m_symbol;
        double m_price;
        int m_shares;
} ;

// Stock.cpp
#include <iostream>
using std::cout;
using std::endl;
#include "stock.h"

Stock::Stock( string symbol, int shares, double price )
     : m_symbol(symbol), m_shares(shares), m_price(price)
{ }
string Stock::GetStockSymbol()
{
    return m_symbol;
}
double Stock::GetPrice()
{
    return m_price;
}
void Stock::SetPrice( double price )
{
    m_price = price;
}
int Stock::GetShares()
{
    return m_shares;
}
// Chap_15_Debugging.cpp
#include <iostream>
using std::cout;
using std::endl;

#include "stock.h"
```

```
void DisplayStock( Stock & s );
void DisplayStock( Stock * s );
void SetStockPricesEqual( Stock & s1, Stock & s2 );

int main()
{
        //Stock s1();
        //s1.setPrice ( 12.34 );
        Stock s2( "MSFT", 100, 28.50 );
        Stock s3( "INTC", 200, 21.25 );
        Stock * s4 = new Stock( "CSCO", 300, 24.75 );

        DisplayStock( s2 );
        SetStockPricesEqual( s2, s3 );
        DisplayStock( s3 );
        DisplayStock( s4 );

        // Breakpoint 1
        return 0;
}

void DisplayStock( Stock & s )
{
        cout << "\nStock: " << s.GetStockSymbol()
            << " Shares: " << s.GetShares()
            << " Price: "  << s.GetPrice() << endl;
}

void DisplayStock( Stock * s )
{
        cout << "\nStock: " << s->GetStockSymbol()
            << " Shares: "   << s->GetShares()
            << " Price: "    << s->GetPrice() << endl;
}

void SetStockPricesEqual( Stock & s1, Stock & s2 )
{
        s1.SetPrice( s2.GetPrice() );
}
```

15.13 Programming Exercises

The following programming exercises are to be developed using all phases of the development method. Be sure to make use of good programming practices and style, such as constants, whitespace, indentation, naming conventions, and commenting. Make sure all input prompts are clear and descriptive and that your output is well formatted and looks professional.

1. Implement the class described by the following UML class diagram:

```
                              Fraction

-m_numer:int
-m_denom:int

+Fraction (in numer:int = 1,in denom:int = 1)
+Add (in left_frac:Fraction, in right_frac:Fraction)
+Subtract (in left_frac:Fraction, in right_frac:Fraction)
+Multiply (in left_frac:Fraction, in right_frac:Fraction)
+Divide (in left_frac:Fraction, in right_frac:Fraction)
+Display()
-Reduce()
+SetNumer (in numer:int)
+SetDenom (in numer:int)
+GetNumer():int
+GetDenom():int
```

Figure 15.13.1 Fraction class diagram

Microsoft Visio, which was used to develop this diagram, shows how each parameter is to be passed to the method. Each parameter is prefaced with either "in", "out"; or "in out". If a parameter is to be passed by value, "in" is specified. If a parameter is to be passed by reference but the initial value is not used, "out" is specified. If a parameter is to be passed by reference and the initial value is used, "in out" is specified. Visio is a tool that can be used to develop a wide variety of diagrams, including UML.

Other supporting methods can be added to the class diagram as needed. What follows is a code fragment that demonstrates how the mathematical method calls should be performed.

```
Fraction f1( 1, 2 ),
         f2( 3, 4 ),
         f3;

f3.Multiply( f1, f2 );

f1.Display();
cout << " * ";
f2.Display();
cout << " = ";
f3.Display();

// Output
1/2 * 3/4 = 3/8
```

Notice that the results of the mathematical operation are stored in the object that is used to call the method. Implement this class and test the functionality appropriately using the code fragment as a guide.

2. Using the following class diagram, implement a deck of cards.

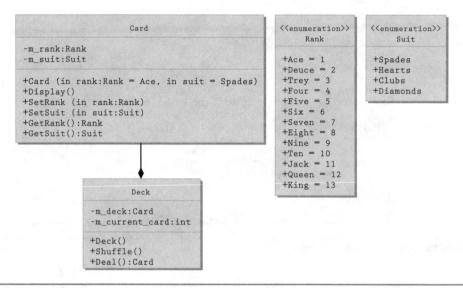

Figure 15.13.2 Deck class diagram

The blackened diamond is a UML convention to show that a class contains an object of a different class. In the diagram above, a Deck will contain 52 Cards.

3. Using a UML class diagram, design a program to store information about a course at your school. Your program should contain the following classes.

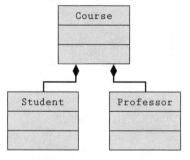

Figure 15.13.3 Class diagram

A course will have a maximum of 30 students and only one professor. Determine what other information and functionality each class should include. Once the class diagram has been completed, write the classes as well as the program that tests the functionality of the classes.

15.14 Team Programming Exercise

It seems our old friend Troy has once again been assigned to work on your team and has completed some of the preliminary design on a project for a system that will eventually be used to manage a movie database. The UML diagram for the `Movie` class follows. Notice that the diagram has been expanded and includes the initial values required for a couple of the data members, and that it also includes a three-argument constructor. To conform to UML standards, Troy has added the + symbol, to represent public access, and the - symbol, to represent private.

```
                   Movie

    -m_name:String
    -m_length:Float=0
    -m_cost:Float=12.99
    -m_rating:String

    +Movie(name:String,
       length:Float,rating:String)
    +getName():String
    +getLength():Float
    +setCost(Float cost)
    +getCost():Float
    +getRating():String
```

Figure 15.14.1 `Movie` class diagram

Your job is to write the necessary source code to create the `Movie` class. Make sure you include all of the attributes and methods listed within the class diagram. You must separate the interface file (`.h`) from the implementation file (`.cpp`). Include within your project a separate `.cpp` file that includes `main` and acts as a driver in which you actually instantiate and test your class. Make it a point to instantiate two different objects and exercise each of the class methods.

To further test the functionality of your class, create a nonmember function and pass an object by const-ref. Once again test all of the methods, this time from the const object. This will cause compiler errors using the current class diagram because there are no const methods. Update the class diagram and code to reflect that the getters need to be const methods.

15.15 Answers to Chapter Exercises

Section 15.1

1. a. True

   b. False

   c. True

    d. False

    e. False

2. a. `float GetShoeSize();`

    b. `void SetAge( short int age );`

    c.
```
short int Sample::GetAge()
{
      return m_age;
}

float Sample::GetShoeSize()
{
      return m_shoe_size;
}

void Sample::SetAge( short int age )
{
      m_age = age;
}
```

Section 15.2

1. a. `Sample s1;`
   b. `cout << s1.GetAge();`
   c. `Sample s2[10];`
   d. `cout << s2[1].GetAge();`
   e. `Sample * s3 = new Sample;`
   f. `cout << s3->GetAge();`
   g. `delete s3;`

Section 15.3

1. The four manager functions are: constructor, destructor, copy constructor, and the assignment operator.

2. Constructor, or ctor.

3. Default constructor; it is called without any parameters.

4. The purpose of a constructor is to provide initial values to data members and to allocate any needed resources for the class.

5. The destructor is automatically called when an object is destroyed.

Section 15.4

1. `.cpp`

   `.h`

2. `#include "sample.h"`

3. interface

Section 15.5

1. `#ifndef`

2. `#endif`

3. `define SAMPLE_H` should be: `#define SAMPLE_H`

   `#end` should be `#endif`

Section 15.6

1. It is required that base member initialization be used when:

   a. the class has a const data member;

   b. the class has a reference data member;

   c. it is necessary to invoke a base class constructor other than the default constructor.

2. False—base member initialization can only be used with constructors.

3. ```
   Sample::Sample( int age, float shoe_size )
   : m_age(age), m_shoe_size(shoe_size)
   {   }
   ```

Section 15.8

1. Passing parameters by const_ref allows a parameter to be passed by reference but provides the safety of passing by value because the object cannot be changed.

2. Const objects can only call const methods.
   ```

Miscellaneous Topics

Chapter Objectives

By the end of the chapter, readers will be able to:

- Understand and discuss the use of the `auto`, `register`, `static`, and `extern` storage classes.
- Explain the value of command-line arguments and demonstrate their usage.
- Understand the usefulness of conditional compilation and apply the more commonly used preprocessor directives.
- Develop macros and explain their advantages and disadvantages.
- Explain the value and characteristics of various bitwise operators.
- Define the basic idea of big-endian and little-endian formats.
- Apply masking techniques and bitwise operators to manipulate data.
- Discuss the characteristics associated with recursion.
- Apply recursive algorithms to solve a specific problem.
- Explain the value of examining the call stack when using recursion.

Introduction

This chapter presents many unrelated short topics that, while very important, do not individually warrant their own chapter. Although the tools discussed may not be used very often, they are important concepts to learn. The topics presented include storage classes, command-line arguments, conditional compilation, macros, bitwise operations, and recursion.

16.1 Storage Classes

Storage classes regulate the lifetime, visibility, or memory placement of a variable. Only one explicitly specified storage class can be used on a single variable. There are four storage classes in C++: `auto`, `register`, `static`, and `extern`.

The `auto` storage class specifies that a variable will only exist in the block in which it is declared. When the block has finished executing, the variable will no longer be available. Sound familiar? The behavior of the `auto` storage class is the default functionality of all local variables.

The `register` storage class requests that the variable be placed into a machine register, if possible. Registers are unique, high-speed sections of memory within the CPU, whose purpose is to hold or store the data that is being operated on. Visual Studio automatically tries to do this when certain optimizations are specified within the compiler. All developer environments allow the programmer to specify how the program is to be optimized. Optimization allows the compiler to decide on a course of action depending on the environment settings. For example, in some applications execution speed may be more important than memory usage. Therefore, the optimization may be set up to make things run faster at execution time. Registers can be used to increase the execution speed.

The other storage class specifiers, `static` and `extern`, are more commonly used and will be discussed in more detail in the following sections.

16.1.1 Static

We have all become accustomed to the fact that when a method or function ends, all local variables cease to exist. If the function is called again, the variables are recreated. One exception to this rule involves the `static` storage class. The `static` storage class specifies that while the variable has local scope, it exists for the lifetime of the program. If a static variable is not explicitly initialized, it is automatically initialized to zero. Example 16.1.1 shows the declaration of a static variable.

Example 16.1.1 Static variable declaration

```
static int counter = 0;
```

While Example 16.1.1 shows a static integer, static can be used with any data type. Even arrays can be declared as static. Like other variables, arrays are automatically initialized.

Remember: A static variable follows scoping rules. A static variable can only be accessed by the function in which it is declared, but it exists after the function ends.

There are many uses of the static storage class. One of the more common is to keep track of the number of times a specific function is called. Example 16.1.2 demonstrates this technique.

Example 16.1.2 Static counter

```
for ( int i = 0; i < 5; i++ )
    TestStatic();

void TestStatic()
{
    static int counter;

    cout << counter++ << " ";
}
// Output
0 1 2 3 4
```

A more complicated situation using static variables is shown in Example 16.1.3. This example uses a static pointer to create our own version of the strtok function. This function only differs from the predefined function in that the second parameter is a single character instead of a cString.

Example 16.1.3 Using a static character pointer

```cpp
int main()
{
    char sentence[] = "This is a test.";
    char * str;

    str = StrTok( sentence, ' ' );
    while ( str != 0 )
    {
        cout << str << endl;
        str = StrTok( 0, ' ' );
    }

    return 0;
}

char * StrTok( char * str, char delimeter )
{
    static char * current_pos = 0;
    char * temp = 0;

    if ( str != 0 )
        current_pos = str;

    temp = current_pos;

    if ( temp != 0 )
    {
        current_pos = strchr( current_pos, delimeter );
        if ( current_pos )
        {
            *current_pos = '\0';
            current_pos ++;
        }
    }
    return temp;
}
// Output
This
is
a
test.
```

Note that the `static` keyword can be used within classes in relation to both individual data members and methods. However, its functionality is much different than what is discussed in this section and is beyond the scope of this chapter.

16.1.2 Extern

When global variables are declared, they are not truly global. They are only visible to functions within the same source code file and therefore have *file scope*. Functions that need to access variables with file scope that are declared in another file need to specify that the variable is declared outside of, or external to, the current file. To do this, the keyword `extern` is used, as shown in Example 16.1.4.

Example 16.1.4 External variables

```cpp
// Filename: main.cpp
int file_scope_var = 0;

void OtherFunc();

int main()
{
    file_scope_var = 10;
    OtherFunc();

    return 0;
}
// Filename: external_file.cpp
#include <iostream>

void OtherFunc()
{
    extern int file_scope_var;

    std::cout << file_scope_var << std::endl;
}
// Output
10
```

In Example 16.1.4, the variable `file_scope_var` is brought into the scope of the function `OtherFunc`. However, because the variable is specified as extern inside of a function, only OtherFunc has access to the variable in external_file.cpp. If it is necessary for other functions to access the variable, either each function that uses the variable has to specify that file_scope_var is declared external to the current scope, or the external specification has to be done at the file level of external_file.cpp.

STYLE NOTE   Global or file scope variables should only be used when absolutely necessary; but as there are situations that require the use of these variables, it is important to learn how to use them, but only use them when truly warranted.

Section 16.1 Exercises

1. How would you declare a variable so that it would retain its value even after a function is finished?

   a. auto

   b. dynamic

   c. static

   d. const

2. What storage class is assigned by default to local variables?

3. True or false: Global variables can automatically be accessed from any source file included in the solution.

4. True or false: A static variable can be accessed by any function in the source file in which the variable was declared.

5. Which of the following are not storage classes?

   a. auto

   b. dynamic

   c. static

   d. register

   e. const

6. What is the output for the following code fragment?

```
for ( int i = 0; i < 3; ++i )
{
```

```
        Function();
}

void Function()
{
        static int var_a(0);
        auto int var_b(0);

        var_a++;
        var_b++;

        cout << var_a << " " << var_b << endl;
}
```

Section 16.1 Learn by Doing Exercises

1. Create a project that has three source code files (.cpp). In the source code file that will contain main, create a global (file scope) two-dimensional array of integers. In main, call two functions: FillArray and DisplayArray. The definition of FillArray is located in fill.cpp, and the definition of DisplayArray is located in display.cpp. Use extern to ensure that the array is visible in each of the other two files.

2. Modify the previous exercise so that an additional function called DisplayArrayReversed is added to the display.cpp source file. First bring the array into the file scope by using the extern specification above the two functions. Once this is working, relocate the extern specification so that it is inside the DisplayArray function. Notice how this makes the array visible only to the DisplayArray function.

16.2 Command-Line Arguments

When a file is double-clicked from within Windows Explorer, that file is opened by an associated program. The operating system has associated files with specific extensions to be opened by certain programs. But how does the program know which file to open? Because the operating system passes the name and path of the file to the program. The program must catch the value in an optional parameter specified in main's function header. Extending this example, if multiple files are selected to be opened by a program, each filename is passed as one row in a ragged array. The number of strings passed to the program is stored in another parameter. These parameters can have any name, but by convention they are usually called argc and argv. The argc parameter contains the number of strings stored in argv.

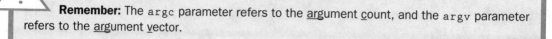

Remember: The `argc` parameter refers to the <u>arg</u>ument <u>c</u>ount, and the `argv` parameter refers to the <u>arg</u>ument <u>v</u>ector.

One thing to be aware of is that the first string stored in `argv` is always the path and name of the program being executed. Example 16.2.1 shows how to use `argc` and `argv`. The example will display all of the strings in `argv`.

Example 16.2.1 Displaying command-line arguments

```
int main( int argc, char * argv[] )
{
    for ( int i = 0; i < argc; i++ )
        cout << argv[i] << endl;

    return 0;
}
```

The term *command line* refers to a textual interface into an operating system. All commands that manipulate the operating system are entered at the command prompt. To see the Windows command-line interface, go to the Start menu, select Run, and then type "cmd". This will start the command-line interface.

Besides opening files when double-clicked, command-line arguments can be used in many situations, such as for allowing program settings to be passed to the program. For example, running the Windows command-line interface and typing "ipconfig /all" will execute the network configuration program. The program ipconfig accepts the "/all" setting and then displays the appropriate information. The operating system uses a space to separate each string and passes that information to the program along with the number of strings.

Example 16.2.2 demonstrates how command-line arguments could be used to pass a series of numbers to a program, which then calculates and displays the sum and average of those numbers.

Example 16.2.2 Running a program from the command line

```
float main( int argc, char *argv[] )
{
    float average;
```

```
    int sum = 0;

    // Valid number of arguments?
    if ( argc > 1 )
    {
        // Loop through arguments ignoring the first, which is
        // the name and path of this program
        for ( int i = 1; i < argc; i++ )
        {
            // Convert cString to int
            sum += atoi( argv[i] );
        }

        // Calculate average
        average = sum / ( argc - 1 );
        cout << "\nSum: " << sum << '\n'
            << "Average: " << average << endl;
    }
    else
    {
        // If invalid number of arguments, display error message
        // and usage syntax
        cout << "Error: No arguments\n"
            << "Syntax: command_line [space-delimited numbers]"
            << endl;
    }

    return 0;
}
// Command-line execution
C:\LearnByDoing\debug>command_line 15 25 35 10 19 40

// Output
Sum: 144
Average: 24
```

In Example 16.2.2, the number of arguments is checked to make sure the user has supplied some data to the program. If he or she has not, an error message is displayed along with the syntax that should be used. This is a common practice for programs that require command-line arguments.

You can also specify command-line arguments to be used in the debugging process. In Visual Studio, right-click on the project in the Solution Explorer. Click on the Properties item at the bottom of the pop-up menu. When the dialog box is displayed, expand the Configuration Properties item and select the Debugging option. Notice that there is an area called Command Arguments. Enter any data necessary to test your program.

Section 16.2 Exercises

1. Write the `main` function header that allows the use of command-line arguments.

2. What does `argc` contain?

3. What is always stored in `argv[0]`?

Section 16.2 Learn by Doing Exercise

1. Using the code presented in Example 16.2.2, create the appropriate project. Debug your solution using your environment's settings to specify the command-line arguments. Once it is working from within your IDE, execute your program from the command-line interface. Be sure to test the program appropriately using a variety of command-line arguments.

16.3 Conditional Compilation

In Chapter 15 we saw two ways of conditionally deciding what pieces of code need to be included when a project is compiled. These two methods are shown in Example 16.3.1.

Example 16.3.1 Conditional compilation review

```
// Method 1
#ifndef ENGINE_H
#define ENGINE_H

...
#endif

// Method 2
#pragma once
```

It makes sense that both of these methods involve preprocessor directives because the preprocessor executes just before the language translator (compiler). Therefore, it is the only application in the compilation process that has a chance to affect what source code gets compiled.

In addition to these methods, there are other preprocessor directives that can be used. Similarly, there are many other situations in which conditional compilation can be used. Example 16.3.2 demonstrates how conditional compilation can be used to set up various program settings based on a #define constant.

Example 16.3.2 Conditional program settings

```cpp
#define DEMO 1
#define SHAREWARE 2
#define FULL 3

#define VERSION FULL

#if VERSION == DEMO
    const int number_users = 1;
    const bool internet_enabled = false;
    const int days_usable = 1;
#elif VERSION == SHAREWARE
    const int number_users = 5;
    const bool internet_enabled = true;
    const int days_usable = 30;
#else
    const int number_users = 200;
    const bool internet_enabled = true;
    const int days_usable = -1;
#endif

int main()
{
    cout << "Number of users: " << number_users << '\n'
         << "Internet enabled: "
         << (internet_enabled ? "True" : "False") << endl;

    cout << "Days usable: ";
    if ( days_usable == -1 )
         cout << "Forever" << endl;
    else
         cout << days_usable << endl;

    return 0;
}
```

```
// Output
Number of users: 200
Internet enabled: True
Days usable: Forever
```

The program shown in Example 16.3.2 determines the version of a program to build depending on a single #define constant. Table 16.3.1 shows most of the preprocessor directives available for conditional compilation.

Another use of conditional compilation is shown in Example 16.3.3. This program will only compile if a C compiler is available.

Example 16.3.3 The #error directive

```
#ifdef __cplusplus
#error C compiler required.
#endif
```

Example 16.3.3 tests for the existence of an identifier, __cplusplus, present in all C++ compilers. (Note: There are two underscores in the identifier

Directive	Description
#if	Preprocessor if statement.
#elif	Preprocessor else if statement.
#else	Preprocessor else statement.
#endif	Ending statement for all preprocessor conditional statements.
#ifdef	Checks to see if an identifier is defined. Evaluates to true if defined.
#ifndef	Checks to see if an identifier is not defined. Evaluates to true if not defined.
#define	Used to create preprocessor constants and identifiers.
#error	Stops compilation and displays an error message.

Table 16.3.1 Preprocessor directives for conditional compilation

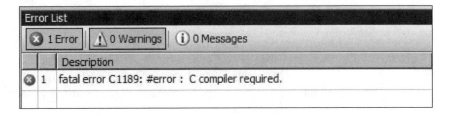

Figure 16.3.1 The #error directive message

__cplusplus.) If it is defined, compilation stops and the error message is displayed in the Error List, as shown in Figure 16.3.1.

Section 16.3 Exercises

1. True or false: Preprocessor directives cannot be used inside of functions.

2. Indicate which of the following are *not* valid preprocessor directives.

   a. #elseif

   b. #endif

   c. #while

   d. #if

   e. #error

   f. #const

   g. #define

Section 16.3 Learn by Doing Exercise

1. Write a program that prints the following text using either C or C++, dependent on a preprocessor setting.

   C: C rocks!

   C++: C++ rocks the world!

   In other words, if the preprocessor identifier is defined, the text will be displayed using printf instead of cout. For ease of testing, use your own identifier rather than the predefined __cplusplus. Be sure to test the program appropriately.

16.4 Macros

Macros are sections of code that physically replace the macro identifier during the compilation process. You have already seen some simplistic macros in use. In C++, macros are created using #define. Therefore, using #define to create a constant in essence creates a macro. The identifier associated with #define is physically replaced by the preprocessor with the supplied value.

Macros are in no way limited to the simple replacement of an identifier with a constant. Very complicated code fragments can be written, including those passing parameters to the macro. Example 16.4.1 shows the creation and use of a more robust macro.

Example 16.4.1 Macro definition and use

```
// Macro definition
#define MAX( a, b ) a > b ? a : b
...
// Using the macro
cout << "Largest value: " << (MAX( 10, 15 )) << endl;

// Output
Largest value: 15
```

Be sure not to place a space between the macro identifier and the opening parenthesis of the parameter list in the macro definition. Your compiler will recognize that situation as an error. Example 16.4.2 shows how the preprocessor would expand the reference to the macro defined and used in Example 16.4.1.

Example 16.4.2 Macro expansion

```
cout << "Largest value: " << (10 > 15 ? 10 : 15) << endl;
```

When writing macros, always keep in mind how the macro will be expanded. Example 16.4.3 shows a macro that will display unexpected results when executed.

Example 16.4.3 Macro problem

```
#define CUBE( a ) a * a * a

int main()
{
    int x = 2;

    cout << CUBE( x ) << endl;        // 2 cubed = 8
    cout << CUBE( x + 1 ) << endl;    // 3 cubed = 27

    return 0;
}

// Output
8
7
```

Notice that the output in Example 16.4.3 is not what was expected. The problem is more evident if you examine the expansion in Example 16.4.4.

Example 16.4.4 Macro expansion problem

```
cout << x * x * x << endl;
cout << x + 1 * x + 1 * x + 1 << endl;
```

As you can see in Example 16.4.4, the order of operations is the cause of the unexpected output. To correct this problem, always make liberal use of parentheses, as shown in Example 16.4.5.

Example 16.4.5 Macro problem solution

```
// Macro definition
#define CUBE( a ) ((a) * (a) * (a))

// Macro expansion using x + 1
cout << ((x + 1) * (x + 1) * (x + 1)) << endl;

// Output
27
```

Sometimes macros may need to span multiple lines to help with the readability and maintainability of your code. However, because of expansion, doing so might cause some problems. The backslash (\ ) can be used to continue a line of code to the next line. Although generally only used with macros, the *line continuation character* can be used at any time. Example 16.4.6 shows the appropriate use of the line continuation character.

Example 16.4.6 Line continuation character

```
#define GETRANDOM( max ) \
    (rand() % (max))

int main()
{
    cout << GETRANDOM( 100 ) << endl;

    return 0;
}
```

16.4.1 Advantages and Disadvantages

So what are the advantages of using macros over functions? As we learned in Chapter 9, every time a function is called, there are quite a few settings—such as the return pointer and the states of all local variables—that are saved on the stack. Because this is done during runtime, the execution speed of your program becomes negligibly slower. Since a macro is expanded during the compilation process, using macros doesn't push anything on the stack resulting in faster execution. However, macros still participate in the modularity of your program.

One disadvantage is that because macros are expanded, if you have a large macro that is used many times, the size of your executable will be expanded accordingly, resulting in a larger executable size. Therefore, macros are usually kept relatively small.

Another disadvantage is that debugging a macro can be a real challenge because you can't use the debugger to step into a macro. Also, syntax errors are more than a little difficult to find because the error appears on the line where the macro is used, not where it is defined.

A final disadvantage is that there isn't any type checking done on the parameters of a macro. This undesirable situation can cost a programmer many hours of debugging.

A common error many of our students make is placing a semicolon at the end of the macro definition. This can cause problems when the macro is embedded within another statement. The additional semicolon would be perceived by the compiler as the termination of the statement.

Because of the disadvantages associated with macros, functions are preferred.

Section 16.4 Exercises

1. What is the output of the following code fragment?

```
#define CUBE( a ) a * a * a

int main()
{
    int x = 2;

    cout << CUBE( x ) << endl;
    cout << CUBE( x + 2 ) << endl;

    return 0;
}
```

2. What makes debugging a macro so difficult?

3. When is a macro expanded?

Section 16.4 Learn by Doing Exercise

1. Write a macro to swap two numbers and another macro to swap two cStrings. Test your program, making multiple calls to the macros.

16.5 Bitwise Operations

There are many times when it is useful to manipulate the individual bits of a piece of data. Although it may not be intuitive when it is necessary to use bitwise manipulations, their use can increase the efficiency of memory resources as well as CPU usage. The following sections discuss the mechanics of bitwise manipulations and demonstrate some of their applications.

Operator	Description
~	Bitwise NOT. Reverse the bit. A 1 results in a 0 and a 0 results in a 1.
>>	Bitwise shift right. Shift all bits to the right by the specified number of bits.
<<	Bitwise shift left. Shift all bits to the left by the specified number of bits.
&	Bitwise AND. The two bits must be 1s to result in a 1.
^	Bitwise XOR. The two bits must be different to result in a 1.
|	Bitwise OR. The two bits must be 0s to result in a 0.

Table 16.5.1 Bitwise operators

16.5.1 Bitwise Operators

The logical operators that were discussed in Chapter 7 also have bitwise counterparts. In addition, there are a few other bitwise operators, some of which have familiar uses. Table 16.5.1 shows the available bitwise operators and their descriptions.

With the exception of the NOT (~) operator, all of the operators in Table 16.5.1 are binary operators and are listed in order of precedence from highest to lowest. Example 16.5.1 demonstrates the use of these operators.

Example 16.5.1 Bitwise operators

```
int i = 0xABAB;   //0000 0000 0000 0000 1010 1011 1010 1011
int j = 0xABCD;   //0000 0000 0000 0000 1010 1011 1100 1101
int result;

result = i & j;   //0000 0000 0000 0000 1010 1011 1000 1001
result = i | j;   //0000 0000 0000 0000 1010 1011 1110 1111
result = i ^ j;   //0000 0000 0000 0000 0000 0000 0110 0110
result = ~i;      //1111 1111 1111 1111 0101 0100 0101 0100
result = i >> 8;  //0000 0000 0000 0000 0000 0000 1010 1011
result = i << 8;  //0000 0000 1010 1011 1010 1011 0000 0000
```

In Example 16.5.1, the bitwise operator is applied to each bit within the operands. The shift left and shift right symbols are also used with `cout` and cin; therefore, if you are embedding any bitwise operations in an input or output statement, you will need to use parentheses to avoid incorrect data or syntax errors.

16.5.2 Bit Fields

A *bit field*, or *bit structure*, allows a programmer to specify that a member of a structure is to occupy only a certain number of bits in an integral type. The syntax for this type of structure follows:

```
struct <struct-name>
{
        <integral-type> <field1> : <number-bits>;
        <integral-type> <field2> : <number-bits>;
...
};
```

The syntax shows that each member is allocated a certain number of bits. Example 16.5.2 shows the declaration of a bit structure.

Example 16.5.2 Bit structure

```
struct IPPacketHeader
{
    unsigned int version         : 4;
    unsigned int net_header_length : 4;
    unsigned int type_service    : 8;
    unsigned int packet_length   : 16;
    unsigned int id_tag          : 16;
    unsigned int fragment_ability : 3;
    unsigned int fragment_offset : 13;
    unsigned int time_to_live    : 8;
    unsigned int protocol        : 8;
    unsigned int check_sum       : 16;
    unsigned int source_ip       : 32;
    unsigned int dest_ip         : 32;
};
```

The bit structure shown in Example 16.5.2 is used to hold the header information for a network packet. The way that Microsoft Visual Studio, running on Intel's architecture, places the individual bits is shown in Figure 16.5.1. Each compiler and architecture may store the information a little differently.

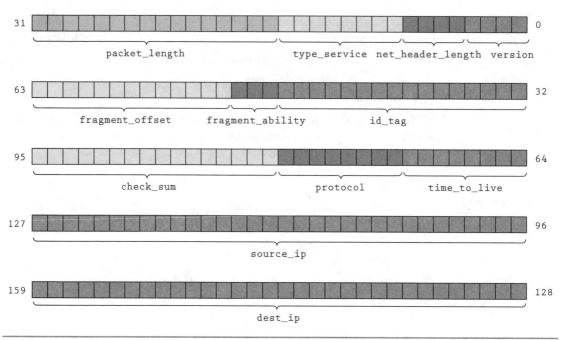

Figure 16.5.1 Memory layout of a network packet

A couple of interesting aspects of bit structures is that the field can be anonymous and the number of bits can be specified as zero. Zero length fields force the compiler to align the next field at the beginning of a new section of memory of the declared type. Example 16.5.3 shows a bit structure using an anonymous field.

Example 16.5.3 Bit structures with an anonymous field

```
struct Anonymous
{
    unsigned short field1 : 4;
    unsigned short field2 : 10;
    unsigned short        : 0;
    unsigned short field3 : 16;
};
```

The third data member in Example 16.5.3 is allocated zero bits and is anonymous. The zero size forces field3 to be aligned with the beginning of

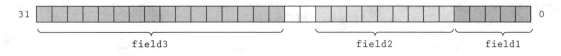

Figure 16.5.2 Memory layout of a bit structure with an anonymous field

the next chunk of memory. Figure 16.5.2 shows the memory layout of the `Anonymous` bit structure shown in Example 16.5.3.

Remember that the size of each portion of memory is determined from the size of the members in the bit structure. Since Figure 16.5.2 shows the layout of a bit structure whose data members are all `unsigned short`, which is two bytes in size, each chunk of memory will be 16 bits.

16.5.3 Masking

Masking is the process of extracting information from a larger set of data using an operator and another piece of data. To set a bit to a 1, use the bitwise OR (|) operator and a mask that has that single bit set as well. Example 16.5.4 demonstrates setting a bit.

Example 16.5.4 Setting a bit

```
unsigned short result = 0;  // result   = 0000 0000 0000 0000
result = result | 2;        // binary 2 = 0000 0000 0000 0010
                            // ----------
                            // result   = 0000 0000 0000 0010
```

Example 16.5.4 sets the second bit from the right to a 1, while all other bits remain the same as the original data. Turning on multiple bits can be accomplished by simply applying the correct mask, as shown in Example 16.5.5.

Example 16.5.5 Setting multiple bits

```
unsigned short result = 10;  // result   = 0000 0000 0000 1010
result = result | 5;         // binary 5 = 0000 0000 0000 0101
                             // ----------
                             // result   = 0000 0000 0000 1111
```

Example 16.5.5 sets the first and third bits from the right. Turning bits off is accomplished in much the same manner except that the bitwise AND (&) operator is used with a zero mask, as demonstrated in Example 16.5.6.

Example 16.5.6 Turning off a specific bit

```
unsigned short result = 15; // result       = 0000 0000 0000 1111
result = result & 0xFFFB;   // binary 65531 = 1111 1111 1111 1011
                            // ------------
                            // result       = 0000 0000 0000 1011
```

In Example 16.5.6, the third bit is turned off, and all other bits remain in their previous state. Toggling bits is accomplished using the bitwise XOR (^) operator. Example 16.5.7 demonstrates how to toggle the state of specific bits.

Example 16.5.7 Toggling bits

```
unsigned short result = 15; // result   = 0000 0000 0000 1111
result = result ^ 4;        // binary 4 = 0000 0000 0000 0100
                            // ----------
                            // result   = 0000 0000 0000 1011
```

Example 16.5.7 turns the third bit on if it was originally 0 and turns it off if it was originally a 1.

Remember: Setting a bit or turning it on means that the bit is assigned a 1. Turning a bit off means changing its state to a zero.

There are many situations in which we can use the concept of masking, one of which is shown in Example 16.5.8.

Example 16.5.8 Determining permissions

```
#define ANONYMOUS 0
#define STUDENT_WORKER 2
#define STUDENT 4
#define ALUMNI 8
#define FACULTY 16
#define ADMIN 32
#define GUEST 64
```

```cpp
int main()
{
    char permissions = 0;

    permissions = AssignPermissions();
    DisplayPermissions( permissions );

    return 0;
}

char AssignPermissions()
{
    char permissions = ALUMNI | FACULTY | ADMIN;
    return permissions;
}

void DisplayPermissions( char permissions )
{
    cout << "You have the following permissions:\n";
    if ( permissions & STUDENT )
        cout << "\tStudent" << endl;

    if ( permissions & STUDENT_WORKER )
        cout << "\tStudent worker" << endl;

    if ( permissions & ALUMNI )
        cout << "\tAlumnus" << endl;

    if ( permissions & FACULTY )
        cout << "\tFaculty" << endl;

    if ( permissions & ADMIN )
        cout << "\tAdministrator" << endl;

    if ( permissions & GUEST )
        cout << "\tGuest" << endl;

    if ( permissions & ANONYMOUS )
        cout << "\tAnonymous" << endl;
}
```

Example 16.5.8 allows you to set up a user with multiple permissions. By using bitwise operators and masking, you can assign multiple access levels while using very little memory. As you can see from the example, you can specify up to 8 different permission levels in a single character. If you were to use a `short`, you could have as many as 16 permissions.

Another situation arises when converting between *big-endian* format to *little-endian* format—terms originating from *Gulliver's Travels*, in which some people open their soft-boiled eggs from the big end, while others open their eggs from the little end. In computer terms, a little-endian computer writes information to memory least-significant-byte (little-end) first, whereas a big-endian computer writes information to memory most-significant-byte (big end) first. Intel-based computers use the little-endian methodology, whereas Motorola typically uses the big-endian format. Converting between formats could be accomplished by reversing the bytes, as shown in Example 16.5.9.

Example 16.5.9 Converting between big-endian and little-endian formats

```
char result[50];
unsigned short number = 0xFBA4;
unsigned short temp = number;

itoa( number, result, 2 );
cout << result << endl;

number &= 0x00FF;          // Clear out MSB
number <<= 8;              // Shift LSB into MSB

temp &= 0xFF00;            // Clear out LSB
temp >>= 8;               // Shift MSB into LSB

number = number | temp;   // Put the two bytes back together

itoa( number, result, 2 );
cout << result << endl;
```

Using bit manipulations are in no way limited to the few examples shown in this section. There are many situations in which bit manipulations can save a significant amount of memory and processing time.

Section 16.5 Exercises

1. What bitwise operation is represented by the ~ operator, and what is its main masking purpose?

2. What value is stored in `i` after each of the following statements? Reset `i` to the original value after each statement.

```
i = 11215; // 0010 1011 1100 1111
j = 54320; // 1101 0100 0011 0000
```

a. i = i | j;

b. i = j << 4;

c. i = i ^ j;

3. Write the statement to perform a bitwise XOR on variables `binary1` and `binary2`, which is then assigned to `result`. Explain what the result (in general) will be for the operation.

Section 16.5 Learn by Doing Exercises

1. Write a function that determines if the integer passed into it is a power of 2. Use bitwise operations to accomplish this task. Be sure to test the program appropriately. **Hint:** A number that is a power of 2 will only have one bit set. What would happen if 1 is subtracted from the number? What bitwise operator could be used with those two values to return a 0? As a programming aid, convert the numbers to binary to help visualize the process.

2. Modify the Swap macro in 16.4 Learn by Doing Exercise to perform number swapping using bitwise operations. **Hint:** Think about how XOR works. Test your macro by nesting it in a simple `if` statement.

16.6 Recursion

In simple terms, a *recursive function* is a function that calls itself. It can also refer to a function that calls another function that already exists on the call stack. Figure 16.6.1 shows the call stack from within Visual Studio for a recursive algorithm.

As you can see in Figure 16.6.1, the function `RecursiveFunction` calls `AnotherFunction`, which in turn calls `RecursiveFunction`. This figure also illustrates another aspect of recursive functions: that the call stack will continue to grow unless something exists to cause the recursion to stop and thus allow the call stack to unwind. Therefore, all recursive functions must have a *terminating condition*. If a terminating condition is not present, the call stack will continue to grow until it runs out of memory. In essence, the lack of a terminating condition creates a very memory-intensive infinite loop.

So recursive functions include a call to themselves or, as we saw in Figure 16.6.1, a call to other functions who will in turn call the recursive function. This recursive call usually has some way of reducing or altering a parameter so that it continues to approach the terminating condition. This is sometimes

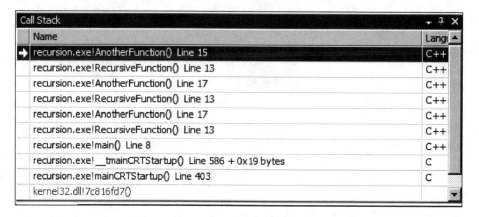

Figure 16.6.1 Recursive call stack

called the *reducing clause*. Example 16.6.1 shows a classic recursive function that calculates the factorial of a number.

Example 16.6.1 Recursive factorial function

```cpp
int main()
{
    cout << Factorial( 5 ) << endl;

    return 0;
}
int Factorial( int n )
{
    if ( n != 1 ) // Terminating condition
    {
        // Recursive call with reducing clause
        n = Factorial( n - 1 ) * n;
    }

    return n;
}
// Output
120
```

Figure 16.6.2 shows the call stack for the execution of the program shown in Example 16.6.1 when the recursion reaches its terminating clause.

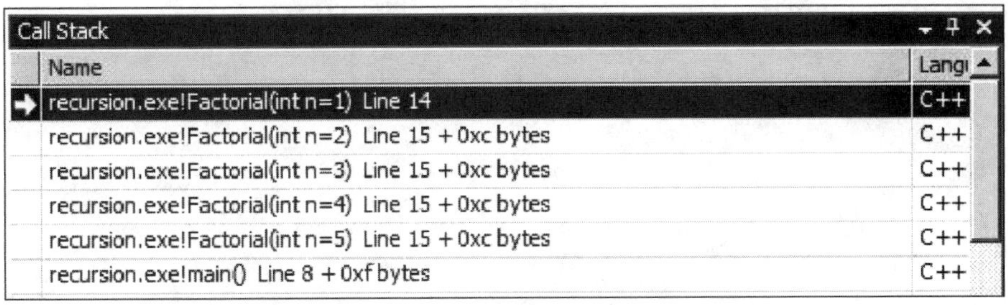

Figure 16.6.2 Factorial call stack

Notice that Example 16.6.1 shows a recursive function that could have just as easily been written using a loop instead. Recursion can always be replaced with iteration, however, some algorithms are more easily written using recursion. When the reducing clause produces something that is essentially the same before as well as after the reducing clause, a solution involving a recursive algorithm will work well.

For example, opening Windows Explorer shows the directory and file structure of your hard drive. Traversing into one of the subdirectories shows an identical structure although with different information. Writing a program that displays all of the directories and files can be accomplished using a recursive algorithm. Just for fun, let's look at one possible solution for accomplishing this task.

There are two predefined C functions that work on a Windows operating system that are helpful in developing this algorithm. The _findfirst function finds the first instance of either a directory or a file in the directory specified in the function call. The _findnext function takes what is returned from the _findfirst function and finds the next directory or file. Example 16.6.2 shows one possible solution to this problem.

Example 16.6.2 Directory traversal

```
// Pass the initial directory and the output file stream
void FindDir( char * dir, ofstream & fout )
{
    _finddata_t find_buf;
    intptr_t rc;
    int success = 0;
    char temp[300];
```

```
strcat( dir, "\\*" ); // Specify the search string

// Find the first file or directory
rc = _findfirst( dir, &find_buf );
do
{
    // If it's a subdirectory, recurse into that directory
    if ( find_buf.attrib & _A_SUBDIR )
    {
        // Ignore the . and .. directories
        if ( strcmp( find_buf.name, "." ) != 0 &&
            strcmp( find_buf.name, ".." ) != 0 )
        {
            strcpy( temp, dir );
            temp[strlen( temp ) - 1] = '\0'; // Remove the *

            // Append new directory name
            strcat( temp, find_buf.name );

            fout << temp << endl; // Output to file

            // Recurse into the subdirectory
            FindDir( temp, fout );
        }
    }
    // Find the next directory or file
    success = _findnext( rc, &find_buf );
} while ( success == 0 );

strcpy( temp, dir );
temp[strlen( temp ) - 1] = '\0'; // Remove trailing *
SearchDir( temp, fout );         // List all files
}
```

The function shown in Example 16.6.2 recursively traverses into each subdirectory. The function then writes each directory to the file. The SearchDir function is not shown here, but it is a nonrecursive function that displays the files within the current directory.

Developing recursive algorithms can be very challenging, although with practice, they can be useful. However, because of the overhead resulting from the ever-growing call stack as well as the possibility of catastrophic errors, use recursion only when necessary.

Section 16.6 Exercises

1. What makes recursive functions so costly?

2. True or false: Though not always as efficient, iteration can replace recursion in all circumstances.

3. What are the two things required by every recursive function?

Section 16.6 Learn by Doing Exercises

1. Write a recursive function that simulates the predefined `pow` function.

2. Write the recursive equivalent of the binary search algorithm discussed in Chapter 11.

3. Write a recursive function that displays any cString character by character, in reverse order.

16.7 SUMMARY

This chapter contained six relatively unrelated topics. The first topic introduced storage classes. As noted, storage classes are simply used to regulate or control the lifetime of a variable. We began our discussion by examining the default storage class called `auto`, which just implies that the variable will cease to exist when the function ends. Next we introduced the `register` storage class, which is a request to the compiler to put the variable into a machine register, with the goal of improving program performance. The third storage class introduced was `static`. The static `storage` class allows the variable to exist for the lifetime of the program. Unlike all other local variables, it does not cease to exist because it has gone out of scope. These variables are automatically initialized to zero if not explicitly initialized by the programmer, and adhere to the normal scoping rules. The final storage class discussed was `extern`. Adding the `extern` keyword allows functions to access a variable physically declared in another file that has file scope.

After discussing the various storage classes, we presented the concept of command-line arguments. Command-line arguments are used to pass information into the `main` function of our programs. While these arguments can technically have any name, they are usually referred to as `argc` and `argv`. The first parameter, `argc`, contains the number of strings stored in `argv`.

The third unique topic presented within this chapter dealt with conditional compilation. While this concept was introduced earlier in the text, some additional preprocessor directives were discussed and demonstrated in various code examples. These directives included #else, #ifdef, #ifndef, and #error.

The next concept examined was macros. A macro is a function-like section of code that is expanded and physically replaces the macro call. This is accomplished by the preprocessor. While macros can be relatively easy to write, it is imperative that the programmer carefully weigh the impact of using macros in place of functions. Such issues as macro expansion, execution speed, file size, and debugging should be considered when determining whether to use macros within your code.

Next we discussed bitwise operations, which provide the programmer with the ability to manipulate the individual bits of a piece of data. In addition to this, bitwise operations are faster in performing various arithmetic functions. To support this, both C and C++ include a number of different bitwise operators. Within this section, we also introduced the concepts of a bit structure, or bit field, and masking. By using a bit field, it becomes possible to specify the number of bits that will be reserved for a member of the structure. Masking allows the programmer to use bitwise operators to extract pieces of information from a larger portion of data.

The final issue discussed in this section was recursion. A recursive function is a function that calls itself. To help visualize the impact of recursion, the call stack was examined. Like so many other actions within C and C++, the programmer must carefully weigh both the costs and the benefits of recursion.

While the topics presented within this chapter are rather unrelated to each other, it is imperative that you be aware of their existence and fundamental use. Even though in some ways they are specialized functions or concepts, they have the potential to become important tools, which you should have in your programming toolbox.

16.8 Programming Exercises

1. Create a program that processes a number of data items passed in via the command line. When your program executes, it will check the command-line arguments for information on how the program is to manipulate the data. If the user passes a `-s` as the first parameter, assume that the data is cStrings; a `-n` specifies that the data will be numbers. If the data is numeric, convert the data to floats and then display the sum as well as the average. Regardless of the data, display all of the arguments except the name of the program.

2. Modify Programming Exercise 1 to add another character sequence to indicate the order in which to display the data. A `-a` will specify ascending order, while a `-d` will specify descending order. You will have only two sort functions—one that sorts cStrings and the other, floats. A function pointer will be passed to the sorting function, which will be used to compare two elements in the array. When the sorting function is called, pass the address of the function that will specify the appropriate order. An example of the sorting function signature follows:

```
void SortStrings( char * ray[], int num_elements,
         int (*Compare)(const char *, const char *) );
```

16.9 Answers to Chapter Exercises

Section 16.1

1. c. `static`

2. `auto`

3. False

4. False

5. b. `dynamic`

   e. `const`

6. 1 1

    2 1

    3 1

Section 16.2

1. `int main( int argc, char * argv[] )`

2. `argc` contains the number of strings in `argv`.

3. The path and name of the program being executed are always stored in `argv[0]`.

Section 16.3

1. False

2. Indicate which of the following are not valid preprocessor directives.

   a. `#elseif`

   c. `#while`

   f. `#const`

Section 16.4

1. 8

    12

2. You are not able to use the debugger to step into a macro.

3. A macro is expanded during the compilation process by the preprocessor.

Section 16.5

1. Bitwise NOT is represented by the ~. Its main purpose is to reverse the bit.

2. What value is stored in `i` after the following code fragment has executed?

   a. `i = i | j;  // i = 65535`

   b. `i = i << 4;  // i = 179440`

   c. `i = i ^ j;  // i = 65535`

3. `int result;`

   `result = binary1 ^ binary2;`

   If the bits are different, the result is 1. If the bits are the same, the result is 0.

Section 16.6

1. Recursive functions are often considered costly because of the additional overhead required from the growing call stack.

2. True

3. In recursive functions, it is important that you have both a terminating condition and a way for altering or reducing a parameter so that you eventually reach the terminating condition.

Binary and Random Access Files

Chapter Objectives

By the end of the chapter, readers will be able to:

- Discuss the overall characteristics, advantages, and disadvantages associated with binary files.
- Explain the options available for opening and closing binary files.
- Develop programs that read from and write to binary files.
- Explain the characteristics of using random access files.
- Compare and contrast sequential files and random access files.
- Illustrate programmatically the use of various methods for manipulating random access files.

Introduction

In Chapter 11, the concepts of using files for data storage and using files for reports were introduced. Up to this point, all of the file-related code examples and programs have had two things in common: (1) they involved text files, and (2) the information in the files was accessed sequentially. In this chapter, the concepts of files and file access are expanded to allow the use of binary files as well as the ability to access information in a nonsequential manner.

17.1 Text Files Versus Binary Files

Text files, as previously discussed, are files written in a way that is readable by humans. This is accomplished by translating the information being written to the file into ASCII or Unicode characters.

Binary files are written in a way that requires no translation. The information is, therefore, virtually unreadable by humans, making binary files unusable for reports. Program executables or documents created using Microsoft Word or some other word processor are examples of binary files. To see how the lack of translation affects the readability of a file, try opening one of your executables using Notepad or some other text editor. Microsoft Visual Studio will actually show a *hex dump* of the binary file. The term "hex dump" refers to showing the contents of a binary file in hexadecimal format as well as offering a translation of those bytes recognizable as ASCII or Unicode characters.

17.1.1 Advantages and Disadvantages of Binary Files

There are a number of advantages that binary files have over traditional text or ASCII files. One advantage is that reading and writing data is much faster when using binary files. With binary files, there is no need to translate all the data stored within a computer's memory into ASCII characters before being written to a file. Instead, the data can simply be stored in the file as it appears in memory. Likewise, when reading data from a binary file, the data can simply be read and placed into memory directly, again without any need for translation. In many cases text files are too limiting, because they don't allow for special formatting symbols or commands to be placed within the file.

While there are a number of advantages to using binary files, there are also some disadvantages. For example, binary files are not directly human-readable because they contain a copy of the actual memory where the data was held. In addition, they are not always portable from one machine to another.

Section 17.1 Exercises

1. What are two disadvantages of binary files?

2. What is the main difference between binary files and text files?

3. What is a hex dump?

4. For each of the following file extensions, state whether the file is typically a text file or a binary file.

   a. `.txt`

   b. `.exe`

   c. `.obj`

   d. `.cpp`

   e. `.h`

17.2 Opening and Closing Binary Files

Opening binary files is similar in many ways to what we demonstrated in Chapter 11 when working with text or ASCII files. As you recall, there are a couple of different options for opening files, as shown in the following syntax:

```
ifstream in_file( filename, mode );
```

```
        -- OR --
```

```
ofstream out_file;
outFile.open( filename, mode );
```

As usual, the filename must be a cString or a string. The optional second parameter represents the mode in which the file is to be opened and can include a combination of the flags presented in Table 17.2.1.

The first three modes in Table 17.2.1 were discussed in Chapter 11. Up to this point we have often been able to omit the second parameter because all files have been text files, which is the default mode. However, when working with binary streams, we are required to include the second parameter, `ios::binary`. Example 17.2.1 illustrates various options for opening binary files.

Mode	Description
ios::in	Open file for input.
ios::out	Open file for output.
ios::app	Open file for output. All new output is added at the end of the file.
ios::ate	Open file with the file pointer initially set at the end of the file. Data can be written anywhere within the file.
ios::binary	Open file in binary mode (the default mode is text).
ios::trunc	Open file for output. If a file already exists, it is replaced by the new file. If using ios::out, this is the default unless you specify ios::app, ios::ate, or ios::in.

Table 17.2.1 File modes

Example 17.2.1 Opening binary files

```
ifstream input( "filename.dat", ios::binary );

ofstream fout;
fout.open( "filename.dat", ios::out | ios::binary );

ofstream data( "c:\\data.dat", ios::out | ios::app | ios::binary );
```

Remember: Regardless of the mode, always check to make sure the file opened successfully before attempting to access it.

Notice in Example 17.2.1 that multiple file mode flags can be combined using the bitwise OR operator (|). The binary data stream in the example was opened so that new information would be appended to the file.

One additional member function that is often helpful is .clear. The .clear function clears, or resets, the I/O state flags for the stream. For example, when you have reached the end of a file, a stream state flag of eofbit is set. If you attempt to reuse a stream object, you will need to clear this flag; otherwise, any attempt to read from the file will fail because the end-of-file (EOF) marker has already been encountered. To reset this state flag, or any of the other I/O flags, use the `.clear` function. The signature of the `.clear` function is as follows:

```
void clear();
```

Just as you have been doing with text files, once you have completed the necessary input and output activities associated with a binary file, always make it a point to close the file.

STYLE NOTE When naming binary data files, it is often common to use the extension `.dat`, as illustrated in our code examples.

Section 17.2 Exercises

1. What is wrong with the following statement?

```
ofstream data( "c:\\data.dat", ios::out & ios::app & ios::binary );
```

2. Indicate which file mode(s) should be used to open a file in the following situations:

   a. To read from a binary file

   b. To write data at the end of a binary file

   c. To open a binary file for both reading and writing

3. What is wrong with the following statement? Assume that you are attempting to open a binary file.

```
ifstream input( "binary.dat" );
```

4. What header file(s) and namespace statements are required to make the following statement compile?

```
ifstream fin( "file.dat", ios::in );
```

Section 17.2 Learn by Doing Exercise

1. Create a word-processing document that has your name in it. Open the binary file in append mode, performing appropriate file operations such as checking for correct opening and closing of the file. Run your program. Reopen the file in your word processor and verify that the information is still there. Now modify your program to open the file in write mode. What should happen to your data? Verify your suspicions.

17.3 Binary File I/O

Reading from a binary file is usually accomplished with an `ifstream` object, while writing to a binary file typically uses an `ofstream` object. To facilitate reading from a binary file, we use the `.read` method, while output is accomplished with the `.write` method. The syntax for both methods is as follows:

```
read( char * buffer, int size );
write( char * buffer, int size );
```

The `.read` and `.write` stream member functions extract or insert a specified number of bytes, as indicated by the second parameter. The information to be written, or the buffer in which to store the information, is designated by the first parameter.

The first parameter is a pointer to the buffer that holds the information read and must be cast to a `char *` (i.e., a character pointer). Does this mean that we can only read or write characters? No. The first parameter is a character pointer because a character takes up a single byte of memory. Therefore, a byte data type can be represented by a character. Since both `.read` and `.write` manipulate a certain number of bytes, they expect an address of a block of memory in which every element is one byte long.

The second argument indicates how many bytes are to be read from or written to the stream. While reading, if the EOF marker is encountered before extracting the number of bytes specified, the read method will simply stop. The `ifstream` member function `.gcount` can be used to retrieve the number of bytes read during the last `.read` statement. The signature for the `.gcount` method follows. The return value, `streamsize`, is simply a `typedef` that equates to a signed integer.

```
streamsize gcount() const;
```

It is important to remember that the contents of a block of memory can be written into a stream with simply one `.write` statement. Likewise, it is possible to read the entire contents of a stream with one `.read` statement. Retrieving or writing a block of information cuts down on the number of storage-device accesses, thus speeding up the I/O process. Example 17.3.1 shows a relatively complete program that includes functions designed to both write to and read from a binary file.

Example 17.3.1 Reading from and writing to a binary file

```
struct Emp
{
    char name[30]; // Use cString, not string
```

```
    short int age;
};
const short int NUM_EMPLOYEES = 3;
...
int main()
{
    Emp ray[NUM_EMPLOYEES];
    FillArrayFromKeyboard( ray );
    WriteToFile( ray );
    ReadFromFile( ray );
    PrintArray( ray );
    return 0;
}
void WriteToFile( Emp ray[] )
{
    ofstream fout( "binary.dat", ios::out | ios:: binary );
    if ( fout.is_open() )
    {
        fout.write( reinterpret_cast <char *> ( ray ),
                    sizeof(Emp) * NUM_EMPLOYEES );
        fout.close();
    }
    else
        cout << "File not opened" << endl;
}
void ReadFromFile( Emp ray[] )
{
    ifstream fin( "binary.dat", ios::in | ios::binary );
    if ( fin.is_open() )
    {
        fin.read( reinterpret_cast <char *>( ray ),
                  sizeof(Emp) * NUM_EMPLOYEES );
        cout << "Number of bytes read is: " << fin.gcount();
        fin.close();
    }
    else
        cout << "File not opened" << endl;
}
```

Notice in Example 17.3.1 that the address of the array is typecast to a character pointer. However, this type of casting is probably unfamiliar to you. The reinterpret_cast is another form of C++ typecasting that is usually used to convert an address to a different type of address. Although discouraged by many programmers because it can be unsafe, it is a necessary evil in this case. Using a `static_cast` will not work and will not even compile in Visual Studio.

Another important aspect of Example 17.3.1 is that the structure contains only fixed-size data members. If the cString data member were to be replaced by a string, it would cause a number of problems. Remember that the string class contains a dynamic cString. Therefore, a member of the `string` class is a pointer. As we discussed in Chapter 13, writing a structure or class that has a pointer data member will create shallow copy issues. The same issues would arise if you were to use `string` data members in a structure used to write to a binary file—only the address would be written and not the data.

Section 17.3 Exercises

1. True or false: Assuming that the file is open, it is possible to read an entire binary file with one statement.

2. What does the `.gcount` member function do, and what is its return type?

3. Write the statement necessary to read from a binary file and store the contents of a single structure into a variable.

Section 17.3 Learn by Doing Exercises

1. Create a text file that has the following information: first name, last name, hourly wage, and hours worked. Write a program that reads the text file, storing this information in an array of structures, and then write the information to a binary file. Before any data from the text file is written to the binary file, write the number of records in your array. Be sure to use cStrings and not strings for the name data members.

> **Remember:** Only use fixed-size data members when writing to a binary file. Do not use pointers or classes that contain pointers as data members.

2. Create another program that reads the information stored in the binary file created in the previous exercise. Remember to read the number of records from the file and create a dynamic array to accommodate the data. Now read the entire data file into the dynamic array using only one read statement. Write the contents of the array to the screen.

3. Modify the previous exercise so that the data is read one record at a time.

4. Modify the previous exercise so that the `first_name` data member is five characters longer. Rerun your program and verify that the information stored in the arrays is invalid. Why did the data get corrupted?

17.4 Sequential Files Versus Random Access Files

So far our focus has been on reading and writing text files in sequential order. For example, when we read data from our files, the only way to get to the third record in the file is to physically read and process the first and second records. It is not possible to randomly jump to the fiftieth record without reading the first forty-nine. To update or modify a sequential file requires actually creating a new file into which all of the data is copied. While reading and writing records in sequential fashion works well for many applications, it is often faster and more efficient to be able to go directly to a specific location within a file. The capability to directly access a specific location within a file is the premise behind *random access* files. To perform random file access requires the ability to actually move the file position marker (FPM).

> ⚠ **Remember:** "FPM" is simply a term we created to indicate the current position within the file.

The following sections examine some of the options available for locating and moving the FPM. Before discussing the methods available to indicate where the FPM is currently located within a specific file, we need to provide some additional background information about stream objects. To begin with, it is important to note that all stream objects have their own internal marker for referencing a specific position within a file. For `ifstream`, this marker is sometimes referred to as the *get pointer* and simply points to the location of the data to be read. For instances of `ofstream`, this marker is called the *put pointer* and indicates the location within the file where data will be written.

17.4.1 Determining Current FPM Location

Two member functions are available to determine where the pointer is currently located within a file. The first method is called `.tellg` and is used with the get pointer; the second method is `.tellp` and is used with the put pointer. In the syntax that follows, notice that both functions return a data type called pos_type. This type is basically a long integer value indicating the current position—the number of bytes—of the FPM from the start of the file.

```
pos_type tellg();
pos_type tellp();
```

Example 17.4.1 demonstrates the use of the .tellg method. In this example, if the sizeof the Student structure is 56, the value returned by the .tellg method would be 112.

Example 17.4.1 Finding current pointer position within an input file

```
ifstream fin( "c:\\temp\\students.dat", ios::in | ios::binary );
...
fin.read( reinterpret_cast<char *> (student_array), sizeof(Student) * 2 );
long int pointer_position = fin.tellg();
```

17.4.2 Moving the FPM

To provide random access of data in a file, the programmer must be able to move or change the position of the marker, or pointer, as needed. The member functions .seekg and .seekp allow the positioning of the pointer to any location within the file. It should come as no surprise that the .seekg method is used with the ifstream get pointer while the .seekp method is used with the ofstream put pointer.

Both .seekp and .seekg can be used with two different options. In the first option, the single parameter represents the number of bytes from the beginning of the file to where you want to move the FPM. This option follows; notice that the parameter type is the same as that used in the .tellg and .tellp methods previously discussed.

```
seekg( pos_type position );
seekp( pos_type position );
```

The second overloaded version of these methods requires two parameters. The first parameter represents the offset relative to some specified starting point, as indicated by the second parameter. This option is as follows:

```
seekg( off_type offset, ios_base::seekdir direction );
seekp( off_type offset, ios_base::seekdir direction );
```

Under the hood, off_type represents a signed integer, while the direction parameter is one of the enumerated values from the seekdir type. Table 17.4.1 shows the options available for use as the second parameter.

Example 17.4.2 shows two examples illustrating how the seek methods can be used to change the position of the pointer within a stream. In the first state-

Direction	Description
`ios::beg`	Seek (change the current read or write position) relative to the beginning of the file.
`ios::cur`	Seek relative to the current FPM position.
`ios::end`	Seek relative to the end of the file.

Table 17.4.1 Enumerations of `seekdir`

ment, the FPM is moved the size of two Student structures from the beginning of the stream. The second example sets the file marker 10 bytes toward the end of the file relative to the stream's current FPM.

Example 17.4.2 Moving the stream pointer

```
fin.seekg( sizeof( Student ) * 2 );
fin.seekg( 10, ios::cur );
```

Example 17.4.3 demonstrates a number of the methods discussed within this section. Notice that the instance of the `fstream` object was opened for both input and output. The code illustrates not only how to move the FPM to a specific record but also how to re-write a record in the file without altering or rewriting the other records.

Example 17.4.3 Modifying the stream pointer

```
void LocateAndModifyRecord()
{
    Emp temp;
    // Opening the stream for both input and output
    fstream emp_file( "binary.dat", ios::in | ios::out |
                                    ios::binary | ios::ate );

    if ( emp_file.is_open() )
    {
        // Move FPM to second record from the front
        emp_file.seekp( sizeof( Emp ) * 1 );
        cout << "\n* Currently at position: "
```

```
                << emp_file.tellp();

        emp_file.read( reinterpret_cast<char *> ( &temp ),
                       sizeof( Emp ) );
        cout << "\n* The name in the second record is: "
             << temp.name;
        cout << "\n* The age in the second record is: "
             << temp.age;

        // Move FPM 0 bytes from beginning of the stream
        emp_file.seekg( 0, ios::beg );

        strcpy( temp.name, "Jamie" );
        temp.age = 41;

        // Write updated data into current (first) position
        emp_file.write( reinterpret_cast<char *> ( &temp ),
                        sizeof( Emp ) );
        emp_file.close();
    }
    else
        cout << "File not opened" << endl;
}
```

The `fstream` class is the parent of the `ifstream` and `ofstream` classes. Therefore, much of the functionality of the children is derived from the parent. The `fstream` class is used because of the default modes of the other two classes. To accomplish the task of both reading and writing to the same stream in Example 17.4.3, we used the `fstream` class.

Section 17.4 Exercises

1. Write the code necessary to move the FPM 10 bytes toward the end of the file from the current position within the file object, `fin`.

2. Explain what `.tellg` and `.tellp` are used for.

3. Explain what `.seekg` and `.seekp` are used for.

Section 17.4 Learn by Doing Exercise

1. Rewrite the program created for Section 17.3 Learn by Doing Exercise 1 so that there is an additional data member in the structure called `record_number`. As the information is read from the text file into the array of structures, increment the record number so that each element of the array has a sequential value for the record number. Now create a program that accepts as input from the user the record number of the person he or she wishes to modify. Read that record only from the file and allow the user to change the data, then rewrite the information out to the file, overwriting the original data. Use the random access methods discussed in this section to accomplish these tasks.

17.5 C—The Differences

As with all I/O, there are numerous differences between C and C++. Although the syntax and functions differ, the concepts remain the same. The following sections present the syntax of these differences.

17.5.1 File Modes

In Chapter 11 we presented the syntax necessary to open files using C. The second parameter to `fopen` is a cString representing the file mode. The only file modes that were discussed were the `r`, `w`, and `a` (read, write, and append) modes. There are several other modes that can be used not only to allow access to binary files but also to allow random access techniques to be used. Table 17.5.1 shows these modes.

In addition to the random access modes listed in Table 17.5.1, a "b" can be appended to any C file mode cString to allow access to binary files. This is shown in Example 17.5.1.

Mode	Explanation
r+	Read and write. File must exist.
w+	Read and write. Will create file if possible. Existing data is destroyed.
a+	Read and append. Will create file if possible. Existing data is retained. All writing will be done at the end of the file.

Table 17.5.1 File modes

Example 17.5.1 Opening binary files

```
FILE * input;
FILE * fout;
FILE * data;

input = fopen( "filename.dat", "rb" );
fout = fopen( "filename.dat", "w+b" );
data = fopen( "c:\\data.dat", "ab" );
```

17.5.2 Binary File I/O with C

The C functions used to read from and write to binary files are `fread` and `fwrite`. The syntax for these functions is as follows:

```
size_t fread( const void * buffer, size_t item_size,
              size_t num_items, FILE * fptr );

size_t fwrite( const void * buffer, size_t item_size,
               size_t num_items, FILE * fptr );
```

As shown in the preceding function signatures, both of these functions require an address of the buffer in which the information is stored or will be stored. Unlike in C++, this address will not need to be typecast because the function accepts a `void` `*`, which you may remember is a pointer to anything. The next parameter is the size of one item that will be written or read. The third parameter is the number of items to be written or read, and the last parameter is the C file pointer. Both of these functions return the number of items, not bytes, completely read or written.

Remember: The `size_t` data type equates to an `unsigned int`.

Example 17.5.2 demonstrates how to use `fread` and `fwrite`. This is a translation of Example 17.3.1 from C++ to C.

Example 17.5.2 Reading from and writing to a binary file

```c
typedef struct
{
    char name[30];
    short int age;
} EMP;
#define NUM_EMPLOYEES 3
...
int main()
{
    EMP ray[NUM_EMPLOYEES];
    FillArrayFromKeyboard( ray );
    WriteToFile( ray );
    ReadFromFile( ray );
    PrintArray( ray );
    return 0;
}
void WriteToFile( EMP ray[] )
{
    FILE * fout;
    fout = fopen( "binary.dat", "wb" );
    if ( fout != NULL )
    {
        fwrite( ray, sizeof( EMP ), NUM_EMPLOYEES, fout );
        fclose( fout );
    }
    else
        printf( "File not opened\n" );
}
void ReadFromFile( EMP ray[] )
{
    size_t num_items = 0;
    FILE * fin;
    fin = fopen( "binary.dat", "rb" );
    if ( fin != NULL )
    {
        num_items = fread( ray, sizeof( EMP ), NUM_EMPLOYEES, fin );
        fclose( fin );
        printf( "Number of bytes read is: %d", num_items );
    }
    else
        printf( "File not opened\n" );
}
```

Identifier	Description
SEEK_CUR	Position FPM relative to the current position of the FPM.
SEEK_END	Position FPM relative to the end of the file.
SEEK_SET	Position FPM relative to the beginning of the file.

Table 17.5.2 The `fseek` function origin identifiers

Remember the first parameter to `fread` and `fwrite` is the address of the data buffer. In Example 17.5.2, the buffer is an array that is already an address. If it were not an address, the address of operator would need to be used.

17.5.3 Random Access Functions

There are three C functions that are used to manipulate the FPM within binary files: `rewind`, `ftell`, and `fseek`. The `rewind` function moves the FPM back to the beginning of the file, `ftell` returns the number of bytes that the FPM is currently away from the beginning of the file, and `fseek` repositions the FPM within the file. The function signatures of these functions are as follows:

```
void rewind( FILE * stream );
long ftell( FILE * stream );
int fseek( FILE * stream, long offset, int origin );
```

The `origin` parameter of `fseek` can have one of three values, as shown in Table 17.5.2.

Example 17.5.3 translates Example 17.4.3 from C++ to C.

Example 17.5.3 Random access file

```
void LocateAndModifyRecord()
{
    EMP temp;
    // Opening the stream for both input and output
    FILE * emp_file = fopen( "binary.dat", "r+b" );
    if ( emp_file != NULL )
    {
```

```
    // Move to the beginning of the file
    rewind( emp_file );

    // Move FPM to second record from the front
    fseek( emp_file, sizeof( EMP ), SEEK_SET );
    printf( "\n* Currently at position: %ld", ftell( emp_file ) );

    fread( &temp, sizeof( EMP ), 1, emp_file );
    printf( "\n* The name in the second record is: %s",
            temp.name );
    printf( "\n* The age in the second record is: %d",
            temp.age );

    // Move FPM 0 bytes from beginning of the stream
    fseek( emp_file, 0, SEEK_SET );

    strcpy( temp.name, "Jamie" );
    temp.age = 41;

    // Write updated data into current (first) position
    fwrite( &temp, sizeof( EMP ), 1, emp_file );
    fclose( emp_file );
  }
  else
    printf( "File not opened" );
}
```

17.6 SUMMARY

Up to this point, all file-related I/O has involved sequential text files. This chapter focused on two additional file formats: binary files and random access files.

Unlike text files, a binary file takes the data directly from the computer's memory and writes it immediately into the stream. Likewise, when reading binary data from a file, the data can be placed directly into memory without the need to do any translation into a human-readable format.

To facilitate binary I/O, we introduced the `.read` and `.write` functions. In addition, we presented a function called `.gcount`, which can be used for retrieving the number of bytes read via the last read statement.

Another topic presented within this chapter centered on random access files. Random access allows the programmer to go directly to a specific location within a file. It is that ability to move the FPM as desired that provides the major framework behind this file format.

To support the ability to randomly access data, we discussed such C++ functions as `.tellg` and `.tellp`, both of which are used to determine where the file pointer is currently located. Two additional functions, `.seekp` and `.seekg`, allow the ability to move the FMP to any desired location, helping to support the increase in data-access speed offered by random files.

The capability to take a stream of data and read or write to an external device is an extremely important aspect of programming. Now that you have been exposed to a number of options for storing and accessing data, be sure to carefully evaluate the needs of your application when making decisions regarding which file organization will work the best for the task at hand.

17.7 Programming Exercise

1. Using Microsoft Visual Studio as a model, create a hex dump utility. Prompt the user for the filename and then display the hexadecimal values as well as the translated ASCII characters.

17.8 Answers to Chapter Exercises

Section 17.1

1. Two disadvantages of binary files are that they cannot be easily read by humans and that they are not always easily transferable from one machine to another.

2. As the data from a text file is read or written, it is translated into either ASCII or Unicode characters, making the file easily read by humans. Binary files are written (and read) in such a way that no translation is required as the data is moved into or out of the memory or the file. However, the resulting file is not in a human-readable format.

3. Hex dump refers to viewing the contents of a section of computer memory or of a binary file in hexadecimal format and providing the translation of those bytes that are recognizable as ASCII or Unicode characters.

4. a. text file

   b. binary file

   c. binary file

   d. text file

   e. text file

Section 17.2

1. Both AND symbols (&) should be replaced by OR symbols (|).

2. a. `ios::in | ios::binary`

    b. `ios::app | ios::binary`

    c. `ios::in | ios::out | ios::binary`

3. When opening binary files, remember to include the second parameter: `ios::binary`.

4. `#include <fstream>`
    `using std::ifstream;`
    `using std::ios;`

Section 17.3

1. True

2. The `.gcount` member function retrieves the number of bytes read during the last read statement. It technically returns a `streamsize`, which is a `typedef` for a signed integer.

3. `fin.read( reinterpret_cast<char *> (&my_var), sizeof(MY_TYPE) );`

Section 17.4

1. `fin.seekg( 10, ios::beg );`

2. Both `.tellg` and `.tellp` are used for determining where within the file the pointer is currently located.

3. Both the `.seekg` and the `.seekp` methods are used to move the FPM.

Introduction to Linked Lists

Chapter Objectives

By the end of the chapter, readers will be able to:

- Explain the overall concept of a data structure.
- Graphically illustrate and discuss the various components associated with a linked list, including nodes, a head pointer, an optional tail pointer, and a trailing pointer.
- Develop and implement various functions for manipulating the individual nodes within a linked list, including inserting, appending, deleting, and traversing the list.
- Write the code to insert nodes into an ordered linked list.
- Distinguish between a singly and a doubly linked list.
- Compare and contrast the concept of a linked list with an array.

Introduction

By now you should be comfortable using arrays to hold information. With all of the practice you have had, you no doubt understand how arrays work as well as their advantages and disadvantages. This chapter introduces another way to store information called *linked lists*.

18.1 Data Structures

A *data structure* is a way to store data so that the information can be used in an efficient manner. There are a variety of data structures, each with its own method of storing data. Figure 18.1.1 shows examples of three of the more common data structures.

As you can see from Figure 18.1.1, an array is an example of a data structure. It has specific characteristics that differentiate it from other data structures. Since an array is a contiguous block of memory, it allows for the random access of any element in the array. The linked list pictured in Figure 18.1.1 shows how the individual elements of the list are connected in a sequential manner. Likewise, the binary tree shows the hierarchical nature of tree data structures.

As we continue our introduction, keep in mind that a data structure is nothing more than a container for information. These containers can be various

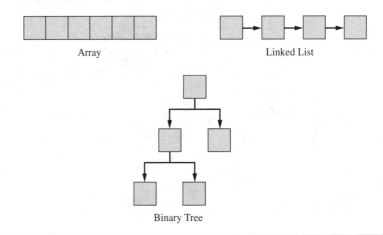

Array   Linked List

Binary Tree

Figure 18.1.1 Simple data structures

sizes and shapes, but certain data structures and their organization clearly work best in specific situations. The focus of this chapter will be on one of the more commonly used data structures: the linked list.

Section 18.1 Exercises

1. What is a data structure?

2. True or false: An array, a linked list, and a binary tree are all examples of data structures.

Section 18.1 Learn by Doing Exercise

1. Research on the Internet different types of data structures not listed in this section. List at least five other data structures.

18.2 Linked Lists

To understand how to create a linked list, you must first be able to visualize a representation of the list. In many ways, a linked list is similar to a passenger train. There is a locomotive at the beginning of the train, followed by a number of cars containing passengers. Each car is coupled together, and at the end of the train there is sometimes a caboose. If you are in the first passenger car and you want to visit somebody in the last car, you need to walk through all of the other cars before you reach your desired destination.

Linked lists contain nodes (cars) that contain information (people) and are connected (coupled) to the next node by a pointer. The front of the list is marked by the *head pointer* (locomotive). The end of the list could optionally be marked by a *tail pointer* (caboose). The last node's pointer will be set to null to signify that there are no other nodes (no more cars). If we start at the first node and want to get to the last node, we have to go through all of the other nodes. In other words, a linked list is accessed sequentially. Figure 18.2.1 shows a detailed diagram of a linked list.

Each node can be either a class or a structure, but no matter which implementation is used, the `node` UDT will contain a pointer to the next node in the list. The `head` and `tail` are `node` pointers that always point to the first node and last node, respectively.

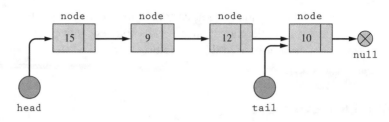

Figure 18.2.1 Linked list

18.2.1 List Implementation Options

There are many implementation possibilities in regard to linked lists. As mentioned previously, a node in the list can be either a structure or a class. Using only structures is more common when developing procedural programs.

A typical OOP methodology would be to have a `node` class and a `linked` list class. The `node` class will contain the data as well as the pointer to the next node. The `linked list` class will contain the head pointer; the optional tail pointer; as well as all of the functions necessary to manipulate the linked list, such as inserting nodes, deleting nodes, and traversing the list.

Normally the object-oriented implementation option would be the preferred method. However, this option requires the programmer to write all four manager functions. Not doing so could result in shallow copy situations, which would cause your program to crash. Since you have not yet learned how to write copy constructors or overloaded assignment operators, this chapter will focus on the more procedural approach.

Another implementation alternative is to keep a pointer to the previous node as well as to the next node in the list. This is called a *doubly linked list*. This is the most common version of linked lists because of the value of being able to traverse the list in both directions. However, since the algorithms are basically the same except for the maintenance of the previous pointers, we will only demonstrate a singly linked list.

18.2.2 Node Structure

As stated earlier, the node will contain the data as well as a pointer to the next node. Example 18.2.1 shows a very simple node structure.

Example 18.2.1 Node structure

```
struct Person
{
    char name[30];
```

```
    int age;

    Person * next;
};
```

In Example 18.2.1, since the pointer must contain an address of another `Person`, the `next` pointer is declared as a `Person` pointer. A pointer embedded in a structure or class that has the same target type as the UDT in which it is enclosed is called a *self-referential pointer*.

Another approach for the implementation of the node structure involves further separation of the data from the necessary linked list components, such as the `next` pointer or a `previous` pointer if we were implementing a doubly linked list. Example 18.2.2 shows the definition of the structures for this implementation option.

Example 18.2.2 Object-oriented node implementation

```
struct Person
{
    char name[30];
    int age;
};

struct Node
{
    Person data;
    Node * next;
};
```

Many programmers feel that the implementation shown in Example 18.2.2 is the preferred option when using structures to create linked lists. The data UDT only contains members to hold pertinent data. Therefore, this is the implementation we will use in all future examples in this chapter.

18.2.3 Head Pointer

The `head` pointer will hold the address of the first node; its declaration is shown in Example 18.2.3.

Example 18.2.3 Head pointer

```
Node * head = 0;
```

It is important, as demonstrated in Example 18.2.3, that `head` be initialized to null. Not doing so will cause difficulties when trying to determine if the list is empty. Because of the initialization, the list can be determined to be empty whenever `head` is null.

18.2.4 Creating a New Node

Before a node can be inserted into the list, a new node needs to be dynamically allocated. A simple utility function that takes the node-related data as its parameter(s) and returns a new node is often very useful. Example 18.2.4 shows two different versions of this function. Although not necessary, the `CreateNode` function has been overloaded to accept the data to be stored in the node in a couple different ways.

Example 18.2.4 Create node functions

```
Node * CreateNode( Person person )
{
    Node * new_node = new Node;
    new_node->data = person;
    new_node->next = 0;

    return new_node;
}

Node * CreateNode( char name[], int age )
{
    Node * new_node = new Node;

    strcpy( new_node->data.name, name );
    new_node->data.age = age;
    new_node->next = 0;

    return new_node;
}
```

Notice that the `CreateNode` function has several tasks. The first is to dynamically allocate a new node, as all nodes in the linked list must be dynamically allocated. The next task assigns the data to the newly allocated node. The third task, and probably the most important, is to make sure the `next` pointer of the node is set to null. This not only places the pointer into a known state but also prepares the node in case it needs to be inserted at the end of the list.

> **Remember:** The next pointer of the last node always needs to contain a null. This allows the programmer to know when the end of the list has been encountered.

The last task of the `CreateNode` function is to return the new node. This node is now fully prepared to be inserted into the list.

Section 18.2 Exercises

1. A linked list is made up of:

    a. arrays

    b. nodes

    c. cars

    d. units

2. True or false: When working with singly linked lists, it is usually necessary to start at the head of the list.

3. The pointer of the last node will contain a:

    a. 1

    b. −1

    c. null

    d. false

    e. 0

4. A linked list that has nodes that contain both a previous and a next pointer is called a:

    a. singly linked list

    b. doubly linked list

    c. problem

    d. binary tree

5. Which of the following are not contained within a node?

   a. data

   b. pointer to the next node

   c. pointer to the head node

   d. pointer to the last node

6. Write the statement to declare a pointer called `head_ptr` and initialize it to 0.

7. True or false: Linked lists are usually accessed or traversed sequentially.

Section 18.2 Learn by Doing Exercises

1. Based on the node created in Example 18.2.2, draw a singly linked list containing three nodes. Include test data within your diagram, along with the necessary connectors linking each of the respective nodes. Make sure you incorporate and clearly label the different components and pointer(s) required.

2. Create a structure that has the following data members:

   ```
   int id;
   char major[35];
   float gpa;
   ```

   Now create a node structure with the appropriate members. Also write `main` and include the declaration of `head`. Next write the appropriate `CreateNode` function, which was discussed in this section.

18.3 Prepending a Node

Before the new node can be inserted into the list, it must be determined where in the list the node is to be placed. The three options are to insert the new node at the head of the list, at the end of the list, or somewhere in between `head` and `tail`.

The easiest place to insert a new node is at the front of the list. Programmers new to linked lists often assume that all that needs to be done is to assign the address of the new node to the `head` pointer. However, if that is the only thing done, all the existing nodes will no longer have any way of being accessed. Prior to reassigning `head`, the new node's next pointer must be assigned to point to the beginning of the current list, and then `head` can be reassigned to the new node's address. This process is demonstrated in Figure 18.3.1.

Step 1: Allocate new node (nn)

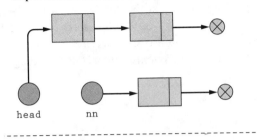

Step 2: Make new node's next point to the first node

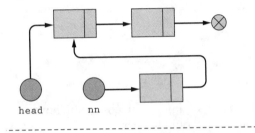

Step 3: Make head **point to the new first node**

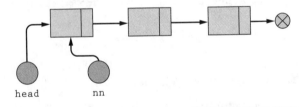

Figure 18.3.1 Prepending a node

Converting the steps illustrated in Figure 18.3.1 into pseudocode is a fairly straightforward process. The resulting pseudocode is shown in Figure 18.3.2.

```
Prepend( head passed by reference,
         new_node a pointer to a dynamically allocated node )

  new_node's next = head
  head = new_node
```

Figure 18.3.2 Pseudocode for prepending a node

The `Prepend` function assumes that the new node has already been created and appropriately initialized, as shown in the `CreateNode` function in Example 18.2.4. But what would happen if we tried to prepend to an empty list? If the list is empty, `head` is null, as previously discussed. Therefore, null is assigned to the new node's next pointer, guaranteeing the integrity of our one-node list.

Section 18.3 Exercises

1. Adding a node to the front or head of the list is called:

    a. appending a node

    b. prepending a node

    c. traversing a node

    d. attaching a node

2. List the four key elements of a `CreateNode` function.

3. What is wrong with the following pseudocode, which was written to prepend a node to a linked list? Explain in detail what would happen if the pseudocode was implemented as shown.

```
Prepend( head passed by value, new_node passed by value )

      head = new_node
```

Section 18.3 Learn by Doing Exercise

1. Expand on the program written for Section 18.2 Learn by Doing Exercise 2 to include a function that prepends a node to the list. Write the necessary function, compile, run, and test your program. Obviously there will be memory leaks, but for now, ignore them. Use your debugger to ensure that the linked list is being created correctly.

18.4 Appending a Node

Another option for inserting a new node involves placing it at the end of the list. This would be a very simple task if we were keeping a tail pointer. However, it is important to know how to perform this type of insertion when there is only a head pointer. Also, just like with the `Prepend` function, a node should be able to be appended to the end of an empty list.

Step 1: Initialize traveling pointer (`travel`)

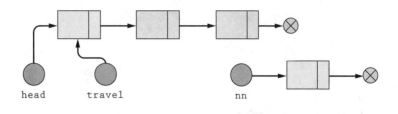

Step 2: Move traveling pointer down list until next pointer is null

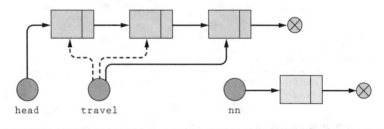

Step 3: Assign address of new node to the traveling pointer's next pointer

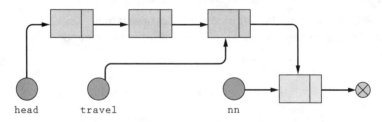

Figure 18.4.1 Appending a node

To find the end of the list, the concept of a *traveling pointer* is introduced. A traveling pointer is a pointer that will be used to traverse the list. This process is shown in Figure 18.4.1.

The only thing the diagram in Figure 18.4.1 doesn't address is the special case of appending a node to an empty list. This only requires a check to see if head is null and then, if so, assigns the address of the new node to head. The resulting pseudocode is shown in Figure 18.4.2.

```
Append( head passed by reference,
       new_node a pointer to a dynamically allocated node )

  If head is null
    head = new_node
  Else
    travel = head
    While travel's next is not null
       travel = travel's next pointer
    End Loop

    travel = new_node
  End If
```

Figure 18.4.2 Pseudocode for appending a node

Section 18.4 Exercises

1. A pointer used to traverse a list is called a _____.

2. What is wrong with the following pseudocode, which was written to append a node to a linked list? Explain in detail what would happen if the pseudocode was implemented as shown.

```
Append( head passed by reference, new_node passed by value )

        travel = head
        While travel's next is not null
            travel = travel's next pointer
        End Loop

        travel = new_node
```

Section 18.4 Learn by Doing Exercise

1. Expand on the program written for Section 18.3 Learn by Doing Exercise 1 to include a function that appends a node to the list. Write the necessary function, compile, run, and test your program. Obviously there will be memory leaks, but for now, ignore them. Use your debugger to ensure that the linked list is being created correctly.

18.5 Inserting a Node into an Ordered List

The last option for inserting a node involves placing it in the middle of a list. Usually this situation only arises when placing a node in an *ordered list*. In an ordered list, each node is inserted into the list in a specified order. Therefore, the list is *always* ordered. This is different than a *sorted list*, in which nodes are placed at the beginning or end of the list and then a sorting algorithm is applied to the list.

When inserting a node into an ordered list, there are four situations we need to be prepared to handle:

1. The list is empty.

2. The new node is to be placed before the current head.

3. The new node is to be placed at the end of the list.

4. The new node is to be placed between two existing nodes.

Since the first three situations have been addressed in the previous sections, we only need to diagram the last situation. There are many ways to accomplish this algorithm, but we have found the approach shown in Figure 18.5.1 to be an easy way for programmers new to linked lists to visualize the necessary steps. This algorithm introduces the concept of a *trailing pointer*. The job of the trailing pointer is to trail one node behind the traveling pointer. The reason for this pointer will become clear as we examine the diagram in Figure 18.5.1.

As stated earlier, the situation diagrammed in Figure 18.5.1 can be accomplished without the trailing pointer; it is just a convenient technique to use. Figure 18.5.2 shows the pseudocode that addresses all four situations of inserting nodes into an ordered list.

As you can see from the pseudocode in Figure 18.5.2, with a little careful planning we can take care of multiple situations in each section of the `if` statement. The `if` statement itself handles situations 1 and 2, and the `else` handles situations 3 and 4.

Notice the `<=` in the `if` statement. This was included to handle the insertion of duplicate data. Without the check for equality, when inserting a duplicate item, the flow of the program would continue to the `else`. The `while` loop's condition would then be evaluated as false, thus never executing the body of the loop and leaving the trailing pointer assigned to null. When an attempt is made to assign the address of the new node to the trailing pointer's next pointer, the program will crash because the trailing pointer is still null.

It is also crucial to understand the `while` loop shown in Figure 18.5.2. Examine the code in Example 18.5.1. Notice that the conditions have been reversed from those given in Figure 18.5.2.

Step 1: Initialize traveling pointer (`travel`) **and trailing pointer** (`trail`)

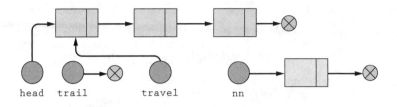

Step 2: Move traveling pointer down list until reaching the node before which the new node is to be inserted

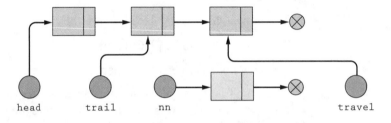

Step 3: Assign address of new node to the traveling pointer's next pointer

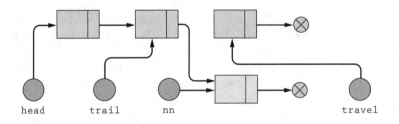

Step 4: Assign address of `travel` **to the new node's next pointer**

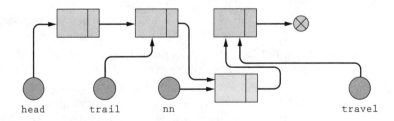

Figure 18.5.1 Inserting a node between two existing nodes

```
InsertOrdered( head passed by reference,
               new_node a pointer to a dynamically allocated node )

   If head is null or new_node's key value <= head's key value
      new_node's next = head
      head = new_node
   Else
      travel = head
      trail = null
      While travel is not null and travel's key < new_node's key
         trail = travel
         travel = travel's next pointer
      End Loop

      trail's next = new_node
      new_node's next = travel
   End If
```

Figure 18.5.2 Pseudocode for inserting a node into an ordered list

Example 18.5.1 Problematic `while` loop

```
while ( travel->data.age < new_node->data.age && travel != 0 )
```

On the surface, both loops appear to work in the same way. However, the loop shown in Example 18.5.1 will cause your program to crash if inserting a node at the end of the list because when inserting the node at the end, the traveling pointer becomes null. Therefore, trying to access the data members of the traveling pointer will cause your program to crash with a memory access violation.

So how does the loop in Figure 18.5.2 work? As discussed in Chapter 7, C++ performs short-circuit evaluation, which means that as soon as the outcome of a condition can be determined, no additional pieces of the condition need to be examined. Therefore, when the traveling pointer is null, the part of the condition that accesses the data member of the traveling pointer is not evaluated.

Section 18.5 Exercises

1. A pointer used to follow behind a traveling pointer is called a _____.

2. Explain short-circuit evaluation.

3. What is wrong with the following pseudocode, which was written to insert a node into an ordered linked list? Explain in detail what would happen if the pseudocode was implemented as shown.

```
InsertOrdered( head passed by reference, new_node passed by value )

    If head is null or new_node's key value < head's key value
        new_node's next = head
        head = new_node
    Else
        travel = head
        trail = null
        While travel's key < new_node's key and travel is not null
            travel = travel's next pointer
        End Loop

        trail's next = new_node
        new_node's next = travel
    End If
```

Section 18.5 Learn by Doing Exercise

1. Expand on the program written for Section 18.4 Learn by Doing Exercise 1 to include a function that inserts a node into the list ordered by the id member. Write the necessary function, compile, run, and test your program. Obviously there will be memory leaks, but for now, ignore them. Use your debugger to ensure that the linked list is being created correctly.

18.6 Traversing the List

As you have seen from the insertion examples in the previous sections, lists are sequential in nature. No matter what you are trying to do, it is necessary to start at the front of the list. We have also seen how to traverse through a list using a traveling pointer to get to some desired location within the list. It is easy to take this concept and use it to display the contents of a list, as shown in Example 18.6.1.

Example 18.6.1 `Display` **function**

```
void Display( Node * head )
{
    Node * travel = head;

    while ( travel != 0 )
    {
        cout << travel->data.name << ' '
             << travel->data.age << endl;
        travel = travel->next;
    }
}
```

The same basic traversal algorithm is used when performing any action on all nodes of the list. Example 18.6.2 shows the code that increments everybody's age.

Example 18.6.2 `HappyBirthday` **function**

```
void HappyBirthday( Node * head )
{
    Node * travel = head;

    while ( travel != 0 )
    {
        (travel->data.age)++;
        travel = travel->next;
    }
}
```

As you can see from the previous two examples, there is a lot of overlapping code. Although this is fine, we can make it better by passing a function pointer that will be called to perform the action required of the traversal. Example 18.6.3 shows a traversal that performs the action by calling a function via a function pointer.

Example 18.6.3 `Traverse` **function**

```
void Traverse( Node * head, void (*visit) (Node *) )
{
    Node * travel = head;

    while ( travel != 0 )
    {
        visit ( travel );
        travel = travel->next;
    }
}
void Display( Node * temp )
{
    cout << temp->data.name << ' ' << temp->data.age << endl;
}
void HappyBirthday( Node * temp )
{
    (temp->data.age)++;
}
int main()
{

    ...

    Traverse( head, Display );
    Traverse( head, HappyBirthday );
    Traverse( head, Display );

    return 0;
}
```

As illustrated in Example 18.6.3, there are many things that can be done by passing a function pointer to the `Traverse` function. The only requirement is that each function accepts a pointer to a specific node in the list.

Another option for traversing the list uses a recursive function. Remember from Chapter 16 that any algorithm written using loops can also be written using recursion. Therefore, we can modify our `Traverse` function, rewriting it as a recursive function, as shown in Example 18.6.4.

Example 18.6.4 `TraverseRecursive` **function**

```
void TraverseRecursive( Node * head, void (*visit) (Node *) )
{
    if ( head != 0 )
```

```
{
    visit( head );
    TraverseRecursive( head->next, visit );
}
}
```

Although the code doesn't change much, the traversal function is now implemented using a recursive algorithm. So why do this recursively when there is so much more overhead? One useful side effect of this algorithm is that simply swapping the two lines in the `if` statement will display the list in reverse order.

Section 18.6 Exercises

1. When traversing the list, you will usually need to start at:

   a. the node containing the null

   b. the front of the list

   c. the end of the list

   d. the current location of the trailing pointer

2. True or false: It is not possible to use a recursive function when traversing the linked list.

Section 18.6 Learn by Doing Exercises

1. Expand on the program written for Section 18.5 Learn by Doing Exercise 1 to include a function that displays the contents of the linked list. Write the necessary function, compile, run, and test your program. Obviously there will be memory leaks, but for now, ignore them.

2. Change the display function from the previous exercise so that it is implemented using recursion.

3. Add a display function that displays the list backward.

18.7 Deleting Nodes

Another task for which it is necessary to provide functionality is the deletion of nodes. The most important deletion activity is destroying or purging the list. Obviously, if this isn't done, your program will contain a multitude of memory leaks. And while it is necessary to be able to insert information into the list, we need to be able to remove it as well.

18.7.1 Deleting All Nodes

As was just stated, it is crucial to purge the list of all nodes when it is time to destroy the list. This function should definitely be called prior to the program exiting. In addition, this function could also be used to remove all of the nodes and return the list back to its original state. Although there are many algorithms that accomplish this task, the one shown here ensures that the head pointer is assigned null when the function is complete. Regardless of the algorithm you choose, always assign null to head when this function is used. Otherwise there won't be any way to determine if the list is empty, and there will be a possibility of making the other list functions work incorrectly.

> **Remember:** When dynamic memory is deallocated, the pointer doesn't change even though the address in the pointer is no longer valid.

Unlike many of the other list algorithms, the purge algorithm uses head as the traveling pointer. We will still use the trailing pointer, as previously seen. The diagram representing one execution of the loop body is shown in Figure 18.7.1.

The process diagrammed in Figure 18.7.1 continues until there are no more nodes. The pseudocode for the Purge function is shown in Figure 18.7.2.

In the pseudocode in Figure 18.7.2, when the function is done, head will be null, thus resetting the head pointer to an empty list state.

18.7.2 Deleting a Specific Node from an Ordered List

The algorithm for deleting a specific node in an ordered list is fairly complicated. However, the algorithm can be broken down into the following situations, based on the location from which the node is deleted.

1. The list is empty.

2. The node to be deleted is head.

3. The node to be deleted is the last node in the list.

4. The node to be deleted is between two nodes.

5. The information to be deleted doesn't exist in the list.

The first and last situations in the preceding list are considered problematic states that need to be handled according to the specifications of your program. This could be a simple error message stating that the item to be deleted doesn't exist. Since deleting head was addressed in the previous section, we will illustrate only the issue of deleting a node from between two nodes, as shown in Figure 18.7.3, which can also be applied to deleting the last node in the list.

Step 1: Initialize traveling pointer (`trail`)

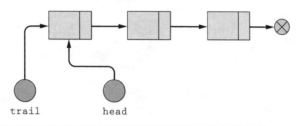

Step 2: Move head **to the next node in the list**

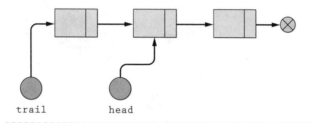

Step 3: Deallocate node pointed to by the trailing pointer

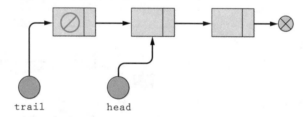

Figure 18.7.1 Purging the list

```
Purge( head passed by reference )

   While head is not null
      trail = head
      head = head's next pointer
      deallocate trail
   End Loop
```

Figure 18.7.2 Pseudocode for purging a list

Step 1: Initialize traveling pointer (`travel`) **and trailing pointer** (`trail`)

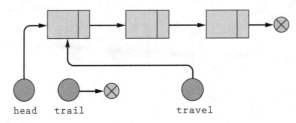

Step 2: Traverse until traveling pointer is pointing to the node to be deleted

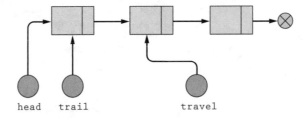

Step 3: Point the trailing pointer's next pointer to the traveling pointer's next pointer

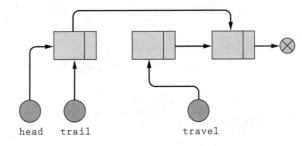

Step 4: Delete target node

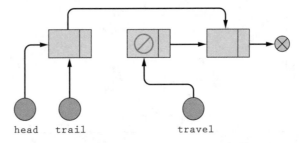

Figure 18.7.3 Deleting a node from between two nodes

```
DeleteNode( head passed by reference,
            target key passed by value )

  If list is empty
     Handle deleting from empty list error
  Else If head's key is equal to target value
     trail = head
     head = head's next
     delete trail
  Else
     travel = head
     While travel not null and travel's key is not equal to target
        trail = travel
        travel = travel's next
     End Loop

     If traveling pointer is null
        Handle target not found error
     Else
        trail's next = travel's next
        delete travel
     End If
  End If
```

Figure 18.7.4 Pseudocode for deleting a specific node

By carefully examining the diagram in Figure 18.7.3, it will become clear that this same algorithm will work even if the node to be deleted is the last one in the list. Combining this algorithm with the other situations presented earlier results in the pseudocode shown in Figure 18.7.4.

Section 18.7 Exercises

1. True or false: Failing to delete one or more of your nodes from a dynamically linked list would result in a memory leak.

2. After the linked list has been deleted, it is important to always set the head pointer to:

   a. true

   b. false

   c. null

   d. -1

   e. 0

3. True or false: Attempting to delete a node that has already been deleted will cause an error.

Section 18.7 Learn by Doing Exercises

1. Continuing with the expansion of the program developed in the Learn by Doing Exercises for this chapter, write the function that deletes all nodes from the linked list. Be sure to use the memory-leak-detection techniques discussed in Chapter 12. Run and test your program.

2. Add the capability to the previous exercise to delete a specific node from the list. Be sure to test all paths through your function to ensure that all five situations discussed in this section are addressed.

18.8 Arrays Versus Linked Lists

Now that you are more familiar with linked lists, it is time to summarize the pros and cons of arrays and linked lists. Table 18.8.1 lists these characteristics.

As shown in Table 18.8.1, if there are elements frequently added to the data structure, a linked list is the better choice. If the size of the data structure is to remain the same and the number of elements is known at compile time, an array is a good choice. Dynamic arrays are good for those situations in which the number of elements will not change, or will change very little, but the number of elements is unknown until runtime. Also, because a binary search can be easily used with an array, searching is much more efficient. The bottom line is that the data structure to be used should be determined by the situation.

18.9 Problem Solving Applied

Throughout the text we have introduced and applied a number of strategies a programmer or software engineer could use to aid in general problem solving and designing programs. To explore one of these strategies in detail, Chapter 2 presented a seven-step development process. The first step of this process involved *defining the problem*, and the second step concerned *developing the*

	Arrays	Dynamic Arrays	Linked Lists
Access	Random and sequential	Random and sequential	Sequential
Memory usage	Static size	Dynamic	Dynamic
Extra memory required	None	None	An extra pointer for each node
Efficiency of adding new element	N/A	Poor	Excellent
Efficiency of deleting an element	N/A	Poor	Excellent
Searching algorithms	Binary or linear	Binary or linear	Linear
Efficiency of order-ing elements	Good	Good	Excellent if using an ordered list; otherwise, poor

Table 18.8.1 Arrays versus linked lists

requirement specification. While both of these steps sound simple enough, it is obvious that as problems or applications become more complex, both of these activities can prove to be challenging. Within this section we make one final attempt at illustrating how to complete the first two steps of the development process.

In this example, Troy has been assigned yet another project. To help fill you in on the details, Troy meets with you and gives you the following information.

The issues he is trying to address revolve around managing the customers for a local small business. Apparently the owner needs an application for a credit company that simply allows for the addition, editing, and deletion of customers. The owner is not looking for an extensive system, but only wants to be able to generate a couple of reports. The first report would list the first and last names of each customer along with their home and work telephone numbers. The second report would include the same information as the first, along with the person's credit limit and their actual credit balance.

Remember that the first step of our design process involves defining the problem. In addition, recall that an error in this first step is likely to be very costly in terms of both money and time. In Step 1, we have condensed our conversation with Troy into the following problem statement.

Step 1: Define the Problem

To design and develop an application for managing the credit information of the customers for a small business.

Now that we have clearly defined the problem, we will move on to the second step in our process, the requirement specification. In developing the requirement specification, we first remove all the ambiguities in our problem statement. Next we have to determine the inputs and outputs for our application. The culmination of this step results in a list of items that our credit program must meet.

After again reviewing the conversation we had with Troy, we developed the list of requirements shown in Step 2.

Step 2: Requirement Specification

The inputs include:
    First name
    Last name
    Home telephone number
    Work telephone number
    Credit limit
    Credit balance

The outputs include:
    Report 1—Customer Contacts
        Last name
        First name
        Home telephone number
        Work telephone number
    Report 2—Customer Credit Limits and Balances
        First name
        Last name
        Home telephone number
        Work telephone number
        Credit limit
        Credit balance

Users should be able to perform each of the following tasks:
        Add new customers
        Edit exiting customer information
        Delete customers
        Generate the two reports requested

Now that the first two steps of the development process have been completed, it would be a good time to talk to Troy to make sure you have understood his requirements. If you have done your job correctly and Troy hasn't changed his mind, you are ready to move on to Step 3 of the development process, the design phase. This example will be continued in the Team Programming section toward the end of this chapter.

18.10 C—The Differences

Since the linked lists in this chapter were created using structures, there really aren't very many differences between C and C++. In fact, the concepts in this chapter are fairly generic and can be implemented with almost any language. Just remember that in C, passing by pointer is the appropriate manner in which to pass a variable so that it can be changed.

18.11 SUMMARY

This final chapter has introduced you to linked lists, one of the more fundamental and powerful data structures associated with programming. The chapter began by briefly reviewing and extending the concept of data structures by graphically illustrating a number of methods for storing data, including an array, a linked list, and a binary tree.

Throughout the remainder of the chapter the emphasis was on visualizing and manipulating a singly linked list. As noted, a linked list is simply a data structure that contains information in nodes that are all connected by a pointer to the next node in the list.

One of the first tasks examined in working with linked lists centered on inserting new nodes. We explored a number of alternatives, including the easiest option, which is simply inserting the node at the front or head of the list.

Another option involved placing the new node at the end of the list. To help support this approach, we introduced the concept of a traveling pointer to help in traversing the list.

The final approach to inserting a new node dealt with putting the node into an ordered list. In this method, the node is actually placed in the list in a specific order, thus ensuring that the list is always ordered.

Next we presented an approach to use when deleting the nodes contained in our list. As discussed a number of times previously in the text, if the programmer allocates any memory dynamically, it is imperative that he or she also delete that memory, including all the nodes within a linked list.

As you can see, the linked list is truly a powerful data structure and another important tool with which the programmer needs to be familiar. It provides some real advantages over arrays—for example, unlike an array whose size is fixed at the time you compile your program, a dynamically allocated linked list is free to grow as needed without any waste-related issues.

It is important for you to realize that linked lists are often used as the basis for a number of other, more advanced data structures that you may indeed encounter in the future.

18.12 Debugging Exercise

Download the following file from this book's website and run the program following the instructions noted in the code.

```
/**************************************************************
 * File: Chap_18_Debugging.cpp
 *
 * General Instructions: Complete each step before proceeding to the
 * next.
 *
 * Debugging Exercise 1
 *
 * 1) Create Breakpoint 1 where indicated in the code.
 * 2) Run the program using the Start Debugging option and run to
 *     Breakpoint 1.
 * 3) Step over the call to CreateNode.
 * 4) Verify that the information stored in the new node is correct.
 * 5) Step over the call to Append.
 * 6) Notice that your program has crashed.
 * 7) Stop debugging.
 * 8) Rerun your program to Breakpoint 1 and step over the call to
 *     CreateNode.
 * 9) This time, step into the Append function.
 * 10) Step over until the current line of execution reaches the while
 *      loop.
 * 11) Look at the value in head. Shouldn't the initial value of head
 *      be null?
 * 12) Fix this problem and repeat Steps 8 - 10. Look once again at the
 *      value of head. If it is not null, you still haven't fixed it.
 * 13) Now look at the value of travel. Can you access a data member of
 *      a null value?
 * 14) This is supposed to be an Append function, which also means that
 *      we need to perform an empty-list check and then change head
 *      appropriately.
 * 15) Put the necessary check into the Append function.
 * 16) Stop debugging, run to Breakpoint 1, and step over the calls to
 *      CreateNode and Append.
 * 17) Look at head after the execution of Append. Why is it still null?
 * 18) How should head be passed to any function that inserts a new
 *      node? Fix this situation.
 * 19) Stop debugging and rerun to Breakpoint 1. Step over the code
 *      until the second node is appended to the list.
 * 20) Why is it crashing now? Look carefully at the new node. What is
 *      the value of the next pointer? Why is there an address in the
 *      next pointer?
```

```
*  21) The next pointer of the last node should always be null. What
*       function is responsible for ensuring this? Fix this situation.
*  22) Disable Breakpoint 1.
*  23) Create Breakpoint 2 where indicated in the code.
*  24) Run to Breakpoint 2 and use the debugger to ensure that all of
*       the information is correct. Click on the plus symbol to the left
*       of the next pointer. Notice that this expands to show the next node in
*       the list. Continue this process until you can see all nodes.
*
* Debugging Exercise 2
*
*  1) Stop debugging, create Breakpoint 3, and run to that line of code.
*  2) Shouldn't head now be null after the call to Purge? Randy sure
*       wrote some buggy code!
*  3) Fix the Purge function as shown in this chapter.
*  4) Rerun your program to Breakpoint 3 and verify that everything is
*       now working correctly.
***************************************************************************/
#include <iostream>
#include <fstream>
#include <string>
using namespace std;

struct Person
{
    string fname;
    int age;
};

struct Node
{
    Person info;
    Node * next;
};

Node * CreateNode( Person temp );
void Append( Node * head, Node * nn );
void Purge( Node *& head );
void Traverse( Node * head );

int main()
{
    Node * head;
    Node * nn = 0;
    Person temp;
    ifstream fin( "data.txt" );

    if ( fin.is_open() )
    {
        fin >> temp.fname >> temp.age;
        while ( !fin.eof() )
```

```
            {
                // Breakpoint 1
                // Put a breakpoint on the following line
                nn = CreateNode( temp );
                Append( head, nn );
                fin >> temp.fname >> temp.age;
            }

            fin.close();
        }
        else
            cout << "Can't open file." << endl;

        // Breakpoint 2
        // Put a breakpoint on the following line
        Traverse( head );
        Purge( head );

        // Breakpoint 3
        // Put a breakpoint on the following line
        temp.fname = "Joe";
        temp.age = 30;

        nn = CreateNode( temp );
        Append( head, nn );

        Traverse( head );
        Purge( head );

        return 0;
    }
    void Traverse( Node * head )
    {
        if ( head != 0 )
        {
            cout << head->info.fname << ' ' << head->info.age << endl;
            Traverse( head->next );
        }
    }
    void Purge( Node *& head )
    {
        Node * travel = head;
        Node * trail;

        while ( travel != 0 )
        {
            trail = travel;
            travel = travel->next;
            delete trail;
        }
    }
```

```
void Append( Node * head, Node * nn )
{
    Node * travel = head;

    while ( travel->next != 0 )
        travel = travel->next;

    travel->next = nn;
}
Node * CreateNode( Person temp )
{
    Node * nn = new Node;
    nn->info = temp;

    return nn;
}
```

18.13 Programming Exercises

1. Create a program that allows a person to keep track of what music is currently on his or her iPod or MP3 player. When the program is executed, it will read a binary file that contains a list of all the music currently loaded on the user's iPod or player. This information will be placed into an ordered linked list. The user will then be able to manipulate the information stored in the list via the following menu.

   1. **Search by Song**—Check to see if a song is currently on the device.

   2. **Search by Artist**—List all songs by a specific artist.

   3. **Add**—Add a song to the linked list.

   4. **Batch Add**—Read a text file and add all music listed in the text file to the list.

   5. **Remove**—Remove a song from the list.

   6. **Batch Remove**—Read a text file and remove all music listed in the file from the list.

   7. **Save**—Save the list to the binary file.

   8. **Exit**—If any changes have been made since the last save, prompt the user to see if he or she wants to save those changes.

   The structure for your data should contain members for such pertinent information as song title and artist. The linked list should be ordered by song title.

2. The computer department needs a program to keep track of equipment checked out to students. When a lab assistant checks out the equipment to a student, he or she needs to keep track of the student's name and major, equipment checked out, and date and time of the trans-

action. The following is an example of a menu that might be displayed when the program is run.

1. Display all equipment checked out
2. Display all equipment checked out to a specific student
3. Display all students that currently have a specific piece of equipment
4. Check out a piece of equipment
5. Check in a piece of equipment
6. Exit

To keep the check-out and check-in procedures running smoothly, use menus to speed up the process. When the program is executed, a text file that has a list of majors and another text file that contains a list of commonly-checked-out equipment will be read. Each one of these files will be stored in its own linked list. During the check-out process, the information from these lists will be displayed in the form of a menu so that the lab assistant can quickly choose the appropriate item from the menu.

There will be times when the item doesn't appear on the list, so the lab assistant will need to be able to choose "Other" from the submenu and then be prompted for the appropriate information. These other entries will then be added to the correct linked list, and upon exiting, the text file will be updated.

The date and time of the transaction—whether checking out or checking in equipment—will be automatically retrieved from the system time. Use the C functions `time`, `localtime`, and `asctime` to determine the date and time.

3. For an added challenge, write Programming Exercise 1 using a doubly linked list.

18.14 Team Programming Exercise

In the Problem Solving Applied section of this chapter, we reviewed and demonstrated the first two steps involved in the development process. Within this section we continue the credit application example and ask you to complete the remaining steps involving the design, implementation, and testing phases of the development process.

Now that Troy has received and approved the requirement specification for this small software program, he needs you to continue developing the application. He has provided some additional information and has asked that you make it a point to clearly document all of the remaining development steps. He is looking forward to seeing your finished application soon.

Additional Software Artifacts and Notes Supplied by Troy

Troy's rough idea of a possible layout for the various records:

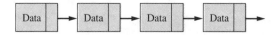

First attempt at one of the possible UDTs for the application:

```
struct Customer
{
        char last[21];
        char first_name[21];
        char home_phone[13];
        char work_phone[13];
        float credit_limit;
        float credit_balance;
        ????  link_field;
};
```

> Maybe a string would be better? Your call. Feel free to change this as desired.
>
> Troy

Format for one of the two required reports:

Customer Contacts

Last Name	First Name	Home Telephone Number	Work Telephone Number
. . . .	. . .		
. . . .	. . .		

Total Customers: *nn*

18.15 Answers to Chapter Exercises

Section 18.1

1. A data structure is a method for storing data so that information can be accessed and used efficiently.

2. True

Section 18.2

1. b. nodes

2. True

3. c. null

   e. 0

4. b. doubly linked list

5. c. pointer to the head node

   d. pointer to the last node

6. `Node * head = 0;`

7. True

Section 18.3

1. b. prepending a node

2. Allocate a new node

   Assign the desired data to the new node

   Set the next pointer to null

   Return a pointer to the new node

3. Any changes made to the head pointer will not remain after the function is terminated because it was passed by value, not reference. In addition, the next pointer for the new node is never assigned the contents of the head pointer, so we have lost the link or connection to the existing members of our list.

Section 18.4

1. traveling pointer

2. The problem with the pseudocode is that it doesn't handle the case of appending a node to an empty list. If implemented as shown and the list were empty, the head pointer would not be assigned the value of our only node, `new_node`.

Section 18.5

1. trailing pointer

2. As soon as the outcome of a condition can be determined, the evaluation process ends. For example, if the first part of an `&&` expression were false, there would be no need to continue because the results would be false.

3. In the first `if` statement, we should have checked for `<=`, not just `<`. Remember, we need to include the equality check to be able to deal with the insertion of duplicate data into the list. If we don't check and we have a duplicate item, the flow of the program continues on to the `else`. The `while` condition would then be evaluated as false, thus never executing the body of the loop and leaving the trailing pointer assigned to null. When an attempt is made to assign the address of the new node to the trailing pointer's next pointer, the program will fail because the trailing pointer continues to be set to null.

Section 18.6

1. b. the front of the list

2. False

Section 18.7

1. True

2. c. null

   e. 0

3. True

ASCII Chart

The following chart shows the ordering of characters in ASCII (American Standard Code for Information Interchange). The internal representation for each character is shown in decimal. For example, the letter *A* is represented internally as the integer 65 in ASCII. The space (blank) character is denoted by a "□".

Left Digit(s)	Right Digit	*ASCII*									
		0	*1*	*2*	*3*	*4*	*5*	*6*	*7*	*8*	*9*
0		NUL	SOH	STX	ETX	EOT	ENQ	ACK	BEL	BS	HT
1		LF	VT	FF	CR	SO	SI	DLE	DC1	DC2	DC3
2		DC4	NAK	SYN	ETB	CAN	EM	SUB	ESC	FS	GS
3		RS	US	□	!	"	#	$	%	&	'
4		(	)	*	+	,	-	.	/	0	1
5		2	3	4	5	6	7	8	9	:	;
6		<	=	>	?	@	A	B	C	D	E
7		F	G	H	I	J	K	L	M	N	O
8		P	Q	R	S	T	U	V	W	X	Y
9		Z	[	\	]	^	_	`	a	b	c
10		d	e	f	g	h	i	j	k	l	m
11		n	o	p	q	r	s	t	u	v	w
12		x	y	z	{	|	}	~	DEL		

Codes 00–31 and 127 are the following nonprintable control characters:

NUL	Null character	VT	Vertical tab	SYN	Synchronous idle
SOH	Start of header	FF	Form feed	ETB	End of transmitted block
STX	Start of text	CR	Carriage return	CAN	Cancel
ETX	End of text	SO	Shift out	EM	End of medium
EOT	End of transmission	SI	Shift in	SUB	Substitute
ENQ	Enquiry	DLE	Data link escape	ESC	Escape
ACK	Acknowledge	DC1	Device control one	FS	File separator
BEL	Bell character (beep)	DC2	Device control two	GS	Group separator
BS	Back space	DC3	Device control three	RS	Record separator
HT	Horizontal tab	DC4	Device control four	US	Unit separator
LF	Line feed	NAK	Negative acknowledge	DEL	Delete

Glossary

access specifier Denotes the level of protection for data members and methods from functions outside the class.

accumulator A variable that adds some value usually other than 1 to itself.

actual parameter Parameter that appears in a function call.

address-of operator An ampersand (&) used in a way that the address of an identifier is returned.

aggregation See *containment*.

algorithm A finite set of instructions that leads to a solution.

ALU See *arithmetic logic unit*.

ANSI Among other things, the American National Standards Institute (ANSI) formed a committee to standardize programming languages.

argument A value passed to a function. Usually called a parameter.

arithmetic logic unit Performs arithmetic computations and logical operations.

array A collection of two or more contiguous memory cells of a homogenous data type.

arrow operator Operator that accesses a data member or member function of a pointer to a structure, union, or class.

ASCII chart American Standard Code for Information Interchange (ASCII) chart associates characters with a number.

attribute Another term for "data member." A variable contained within a class.

base member initialization Mechanism that allows the initialization of data members in a class constructor.

big-endian Writing information with the most significant byte (big end) first.

binary numbering system   Base 2 numbers. Can contain digits 0 and 1.

binary operator   An operator that has two operands.

binary scope resolution operator   Operator that specifies that the identifier on the right belongs to the data type (usually a class) on the left.

binary search   Search algorithm that logically cuts an array in half. Then a comparison is made to see which half the target would be located in, and it too is logically cut in half. This process continues until the target is located. This algorithm assumes that the array is ordered.

bit   Binary digit. Can hold either 0 or 1.

bit field   See *bit structure*.

bit structure   Allows a programmer to specify that a member of a structure is to occupy only a certain number of bits in an integral type.

black box   A stand-alone unit where the processing of the unit is hidden or ignored.

Boolean value   Can either be true or false.

bounds of an array   The valid index values of an array.

break statement   Stops the execution of a control structure prematurely. In the case of a `switch` statement, the `break` is necessary to preempt multiple case statements from being executed.

breakpoint   A debugging tool that stops the execution of a program at a specific line of code in the program. The programmer can then step through the code line by line.

bubble sort   Sorting algorithm that moves the largest element to the end of the array. Once one element is in place, the process restarts back at the beginning of the array to bubble the next largest value to its place within the array. Each pass consists of comparing two elements, and if the first element is greater than the second, the elements are swapped. This continues until the end of the array is encountered.

buffer   A specific area of memory that holds data.

bug   Errors in a program or computer.

building   A process that combines object code files into an executable. Also called linking.

byte   A grouping of eight bits.

call stack   Debugging tool that allows a programmer to view where in the hierarchy of the function calls the current line of execution is located.

central processing unit   Hardware responsible for executing the set of instructions that directs the computer's activities and for managing the various hardware components.

character escape sequence   Violates the rule that a character literal is a single character surrounded by single quotation marks. All escape sequences start with a backslash (\) followed by one or more characters.

character literal   Single character enclosed in single quotation marks, such as 'a'.

class   Mechanism that is the basis for object-oriented programming. Contains data and functions.

class diagram   UML tool that describes the components of a class.

colon init list   See *base member initialization*.

column-major order   The order in which an array is stored in memory column by column.

command-line arguments   Data passed to a program via the command line. This data is caught in `main`'s parameter list.

comment   Lines of code that are ignored by the compiler. Like whitespace, using comments has no impact on the overall behavior, flow, or size of your program. These lines are used to document the source code for you or for other programmers. Comments aid in the readability and maintainability of your code.

compilation   A process that translates the entire program to machine language and creates a file that can be executed by the operating system.

compiler   An application that translates the source code into machine language. Sometimes called a language translator.

composition   See *containment*.

conditional compilation   Ability to specify what statements are compiled, depending on the evaluation of a condition. This is accomplished through the use of preprocessor directives.

console application   A text-based application. Usually doesn't include any of the familiar graphical user interface (GUI) features.

const method   Member function that guarantees that no data members will be changed within the function.

constant   An identifier that has an associated value that will never change. Constants must be initialized.

control variable   A variable with an initial value that controls whether the body of a loop is executed.

constructor   A special function that is automatically called anytime an object is instantiated. The job of the constructor is to build, or construct, the object, including the allocation of any resources.

containment   When a data member is an object instantiated from another class.

control characters   Escape sequences that don't display anything but control the position of the text displayed.

control unit   Responsible for the actual execution of instructions as well as manages when the instruction is executed. The control unit tells the ALU what to do and when to do it.

counter   A variable that is always incremented, adding 1 to itself.

CPU   See *central processing unit*.

cString   A null-terminated character array.

ctor   See *constructor*.

CU   See *control unit*.

dangling pointer   A pointer containing an address that is no longer valid.

data file   A group of related records physically stored on a disk or some other storage media.

data hierarchy   A grouping of data or information. Typically consisting of a bit, byte, field, record, and file.

data members   Variables contained within structures, unions, and classes.

data structure   Organization of data in memory so that the information can be used in an efficient manner.

database   A storage mechanism used to house large amounts of data.

deallocation   Freeing memory dynamically allocated to a program.

debugger   A set of tools that helps the programmer locate errors or bugs.

debugging   Process of removing runtime and logic errors.

decimal numbering system   Base 10 numbers. Can contain digits 0–9.

deep copy   Allocation of additional memory for a pointer data member when two variables created from a structure, union, or class are copied. The data is then copied to the newly allocated memory.

default argument   A value provided in the function declaration that will automatically be inserted if no value is provided in the function call.

default constructor   Constructor that can be called without any parameters.

dereferencing   Using the indirection operator to acquire the value being referred to by the pointer.

desk checking   The process of manually verifying the logic of your solution.

destructor   Member function automatically invoked when an object is destroyed. Its job is to free up any allocated resources.

diamond inheritance   Two parents of a derived class that share a single parent.

dot operator   Operator that accesses a data member or member function of a variable created from a structure, union, or class.

doubly linked list   Linked list where each element also points to the previous node in the list.

dtor   See *destructor*.

dynamic memory allocation   Process of requesting memory from the operating system at runtime.

element   Area within the block of memory where one piece of data will be stored.

embedded system   Computer designed to perform only one or a limited number of tasks. Most embedded systems include both hardware and software together and can be placed collectively on a single microprocessor.

encapsulation   Ability to enclose the data or attributes that describe the object, as well as the functions that manipulate the data, into one container.

enumerated data type   Association of a list of identifiers with a type name. Any variable of this newly created type can have only the values specified in the identifier list.

EOF   End-of-file.

field   A collection of related bytes. Holds all of the characters or data for a specific piece of information.

file pointer   A C term representing a pointer used to access a file once it has been opened. The pointer is returned during the opening process.

file position marker   Often referred to by other names such as file pointer and cursor. This marker designates the current position within the file.

file scope   Identifiers that are only visible within a source code file.

firmware   Software designed for an embedded system. Since the software is located on a chip, it is no longer volatile and performs only predefined tasks, unlike general purpose desktop computers.

flag   A value that represents a specific setting or state.

flagged bubble sort   Variation of the bubble sort algorithm that uses a flag to determine when the list is ordered.

flash drive   Another form of nonvolatile storage. These extremely popular devices, sometimes referred to as pen or thumb drives, are made up of a relatively small circuit board that is encased in a protective plastic housing.

floppy disk   A form of nonvolatile storage that is quickly becoming outdated. Floppy disks are made up of a flexible piece of material containing a magnetic recording surface that can store data.

flowchart   A graphical or pictorial representation of an algorithm. It is a series of standardized shapes, each with its own meaning, arranged to represent the overall flow of the program.

formal parameter   Parameter that appears in a function header.

FPM   See *file position marker*.

function   A group of related statements that together perform a specific task or job.

function body   The statements that specify what the function is to do when it is invoked.

function call   Statement that invokes a function. Transfers the control of the program to a specific function or method.

function declaration   Statement provided so that when the compiler encounters the function call, it can verify the existence of the function name and the required parameters. Sometimes called a function prototype.

function definition   The combination of the function header and a function body.

function header   The first line in a function definition. It is the entry point into the function.

function overloading Ability to have multiple versions of a function with the same name as long as the number and type of parameters are different.

function pointer Pointer that holds the address of a function.

function prototype See *function declaration*.

function signature Method for identifying a specific function based on its name and the order and number of parameters it takes.

functional programming A paradigm that has its roots in mathematics and centers on the program being made up of a collection of mathematical-like functions.

generalization See *inheritance*.

generic programming Feature of object-oriented languages allowing a programmer to specify that a class will contain data members whose data type can change to meet the programmer's needs.

getter Member function that returns the value of a specific data member.

gigabyte Abbreviated as GB. Roughly 1 billion bytes.

global Declared outside of all functions. Can be accessed by any function within the source-code file.

graphical user interface Uses pictures and other graphic symbols to help make a program—including operating systems—easier to use.

GUI See *graphical user interface*.

hacking An undesirable form of trial-and-error programming.

hard disk A nonvolatile form of storage. Usually stores the operating system and other applications.

hardware The physical components of a computer.

"has a" relationship Refers to the relationship between a class and a data member that is an object of another class.

head pointer Pointer to the beginning of a list.

header file External or separate files containing information necessary to access predefined routines. Can also be created by the programmer.

heap Memory not currently being used by the operating system or running programs.

hex dump Showing the contents of a binary file or memory in hexadecimal format as well as offering a translation of those bytes recognizable as ASCII or Unicode characters.

hexadecimal numbering system Base 16 numbers. Can contain digits 0–9 and A–F.

IC See *integrated circuits*.

IDE See *integrated developer's environment*.

implementation hiding Concealing the details of the class from the user of the class.

indirection Method of referencing a variable in a roundabout way rather than directly accessing the variable by its name. Accessing a variable's value via its memory address rather than its name is an example of indirection.

infinite loop   A loop that continuously executes. The program or loop has to be terminated by the user or programmer.

information hiding   Ensuring that only the class's methods can change the state of its data members.

inheritance   Ability to take an existing class and extend its functionality to form another class.

initialization   The process of giving a variable a value during its declaration. As a result, the variable will always be in a known state.

input device   Provides a mechanism with which the user communicates with the computer.

instantiation   Creating or declaring a variable using a class as its data type.

integral data type   Any data type that can only hold whole numbers. The char data type is an integral data type because under the hood a char holds an ASCII number representing a character.

integrated circuits   Often referred to as ICs. Can contain a large number of different components such as resistors, transistors, and capacitors.

integrated developer's environment   Combines many development tools into one application.

interpretation   The source code is translated line by line and immediately executed. This takes place when the program is running, so interpreted programs tend to execute slower than other forms of language translation.

IPO   Acronym for input-process-output.

"is a" relationship   Refers to the relationship between a derived class and its parent.

iteration   The process of looping or repetition.

key value   A piece of data that is used to uniquely identify a record.

language translator   An application that translates the source code into machine language. Sometimes called a compiler.

levels of indirection   Number of intermediate pointers before reaching the actual data.

lexical analysis   Character-by-character comparison.

linear search   Search algorithm that starts at the first record, comparing a value from within arrays, or some other data structure, to a user-specified target. If the value matches the target record, process the information; otherwise, move to the next record.

linked list   Data structure that organizes its data so that one element points to the next element in the data structure.

linker   An application that combines object code files into an executable.

linker error   Errors produced by the linker because of inaccurate or missing definitions.

linking   A process that combines object code files into an executable. Also called building.

literal   A value that is interpreted exactly as it is written.

little-endian   Writing information to memory least-significant-byte (little end) first.

local variable   A variable declared in the body of a function or control statement. The variable will only be accessible from within that body. When the execution leaves the body, the variable is destroyed.

logic error   Error that causes a running program to produce incorrect results.

logical operator   An operator that is used to make compound conditions.

l-**value**   The appropriate constructs that can be placed on the left side of an assignment operator. Variables are *l*-values; constants are not.

macro   Sections of code that physically replace the identifier during the compilation process.

manager functions   Special functions that perform fundamental tasks associated with a class, such as assignment, copy, and initialization. The four manager functions are constructor, destructor, copy constructor, and the assignment operator.

manipulator   A command that is directly placed into the stream.

masking   Process of extracting information from a larger set of data using an operator and another piece of data.

megabyte   Abbreviated as MB. Roughly 1 million bytes.

member function   A function that is defined as a part of a class.

memberwise copy   Duplicates the contents of the data members by performing a bitwise replication of the variable.

memory leak   Happens when memory is allocated but is not deallocated. If this situation continues, your computer will eventually run out of memory and will need to be rebooted.

method   Another term for a member function. A function contained within a class.

microprocessor   An IC containing components that execute a program.

motherboard   Used to connect all of the various hardware components together.

multiple inheritance   Inheriting from more than one class.

mutator   Method that changes the state of an object's data members.

name decoration   See *name mangling*.

name mangling   Process the compiler takes to ensure that each function has a unique name. When a C++ compiler translates a function into object code, the data type of each parameter is used in conjunction with the function name to create a unique identifier.

namespace   A method provided in C++ that allows the grouping of related entities inside one category. Literally, it is a named space.

narrowing conversion   Automatic process of converting a data-type value to a smaller data type. Data could be lost.

nested loop   A loop embedded in another loop.

nesting   The placement of one construct in the body of another construct.

node   Element in a list.

null   Value used to initialize pointers.

null character   ASCII value 0. Used, among other things, to give a character variable an initial value. Also used to terminate a cString.

object   Variable created using a class.

object code   Binary file produced by a compiler.

object-oriented programming   In the OOP paradigm, the central component is considered an object. In this paradigm, the focus is on the objects and their relationships and interactions.

octal numbering system   Base 8 numbers. Can contain digits 0–7.

OOP   See *object-oriented programming*.

operating system   Responsible for managing the various tasks on your computer. These tasks include such activities as preparing the computer when the machine is turned on, dealing with various input requests from such devices as the keyboard and the mouse, managing output requests to the display or printers, and managing the overall storage system.

order of precedence   Established order that must be adhered to when evaluating expressions with multiple operations.

ordered list   List in which each node is put in the appropriate place within the list.

ordinal data type   Those data types that can be translated into an integer to provide a finite number set.

out of bounds   Accessing an element, or memory cell, that does not belong to the array.

output buffer   Holds information until a signal is received to write the entire buffer to the output device.

output device   Used to communicate information or processed data from the computer to a user.

overloading   Process of providing an alternative definition for a function or an operator.

padding   Placing spaces on either side of the displayed data.

parallel arrays   Arrays where one element or row corresponds to a specific field in a record.

parameter   A value passed to a function.

passing   Giving a value to a function.

passing by const-ref   Allows a parameter to be passed by reference to avoid the performance cost of making a copy of the object, but still has the safety of passing by value because the object cannot be changed.

passing by pointer   Process of passing an address of an actual parameter to a function. Any changes to the parameter in the called function will be reflected in the actual parameter.

passing by reference   Process of passing a reference or alias to the parameter. Any changes to the parameter in the called function will be reflected in the actual parameter.

passing by value   Process of making a copy of a parameter and passing the copy. The original value will be retained when the function ends.

pointer   Variable that holds an address.

polymorphism   Ability of different objects to respond differently to the same message.

post-test loop   A loop whose condition is evaluated after the first execution of the body of the loop.

predefined routine   Not part of the core language but an extension to the language. These routines are a part of the C++ standard and are accessed through header files.

preprocessor   An application that executes prior to language translation.

preprocessor directive   A command executed by the preprocessor. All preprocessor directives start with a # symbol.

pre-test loop   A loop whose condition is evaluated prior to the execution of the body of the loop.

priming read   Ensures that the control variable of a loop has a user-provided value before evaluating the condition. Can also refer to the initial access of a file before entering the loop.

primitive data type   A data type whose definition is built into the language.

procedural programming paradigm   Paradigm that focuses on breaking down a particular programming problem into various pieces, subprograms, or routines. Each of these individual components performs a specific function and is executed as needed.

processor   See *microprocessor*.

program   The set of instructions to be performed by the computer; often called computer software.

programming language   A language containing a finite list of keywords and constructs that can be used by a programmer to direct the operations of a computer.

programming paradigm   Different approaches for visualizing a problem's solution or an overall project structure.

prompt   Text displayed to the user asking (prompting) him or her to do something.

property   Another term for "data member." A variable contained within a class.

pseudocode   A written list of the individual steps needed to solve the problem independent of any programming language.

ragged array   Array of character pointers in which each element points to a different-length cString.

RAM   See *random access memory*.

random access memory Memory within a computer that is used for holding the program and any information needed to perform the necessary processing. It is often referred to as short-term memory because the data contained within RAM will be lost when the computer is shut off or loses power.

record A group of related fields.

recursive function A function that calls itself.

register Unique high-speed sections of memory within the CPU.

relational operator An operator that is used to compare two values.

report Generated for human consumption; usually includes title information, column headings, and other formatting.

reserved word Has a special or predefined meaning within the language and therefore cannot be used as a user-defined identifier.

return Statement that gives back a value to the calling function.

row-major order The order in which an array is stored in memory row by row.

run time error Error that causes a program to abruptly terminate, or crash, during execution.

r-value The values that appear to the right of an assignment operator.

scope Where, within your code, the variable can be referenced and used.

selection statement Conditional statement that chooses a single outcome. The C++ `switch` statement is an example.

self-contained The ability of an object to stand alone.

self-referential pointer Pointer whose data type is the same as the one in which the pointer is declared.

sequential search See *linear search*.

setter Member function that is passed a parameter, which will then be assigned to a specific data member.

shallow copy Memberwise copy of pointers contained within a structure, union, or class, resulting in two pointers pointing to the same piece of memory.

short-circuit evaluation The early termination of a compound condition evaluation once the result is determined.

software The instructions that tell the computer what to do.

sorted list List that is created and then ordered.

source-code file File containing the program written by the programmer.

specialization Relationship between parent and child class.

stack A place in memory where a program's variables are stored. Also a type of data structure.

stepwise refinement Breaking the program into smaller, more manageable, and detailed pieces. Each piece is then designed, implemented, and tested.

storage classes Regulate the lifetime, visibility, or memory placement of a variable.

stream A flow of information.

string literal Multiple characters surrounded by double quotation marks ("/").

structure Encapsulation of variables of any type into one UDT. Some languages call this concept a record.

structure chart A graphical design tool that specifies where the functions in the program are called from. It specifies the hierarchy of the functions in a program.

subscript Specifies the offset from the beginning address of an array.

syntax error Caused by something incorrect in the mechanics of the statement(s). An executable cannot be created until all syntax errors are corrected.

symbol table A table that holds all of the literals (symbols) needed for a program.

system software Manages the various hardware components of a computer, and coordinates the loading and execution of application programs.

tail pointer Pointer to the end of the list.

template C++ mechanism to achieve generic programming.

ternary operator An operator with three operands. The conditional operator is an example.

tokenizing Process of separating data into pieces of information based on a specific delimiter.

trailing pointer Pointer used to follow one node behind a traveling pointer.

traveling pointer Pointer that will be used to traverse the list.

truth table The Boolean results produced when an operator is applied to the specified operands.

typecasting Used to force a value to be converted from one type to another.

UDT See *user-defined data type*.

UML See *Unified Modeling Language*.

unary operator An operator that has one operand.

Unified Modeling Language Includes standardized symbols for use in developing, documenting, and modeling a software system or application. UML includes a number of different types of diagrams for modeling or representing a software system, each providing a different perspective on the system. These diagrams include such tools as use cases, class diagrams, sequence diagrams, and state diagrams.

union Mechanism allowing for the creation of a UDT that contains many data members but can store only one. The amount of memory allocated for the variable is dependent on the largest data member of the union.

user-defined data type Data type created by the programmer.

variable A placeholder whose contents can change.

void In C and C++, it literally means "nothing." Therefore, if a function has a void return type, the function will return nothing.

watch   A debugging tool that allows the programmer to view the contents of a variable.

whitespace   Usually refers to empty spaces inserted around related items. In the area of computer science and programming, the term refers to an empty or nonvisible character (i.e., space or tab), including blank lines.

widening conversion   Automatic process of converting a data type value to a larger data type. No data will be lost in this conversion.

Index

/******** - ********/
-, 146
--, 148
-=, 150

/******** ! ********/
!, 174
!=, 172

/******** # ********/
#define, 91, 544
#elif, 544
#else, 544
#endif, 544
#error, 544
#if, 544
#ifdef, 544
#ifndef, 523, 544
#include, 65, 521
#pragma once, 523

/******** % ********/
%, 146
%=, 150

/******** & ********/
&, 297, 393
&&, 174